THE 1929
STOCK MARKET
CRASH

Essential Events

THE 1929
STOCK MARKET
CRASH
BY MARTIN GITLIN

Content Consultant
Richard Sylla
Professor of the History of Financial Institutions and Markets
New York University

ABDO
Publishing Company

CREDITS

Published by ABDO Publishing Company, 8000 West 78th Street, Edina, Minnesota 55439. Copyright © 2008 by Abdo Consulting Group, Inc. International copyrights reserved in all countries. No part of this book may be reproduced in any form without written permission from the publisher. The Essential Library™ is a trademark and logo of ABDO Publishing Company.

Printed in the United States.

Editors: Jill Sherman and Sara M. Hamilton
Copy Editor: Paula Lewis
Interior Design and Production: Nicole Brecke
Cover Design: Nicole Brecke

Library of Congress Cataloging-in-Publication Data
Gitlin, Martin.
  The 1929 Stock Market Crash / Martin Gitlin.
     p. cm.
  Includes bibliographical references.
  ISBN 978-1-60453-050-6
  1. Stock Market Crash, 1929. 2. United States—Economic conditions—1918-1945. 3. Depressions—1929. I. Title.

  HB37171929 .G 2008
  973.91'6—dc22

                              2007031212

TABLE OF CONTENTS

President Herbert Hoover delivers his inaugural address in 1929.

THE CALM BEFORE THE STORM

In 1928, most Americans were feeling carefree and giddy. Amelia Earhart was showered with praise as the first woman pilot to fly across the Atlantic Ocean. Walt Disney created his first animated film featuring Mickey Mouse, called

Plane Crazy. Babe Ruth was slugging majestic home runs for the New York Yankees.

Though Prohibition had outlawed the consumption of alcohol, people danced the night away at nightclubs across the country. Wild, spirited dances such as the Charleston and the jitterbug reflected the unbridled enthusiasm and spirit of Americans in the late 1920s.

All seemed right with the nation on December 4, 1928. On that day, outgoing Republican President Calvin Coolidge gave his last State of the Union address to Congress. It reflected the mood of the country:

> *No Congress of the United States ever assembled, on surveying the state of the Union, has met with a more pleasing prospect than that which appears at the present time. In the domestic field there is tranquility and contentment ... and the highest record of years of prosperity.*[1]

Talkies

The late 1920s was an eventful period in the movie industry. Until 1927, all films were silent. That year, the film *The Jazz Singer* became the first talkie, or a movie with sound, to be shown at theaters. The first Academy Awards ceremony, honoring the top film performances of the year, was held in 1929 and has been a much-anticipated annual event ever since.

Such words served to strengthen a feeling of well-being heading into the new year. The prevailing view was that there was enough wealth for everyone to share. A popular song of the time was titled "My God, How the Money Rolls In."

POSTWAR UNITED STATES

World War I (1914–1918) had ended in the previous decade and had become a distant memory. The Kellogg-Briand Pact, which denounced war as a means to end conflict, had been ratified by 41 nations by 1929. Many believed that they would never experience another war.

The United States played a relatively minor role in World War I. Many European countries had been fighting since 1914, but the United States did not formally enter the war until 1917. Its soldiers, however, helped Britain and France defeat Germany.

Though the war briefly turned Americans' attention overseas, the victorious conclusion allowed them to look inward again. Moreover, the United States was now considered a world power. Americans began viewing themselves with greater pride. While much of Europe had been destroyed, the United States had remained unblemished, and its contributions during the war were considered heroic.

For the United States, the immediate postwar era was a time of financial prosperity. Not only did Britain, France, and Germany borrow millions of dollars to repair their battered lands, but they also had to repay the United States for war loans. Germany also owed reparations—money that defeated nations are ordered to pay the victors. Britain and France even borrowed more money from the United States to rebuild their countries.

After the War

Britain and France were in no mood to let Germany off the hook in 1918. They forced the Germans to sign the Treaty of Versailles in November 1919. The agreement stipulated that Germany must give up territory to surrounding nations and pay for damages inflicted on these countries during the conflict. The Treaty of Versailles reduced the German army to 100,000 men and severely curtailed its naval fleet.

But it was the reparations, which Germany simply did not have the resources to pay, that hurt the most. After the war, Germany fell into a deep economic slump. It recovered in the late 1920s, only to struggle again in the early 1930s.

Many parts of Europe had been ravaged by the war. The United States made loans to countries such as Britain, France, and Germany to help them rebuild. In the late 1920s, the growth in the American economy began to show signs of slowing down. Bankers hoped to receive repayments of money they had loaned to foreign governments. However, by the time these countries had finished rebuilding, they only had enough money left to run their countries. They were also beginning to experience an economic recession. Repaying the United States was not a priority on their agendas.

U.S. manufacturers thrived in 1917 and 1918 building war equipment, but they did not slow down after peace finally settled upon Europe. European nations were unable to produce their own goods for export. Instead, they depended on the United States for many imported goods. This dependence helped the United States achieve financial dominance in the years following the war.

In addition, U.S. manufacturers produced and marketed goods and services that were either new to Americans or that elevated their sense of self-worth. Automobiles were one of these products. Few Americans owned cars before the war. But between 1918 and 1929, the number of registered cars in the United States leaped from 7 million to 23 million. Economist Stuart Chase wrote:

> *Besides the elation of sheer speed and its power to determine social position, (the car promised) romance, adventure, and escape from the monotony which all too often characterizes modern life. It has captured our psychological interest as nothing has ever done before, and as perhaps nothing will do again.* [2]

Other inventions, such as refrigerators and household appliances, elevated the lifestyle of

Americans as well. The business boom jump-started the construction of new office buildings, factories, and stores. People moved into newly built homes—a first for many.

The entertainment industry also changed dramatically. Even though only silent films were being produced, the number of movie theaters rose considerably during the first half of the 1920s. People were listening to radios in larger numbers. By 1923, approximately 400,000 Americans had radios in their homes, up from 60,000 the year before. Through radio, businesses could market their products to people in their own homes, boosting the advertising industry and spurring the economy.

Radios in America

KDKA in Pittsburgh, Pennsylvania, became the first commercial radio station in 1920, and many Americans decided they wanted a radio in their homes. Radio sales jumped from $60 million in 1922 to $426 million in 1929. By 1922, a total of 576 radio stations jammed the airways.

INVESTING

Before World War I, the vast majority of Americans simply put their money in banks. But in 1917,

Silent film actor Charlie Chaplin helped promote the sale of Liberty Bonds in the 1920s.

the U.S. government began promoting Liberty Bonds to help pay for the war effort. This was the first experience many Americans had with investing.

A bond is similar to a loan to the government. Investors who purchased the bonds were promised their money returned with interest at a later date. The government authorized the issue of Liberty Bonds four times during the war at interest rates between 3.5 and 4.5 percent. If a person bought a $100 bond that earned 3.5 percent interest, he or she would be loaning the government $100 for the war effort. If the person held on to the bond for ten years, he or she would earn $41.06 for that loan in addition to receiving the initial investment of $100 back. The bonds helped both the U.S. government and the investors who bought the bonds.

More than 65 million Americans purchased Liberty Bonds during the war. The U.S. government raised more than $17 billion to fund the war through the sale of these bonds.

Promoting Bonds

Popular silent film actor Charlie Chaplin strongly supported the purchase of Liberty Bonds in order to support the war effort. He made public appearances to promote the bonds. He even made a short film called *The Bond* to encourage people to purchase Liberty Bonds.

LOOKING TO THE FUTURE

The United States had recovered from a slow economic period following World War I. Americans felt comfortable and happy with the status quo. In 1928, they elected Herbert Hoover as President. At his inauguration in March 1929, Hoover spoke about continuing the country's prosperity into the 1930s:

In no nation, are the institutions of progress more advanced. In no nations are the fruits of accomplishment more secure. In no nation is the government more worthy of respect. No country is more loved by its people. I have an abiding faith in their capacity, integrity and high purpose. I have no fears for the future of our country. It is bright with hope. [3]

Many people believed the good times would last forever. Americans who had been introduced to the idea of investing with Liberty Bonds began to put their money into riskier

Spending in the 1920s

In 1929, Americans spent $500 million on sporting goods; $114 million on toys, games, and playground equipment; and $75 million on record players. Greater wealth allowed people to purchase cars and increased the number of visitors to national parks from 196,000 in 1910 to 2.7 million in 1930.

An advertisement for liberty bonds

investments in the stock market. They also began to purchase goods on credit. They did not have enough money to purchase cars, homes, or luxuries, such as appliances, for their homes, but they were confident in the economy. Americans felt that they could purchase these items on credit, using installment plans to pay off their purchases over a period of time. They believed they would be able to pay for these items later. This exuberance for new products and the availability of money in the form of credit pushed manufacturers to keep putting out newer and more modern products to sell.

However, manufacturers were soon producing more goods than could be sold. American farmers faced similar problems. New equipment allowed farmers to produce more food at a faster rate. At first, farmers were selling their crops abroad to recovering European nations. But as time went on and Europe recovered from the war, demand began to dwindle. By the mid-1920s, Britain, France, and Germany were becoming self-sufficient. Farmers were now left with an overabundance of crops.

While some problems were clearly looming in the U.S. economy, they were easy to ignore during this period of abundance. Americans' outlooks on the future were as bright as the words of President Hoover. ⌐

Herbert Hoover and Amelia Earhart

The floor of the New York Stock Exchange

STOCKS AND BONDS

The introduction of Liberty Bonds in 1917 helped open up the idea of investing for many Americans. They realized they did not have to simply put their money in a bank. Instead, they could invest it. This idea appealed to many new investors who were excited by the idea of large returns on their investments. To them, the stock market appeared to be a fantastic way to increase their savings. Finally, even middle-class investors would be able to afford automobiles, radios, and the newest appliances.

Generally, most investors put their money into two types of financial investments: bonds (such as Liberty Bonds) or company stocks. An investor who purchased a bond, either through a company or the government, was guaranteed to receive that money back at a later time, plus the interest that had built up during that time. If an individual purchased a $1,000 bond at 4 percent interest and allowed the bond to accrue, or accumulate, interest for ten years, that person would receive back $1,480.25—a $480.25 profit—after the ten-year period.

Investing in the Stock Market

Investing in bonds, however, is a slow way to make money. Many new investors in the 1920s were more interested in investing in the stock market, where their investments could grow within days. Investing in shares of stock can be a good way to make money, but it is also much riskier. When an investor purchases shares of stock from a company, that investor is buying a part of the company. A company sells stock, or shares of ownership, as a way to raise money that is used to improve the business. This money can be used to expand the business or purchase new technology. Whatever the money is used for, it is intended to help the business in some way.

If a company does well, its stock value goes up. If it does poorly, stock value goes down. Investors want the company's stock to go up because that is how investors make money. If the value of their stock goes up, they can make a profit by selling that stock. For example, if an investor buys 100 shares of stock at $15 each (a total of $1,500) and the company's stock increases in value to $25 a share, that investor could sell his or her stock—which would be then valued at $2,500—and make a $1,000 profit. However, if the

Land in Florida

One example of speculation at its worst in the mid-1920s was the buying and selling of land in Florida. Land was divided into building lots and sold for a 10 percent down payment. It did not matter that much if the land bought and sold was uninhabitable. The mere idea of people swarming to that warm state in the winter caused a market craze, even to those who had no intention of moving there.

company does poorly, and the shares decrease in value to five dollars each, that investor would lose $1,000 if he or she were to sell at that time. If the investor does not sell, he or she can hold on to the stocks. Later, the value could increase to where the investor could make a profit, or it could drop even further. Although stock investments can be very profitable, they can also be very risky investments because profits are not guaranteed.

Many people in the 1920s, however, did not recognize the risk of investing in the stock market. They saw only that businesses had been doing well throughout the past decade and that the economy appeared strong. The past success of the stock market made many new investors believe that anyone could become rich through investing. They did not want to miss out on this opportunity. At the time, most people were optimistic about the

A Bull or Bear Stock Market

Often times, the stock market is referred to as being either a bear or a bull market. In a bear market, stock prices are generally declining and the market is not doing well. A bull market is simply the opposite—when stocks are rising and the market appears good.

future of the country and believed they were in an era of what President Hoover called permanent prosperity.

TRADING ON THE NEW YORK STOCK EXCHANGE

Such optimism was on full display at the center of the American economic world at the New York Stock Exchange (NYSE). The stock exchange is located on the corner of Broad Street and Wall Street in New York City. Traders gather there daily to buy and sell stocks.

On the floor of the stock exchange, traders

New York Stock Exchange

On May 17, 1792, the historic Buttonwood Agreement was signed by 24 stockbrokers outside 68 Wall Street in New York City. The meeting took place under a buttonwood tree. The agreement specified that the brokers were to deal only with each other, and it set commissions at .25 percent.

In 1817, the group named itself the New York Stock & Exchange Board, later shortening the name to New York Stock Exchange (NYSE). By then, the stock exchange was trading the stocks and bonds of the country's largest corporations, such as railroads. The NYSE would become the largest stock exchange in the world.

As of December 2006, the NYSE traded the stock of 2,764 companies worldwide. The NYSE is sometimes referred to as the "big board" because it lists more large companies than any other stock exchange. In 1929, the NYSE traded an average of 10 million shares a day. By 2007, that number had increased to 5 billion shares.

The stock exchange building is currently located at the corners of Broad Street and Wall Street in New York City. It is a prominent landmark in New York City's financial district.

would buy and sell shares of stock for other investors. Groups of traders would gather around posts and call out prices on stock shares while specialists at the posts would take the bids and ultimately make the stock trade. Usually this activity was fairly calm. But by the late 1920s, the stock exchange floor became increasingly busy, as more and more Americans were investing in the stock market.

Not everyone had direct access to a trader at the stock exchange. So, across the country there were brokerages (also called commission houses). There, investors could hire a stockbroker to buy or sell stock for them. The broker would send the investor's order by telephone to the New York Stock Exchange.

Investors across the country could see how the general stock market was doing by checking the Dow Jones Industrial Average. The Dow Jones is a popular index that many investors

The History of the Dow

In 1896, Charles Dow, a financial journalist, and his business partner, Edward Jones, created the Dow Jones Industrial Average stock index. The index was created as a way for investors to see how the general market was doing on any particular day. At first, the Dow only represented 11 well-known industrial companies. Each company's stock price would be added up with the other companies' and divided by 11 in order to get the average for the day. That average could be compared to other days to determine if general stock prices went up or down on that particular day. In 1916, the Dow index represented 20 different companies' stocks. By 1929, it expanded to 30—the amount it still uses today.

Stock certificate for North Butte Mining Company

used, and still use today. It lists the value of 30 major stocks. The average value of the 30 stocks represents how the general stock market is doing on any given day. If the Dow goes up, overall stock prices go up. If the Dow goes down, stock prices as a whole are also down.

Buying Stocks on Margin

As consumers across the United States purchased items such as refrigerators and automobiles on credit or installment plans in the 1920s, many also did the same with stocks. Many brokerages allowed investors to pay only a small portion of the value of the shares of stock they wanted to purchase. The rest would be backed by loans from the commission houses. This is called buying stocks on margin.

Many investors were eager to buy stocks on margin because it allowed them to make larger investments with less money as a down payment. The false promise of large returns caused many to believe they would have no trouble repaying the loan after their stocks went up.

If an investor only had $500 to put toward stock shares but wanted to purchase $5,000 worth of shares, the broker would loan the remaining $4,500. The broker would then purchase the total amount of shares worth $5,000. The broker also kept the stock certificate (which showed the amount of shares the investor owned) as backing for the loan. If the stock went up, the investor could use those gains toward paying off the loan to receive the full amount of shares. But if the stock went down, the investor had to either pay the broker more money to continue holding the stock, or the broker would sell the shares and the investor would have to pay off the remaining loan.

Buying stocks on margin was extremely popular for many Americans—especially those who were new to the stock market. For the first time, working-class Americans were able to invest in the stock market by purchasing stocks on margin. Few were concerned with the risk involved. After all, although there were slight dips in the stock market from time to time; for the most part, stock shares seemed to be going up. People continued to borrow money to buy stocks. By the end of 1928, stock exchange brokers had more than $6 billion in outstanding loans from those who had bought stocks on margin.

SPECULATION

Such frenzy within the stock market also led to increased speculation. In the past, an investor bought shares of stock in a company to help the business expand and grow

Favored Investments

The growth of the automobile industry played an important role in the increased interest in buying stocks following World War I. Shares in General Motors rose 50 percent in the spring of 1919 alone. The relatively new invention of radio also became a popular investment in the 1920s. The Radio Corporation of America (RCA) was a particular favorite.

Wall Street is the heart of New York City's financial district.

through a long-term investment. As the business
expanded and became more profitable, the shares
of stock the investor owned would increase in value.
Through long-term investing, both the investor
and the business would profit. Speculators, on the
other hand, only bought stocks to make a profit
off day-to-day changes in the value of shares. They
would watch a stock's value, selling it when the
value went up enough in price to make a profit. As

a result, speculators did not help businesses or the economy grow, as they were not investing in the long-term health of a company. Still, the presence of speculators added liquidity to financial markets, making it easier for non-speculators to buy and sell.

The rapid speculation in the stock market and the ever-increasing amount of stocks being bought on margin concerned the government and the Federal Reserve Board. They understood that the value of the stocks would not go up forever. When the prices dropped, billions of dollars in loans would, possibly, not be able to be paid back. Millions of investors could end up in debt, and the nation's economy would be devastated. The Federal Reserve Board knew they had to do something, and they knew they would have to act fast. ⌐

The New York Stock Exchange

First U.S. Secretary of the Treasury Alexander Hamilton

THE FEDERAL RESERVE
TAKES ACTION

Virtually since the stock market began, speculators have been attracted to it. These investors are often willing to take great financial risks in the hopes of achieving greater financial wealth. They are unconcerned with the growth and future of the companies in which they invest. Speculators buy large amounts of stocks, often borrowing the money to do so, with the goal of selling them soon after for a higher price. In 1792, first U.S. Secretary of the Treasury Alexander Hamilton expressed his disgust in one such investor,

> 'Tis time there should be a line of separation between honest Men & knaves, between respectable Stockholders and dealers in the funds, and more unprincipled Gamblers.[1]

Hoover Tries to Limit Speculation

Almost 140 years later, newly elected President Herbert Hoover was concerned over the same issue of speculators in the stock market. He, and many in Congress, felt that speculators were creating overvalued shares of stock. Generally,

Alexander Hamilton

Throughout his lifetime, Alexander Hamilton served as an Army officer, a statesman, a lawyer, and even helped write the U.S. Constitution. Yet one of his most important roles was serving as the first U.S. secretary of the treasury. Hamilton served from 1789 to 1795 and was responsible for the economic policies of the country. He also established the first central bank.

a stock's value is directly related to how well a company is doing. But sometimes, stocks become overvalued or undervalued by investors manipulating the price of the stock. Many in the U.S. government feared that speculators were driving up the prices of stock, making each share much more expensive than what it was worth. An overvaluation of stock prices creates a "bubble."

Hoover was concerned about what would happen when the bubble eventually burst and investors realized their shares of stock were worth less than their actual value. Hoover and his advisors anticipated a selling frenzy in which few people would be willing to buy. This would mean that the borrowers would not be able to pay back their loans for the stocks they had purchased on margin. Hoover and his advisors feared this could cause the stock market to crash.

Herbert Hoover

Herbert Clark Hoover was the thirty-first president of the United States. Before becoming president, Hoover was an active humanitarian and also served as the U.S. secretary of commerce under President Harding and President Coolidge. Hoover won a landslide victory for the presidency in 1929. He lost the election for a second term mainly due to the challenges he faced in trying to bring the country out of the Great Depression.

Hoover attempted to reduce the amount of speculation in the market. He contacted editors and publishers and asked them to warn Americans about speculation. He spoke with bankers, asking them to decrease such easy lending to investors. Hoover even sought out Richard Whitney, vice president of the New York Stock Exchange, to see if Whitney could limit the amount of speculation by his members in the stock exchange. Hoover's efforts had little effect. It seemed more action was needed.

THE FEDERAL RESERVE RAISES INTEREST RATES

In 1913, the U.S. government created the Federal Reserve. Its purpose was, and still is, to regulate monetary policy so that the U.S. economy remains stable and healthy. The

Stock Pools

With increased speculation, stock prices became overvalued. Speculators drove up the price of stocks in ways that were unrelated to the actual business growth of the companies. Speculators bought stock with the intention of selling soon after the stock had increased in value.

Many speculators formed pools to promote stocks. The investors within the pool bought shares of a particular stock and then promoted that stock to unknowing investors, often by using the media to write glowing reports about the particular stock. When the stock became popular enough and the price was high enough, the original pool of investors quietly sold their shares—making a hefty profit in the process. The price of that stock had little to do with the actual growth of the company that it represented, so it became overvalued.

The Federal Reserve

Federal Reserve has the authority to raise or lower
interest rates on bank loans. If a person takes out a
loan through a bank, he or she is required not only
to repay the loan but also to pay interest on the loan.
If a person takes out a $5,000 loan that is to be

paid off over a ten-year period with 10 percent interest, that person will ultimately pay $7,929.60—$5,000 for the original loan plus $2,929.60 in interest.

In March 1929, the Federal Reserve raised the interest rates on stock loans to 20 percent in the hopes of discouraging investors from buying on margin. That same $5,000 at 20 percent interest over a ten-year period would then cost an investor $11,595.60. It appeared as if the Federal Reserve's increase on interest rates had worked. Stock prices plummeted, as few were willing to take out loans to buy stocks at such high interest rates.

SPECULATION AND MARGIN-BUYING CONTINUES

But the tycoons of Wall Street had their own plan. They did not like the government getting involved in what they felt was none of its business. On

National City Bank Provides Loans

When the Federal Reserve raised interest rates in late March 1929, the stock market experienced a sharp decline. Yet as soon as banks, such as National City Bank, stepped in to provide loans to brokers, the panic stopped and the stock market once again went up.

W.A. Lyon of the *New York Herald Tribune* wrote of these loans, "Assured that the New York banks were ready with their boundless resources to prevent a money crisis, the public and the professional trader set out to repair the damage done to prices on Monday and the major part of Tuesday."[2]

March 26, 1929, Charles E. Mitchell, chairman of National City Bank, announced that his bank would lend approximately $25 million to brokers. This allowed speculators to continue to buy stocks on margin. Stock prices, once again, continued to rise. It seemed that there was little the Federal Reserve could do to keep Wall Street's power in check.

Over the next few months, stock prices remained relatively stable. But in June, borrowing money for buying stocks suddenly became much easier. Corporations started lending their own money to investors. Instead of using their money to improve their companies, they were loaning it to speculators for an easy profit. With cheap loans available, the stock market once again soared.

Although the stock market was doing well, the economy showed further signs of a recession, or decline. Housing construction and automobile manufacturing were slowing down. Retail sales were decreasing. Farmers were also not doing as well, and many were facing extreme amounts of debt. By 1929, the difference in income between the rich and the poor in the United States was immense. One study showed that the top 0.1 percent of the population enjoyed a total income equal to the total incomes

National City Bank

of the bottom 42 percent of the population. That
same wealthy group of 0.1 percent of the population
controlled 34 percent of the money in savings.
Meanwhile, 80 percent of Americans had no savings
at all.

To make matters worse, the gap between the rich and poor was extreme. Over the ten-year span from 1919 to 1929, production of goods increased over 40 percent, but the workers' earnings did not increase. There were more products available than those who could afford to buy them. The nation relied on its wealthiest individuals to keep the economy afloat. But many did not consider what would happen to the economy if the nation's wealthiest people were to lose all of their investments. ⌐

In 1929, the wealthy controlled 34 percent of the money in savings in U.S. banks.

People gather outside the New York Stock Exchange on October 24, 1929.

BLACK THURSDAY

Throughout the 1920s, the U.S. economy experienced incredible growth. But by 1929, the economy was heading into a natural state of decline. Only so many houses and automobiles can be built before there are not as many buyers to purchase what is produced. An economic recession seemed to be approaching. Despite this, business magazines continually noted great economic success from January to October. E.K. Berger and A.M. Leinbach of the *Magazine of Wall Street* reported in June 1929, "Business so far this year has astonished even the perennial optimists."[1] For the most part, those involved in the stock market remained optimistic and continued to buy shares of stock. Industries that held promise for growth, such as radio, electrical equipment, and utilities, were especially popular.

THE MARKET DROPS

Stock market activity decreased slightly over the summer months as many successful investors enjoyed their profits at various vacation spots. But by autumn, investors were back in the swing of things and ready to

Predictions

On September 5, 1929, only two days after the stock market reached a record high, statistician Roger Babson gave a speech warning Americans, "Sooner or later, a crash is coming and it may be terrific."[2] While the market took a dip after his speech, it soon rebounded, only to experience one of the nation's greatest crashes a month later.

Reports on Black Thursday

Although virtually all of Wall Street's top bankers and brokers were extremely nervous with the recent selling frenzy, they tried to remain optimistic and secretly encouraged reporters to be so as well. The day after Black Thursday, a reporter for the *New York Times* wrote that the mass amount of selling in the stock market was largely due to panic rather than to a poor economy:

"Much of the selling of the last few days, the brokers felt, was induced by hysteria. The views of all of the brokers present were heard, and none knew of anything disturbing to the general market situation ..."[4]

purchase more stocks. On September 3, the Dow peaked at 381.2 points—a record high in the stock market. Throughout the next two months, the Dow went up and down. The most significant price declines occurred on October 3, October 4, and October 16.

Philip Snowden, England's chancellor of the exchequer (the British equivalent to U.S. secretary of the treasury), visited the United States in early October. After observing American investors, Snowden remarked that the American stock market was a place of "speculative orgy."[3] His comment confirmed what many already feared—that stock market shares were overvalued. American investors were overly greedy, and it seemed that sooner or later, their investment tactics would result in a market collapse. Harold Bierman Jr. of Cornell University wrote:

The stock market went down on October 3 and October 4, but almost all reported business news was very optimistic. The primary negative news item was the statement by Snowden regarding the amount of speculation in the American stock market. ... There is a possibility that the Snowden comment ... was the push that started the boulder down the hill ...[5]

Snowden's comment was undoubtedly the beginning of the market's instability. His phrase "speculative orgy" concerned British investors, who then began to sell their stocks, essentially pulling their money out of the U.S. stock market.

On October 16, however, something else pushed the market downward. Many speculators had been investing largely in public utilities. In the fall of 1929, news had not been good in that sector. New government regulations, among other things, had weakened

Chancellor of the Exchequer

Philip Snowden served as Great Britain's chancellor of the exchequer on and off from 1924 to 1931. Britain's chancellor of the exchequer is very similar to the U.S. secretary of the treasury. The chancellor is responsible for the monetary and fiscal policies of Great Britain. The office of chancellor of the exchequer is the third-oldest major office in British government. In recent years the chancellor has gained considerable influence in political power.

the public utility market. Because speculators had bought the stocks on margin, as utilities decreased in price, these investors could not afford to keep them. A selling frenzy started as investors rushed to sell their shares of utility stocks before prices went down even further.

Investors were becoming increasingly uncertain. In the last hour of trading on Wednesday, October 23, 1929, stock prices fell dramatically. Some stocks were dropping more than $15 a share, and no one was willing to buy them. At the New

Stock Ticker Falls Behind

A stock ticker keeps track of the value of stocks. In 1929, the ticker did this by punching the information into long strips of paper. Today, stock tickers are digital. The 1929 stock ticker was known to keep up quite well with prices of stocks that were bought and sold. But even a delayed stock ticker generally means little. Investors know the approximate value of a stock when there is little fluctuation in the market.

However, the ticker could not keep up with the tremendous volume of trading in late October. Because stock prices were collapsing rapidly, investors did not know the prices of the stocks they were selling or buying.

The psychological effect of not knowing the prices proved to be immense. With prices dropping and panic selling overtaking the market, investors generally feared the worst. The late ticker helped convince them to sell their stocks at whatever cost the market would bring, even if it meant an enormous loss.

Brokers and investors outside New York had to catch up with the massive amount of trading. The heavy trading activity at the New York Stock Exchange caused an additional communication gap. Without knowing exactly what was going on, investors around the country feared the late information of the ticker.

Stock ticker

York Stock Exchange, traders became frantic. In that final hour of the trading day, more than 2.6 million shares of stock traded hands resulting in a market decline of $4 billion. October 23 was a record-breaking day of bad news in the stock market, but it was nothing compared to what was about to come.

BLACK THURSDAY HITS

With the opening gong sounding at the New York Stock Exchange on Thursday, October 24, traders rushed around posts ready to sell. With few investors willing to buy, stock prices plummeted. So much trading was taking place that by midday the stock ticker was nearly two hours behind. Commission houses across the country were becoming increasingly anxious because there was no reliable, up-to-date information for the current prices of stocks. All over the country, panicked investors put in orders to sell, trying to get rid of their shares before prices dropped even lower. Even across the Atlantic, panicked investors were starting to sell. As the London Stock Exchange was already closed for the day, brokers set up shop on the sidewalks instead so investors could have a chance to sell their American stocks before prices plummeted even

A Record-breaking Day

The amount of shares traded on Black Thursday, October 24, 1929, was a record-breaking 12,894,650 shares. The previous record-breaking day was the previous March, when just over 8 million shares had been traded.

more. The market experienced a free fall in stock prices. In Washington, D.C., officials at the Federal Reserve met with U.S. Secretary of the Treasury Andrew Mellon to discuss what could be done. Although they knew the stock market was in a dire position, officials were reluctant to do anything rash. Instead, they decided to wait and see if conditions would improve without action from the government.

By late afternoon, a glimmer of hope appeared. Thomas W. Lamont, a senior partner at the prominent J.P. Morgan bank, called a meeting with Wall Street's tycoons. New York City's top bankers gathered for a meeting that would last for only 20 minutes but would manage to save the market from even further calamity that day. The bankers agreed to put several million dollars of their banks' funds into the stock market. The bankers strolled around the trading floor of the exchange shouting out bids to buy shares, sometimes for more than they were valued. Richard Whitney, vice president of the New York Stock Exchange, put in an order for 25,000 shares of U.S. Steel for $205 a share—even though they were valued at $190 a share.

The actions of Wall Street's most prominent men spurred other traders to start buying. At the closing gong that day, some stocks actually ended up at a higher price than they had been at the beginning of the day. Although the day would be remembered by many as Black Thursday, the bankers' strategy seemed to help save the market from collapse—at least temporarily.

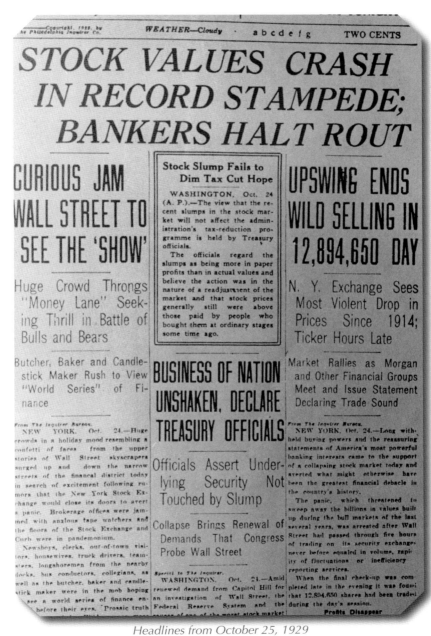

Headlines from October 25, 1929

Workers answer calls at the exchange.

INVESTORS HOLD ON

ompared to the events of Black Thursday, trading on Friday, October 25, 1929, was relatively calm but still heavy. Wall Street's tycoons did not put more money into the market, but they did not need to. There were enough traders that day to buy. By the end of the day, the Dow Jones Industrial Average was up.

Even with the stock market appearing somewhat stable, many were worried—including President Hoover and the Federal Reserve Board. Yet, they felt they could do little to improve the situation.

SPECULATORS AND MARGIN BUYERS

Newspapers and other reports attacked speculators and margin buyers for their role in the stock market's downward spiral. Much of the public began to agree with the government and officials such as Chancellor Snowden. Speculation was ruining the market, and soon the bubble would burst. This fear became even more widespread. Although trading on October 25 was not too extreme, by Saturday, October 26, the market took another turn for the worse.

Headlines

Across the country, Americans learned about the crash in the newspapers. After the crash on Black Thursday, the headlines on the front page of the *New York Times* read:

PRICES OF STOCKS CRASH IN HEAVY LIQUIDATION, TOTAL DROP OF BILLIONS

PAPER LOSS $4,000,000,000

2,600,000 Shares Sold In The Final Hour In Record Decline

MANY ACCOUNTS WIPED OUT

But No Brokerage House Is In Difficulties, As Margins Have Been Kept High

ORGANIZED BANKING ABSENT

Bankers Confer On Steps To Support Market Highest Break Is 96 Points[1]

In 1929, many types of people were investing in the market. Some were wealthy businessmen who knew the ups and downs of the market and its fundamentals. Others were newcomers, hoping to make quick money by purchasing stocks on margin. Those purchasing on margin were hit hard that Saturday. They did not realize how quickly their fortunes could change. It was an easy way to get rich quick, and few truly understood the risk involved.

Brokers demanded that margin buyers come up with more cash in order to keep their shares of stock in the market. Many could not afford to do so as they already had taken out loans to buy the initial shares. Most of these investors were

Companies Hit Hard during the Crash

Investors were not the only ones to lose out during the stock market crash. Many companies relied on the support of investors to help further their businesses. Some well-known companies that were hit hard during the stock market crash of 1929 include:

- Chrysler
- General Electric
- General Motors
- Ford Motors
- Paramount
- Radio Corporation of America
- Sears, Roebuck & Co.
- Standard Oil
- U.S. Steel

Many of the companies devastated in the crash of 1929 managed to keep going and continue to be profitable businesses today. Others were not as lucky. Some companies could not withstand the loss of so many investors after the crash and were forced to declare bankruptcy.

forced to simply sell their remaining shares. A few others believed that the market would soon recover. In desperation, they were able to come up with the money to pay their brokers enough to keep holding on to their shares of stock. They turned to relatives to borrow money or sold their jewelry and other valuables at pawnshops.

Throughout the 1920s, stocks seemed to effortlessly go up in price. Although the market had been hit hard in the prior days, few recognized the possibility that their stocks might not go up in price again anytime soon. As prices continued to drop through the trading day on Saturday, more speculators were forced to sell the stocks they were so desperately trying to keep. The market was once again plummeting, and more and more investors were losing all that they were worth.

Desperate Investors

During the days of the crash, thousands of brokers told margin buyers they needed to come up with more money in order to keep their shares in the market. As a result, pawnshops, savings banks, and insurance companies were bombarded with those trying to obtain any amount of money with which to pay their brokers. Many investors mistakenly thought that the stock market would soon rebound so they were willing to cash out their insurance policies and sell their valuables in order to keep their stocks.

A Day to Rest

The closing gong on Saturday, October 26, marked the end of an extremely tumultuous week at the stock exchange. Investors everywhere were bracing themselves for the start of the trading week that Monday. However, those who worked at the stock exchange had little time to rest. Brokers and stock exchange workers labored around the clock to prepare for the week ahead. Although Sunday was their only day off, few were able to leave Wall Street. With all of the mayhem that had occurred within the previous week, commission houses in New York and throughout the country spent the day trying to catch up and straighten out their accounting books.

Cots were put up in hotels and gyms near Wall Street so employees could get a few hours of sleep. Restaurants stayed open much later than usual to give exhausted workers

Rumors of Suicide

During the days of the stock market collapse, rumors of investors taking their lives were rampant throughout New York City's financial district and across the country. Although some did commit suicide in the wake of the crash, data shows that suicides were more prevalent that summer when the stock market had been doing well.

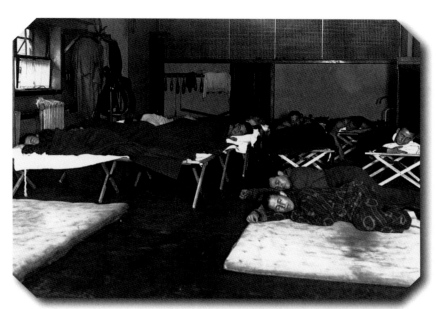

Workers catch a few hours of sleep in the days following Black Thursday.

a chance to get a quick bite to eat. Workers were tired and there were reports of people passing out at their desks in exhaustion.

While those on Wall Street and at commission houses were busy getting their books in order, investors across the country were reading the Sunday newspapers. The papers were filled with articles giving more bad news concerning the public utility sector. For example, one article in the *New York Times* was titled "Bay State Utilities Face Investigation."[2]

Utility stocks had been faring poorly that month and news of further regulations did not bode well. Although many investors remained hopeful that the worst was over, many others were doubtful and getting ready to pull their investments out of such a shaky market. The New York Stock Exchange had already experienced a few very chaotic days of trading, and many investors were going to experience a few more. ⌒

Brokers in London keep track of exchange rates.

Investors outside the Exchange on October 29, 1929

THE COLLAPSE

The opening gong on Monday, October 28, 1929, sparked another intense day of selling. While much of the trading the prior week had been focused on smaller, relatively unimportant company stocks, this day was different. Traders were selling the blue chip stocks—stocks issued from the best companies. U.S. Steel, General Electric, and other high-ranking stocks were falling at a dramatic rate. By late that morning, the stock ticker was already a half hour behind. By the end of the day, so much trading had occurred that the ticker was two-and-a-half hours behind. Many brokerages did not even bother to look at the ticker, but instead called the exchange directly to learn the current stock prices.

By the end of the trading day, more than 9 million shares had traded hands—3 million shares had traded in the last hour alone. The Dow Jones Industrial Average had declined 12.8 percent—the largest decline the U.S. stock market had ever experienced. Wall Street's top businessmen and bankers met to discuss the day's events. They would continue to try to keep the market from bottoming out, but they knew

Busy Day of Trading

New York hotels were crowded from Black Thursday to Black Tuesday. Trading was so heavy that few employees of the New York Stock Exchange had time to go home before they had to return to work. Restaurants in the financial district were also open 15 to 20 hours a day to keep up with business.

they could not keep it afloat forever. Bankers tried to put up an optimistic and reassuring front despite the grim outlook.

Black Tuesday

On Tuesday, October 29, it seemed everyone was prepared for the worst. New York Stock Exchange Superintendent William R. Crawford witnessed the chaos that day. He sounded the gong that signaled the start of trading, which was a well-known daily ritual. He described the activity of the thousands of panicked brokers, and investors:

They roared like a lot of lions and tigers. They hollered and screamed, they clawed at one another's collars. It was like a bunch of crazy men. [1]

As had happened during previous periods of panic selling, the stock market ticker again could not keep up with the activity. Among the first stocks to collapse that fateful morning was U.S. Steel. More than 650,000 of its shares were sold in the first three minutes of trading. Even as its price plummeted, few seemed interested in buying.

Communication stocks such as International Telephone and Telegraph and the Radio

Corporation of America also fell rapidly. Stock in other large corporations such as General Motors and General Electric fell as well. Investment trusts Allegheny, Blue Ridge, and United Corporation dropped. So did movie industry stocks Paramount, Fox, and Warner Brothers.

Over the screaming of the frightened masses stampeding around the floor, the New York Stock Exchange acting president, Richard Whitney, called for the 40 governors of the stock exchange to hold a meeting. The meeting was called to discuss

Memories of the Crash

In October of 1929 I was just being broken in on the phones on the floor of the Stock Exchange, cold. The wires from the order room and from any special customer or any registered rep that had a direct wire to me, would put an order in and I had to take the order—buy a thousand shares of Auburn Motors or whatever. Give it to a broker. But at that time I was just a clerk. I was brought down two months before that crash took place to learn the wires. So when the crash took place, I didn't know enough about what was going on. And it was just like a nightmare. I couldn't believe what was going on. In those days, every buy order was on a black pad. And every sell order was on a red pad. And all I saw was members running around with a fistful of red orders. I couldn't find any bids. I'd come back to the phone and say, "there's no bid for New York Central, it's down ... it's selling down 15 points." The tape ran ... in those days the market was open from 10 until 3. That's during the five day week and on Saturday, from 10 to 12 on Saturday, we had a short weekend. Anyhow, the tape ran two and a half hours late in a five-hour session and didn't stop running until 8:30 at night the day of the crash.[2]

—Horace Silverstone

whether or not they should close the stock exchange for some time until the chaos could die down. The meeting was discretely held in the basement of the New York Stock Exchange, rather than in the usual meeting room. Moving in twos or threes, to not attract attention, the 40 governors made it into the basement. Whitney later described the atmosphere of their meeting:

> *The feeling of those present was revealed by their habit of continually lighting cigarettes, taking a puff or two, putting them out and lighting new ones—a practice which soon made the narrow room blue with smoke and extremely stuffy.*[3]

Amid the noise of panicked traders above them, the 40 governors discussed the situation. Some felt the stock exchange would collapse if they did not close for the remainder of the day. They thought that the system could not handle so much

Movies

In October 1929, New York City Mayor Jimmy Walker presided over a convention of movie exhibitors and asked them not to show newsreels of the panic in New York City while the stock market crash continued. Newsreels were short documentary-type movies about current events that were shown before a movie. To keep morale up, Mayor Walker urged movie theater owners to "Show pictures that will reinstate courage and hope in the hearts of the people. Give them a chance to forget their financial losses on the stock market and look with hope to the future. The morale of the people must be maintained, and you can do it."[4]

trading at one time. Others felt it was necessary to keep the stock exchange open, so as to not panic traders and investors even further. They argued that if it were to close, it might result in traders selling their shares illegally on "sidewalk markets" where the trading would become even more unregulated. Ultimately, the governors agreed to keep the New York Stock Exchange open and headed back upstairs to the pandemonium of the trading floor.

The selling frenzy was feeding off itself. The savings of many investors were wiped out. Rumors of suicides were rampant throughout New York City's financial district, although few actually occurred on Wall Street that day. Investors of every religion packed the nearby Trinity Church to pray. They were stunned and depressed. By noon, more than 8 million shares had been traded, and prices were still falling.

Close the NYSE?

The governors of the New York Stock Exchange voted against closing the stock market on October 29. Many believed that by allowing the market to remain open, investors would be reassured. The decision to keep the stock exchange open is still debated today.

By late afternoon, stock prices had dropped far enough for some of the wealthiest investors to take a chance at buying. Stock market giants such as Bernard Baruch, a large-scale financier, and Billy Durant of the automotive industry purchased shares of U.S. Steel.

The market recovered somewhat during the last couple hours of the session. But by the end of the day, an incredible 16.4 million shares had been traded on Wall Street and $15 billion had been lost. Millions of people had been affected by the collapse, and there was nothing to do now but assess the losses and keep going. ⌐

Newspapers

Among the only businesses that profited, at least temporarily, from the events of October 29, 1929, were newspapers. Many people first learned about the crash from the evening editions of newspapers. Hundreds of people gathered to read the extra editions that were sold by newsboys on the streets.

Investors crowd the streets after Black Tuesday.

An investor tries to sell his car after losing his savings.

IN THE WAKE
OF THE CRASH

he bull market of the 1920s had drawn
in millions of investors and made many
believe they were invincible. During the last week
of October 1929, that all came crashing down.
Approximately 64.4 million shares had been traded

over the course of one week—an amount greater than the total bought and sold during any month since March 1928. The massive profits of 1929 were wiped out, and many Americans' savings were lost with them.

Stories of once prominent men suddenly taking their lives spread across the country. These stories have been exaggerated over the years, but such tragedies did occur during the stock market crash of 1929. Some simply could not handle the prospect of suddenly being both broke and hopelessly in debt.

Losing It All

With the crash, many celebrities had lost their savings or gone into debt. Singer Eddie Cantor had only $60 to his name and owed $285,000 in loans on his failed stocks. The rich became poor overnight. Newspaper editor Herbert Bayard Swope had

Defining a Crash

There is no specific dollar amount or percentage that defines a stock market crash. However, economists characterize a market crash as a steep, double-digit decline in the value of the stock market index in a matter of a few days. A stock market index measures the value of all stocks being traded. The Dow Jones Industrial Average is the market index that American investors used and still use.

started October with a fortune of $14 million. By the end of the week, he was $2 million in debt. Heavyweight boxing champion Jack Dempsey went broke. Composer Irving Berlin lost nearly everything. He expressed the fright many felt during that week of financial collapse, admitting,

> I was scared. I had all the money I wanted for the rest of my life. Then all of a sudden I didn't. I had taken it easy and gone soft and wasn't too certain I could get going again.[1]

Among the victims were famed comedian brothers Groucho and Harpo Marx. Groucho was so crushed after the collapse that he refused to go on stage for two days in Pittsburgh to perform in the play *Animal Crackers*. Groucho later quipped, "All I lost was two hundred and forty thousand dollars, I would have lost more, but that was all the money I had."[2]

Bernard Baruch

Before the stock market collapse, financial investor Bernard Baruch advised many investors, such as humorist Will Rogers, to sell their stocks when stock market prices were still high, saying "When good news about the market hits the front page of the *New York Times*, sell."[3] Baruch was a stock market speculator who, by the age of 30, had amassed a fortune speculating in the sugar market.

Those who had recognized the warning signs and sold their stocks before the stock market crash managed to survive. Humorist Will Rogers took the advice of Bernard Baruch and sold his stocks months earlier. But most investors had ignored the warning signs and were now terrified.

INVESTORS TAKE ADVANTAGE OF THE FALLEN MARKET

In the days following the crash, John D. Rockefeller, one of America's richest men, announced that he and his son would continue investing in the market. They believed that the fundamentals of business and economics in the United States were generally sound and that the crash did not warrant any halt in purchasing stocks. His comment buoyed many investors to continue purchasing. In a *New York Herald Tribune* article, reporter

Continuing to Invest

John D. Rockefeller, one of the wealthiest men in America, tried to calm investors on October 29 by announcing he had purchased "sound common stocks." Entertainer Eddie Cantor replied by joking, "Sure, who else had any money left?"[4] It was amazing Cantor was in any mood to make a humorous remark. He was one of many in show business who was in the process of losing a fortune.

Ferdinand Lundberg wrote:

> *Revived by spontaneous investment buying and declarations*
> *of large extra cash dividends by leading companies ... the stock*
> *market yesterday received a fresh start and scored a record*
> *comeback. ... The high spot of the day from a stock market*
> *viewpoint was the statement by John D. Rockefeller that there*
> *was no need to destroy values and that he and his son ... had*
> *been heavy buyers of stocks for investment in the last few days,*
> *and would continue to buy at present prices ...*[5]

While many Americans had lost their savings
and were in debt from the previous week's crash,
others were taking advantage of the fallen market.
On Wednesday, October 30, many bargain buyers
bought into the stock market hoping to make money
by buying very cheap stock shares that were offered
at the time. At the opening gong, trading was once
again heavy. This time, however, stock shares were
going up. Investors and traders were relieved and
hopeful that the stock market was finally starting to
rebound. But the collapse had tired workers and
traders alike. Acting president Richard Whitney
decided to make Thursday's trading day a short one.
He closed the market that Friday and Saturday so
workers could catch up on some much needed rest.

THE MARKET BEGINS TO RECOVER

Trading resumed the following Monday, November 4. Over the next week, stock prices continued to go up and down. On November 11, stock prices once again experienced a dramatic drop.

That evening, Wall Street's top bankers held a meeting. Although the market was still experiencing some violent swings, the bankers decided that it was stable enough that they did not have to continue buying stocks to hold it up. The next day, stocks again took a dive, but this time, the bankers were not there to buy. On November 13, 1929, the Dow

Bad Memories

The events of late October 1929 gave older investors a horrible sense of déjà vu. Those who had been involved in the stock market two decades earlier remembered the stock market crash of 1907.

The stock market took two major dips in 1907—one in March and another in October. After strong times in 1906, stock prices fell 50 percent the following year, which contributed to a period of reduced economic activity or recession. The practices of speculation and purchasing stocks on credit played a role in the panic of 1907. It also resulted in the closing of many banks and other businesses.

Fortunately, disaster was averted. Wealthy businessman J.P. Morgan organized a team of bankers and trust executives to buy devalued stocks of healthy corporations and the U.S. Treasury transferred $35 million to various banks around the country.

Soon the panic passed. By 1908, the American economy was thriving again. But in 1929, many older investors could not help but remember the stock crash 22 years earlier with a terrible sense of foreboding.

Jones Industrial Average closed at 199—lower than on Black Thursday and Black Tuesday. The stock market collapse of 1929 was at its lowest point.

After November 13, the stock market began to make its slow recovery. The market shakily moved back up, although the wealth of many investors did not do the same. Approximately 3 million people were directly affected by the crash, but hundreds of thousands would feel its effects as well.

America's wealthiest consumed much of the luxury goods produced at the time. After the market crash, they were no longer able to spend their money on such goods. Because businesses could no longer sell as much as they had been, they began to fire their employees. Unemployment rates began to climb.

President Hoover took immediate action after the crash. He lowered

Unsympathetic Response

Not every publication was sympathetic during the crash. The *New Yorker* magazine criticized the United States for its perceived greed, stating, "the collapse of the market, over and above the pain, couldn't help but be amusing. It is amusing to see a fat land quivering in paunchy fright."[6]

income tax rates in the belief that cutting taxes would allow people to purchase more goods and invest again. This approach had little effect since taxes at the time took little out of income. The president also called together business leaders and encouraged them to maintain employment and salary levels.

LOOKING AHEAD TO THE 1930s

Times were not as easy as they were throughout most of the 1920s, yet the general outlook for 1930 seemed good. A December 15, 1929, article from the *World* stated:

> *That 1930 may be a very prosperous year, industrially and otherwise, without the peak conditions that made 1929 an exceptional year for business prosperity, is an observation made by Louis Guenther, publisher of the Financial World, in a statement based upon Secretary Mellon's fiscal report ...*[7]

Hoover Criticism

Hoover was often criticized during his presidency for his policies during the stock market crash and the Great Depression that followed. Many people criticized Hoover's lack of action.

Hoover preferred a central government that had a limited role in people's lives and was tentative about exerting too much control. Despite this, Hoover implemented more programs to relieve citizens' economic burdens than any U.S. president before him.

People were cautious but optimistic. And that optimism was seen in the stock market in the first few months of the new year. By April 17, 1930, the Dow Jones Industrial Average reached 294—essentially a full recovery from the collapse six months earlier. Although the stock market had rebounded from the original crash, the results of the crash would continue to affect both the stock market and the lives of millions throughout the United States in the coming decade. ⌐

*John D. Rockefeller was one of the few people
still investing after the crash.*

This political cartoon shows investors reaching to grab stock market bubbles.

LOOKING BACK ON
THE CRASH

In the 1920s, a popular song was "My God, How the Money Rolls In." By the 1930s, it was E.Y. "Yip" Harburg's "Brother, Can You Spare a Dime?" With the crash of 1929, the economic fortunes of millions of Americans had drastically changed in less than one year's time. And countless people were left wondering how it all had happened.

SPECULATION

People were quick to blame the excessive speculation within the market, as well as the actions, or lack thereof, of the Federal Reserve. Many felt that the speculation and the belief in permanent prosperity caught up with the greedy investor and the market as a whole. Alexander Dana Noyes, a leading financial writer of the time, wrote:

> *Wild speculation and panic of 1929 [brought a] sudden recognition of economic realities. It punctured, almost overnight, the ill-fated Stock Exchange illusions. No more was heard of the new economic era.*[1]

Over the years, several leading economists have agreed that speculation in the market was a major cause of the crash.

BAD NEWS IN THE ECONOMY

There were other days of major declines before the October crash

Optimism for the Future of the Nation

After the crash, President Hoover remained optimistic that the country would be able to recover. In a speech he gave in March 1930, Hoover stated, "Any lack of confidence in the economic future or the basic strength of business in the United States is foolish. Our national capacity for hard work and intelligent cooperation is [amply] guaranty of the future."[2]

that did not result in such a collapse. What was different about that October? Some economists and financial historians believe that the 1929 crash was the result of several contributing factors that turned the "dip" in the market to a full-blown crash. During previous declines in the market, investors remained confident that stock prices would once again rise. In September and October 1929, however, there were reports reflecting bad news in utilities, as well as comments, such as Snowden's, about a "speculative orgy." There were also rising interest rates and a slowing of production in the economy. Some economists feel that it was these factors—

Galbraith's Warning

John Kenneth Galbraith is a leading economist and author of *The Great Crash*. He believes that speculation was indeed a major factor in the crash of 1929. Although many scholars disagree with him, Galbraith remains influential and continues to speak about the dangers of stock speculation, as he did at Harvard University in 1998:

One of the great facts of our time is that there is still, in the investment structure, in the stock market, a commitment to what we should call, "the speculate bubble." The possibility that bubble will break is something that everybody should have in mind.

There's one thing that should warn everybody. If you forget everything else tonight remember this, that when you hear someone say, "We have entered a new era of permanent prosperity," then you should immediately take cover, because that shows that financial idiocy has really taken hold and that history, all history, is being rejected.[3]

combined with the excessive speculation—that caused the crash.

A leading economist during the time of the crash, Irving Fisher, believed speculation was not as rampant as many thought. Fisher thought that stock prices reflected the genuine growth in the economy. Over the years, there have been many who support his view. Economist Harold Bierman Jr. states:

> *Although it can be argued that the stock market was not overvalued, there is evidence that many feared that it was overvalued—including the Federal Reserve Board and the United States Senate.*[4]

Perhaps, speculation was not really as rampant as many claimed. However, the fear and the uncertainty that it created for the government, the general public, and investors in the stock market was real. This may have been enough to cause the severe crash that was experienced that October.

THE ROLE OF THE FEDERAL RESERVE

The Federal Reserve Board has also been blamed for the 1929 crash. Many believe that the Federal Reserve did not raise interest rates soon enough in order to stop margin buying. In 1927, the Federal

Reserve loosened its credit policies, making it easier for margin buyers to purchase stocks.

Later, one of the board's own members, Alfred Miller, said that the loosening of credit policies had been one of the most costly mistakes ever committed by the Federal Reserve—or any other bank—within the last 75 years leading up to the crash. Some defend the Federal Reserve's "easy money" policy in 1927. During the time, the loosening of credit seemed very reasonable, as average prices, employment, and construction were at their lowest point in two years. The policies were meant to spur the economy and avoid a deep recession. In actuality, they did little else than create an even more unstable market. Although the Federal Reserve did attempt to raise interest rates and tighten its credit policies in March 1928, banks, and later, commercial lenders stepped in to continue

Andrew Mellon

Andrew Mellon, who served as secretary of the treasury during the Harding, Coolidge, and Hoover administrations, was also the chairman of the Federal Reserve Board during the 1929 stock market collapse. Mellon influenced the board's decision not to raise interest rates, which left bankers free to lend speculative investors more money. Many people blamed Mellon and the Federal Reserve Board, believing that higher interest rates would have slowed speculation and perhaps even prevented the stock market collapse.

lending at lower rates. The Federal Reserve did little to offset the actions by commercial lenders, most likely due to the potential criticism the board would face from others within the government or financial sector. Interestingly, other critics were also quick to blame the Federal Reserve for tightening credit too much. It seemed the Federal Reserve did little to stop the crash, yet there may have been little else they could have done.

OTHER CONTRIBUTING FACTORS

Many other factors contributed either directly or indirectly to the stock market crash. The nation was experiencing an unwarranted increase in currency, which led to unnecessary inflation. There was also an extremely weak banking structure, with many banks facing closures and wiping out the savings of thousands. Others point to financial crises abroad, such as trade

The Million-dollar Playground

The stock market crash changed the mind-set and lifestyle of millions of Americans. Harpo Marx, a comedian who had lost millions in the stock market crash himself, noted, "Life would no longer be, ever again, all fun and games. The bam-bang-sock-and-pow part was over, and so was the permanent New Year's Eve party. Our million-dollar playground had been condemned."[5]

restrictions and war debts that were not being paid off, as contributing to the already weak economy. In addition, the stock market was wrought with fraud and illegal activity, particularly involving stock pools that created overvalued shares of stock. Although leading authorities disagree as to the actual cause or causes of the crash, what can be taken away from the event is the lesson, as Bierman noted, that, "the balance between stock market optimism and pessimism is very delicate."[6] People were caught up in the idea of ever-increasing wealth. Many gave little thought to the risks involved or the chance that stock prices could go down and possibly not go back up. When the bad news struck that autumn, stock prices continued to plummet. The original optimism turned to a deepening pessimism—a pessimism that rocked the nation and affected the wealth and lives of millions.

London Stock Exchange

The U.S. stock market was not the only stock market suffering in 1929. The British stock exchange also had enjoyed a strong decade, but prices began dropping markedly on the London Stock Exchange in mid-September. Interest rates were raised in an attempt to cool speculation, but the U.S. stock market crash on October 29 had a major effect in Great Britain and throughout Western Europe. Foreigners everywhere invested in the stock market, and stock exchanges worldwide were affected.

Wall Street

The Great Depression left many Americans homeless.

THE GREAT DEPRESSION

Within two years of the stock market crash, the country had fallen into the Great Depression. Americans did not know how to regain control of their lives. Many people waited in unemployment lines for hours to apply for the few available jobs. Soup kitchens and breadlines fed the growing number of hungry people in major cities across the country. Homeless people built tar-paper shacks for housing. Adding to the misery, a drought struck the heartland, making it difficult for farmers to grow their crops. Bank after bank closed, wiping out the savings of millions of people.

The Myth of the Crash

Over the years, many people have come to believe the myth that the stock market crash of 1929 caused the Great Depression. The Dow Jones Industrial Average reached its lowest point, at 199 points, on November 13, 1929, two weeks after Black Tuesday. By April of 1930—just five months later—the Dow reached precrash levels, rising to 294 points. Within that five-month period, the stock market effectively rebounded to its original standing. Within another

Unemployment Statistics

Unemployment figures have been disputed. Even today's experts are unsure of exact counts. In the early days of the Great Depression, discrepancies were common. In 1930, Commerce Secretary Robert P. Lamont estimated that 2.3 million Americans were out of work. In contrast, National Unemployment League representative Darwin J. Meserole calculated the number of unemployed at 6.6 million.

few months, the Dow once again plummeted—
however, this was unrelated to the 1929 crash and
caused by other economic factors.

While the crash of 1929 was not a direct cause
of the ensuing economic depression, the lack of
faith in the stock market and the uncertainty many
people felt after the stock market crash most certainly
contributed to the depression that followed. Craig
Mitchell, the son of Wall Street tycoon Charles E.
Mitchell, recalls how the crash of 1929 and the Great
Depression affected those around him:

> *Looking back it seems like a complete dichotomy between
> the days up until the great crash of '29 and the subsequent
> depression. ... I think one example is the experience of a great
> friend of my father, Reggie Waterbury, who was almost a
> member of the family. ... When the Depression came, after
> the crash and when we got into 1930, Father received a
> letter from him saying... "Dear Charlie ... a new world is
> coming and I'm not prepared to live in it and I'm dropping
> out ..." ... he would go from town to town one step ahead of
> the detectives my father would send to try to find him. And he
> was never again located and he was never able to make that
> transition.*[1]

In the 1920s, people were caught up in the illusion that the American economy and way of life would only get better. With the crash of 1929, many realized that they were vulnerable. That vulnerability continued well into 1930, and by 1931, most Americans felt hopeless.

BANK CLOSINGS

This loss of hope was related to several factors—the stock market was only one factor. In the late 1920s, banks started closing. At that time, there where no laws protecting people's savings within the banks. When a bank closed, a person could lose their entire life savings. By late 1930,

A New Reality

When the stock market crashed in 1929, the dreams and illusions of many Americans crashed with it. People no longer believed in the "New Era"—an era of permanent and ever-rising prosperity. The shock of the crash and the economic troubles that followed changed the way the whole of American society viewed their lives and the world they lived in. This change in attitude and lack of confidence only worsened as the Great Depression took a greater hold of the American psyche.

Frederick Lewis Allen wrote of this changing outlook in his book, *Only Yesterday*, published in 1931—before the Great Depression was fully underway:

Prosperity is more than an economic condition; it is a state of mind. The Big Bull Market had been more than the climax of a business cycle; it had been the climax of a cycle in American mass thinking and mass emotion. ... With the Big Bull Market gone and prosperity now going, Americans were soon to find themselves living in an altered world which called for new adjustments, new ideas, new habits of thought, and a new order of values.[2]

banks across the country experienced closures—and hundreds of thousands of individuals went broke in the process. Bank runs occurred because people feared their banks would run out of money. People would line up at the banks to withdraw their savings. Banks do not keep 100 percent reserves in their vaults, so often a bank run would leave banks without a penny in the safes.

In addition to the bank closures, the economy was still not doing well. When businesses were unable to sell as many products, they were forced to lay off employees that they could no longer afford to pay. It was a vicious cycle. People were poor and could not buy the goods produced. In turn, businesses could not keep the workers who made the goods, which resulted in more people losing their jobs and losing any way of making a living.

When people lost their jobs or lost savings from a bank closure,

"Economic depression cannot be cured by legislative action or executive pronouncement. Economic wounds must be healed by the action of the cells of the economic body—the producers and consumers themselves."[3]

—*President Hoover*

*Many people lost their savings in bank closings
in the years following the crash.*

they could no longer pay all of their bills. The
products they had purchased on credit during the
1920s were then taken away from them—even if they
only had one or two payments left on the purchase.
Thousands of people became homeless, as they
could no longer afford to keep their homes. Many
homeless moved to shantytowns or "Hoovervilles"—

People waited in breadlines during the Great Depression.

nicknamed after President Hoover, who many felt did little to help people during the depression. Shantytowns were gatherings of makeshift shelters, often made of cardboard. Hundreds of unemployed and homeless people were forced to relocate to these communities during the depression.

In addition to the bank closures and businesses doing poorly, problems abroad also arose. At the time, the international monetary system was the gold-exchange standard. After World War I,

the United States insisted that
reparations be paid with gold, but
by the end of the 1920s, the United
States controlled most of the world's
gold supply. When one country
experienced economic troubles,
other countries that adhered to the
same system would experience many
of the same problems. Because the
United States controlled most of
the world's supply of gold, Western
European countries could not afford
to pay back their debt. And if they
could not pay back their debt, they
also could not purchase U.S. goods,
which further hurt the economies of
both Europe and the United States.

The Dust Bowl

Farmers were among those
the most affected by the Great
Depression. In the early 1930s,
a series of dust storms destroyed
farmland in the Great Plains areas of
the United States. Extensive farming

"The Great Depression,
like most other periods
of severe unemployment,
was produced by govern-
ment mismanagement
rather than by any inher-
ent instability of the private economy."[4]
—*Milton Friedman,
economist*

of cotton, corn, and wheat crops without crop rotation had depleted the soil, and the drought of 1930 only added to the problem. Winds kicked up the dried, exposed soil and covered everything in dust. Crops across the plains area were destroyed. The soil left was unfit for growing crops. The Great Plains turned into a giant dust bowl.

Farm income in the United States fell from $12 billion to just $5 billion. It often cost farmers more to grow the crop than what they could get when they sold the crop. Because other countries were also faring badly, they could no longer afford to buy American crops. The worldwide economic slump decreased demand and decreased crop prices.

Throughout the Great Depression, millions of people lost their jobs, lived on the streets or in shantytowns, waited in breadlines for meager servings of food, and

The Grapes of Wrath

Many farmers migrated to California, having learned that they could receive high wages picking crops such as grapes, apples, and oranges. However, migrant workers often found they had to compete with other migrants for work and wages that were lower than promised.

John Steinbeck's novel *The Grapes of Wrath* follows a family of farmers during the Great Depression as they lose their farm and travel to California in search of work. Steinbeck's novel has been praised for its accurate description of the economic and personal hardships people faced during the Great Depression.

Dust storms in the Great Plains, which left everything covered in dirt, destroyed many farms.

desperately sought any small way to make a living. The economic prosperity of the 1920s seemed far behind. The American people were in the grip of a crisis.

The Great Depression was—and remains—the worst economic depression the United States has ever witnessed. Between the two world wars, the crash of 1929 and the Great Depression was a unique time in American history.

Could a crash such as the one that occurred in 1929 or the subsequent Great Depression happen again? Given the right conditions, the answer would be yes. But as writer Maury Klein puts it:

> It amounts to a refined version of the old saw that history is just one … thing after another. The crash and the depression can be viewed as aberrations, and their relation the product of an unlikely and unpredictable sequence of events—the random coming together of a confluence of unfortunate forces. The accumulating effect of these forces not only created the crisis but prolonged and deepened it, much like the strengthening of a routine storm into a killer hurricane or blizzard when a variety of unfavorable factors, each one unpleasant but not lethal in itself, combine on rare occasions to forge the worst-case scenario. In short, the crash and its aftermath was the perfect storm.[5]

An investor taps a statue of a bull,
which represents a bull market, for good luck.

TIMELINE

1792	1913	1917
Stockbrokers sign the Buttonwood Agreement on May 17, forming the New York Stock Exchange.	The U.S. government creates the Federal Reserve.	Liberty bonds help fund World War I. Americans are introduced to the concept of investing.

1929	1929	1929
On October 3, Philip Snowden calls the American stock market a "speculative orgy."	Market dips after utilities stocks decrease in value on October 16.	Stock prices fall on October 23. More than 2.6 million shares of stock are traded.

1928	1929	1929
Herbert Hoover is elected president of the United States on November 6.	National City Bank announces on March 26, it will lend $25 million to stockbrokers after the Federal Reserve raised interest rates on stock loans.	The Dow Jones peaks at 381.2 points on September 3.

1929	1929	1929
On October 24, Black Thursday causes widespread panic as stock prices fall dramatically.	Trading is heavy following Black Thursday. By the end of October 25, the Dow Jones has increased.	On October 26, brokers demand payment from margin buyers. Many investors are forced to sell their stocks at a loss or borrow money to keep them.

TIMELINE

1929

The exchange
is closed on
October 27.
Commission houses
work to bring their
books up to the
current holdings.

1929

On October 28,
heavy selling occurs
on the exchange
floor and blue chip
stocks are beginning
to be sold. Dow Jones
declines 12.8 percent.

1929

The Dow Jones closes
at 199 points on
November 13. The
market reaches its
lowest point in
the crash.

1930

The Dow Jones
reaches 294 points
on April 17, making a
full market recovery.

1929

Stocks plummet as
panic selling ensues
on October 29.
Exchange governors
keep the market open
and $15 billion is lost.

1929

The exchange closes
early on October
31 and remains
closed until Monday,
November 4.

1930

Drought and dust
storms hit the Great
Plains area and
devastate crops.

late 1930s

Bank closures become
common throughout
the United States.

ESSENTIAL FACTS

DATE OF EVENT

October 29, 1929

PLACE OF EVENT

❖ New York Stock Exchange

❖ Exchanges and brokerages throughout the United States

KEY PLAYERS

❖ Herbert Hoover, thirty-first president of the United States

❖ Richard Whitney, acting president of the New York Stock Exchange

❖ The Federal Reserve Board

❖ Banking industry

❖ Brokers

❖ American and foreign investors

HIGHLIGHTS OF EVENT

❖ Speculative investors bought and sold stocks in the late 1920s to make quick profits. This caused instability in the market.

❖ Panic selling intensified in late October 1929. The fear of a crash prevented buyers from coming forth, causing a severe drop in stock prices.

❖ The stock market rebounded by April 1930 but soon worsened as the United States slipped into the Great Depression.

QUOTE

"Sooner or later, a crash is coming and it may be terrific."
—*Roger Babson*

ADDITIONAL RESOURCES

SELECT BIBLIOGRAPHY

Bierman, Harold, Jr. "The 1929 Stock Market Crash." *EH.Net Encyclopedia*. Robert Whaples, ed. <http://eh.net/encyclopedia/article/Bierman.Crash>.

Blumenthal, Karen. *Six Days in October: The Stock Market Crash of 1929*. New York: Simon & Schuster, 2002.

Klein, Maury. *Rainbow's End: The Crash of 1929*. New York: Oxford University Press, 2001.

Klein, Maury. "The Stock Market Crash of 1929: A Review Article." *The Business History Review* 75.2 (2001).

Romer, Christina D. "The Great Crash and the Onset of the Great Depression." *The Quarterly Journal of Economics* 105.3 (1990).

FURTHER READING

Blumenthal Karen. *Six Days in October: The Stock Market Crash of 1929*. Atheneum Books for Young Readers: New York, 2002.

Goodman, Paul. *America in the Twenties: the Beginnings of Contemporary America*. Holt Reinhart and Winston: New York, 1971.

Terkel, Studs. *Hard Times: An Oral History of the Great Depression*. Pantheon Books: New York, 1986.

WEB LINKS

To learn more about the stock market crash of 1929, visit ABDO Publishing Company on the World Wide Web at **www.abdopublishing.com**. Web sites about the stock market crash of 1929 are featured on our Book Links page. These links are routinely monitored and updated to provide the most current information available.

Places To Visit

Federal Reserve Bank of New York
33 Liberty Street, New York, NY 10045
212-720-6130
http://www.newyorkfed.org/aboutthe fed/ny_tours.html
Visitors may tour the Federal Reserve Bank of New York and learn about the functions of the bank and its role in the economy.

Herbert Hoover Presidential Library and Museum
210 Parkside Drive, West Branch, IA 52358
319-643-5301
http://hoover.archives.gov/exhibits/Hooverstory/gallery06/gallery06.html
Gallery Six deals specifically with the stock market crash of 1929 and the Great Depression.

Museum of American Finance
48 Wall Street, New York, NY 10005
212-908-4110
http://www.financialhistory.org
Visitors may view many artifacts related to American finance, including photographs; antique stocks, bonds and currency; and equipment once used on Wall Street.

GLOSSARY

accrue
To accumulate or build up over a period of time.

bear market
A period of dropping stock prices.

bond
A type of security investment generally sold by the government or corporations.

broker
A financial expert hired by investors to maximize profits in the stock market.

bull market
A period of rising stock prices.

crash
A significant and sudden decline in the market index.

credit
Money paid by a bank for a consumer to purchase goods, with the understanding that the money will be repaid in the future.

debt
Money owed.

depression
A sustained period of deep economic hardship.

dividend
Timely payments made by companies to their stockholders.

Dow Jones Industrial Average
An index averaging the value of shares on the New York Stock Exchange.

economy
A country's wealth and resources in relation to its production, distribution, and consumption of goods and services.

Federal Reserve Board
An independent agency that helps control the U.S. money supply as well as supervises banking and deals in the securities market.

interest
> Money paid at a regular rate for delaying the full payment of money borrowed.

invest
> To commit money in the expectation of a larger financial return.

loan
> Money that has been borrowed and will be repaid with interest.

margin
> An up-front deposit put down by investors for shares in the stock market.

margin buyer
> A person who takes out a loan to buy shares in a stock.

New York Stock Exchange (NYSE)
> The most noted location in the United States for the buying and selling of securities.

share
> A percentage of a company's stock.

speculation
> The buying and selling of securities with the prospect of making a quick profit.

stock
> The ownership of a part of a company or corporation in which dividends are paid.

stock bubble
> A temporary overvaluation of stock prices.

stock pool
> A group of investors who agree to purchase the same stock to increase its value and then sell the stock for a profit.

stock ticker
> The machine that keeps investors informed by printing out current stock prices.

Source Notes

Chapter 1. The Calm before the Storm
1. John Kenneth Galbraith. *The Great Crash*. Boston: Houghton Mifflin Company, 1954. 6.
2. Maury Klein. *Rainbow's End: The Crash of 1929*. New York: Oxford University Press, 2001. 113.
3. "Herbert Hoover: Inaugural Address." *Inaugural Addresses of the Presidents of the United States*. Bartleby.com. 15 Mar. 2007 <http://bartleby.com/124/pres48.html>.

Chapter 2. Stocks and Bonds
None.

Chapter 3. The Federal Reserve Takes Action
1. Karen Blumenthal. *Six Days in October: The Stock Market Crash of 1929*. New York: Simon & Schuster, 2002. 81.
2. W.A. Lyon. "Stocks Soar As Bank Aid Ends Fear of Money Panic." *New York Herald Tribune*. 28 Mar. 1929. American Experience. 1929 Headlines. 21 Oct. 2004. 14 Sept. 2007 <http://www.pbs.org/wgbh/amex/crash/sfeature/sf_headlines.html>.

Chapter 4. Black Thursday
1. Harold Bierman, Jr. "The 1929 Stock Market Crash." *EH.Net Encyclopedia*. Robert Whaples, ed. 11 Aug. 2004. 12 Sept. 2007 <http://eh.net/encyclopedia/article/Bierman.Crash>.
2. Barbara Feinberg. *Black Tuesday: The Stock Market Crash of 1929*. Brookfield, CT: The Millbrook Press, 1995. 23–25.
3. Harold Bierman, Jr. "The 1929 Stock Market Crash." *EH.Net Encyclopedia*. Robert Whaples, ed. 11 Aug. 2004. 12 Sept. 2007 <http://eh.net/encyclopedia/article/Bierman.Crash>.
4. "Brokers in Meeting Predict Recovery." *New York Times*. 25 Oct. 1929. American Experience. 1929 Headlines. 21 Oct. 2004. 14 Sept. 2007 <http://www.pbs.org/wgbh/amex/crash/sfeature/sf_headlines.html>.
5. Harold Bierman, Jr. "The 1929 Stock Market Crash." *EH.Net Encyclopedia*. Robert Whaples, ed. 11 Aug. 2004. 12 Sept. 2007 <http://eh.net/encyclopedia/article/Bierman.Crash>.

Chapter 5. Investors Hold On
1. "Black Thursday: October 24, 1929—The Crash" 16 Oct. 2007 <http://sweb.uky.edu/~msunde00/hon202/p4/thursday.html>.
2. Harold Bierman, Jr. "The 1929 Stock Market Crash." *EH.Net Encyclopedia*. Robert Whaples, ed. 11 Aug. 2004. 12 Sept. 2007 <http://eh.net/encyclopedia/article/Bierman.Crash>.

Chapter 6. The Collapse
1. Gordon Thomas and Max Morgan-Witts. *The Day the Bubble Burst: A Social History of the Wall Street Crash of 1929*. Garden City, NY: Doubleday and Company, 1979. 388.
2. "A Fistful of Red Orders." *American Experience*. Crash Memories. 21 Oct. 2004. 15 Sept. 2007 <http://www.pbs.org/wgbh/amex/crash/sfeature/sf_excerpts.html>.
3. Karen Blumenthal. *Six Days in October: The Stock Market Crash of 1929*. New York: Simon & Schuster, 2002. 115.
4. William K. Klingaman. *The Year of the Great Crash: 1929*. New York: Harper and Row Publishers, Inc., 1989. 283.

Chapter 7. In the Wake of the Crash
1. William K. Klingaman. *The Year of the Great Crash: 1929*. New York: Harper & Row, Publishers, Inc., 1989. 287.
2. Maury Klein. *Rainbow's End: The Crash of 1929*. New York: Oxford University Press, 2003. 231.
3. "Bernard Baruch Quotes." Brainy Quotes. 9 Oct. 2007 <http://www.brainyquote.com/quotes/authors/b/bernard_baruch.html>.
4. John Kenneth Galbraith. *The Great Crash*. Boston: Houghton Mifflin Company, 1954. 119.
5. Ferdinand Lundberg. "Stocks Up in Strong Rally; Rockefellers Big Buyers; Exchanges Close 2-1/2 Days." *New York Herald Tribune*. 31 Oct. 1929. American Experience. 1929 Headlines. 21 Oct. 2004. 14 Sept. 2007 <http://www.pbs.org/wgbh/amex/crash/sfeature/sf_headlines.html>.
6. William K. Klingaman. *The Year of the Great Crash: 1929*. New York: Harper & Row Publishers, Inc., 1989. 287.

Source Notes Continued

7. "Very Prosperous Year Is Forecast." *World 15*. Dec. 1929.
American Experience. 1929 Headlines. 21 Oct. 2004. 14 Sept.
2007 <http://www.pbs.org/wgbh/amex/crash/sfeature/sf_headlines.
html>.

Chapter 8. Looking Back on the Crash
1. Maury Klein. "The Stock Market Crash of 1929: A Review
Article." *Business History Review* 75.2 (2001). 329. JSTOR. 17 Sept.
2007 <http://jstor.org>.
2. William K. Klingaman. *The Year of the Great Crash: 1929*. New York:
Harper & Row Publishers, Inc., 1989. 300–01.
3. "Galbraith Warns of Stock Speculation and Tells some Delightful
Anecdotes." *Nieman Foundation Seminars*. 14 Oct. 1999. 4 Apr. 2007
<http://nieman.harvard.edu/events/seminars/galbraith2.html>.
4. Harold Bierman, Jr. "The 1929 Stock Market Crash." *EH.Net
Encyclopedia*. Robert Whaples, ed. 11 Aug. 2004. 12 Sept. 2007
<http://eh.net/encyclopedia/article/Bierman.Crash>.
5. Ibid.
6. Maury Klein. *Rainbow's End: The Crash of 1929*. New York: Oxford
University Press, 2001. 239.

Chapter 9. The Great Depression

1. "A New World Is Coming." *American Experience*. Crash Memories. 21 Oct. 2004. 15 Sept. 2007 <http://www.pbs.org/wgbh/amex/crash/sfeature/sf_excerpts.html>.

2. Maury Klein. "The Stock Market Crash of 1929: A Review Article." *Business History Review*. 75.2 (2001). 341. JSTOR. 17 Sept. 2007 <http://jstor.org>.

3. Herbert Hoover Quotes. *Brainy Quote*. 5 Aug. 2007 <http://www.brainyquote.com/quotes/authors/h/herbert_hoover.html>.

4. Milton Friedman quotes. *ThinkExist.com*. 5 Aug. 2007 <http://thinkexist.com/quotation/the_great_depression-like_most_other_periods_of/215920.html>.

5. Maury Klein. "The Stock Market Crash of 1929: A Review Article." *Business History Review*. 75.2 (2001). 351. JSTOR. 17 Sept. 2007 <http://jstor.org>.

INDEX

ABOUT THE AUTHOR

Martin Gitlin was a writer for two newspapers in northeast Ohio for 20 years before becoming a freelance writer. During those two decades, he won more than 40 writing awards, including first place for general excellence from Associated Press in 1995. That organization also named him one of the top four feature writers in the state of Ohio in 2001.

PHOTO CREDITS

AP Images, cover, 3, 6, 12, 17, 18, 30, 34, 40, 45, 58, 75, 84, 89, 90, 93, 96 (bottom), 99 (bottom); Library of Congress, 15, 29, 37, 50, 76, 83, 96 (top), 98; Bettmann/Corbis, 24, 55, 66, 99 (top); Jupiterimages/AP Images, 27; Library of Congress/AP Images, 39; Frederic Lewis/Getty Images, 49; London Express/Getty Images, 57, 97; Keystone/Getty Images, 65; Emile Wamsteker/AP Images, 95.

Echoes and Inscriptions

Echoes and Inscriptions

Comparative Approaches
to Early Modern Spanish Literatures

Edited by

Barbara A. Simerka
and Christopher B. Weimer

Lewisburg
Bucknell University Press
London: Associated University Presses

Associated University Presses
440 Forsgate Drive
Cranbury, NJ 08512

Associated University Presses
16 Barter Street
London WC1A 2AH, England

Associated University Presses
P.O. Box 338, Port Credit
Mississauga, Ontario
Canada L5G 4L8

The paper used in this publication meets the requirements of the American National Standard for Permanence of Paper for Printed Library Materials Z30.48-1984

Library of Congress Cataloging-in-Publication Data

Echoes and inscriptions : comparative approaches to early modern Spanish literatures / edited by Barbara A. Simerka and Christopher B. Weimer.
        p.   cm.
    Includes bibliographical references and index.
    ISBN 0-8387-5430-9 (alk. paper)
        1. Spanish literature—Classical period, 1500–1700—History and criticism.   2. Spanish American literature—History and criticism.   3. Literature, Comparative—Spanish American and European.   4. Literature, Comparative—European and Spanish American. I. Simerka, Barbara, 1957–   .   II. Weimer, Christopher B., 1963–
PQ6066.E34   2000
860.9′003—dc21   99-098198

Contents

List of Illustrations

7

Introduction

This volume of comparative approaches to early modern Spanish literatures seeks to explore the many unrecognized connections between Golden Age texts and the cultural productions of other places and other eras. In this undertaking, we hope to resuscitate and re-signify Iberian Renaissance and Baroque writings, not merely by illuminating the underappreciated influence of sixteenth- and seventeenth-century Spanish works upon western culture, but more importantly, by positioning Cervantes, María de Zayas, and the other authors examined here within an artistic continuum ranging over a wide variety of time periods, genres or mediums, and geographical locales.

Such an undertaking does require that oft-maligned critical questions of influence be considered in a new light. As a general trend, the fall from favor of influence studies, because of their positivist and authoritative connotations, and the rise of post-structuralist explorations of intertextuality have been beneficial to the discipline of textual study. However, that shift in paradigm has not eliminated the narratives of origin of literary styles and genres that still play a significant role in undergraduate education; in this context, the identification of early modern Iberian influences upon canonical and emerging texts can be seen as one component in the ongoing project of reexamining the process of canonization in order to take into account many forms of previously marginalized writing. Ironically, it is Renaissance humanism, that sacrosanct ideological space inhabited and guarded almost exclusively by the critically infamous Dead White European Males, that might provide us with an applicable perspective on questions of influence. While the traditional influence studies mentioned above often tended to emphasize similarities over divergences and the impact or function of a given textual model over those of texts derived from it, it is also possible to regard works that draw upon preexisting texts as examples of *imitatio* and *renovatio*. As Thomas Greene has pointed out, Renaissance theories of imitation extend far beyond the slavish reproduction of earlier works, instead calling attention to the many

9

modes and registers of what we today would label intertextuality. "Imitative" texts can, among other strategies, position themselves in deconstructive opposition to their alleged models or breathe new life and fresh meaning into those models. In neither case can the prior texts be seen as exerting authority over, or limiting, the functions and dynamics of those incorporating them for their own specific purposes.

Of course, comparative studies can just as productively address relationships between works lacking any such direct connections; indeed, in many cases one author might produce a text that can be fruitfully examined when juxtaposed with another of which he or she had no knowledge. Nearly all comparative studies, however, must explicitly or implicitly address a process that might be termed textual osmosis. Like scientific studies of osmosis that define the conditions that encourage or prohibit the transfer of liquid through a semipermeable membrane by studying the liquids and the membranes, the essays in this collection seek in a number of ways to identify the cultural conditions that facilitate or block the movement of texts or textual elements between various cultures, time periods, genres, and even mediums; those texts and textual elements that have permeated these "membranes"; and the transformations wrought by their movements.

In his opening consideration of the status of comparative studies with regard to early modern Spain, Walter Cohen revisits the debates about the peninsula's place in western Europe, which have often centered on its supposed uniqueness. Drawing on universally known features of Iberian history, this essay seeks to arrive at less-well-known conclusions. Cohen repositions Spanish literature within the history of European literature and redefines Spain as the most typical of European countries.

The next section of the anthology consists of studies that compare the stylistic strategies of the texts under consideration. Margaret Greer examines the function of the embedded narrative and its effect on the narratees of the frame tales in works ranging from an eighth-century Indian collection of novellas to María de Zayas's exemplary novels, Boccaccio's *Decameron*, and the recent Hollywood film *The Princess Bride*. Amy R. Williamsen also turns to María de Zayas in her comparative analysis of comedy in the early-modern *novelas* and Rosario Castellanos's contemporary Latin American feminist satires. Williamsen's article addresses an area of comparative inquiry that is often neglected because of a shared language, the relationship between Spanish and Latin American writings, where the process of reinscription is complicated by issues related to the colonial experience. Likewise, Salvador Oropesa explores the complex relationship between early-modern peninsular texts and those of modern day Latin America, as manifested by the neo-Baroque poetry of Xavier Villaurrutia. Sidney E. Donnell broadens the comparative field with his study of Luis Buñuel's film *La vida criminal de Archibaldo de la Cruz* [The Criminal Life of Archibaldo de la Cruz], focusing on Baroque imagery, picaresque narrative, and honor plays as cultural sources for this 1950s *film noir*. Both Salvador J. Fajardo and James A. Parr analyze diegetic discourse in *Don Quijote* and French Baroque literature. Fajardo scrutinizes the embedding of the knight errant's adventures in Saint-Amant's burlesque poem, La chambre de débauché [The Wastrel's Room], while Parr employs the theories of Gerard Gennette and Gerald Prince in his investigation of Furetière's *Le Roman Bourgeois* [The Bourgeois Novel]. A narratological approach is particularly appropriate for these works, which foreground an iconoclastic scrutiny of the entire creative enterprise.

Part three foregrounds questions of subjectivity and identity. The first three essays emphasize gendered subjectivities. Anne J. Cruz utilizes the theories of Jacques Lacan to reflect upon the construction of identity in the poetic voices of mystics including San Juan de la Cruz, Santa Teresa, Luisa de Carvajal, and Angela de Foligno. Amy Pawl considers the figure of the female Quixote as reinvented by Charlotte Lennox and other eighteenth-century British authors whose protagonists became vehicles for fantasies of female power and importance. Thomas P. Finn explores self-fashioned identities in *La dama boba* [The Foolish Lady], *Don Gil de las calzas verdes* [Don Gil of the Green Stockings], and *Le bourgeois gentilhomme* [The Bourgeois Gentleman]. Finn's essay studies the underlying belief of the protagonists that human identity is more constituted than constitutive. William R. Blue seeks to dispel the popular critical myth of plot's primacy over characterization in early modern British and Spanish drama with his comparative study of *A Comedy of Errors* and *La dama duende* [The Phantom Lady].

The fourth section's essays confront implicitly and explicitly political issues in a variety of texts and other mediums. Diana de Armas Wilson rethinks the intertextual and cultural relations between English utopian thought and the Spanish "utopian" society that, according to José Antonio Maravall, Cervantes allegedly opposes. De Armas Wilson argues instead that *Don Quijote* and the *Persiles* move ideologically from utopia to dystopia and, finally, to a vision of "heterotopia." Perry Gethner compares Marie-Catherine Desjardins's *Le favori* [The Royal Favorite], the first play by a woman to receive a command performance at the French court, with its direct source, Tirso de Molina's political comedy *El amor y el amistad* [Love and Friendship]. This study contextualizes Desjardins's adaptation of Tirso's *comedia* within the political disparities between early-modern France and Spain. Barbara A. Simerka combines Raymond Williams's notion of the competition among discourses with contemporary reception theory to demonstrate that a challenge to orthodox Christian theology can be seen in the problematic representation of divine intervention in Tirso's *El burlador de Sevilla* [The Trickster of Seville] and Shadwell's *The Libertine*. Christopher B. Weimer foregrounds the politics of rewriting in his analysis of the contemporary Chilean playwright Isidora Aguirre's adaptation of *Fuenteovejuna* [Sheep's Well], written and performed in the shadow of the Pinochet dictatorship. Frederick A. de Armas addresses questions of *imitatio* in his examination of imperialist discourse in Rojas Zorrilla's diptych *Numancia cercada* [Numancia Beseiged] and *Numancia destruida* [Numancia Destroyed]. De Armas illuminates the manner in which Rojas Zorrilla transforms and problematizes his sources, including the Cervantine drama of the same name and a group of paintings and tapestries that address related themes.

Christopher B. Weimer would like to thank the College of Arts and Sciences, Oklahoma State University for funding provided by a Dean's Incentive Grant. Barbara A. Simerka would like to acknowledge support extended by the faculty summer research grant program, Office of the Provost, University of Texas, San Antonio, and also to express appreciation to graduate research assistants Shelley Dellert, José Luis Ramirez, and Pilar Puente, to technical assistant Karla Marsh, and especially to Administrative Assistant Sylvia Hernandez, whose dedication and hard work was essential to assuring that a half-time administrative position did not devour every moment of the day.

Part I
The Politics of Discourse

Echoes and Inscriptions

The Uniqueness of Spain

WALTER COHEN

Since the Enlightenment at the latest, Spain has often been considered the odd-man-out in western Europe by friend and foe alike. Debates have sometimes turned on whether or not Spain is unique, and sometimes even on what the specificity of the uniqueness is. I want to take up the notion of uniqueness from a sociocultural perspective and drive it to a paradoxical conclusion. Drawing on central and familiar features of Spanish history, I hope to arrive at slightly less-well-known conclusions. My aim is to reposition Spanish literature within the history of European literature and in so doing, to reorient that history, however modestly.

Traditionally, Spanish history, culture, and literature have been treated with a combination of condescension and neglect, especially in the anglophone world, and above all in the United States. These attitudes have something to do with the U.S.'s primary cultural heritage, which brings with it a northwest European, Protestant, anti-Catholic bias. The Spanish-American War may also have played a part, as has the imperialist and racist view of Latin America in this country. The relative historical backwardness of Spain—at least compared to the other large nations of western Europe (England, France, Germany, and Italy)—has surely been of major significance. That backwardness arguably culminates in the Franco regime, which outlasted by three decades the Fascist periods in Italy and Germany. While those countries rejoined western Europe in the postwar period, Spain (and Portugal) became ever more peripheral. One scholarly consequence was that many of the best historical and critical works during these years were foreign or Catalonian, in the latter case drawing on or drawn to the republican and anarchist heritage of the region. One thinks of Noël Salomon, Pierre Vilar, Jaime Vicens Vives, and J. H. Elliott; and, in a somewhat different way, of British *calderonistas* like Edward M. Wilson.[1] Another, more predictable, consequence was the ignorance of Hispanic letters among speakers of English. As recently as 1965, *Don Quixote* was the only work composed in Spanish that was known (or, often, even

17

heard of) in the anglophone world—not just among the general reading public but also and more strikingly among Ph.D.s in English. This was bizarre and unfortunate considering the stature of this writing. And it was ironic in a country with a large and growing Hispanic population.

During the past fifteen years, however, the situation has changed dramatically. A secondary explanation for the shift is the death of Franco, which enabled Spain to become a typical western European country. Far more important has been the Latin American "boom," whose international celebrity, though centered on García Márquez's *One Hundred Years of Solitude*, has inspired a steady stream of translations into English. In Spanish departments at North American colleges and universities this has led to a hierarchical reversal, with Latin America becoming for the first time the dog that wags the Spanish tail. But that reversal has also had—to change the metaphor—a limited upward draft on interest in peninsular literature as well, though that effect has become crucial only because of a further, related development. Partly because of a recurrent thematic orientation of Latin American literature, but perhaps even more because of the general shift to the left in anglophone criticism (especially in the United States, where things Hispanic are likely to matter most), the celebration of Latin American literature has been yoked to a distinctive ideological position, in which a celebration of the Third World is equated with a critique of Eurocentrism, and politics, culture, and literature are brought into close relation with one another. These are plausible intellectual moves, but the crucial point is that they are by no means necessary ones. It would be just as reasonable, for instance, to argue that Latin American literature at its best, including the moments when it is most critical of Europe or North America, reveals not the limits but the inexhaustibility of the European tradition.

Since, however, this has been the road not taken, one might expect Spain, and especially Golden Age literature, to be relegated to the dustbin of history as the repository of reaction. This has not happened, but in many respects the neglect and condescension continue. Though familiarity with texts composed in Spanish has increased among readers of English, *Don Quixote* remains the only widely known peninsular literary text, and the dominant figures in American or international criticism of the last twenty years are neither from Spain nor specialists in peninsular literature. (They are only rarely from Latin America and only rarely specialists in Latin American literature.) That this is not an inevitable situation can be recognized by recalling the prominent role of Spanish literature in

the criticism of the leading German Romance philologists of an earlier generation—Auerbach, even more Spitzer, and above all Curtius. Their focus on the Romance languages resulted, however, in a
neglect of the relationship between Spanish and English literature.
Most crucially, there is still little understanding of the role of Spanish Golden Age fiction in the development of the novel.

Yet in one important respect, early-modern Spanish letters have
newly come into view as a consequence of both the prominence and
the orientation of Latin American studies. Though the presentist
predilection of contemporary criticism has vitiated interest in the
literary past, there is no way to understand the conquest—and
hence, to some extent, the nature—of Latin America without studying the conquerors. The huge surge of interest in sixteenth- and
seventeenth-century Spanish discourse about the New World is part
of the general emergence of colonial and postcolonial studies. The
scholarship in this area has had relatively little to do with the literary canon of the *Siglo de Oro* [Golden Age], at least as traditionally
understood. But Columbus and his successors have accomplished
what Lope de Vega has not: they have attracted the attention of
leading intellectuals from outside the field of Hispanic letters.
Tzvetan Todorov and Stephen Greenblatt are perhaps the best
known examples of this trend.

On related grounds, the Islamic and Jewish legacies of Renaissance Spain, though obviously more central to the Middle Ages, are
ripe for reevaluation after a hiatus of at least two decades. Accord-
ingly, in what follows I discuss Spanish letters of the early modern
period in relation to the European novel, and more briefly in relation to European global expansion and the European confrontation
with Islam. In each instance, the aim of a comparative perspective
is to help suggest both the nature of Spanish literature's distinctive-
ness and the more general character of European literature.

I

Two of the problems posed by Spanish fiction of the *Siglo de Oro*
are the establishment of its place in the international transmission
of genres and an explanation for its apparent modernity, given the
comparatively reactionary cast of the country's economic, social,
and cultural structures. On the one hand, such questions cannot
even really be addressed within the confines of Spanish literary history. On the other, failure to address them distorts European literary
history as well.

Any attempt to locate a turning point in the history of European fiction risks arbitrariness. Yet the mid-fourteenth century witnessed a genuine break with the past, the emergence of a self-consciously artistic practice of prose fictional narrative that culminated four hundred years later in the dominance of the novel.[2] This writing expressed a new ideology felt to be subversive and subordinate. Novelistic fiction moved gradually from this counterhegemonic position to the hegemonic status among literary forms it continues to occupy today, from opposition to aristocratic values to a close connection with the triumph of the middle class. It also moved across linguistic and national boundaries—from Italy to Spain to France to England. The names Boccaccio, Cervantes, Lafayette, Richardson, and Fielding mark a historical trajectory that at every point involved influence as well as affinity.

Recognition of this pattern may make it possible to resolve an ongoing critical conflict. Attempts to connect the rise of the novel to the rise of the middle class have often been confined to England. Insistence that there were continental novels before there were eighteenth-century English novels has regularly resulted in the rejection of sociological inquiry. Even if one claims that Golden Age Spain produced no true novels, its prose fiction was undoubtedly far more novelistic than Renaissance England's, whereas its middle class was far weaker. The very retardation of the Spanish middle class behind its English counterpart during the sixteenth and seventeenth centuries may, however, account for the precocity of Golden Age fiction, for its counterhegemonic efficacy. Expressive of socially marginal ideologies, the Spanish picaresque is a kind of protest literature, a countergenre to the norms of pastoral or chivalric romance that is connected to the discontents and frustrations of the middle class. The picaresque's serious treatment of urban lower-class protagonists registers a consciousness that, though potentially assimilable in sixteenth-century Italy or England or France, remained alien in Spain. The relative backwardness of Castile within a western European context makes possible the critical, oppositional perspective of the form.

From this perspective, the hypothesis of *converso* influence on Golden Age fiction acquires a certain logic. The *conversos* constituted much of the Spanish bourgeoisie. Their peripheral position may have contributed a crucial cultural tone that could be exploited in the formation of an ultimately hegemonic genre. Whether religiously inspired or not, the ideology of *Lazarillo de Tormes* is essentially negative. A unified, positive vision along Counter-Reformation lines perhaps occurs in *Guzmán de Alfarache*, but as

Lesage's selective cutting in the eighteenth century suggests, Alemán's solution does not anticipate subsequent strategies. The process of secularization already evident in Boccaccio remains central to the entire tradition of insurgent prose fiction in this period. Appropriately, then, novelistic fiction achieved a hegemonic position only when it settled in postrevolutionary, eighteenth-century England during the initial era of bourgeois hegemony. Discontinuity of ideological function, linguistic medium, sociological milieu, and geographical terrain defines the tradition.

An international perspective also helps locate that tradition's generic peculiarity. The novel has justifiably accumulated an impressive array of antecedents in the critical literature. Yet if one operates at an intermediate level of generality, the novella emerges as the decisive form connecting four hundred years of insurgent novelistic fiction. The movement from counterhegemonic to hegemonic status coincides from this perspective with the gradual absorption of the novella into the novel. Yet there is no generic purity to this process. Though the fifth *tratado* of *Lazarillo de Tormes* bears comparison to the fourth tale in Masuccio da Salerno's *Il Novellino* [The Little Novel], a fifteenth-century Boccaccian novella collection, most readers of *Lazarillo de Tormes* feel the disjunction between the developmental pattern of the first three *tratados* and the self-contained character of the fifth. *Lazarillo de Tormes* lacks the framing technique of the *Decameron*. On the other hand, its progressive movement goes well beyond anything either in the *Decameron* as a whole or in its individual tales. The picaresque is thus partly independent of the novella and the novella collection. Its innovative dynamism has more in common with later fiction—with the works of Defoe and Smollett, for example—than do any aspects of Boccaccio's masterpiece.

Though *Don Quixote* is plausibly seen as a synthesis of chivalric romance and the picaresque, this model obscures the role of the novella. Cervantes's *Novelas ejemplares* [Exemplary Novels] as well as the inset novellas in part one of *Don Quixote* derive from the Boccaccian tradition and particularly from the more serious, aristocratic novellas, novellas that if purged of their class specificity might help constitute a hegemonic form. "La gitanilla" [The Gypsy Girl] unfolds a romance pattern, complete with the renunciation of class differences, in an idealized, utopian gypsy milieu. In "El amante liberal" [The Generous Lover], the adventures of a Christian held captive by Turks have the pattern of Greek romance.

The opening five chapters of *Don Quixote* have also been seen as a novella. Despite the difficulties with this theory, Cervantes's

masterpiece may have begun as one more novella before turning
into something qualitatively different. This hypothetical novella
would have parodically demystified chivalric romance by demon-
strating its inadequacy in the face of everyday life. Cervantes's actual narrative goes well beyond this by introducing both Sancho
Panza and a self-conscious authorial voice. The work turns on the
interaction between the experiences of the characters and the repeated intrusion of that voice. In part one, this interaction is based
on structural indeterminacy. The main, realistic plot does not
arouse expectations strong enough to preclude inset novellas or artistic self-referentiality. Concerns about Don Quixote and Sancho
are largely limited to the individual episode. In other words, the plot
consists of a series of independent novellas connected by at least
two recurring figures. The inset tales violate this structural principle
by shifting the cast of characters, but not by being self-contained.
The first half of the work is, in this sense, an expanded novella composed of novellas in which the protagonists are either the actors or
the audience. The innovative complexity of the form is a legacy of
the novella tradition.[3]

Part Two of *Don Quixote*, published a decade after Part One,
moves even further away from a simple model of demystification.
It is really a fresh start that in a sense reverses the ideological orientation of its predecessor, implicitly validating Don Quixote's
medieval vision at the expense of the modern, realistic outlook of
his tormentors. Moreover, even more than Part One, Part Two calls
into question the primacy of reality over fiction and thus undermines the majority of the narrative. Characters in Part Two strictly
distinguish between the reality of the knight and squire they meet
and the fictionality of the earlier adventures of those characters—
the very distinction denied to readers of both parts. Cervantes developed unprecedentedly persuasive techniques for rendering
secular reality such that literature might be taken for reality by sane
and mad alike. Although in later centuries these techniques became
naturalized as literary realism, their novelty in the early seventeenth
century gave them an artificial character. Realism and self-consciousness arose simultaneously, the latter as the inherent, contradictory reflex of the former within an emergent ideology that did
not yet appear seamless, that had not yet become hegemonic.

Part Two, in which the novella becomes a weaker structural principle, does not, however, mark the supersession of the Boccaccian
heritage in insurgent fiction. The *Novelas ejemplares* and its many
imitators in seventeenth-century Spain are a crucial impetus behind
the rise of the French *nouvelle* after 1670. Compared to earlier

French fiction, the new form tends away from romance and toward brevity, simplicity, immediacy, and, somewhat ambiguously, realism. Lafayette's *La Princesse de Clèves*, arguably the central work in this tradition, is indebted to the novella both for its overall structure and for a series of interpolated tales somewhat reminiscent of the inset novellas in Part One of *Don Quixote*. In turn, among the major influences on Richardson's fiction are translations and adaptations of the French *nouvelle*. Thus both Fielding and Richardson are indebted to Cervantes, Fielding directly and indirectly to *Don Quixote* and Richardson indirectly to the *Novelas ejemplares*. Sterne's *Tristram Shandy* consciously evokes *Don Quixote* as does some of Smollett's fiction. The title of Charlotte Lennox's *Female Quixote* gives some sense of the prominence of the work.

As previously noted, much of the fiction of Defoe, whose main novels appeared between 1719 and 1724, and of Smollett is rooted in the Spanish picaresque, which was a secondary influence on Fielding as well. Among English translations of the Spanish picaresque, *Lazarillo de Tormes* appeared in 1688 and 1708, and its popular second part by Juan de Luna in 1669–70. Alemán's *Guzmán de Alfarache*, the most influential Spanish picaresque text in England, was printed three times in the late seventeenth century and again in 1708. Quevedo's *Buscón* [The Vagabond] came out twice between 1650 and 1700, as well as in 1707 and 1709. His *Sueños* [Dreams] went through at least eleven editions between 1668 and 1715, three of them in the eighteenth century. García's *La desordenada codicia de los bienes agenos* [The Chaotic Greed for Others' Property] was published three times in the 1650s, Salas Barbadillo's *La hija de Celestina* [Celestina's Daughter] in 1657 and 1667, and the same author's *El necio bien afortunado* [The Lucky Fool] in 1670. It was the turn of the *Novelas ejemplares* in 1694 and 1709, of *Estebanillo González* and López de Ubeda's *La pícara Justina* [Justina the Vagabond] in 1707, and of Castillo Solórzano's *La garduña de Sevilla* [The Marten of Seville] in 1665 (as *La Pícara* [The Vagabond]), c.1700, 1712, and 1717.[4]

These translations, especially of Alemán, inspired numerous borrowings and imitations, the most important of which was Head and Kirkman's *The English Rogue* (1665–71, with sequels through 1689). (*Guzmán de Alfarache* had been translated as *The Rogue*; after the appearance of *The English Rogue* it was retitled *The Spanish Rogue*.) Also important for our present purposes are *The French Rogue* (1672) and Smith's *History of the Lives and Robberies of the Most Notorious Highwaymen* (1714–19), because these, like *The Rogue*, were read by Defoe and influenced him. Smith's criminal biographies had a direct effect on Defoe's nonfictional work and may have had a general impact on his fiction. Both *Robinson Crusoe* and *Roxana* seem to owe something to *The English Rogue*, and *Colonel Jack* to *The French Rogue*. There are, in addition, significant resemblances between *Captain Singleton* and *Lazarillo de Tormes*.[5] The most tantalizing and also the most uncertain relationship is between *Moll Flanders* and works featuring a *pícara* protagonist, especially *La garduña de Sevilla* and *La pícara Justina*, both of which, as just noted, were printed in the early eighteenth century. It is tempting to see Defoe's novel as a synthesis of *La pícara Justina*'s first-person narration and *La garduña de Sevilla*'s conflict between efforts at moralizing judgment and interest in worldly profit. Though it has been suggested that *La pícara Justina* is the most likely source for *Moll Flanders*, I should confess that the English versions of the two Spanish works do not much remind me of Defoe's novel. But whatever the truth of this particular matter, Defoe was a typical eighteenth-century English novelist: his models came from Spain.

In short, eighteenth-century English fiction derives from Golden Age Spanish fiction, just as *Don Quixote* and the *Novelas ejemplares* probably are indebted to the *Decameron*. The crucial moments in the formation of the novel are connected, with Cervantes's work occupying the pivotal position.

II

If the role of Spanish fiction in the formation of the modern European novel remains underappreciated and even misunderstood, the same could never have been said of its importance to European global expansion beginning in the Renaissance.[6] But the specifically discursive dimensions of that expansion have only recently been subjected to close analysis, and so it is that, despite the spate of recent scholarship, assessment of the significance of Hispanic letters in the rise of modern European imperialism remains a work-in-progress. It may be useful to begin with what Spain shares with other European writing of the time. Spain is typical in the frequent recourse to classicizing rhetoric to render America. The pronouncedly masculinist tenor of the literature of expansion, even in comparison to other literature of the time, is equally international. I noted earlier the modest amount of narrowly literary interest in Spanish overseas conquest, especially if one looks only to the standard masterpieces of the age. Here, too, Spain approaches the norm.

It may be that Europeans found the New World too exotic, too strange to grasp. But there may also be a more distinctively literary explanation that is not limited to the Renaissance. Those genres that purport to capture contemporary life—in the Golden Age, most notably the prose fiction discussed above and some of the drama—seem to require a familiarity with the immediate surroundings that a distance of thousands of nautical miles apparently precluded. And despite the enormous amount of recent work arguing for the imperial vocation of European literature in subsequent centuries, the curious evasion characteristic of the Renaissance is maintained, especially in the history of the novel. Only in the very late stages of European expansion, when the settler colonies finally acquired sufficient density, were European novelists able to understand the overseas possessions of their countries with anything like the same depth they were capable of when writing about domestic or at least European locales.

It might appear, however, that early-modern Spain would enjoy a comparative advantage along this axis. Though it lacks the demystifying strain of French letters or the utopian speculation of English writing, its vast territorial acquisitions, combined with the early establishment of sizable settler colonies, would seem to give its authors precisely the necessary social density that a more commercially oriented imperial power would inevitably be unable to provide. And in significant ways this is in fact the case. There is little in other European languages to compare, for instance, with Ercilla's *La Araucana*, and when one turns to Hispanic letters more generally the disparity is simply overwhelming, whether the subject is geographical, biological, or ethnographic. Furthermore, the incomparably genocidal consequences of the Spanish conquest of America have as their reflex the most thoroughgoing denunciation of European imperialism of the time in the work of Las Casas. Finally, Spain's colonizing strategy eventually resulted in the recording of the apparently preconquest views of "native informants" and the production of autoethnographic indigenous texts for which, again, there are few analogues.[7] The writings of Fernando de Alva Ixtlilxochitl and of the Inca Garcilaso de la Vega may stand as examples. In short, the very scope and density of Spanish imperialism was answered by an unparalleled discursive richness.

III

The conquest is often seen as a continuation of the Reconquest. The relation of Catholic Spain to its Semitic heritage is, of course, the subject of a major reinterpretation by Américo Castro beginning shortly after World War II.[8] Before turning to the debate that Castro's writings have inspired, it may be useful to situate him in an international context, to place him in the company of the Germanic philologists mentioned earlier as well as of Bakhtin and Lukács. The lives and work of these critics were marked by one or both of the twin catastrophes of Stalinism and fascism, to which their loving accounts of European literature are honorable responses. Seeking the reconciliation of nation-states, Curtius finds the principle of European unity in medieval Latin Christianity. It is hard to miss the moral obtuseness of tacitly ignoring, in the late 1940s, the deaths of millions of Jews, Eastern Christians, and Moslems at the hands of the former leaders of his own country. By contrast Auerbach, who like Lukács and Spitzer was Jewish, was at pains to emphasize, in both his essay "Figura" and in *Mimesis*, the untranscendable Jewish element in Western literature. A still bolder departure occurs, however, in Castro, who "enjoyed" an exceptionally prolonged experience of fascism. Rewriting the history of medieval Spain as the interaction of three cultures—Christian, Moslem, and Jewish—and then extending this approach to the literature of the sixteenth and seventeenth centuries, he breaks with a prevalent intra-European essentialism.

But the claim that Castro's approach is morally more sensitive than those of his contemporaries is by no means equivalent to the assertion that it is historically more accurate. My view, however, is that it is. Critics of the Semitic hypothesis have often tried to show that what looks like Arabic or Hebrew influence can be adequately explained by reference to the western tradition. The choice, then, would seem to be—falsely, in my estimation—between a Spain that is unique because of the Islamic conquest and a Spain that is a typical European country. Castro and other scholars who have developed his ideas have surely aided their intellectual foes by overarguing from the available evidence, by resorting to dubious allegorical interpretations in which every conflict is ultimately a screen for the only real (religious) one, and by understanding the three religious groups through the conceptually problematic notion of castes. Yet whatever the debate over individual writers, texts, or cultural practices, there ought to be no rational disagreement about Castro's central thesis: Christian and Semitic Spain significantly interacted with each other. For instance, it has been claimed that Provençal lyric may derive from the Mozarabic *kharjas*, and in a perhaps more compelling rebuttal that these Arabic or Hebrew macaronic poems instead borrowed from earlier European poetry. But whichever way influence ran, medieval Semitic and Romance-language poetry clearly belonged to the same cultural matrix. Similarly, there can be no doubt about the eastern origin of the frame tale collections that appeared on both sides of the religious divide in medieval Spain, of the extraordinary volume of translation from the Arabic and the Hebrew in medieval Christian Spain, of the recurrent thematic treatment of the relationships among the three religious groups at least as early as the *Cantar de Mio Cid* [Song of the Cid] and continuing through the canonical authors and texts of the *Siglo de Oro*, of the *converso* lineage of some of the leading writers of the age, and—more broadly—of the pervasive cultural intermingling, especially in the Middle Ages, emblematized by the widespread and related practices of religious intermarriage and of religious conversion and reconversion.

Yet it does not follow from this history that Spain is therefore unique, except in the obvious sense that every country is different from every other country. The inference that the Semitic heritage renders Spain anomalous rests on the prior assumption that the rest of Europe developed autochthonously. That assumption is hard to sustain, however, whether one looks at the formation of individual nation states or at the development of the continent as a whole. Even if one ignores the Islamic conquest, the complex emergence and continuing vicissitudes of Spain in relation to Portugal, Catalonia, and the Basque country—to take only the most obvious regions—have analogues in England, France, Germany, and Italy, among many others. A similar pattern holds if one moves from a national to a continental scale. Islamic domination extended to parts of Italy and, later, to southeastern Europe. Earlier, much of eastern Europe belonged to Eastern Orthodoxy, and nearly all of eastern Europe was subjected to repeated nomadic invasions from Asia. One finds the same international and intercontinental relations if attention is confined to literature. National literary languages are formed by both the absorption and the suppression of regional literatures, and by both the acceptance and the rejection of foreign influences. In Spain, the example of the *kharjas* can be supplemented by the Galician-Portuguese lyric, the plays of Gil Vicente, *Tirant lo Blanc* (admired by Cervantes), and the possible Valencian roots of the *comedia*, among others. In Europe as a whole, literature developed in relation to a pre-Christian past and to a Byzantine and Semitic present. Those ostensibly non-European presences on the periphery of Europe had the additional function of providing a conduit for materials from further east. It is this porousness and hybrid-ity that has defined European literature from the beginning to the present day.

IV

In a well-known essay on Laurence Sterne's *Tristram Shandy*, Victor Shklovsky emphasizes that novel's apparently unnovelistic laying bare of its technique, obtrusiveness of its formal devices, self-consciousness, and self-referentiality. He provocatively concludes: "*Tristram Shandy* is the most typical novel in world literature."[9] Shklovsky's point is that the very extremism of *Tristram Shandy* reveals the essence of the category to which it belongs. So it is with Spain. Both conquered by and conqueror of non-Christian non-Europeans, it was formed not only out of these intercontinental conflicts but also out of historical sedimentation and internal struggle: this is the supposed uniqueness of Spanish history. Uniquely positioned in the formation of the European novel, uniquely situated to provide a multidimensional account of early-modern European imperialism, uniquely influenced by Semitic culture in the European Middle Ages and Renaissance, Spanish literature is the most typical literature in Europe.

NOTES

1. See Salomon 1965, Vilar 1971, Vicens Vives 1969, and Elliott 1964.
2. The following discussion of prose fiction partly draws on my 1988 article "The Novel and Cultural Revolution." The journal in which it appeared did not circulate widely and is difficult to obtain.
3. For studies of the novella and *Don Quixote*, see Jones 1971 and Shklovsky 1965, 189–91.
4. See Chandler 1907, 2: 285–341, and 1899, especially 399–469. See also Randall 1963, especially 234–9, and Bjornson 1977, 139–65 and 273, n. 15.
5. See Bjornson 1977, 161; Chandler 1899, 422–4 and 262- 63; Novak 1983, 126–30, 3, 7, and 8; Novak 1973, 133; and Zimmerman, 56–57.
6. This section draws partly on portions of my 1995 essay The Discourse of Empire in the Renaissance.
7. See Alva Ixtlilxochitl (1969) and Inca Garcilaso de la Vega (1963).
8. See Castro 1954 and 1971.
9. See Shklovsky 1965, 57.

WORKS CITED

Alva Ixtlilxochitl, Fernando de. 1969. *Ally of Cortes (Account 13: Of the Coming of the Spaniards and the Beginning of the Evangelical Law)*. Translated by Douglass K. Ballentine. El Paso: Texas Western Press.

Bjornson, Richard. 1977. *The Picaresque Hero in European Fiction*. Madison: University of Wisconsin Press.

Castro, Américo. 1954. *The Structure of Spanish History*. Translated by Edmund L. King Princeton: Princeton University Press.

———. 1971. *The Spaniards: An Introduction to Their History*. Translated by Willard F. King and Selma Margaretten. Berkeley: University of California Press.

Chandler, Frank Wadleigh. [1899] 1961. *Romances of Roguery, an Episode in the History of the Novel: The Picaresque Novel in Spain*. Reprint, New York: Burt Franklin.

———. 1907. *The Literature of Roguery*. 2 vols. Boston: Houghton Mifflin.

Cohen, Walter. 1988. "The Novel and Cultural Revolution." *Wissenschaftliche Zeitschrift der Pädagogische Hochschule "Karl Liebknecht" Potsdam* 32: 29–47.

———. 1995. "The Discourse of Empire in the Renaissance." In *Cultural Authority in Golden Age Spain*, edited by Marina S. Brownlee and Hans Ulrich Gumbrecht. Baltimore: Johns Hopkins University Press.

Elliott, J. H. 1964. *Imperial Spain, 1469–1716*. New York: St. Martin's Press.

Inca Garcilaso de la Vega. 1963. *First Part of the Royal Commentaries of the Yncas*. Translated by Clements R. Markham. 2 vols. New York: Burt Franklin.

Jones, R. O. 1971. *The Golden Age: Prose and Poetry (The Sixteenth and Seventeenth Centuries)*. Vol. 2 of *A Literary History of Spain*. London: Ernest Benn.

Novak, Maximillian E. 1973. "Some Notes Toward a History of Fictional Forms: From Aphra Behn to Daniel Defoe." *Novel* 6: 120–33.

———. 1983. *Realism, Myth, and History in Defoe's Fiction*. Lincoln: University of Nebraska Press.

Randall, Dale B. J. 1963. *The Golden Tapestry: A Critical Study of Non-chivalric Spanish Fiction in English Translation, 1543–1657*. Durham, N. C.: Duke University Press.

Salomon, Noël. 1965. *Recherches sur le thème paysan dans la "comedia" au temps de Lope de Vega*. Bordeaux: Fret.

Shklovsky, Victor. (Chklovski, V.) 1965. "La construction de la nouvelle et du roman." In *Théorie de la littérature*, edited by Tzvetan Todorov. Paris: Seuil.

———. 1965. "Sterne's *Tristram Shandy*: Stylistic Commentary." In *Russian Formalist Criticism: Four Essays*, edited and translated by Lee T. Lemon and Marion J. Reis. Lincoln: University of Nebraska Press.

Vicens Vives, Jaime. 1969. *An Economic History of Spain*. In collaboration with Jorge Nada Olla. Translated by Frances M. López-Morals. Princeton: Princeton University Press.

Vilar, Pierre. 1971. "The Age of Don Quixote." *New Left Review* 68 (July–August): 59–71.

Zimmerman, Everett. 1975. *Defoe and the Novel*. Berkeley: University of California Press.

Part II
Textual Strategies

Who's Telling This Story, Anyhow?
Framing Tales East and West:
Panchatantra to Boccaccio to Zayas

MARGARET GREER

My central interest in this essay is the use of the frame tale by the Spanish Baroque writer María de Zayas y Sotomayor in her two-volume collection of stories, the *Novelas amorosas y ejemplares* [Amorous and Exemplary Stories] and the *[Desengaños amorosos] Parte segunda del Sarao y entretenimiento honesto* [(Amorous Disillusions) Second Part of the Soire and Honest Entertainment] published in 1637 and 1647, respectively. To understand Zayas's particular use of the frame tale, however, I will approach it through a brief consideration of the function of artistic frames in a larger sense, and of the nature and function of the frame tale as it was employed, or omitted, by Zayas's predecessors in the novella tradition.

First, let us imagine a fond father or mother who in a burst of parental enthusiasm puts a child's first tempera painting in a real frame and hangs it on the wall. What is the significance of that frame? In the mind of parent and child, at least, it says: this is not just a four-year old's play with color, this is important; this is ART. Now, working in reverse, if we call to mind a favorite painting, whether it be Velázquez, Monet, or Picasso and, in our mind's eye, remove its frame, does it diminish it in some way? Does it make more tenuous the stature of that image as a work of art? I would be tempted to say that it does, until I think of a small print I have of one of my favorite paintings, La Tour's *Education of the Virgin*.[1] It has no frame, just two tacks holding it to the wall above my desk in my office, yet looking at it transports me to another realm of aesthetic as well as educational purity. I would deduce from this mental exercise that the declaration of aesthetic value can be either internally or externally coded.

If we turn to theater, we find the same to be the case. Theaters with a proscenium arch and a stage curtain need no mediating *dramatic* frame or prologue to define the dramatic world. But dramatic prologues are an important constituent of Spanish Renaissance drama from Juan del Encina forward, when plays were performed in improvised theaters and playwrights were defining the conventions of drama for their audiences. Although prologues gradually disappeared from *corral* [public theater] performances once permanent theaters were established, they continued in vigor as a vital part of the street performances of the *autos sacramentales* [allegorical religious dramas] for the annual Corpus Christi celebration.[2] Informal street theater today, too, requires some kind of frame definition. This may be effected by a barker, or a lone performer who attracts a group of spectators. On the other hand, the separate, aesthetic realm may, in this case, be worked internally by opening the dramatic action with a heightened theatrical rhetoric— "overacting"—that marks this interaction as distinct from the everyday world of the street itself. Once a semicircle of spectators forms, the semicircle itself marks out the limits of the aesthetic "object," within which space, time, and being have the peculiar doubleness of drama. While most mature human beings respect the integrity of the object thus demarcated, the frame is not impermeable. Naive spectators do sometimes behave like Don Quixote before Maese Pedro's puppet show; Henry Sullivan (1983, 386) cites two cases of twentieth-century spectators of a German version of Calderón's *La dama duende* [The Phantom Lady] who intervened across the frame at least verbally. And the Argentine dramatist Osvaldo Dragún told me that when, in the last days of the military regime that ruled Argentina from 1976 to 1983, his troop, using theater as a political weapon, performed his works wherever they could gather a crowd in the streets of Buenos Aires, one play in particular caused "framing" problems. In his brief play, *Historia de un hombre convertido en perro* [Story of a Man Transformed into a Dog], as the title indicates, the main character is transformed from a speaking human being into a barking dog. As he was reduced to barking, the spectators might understand the political point being made, but all the neighborhood dogs saw was a new interloper in their territory, and the only way the troop could keep them from attacking was by, shall we say, turning up the theatrical rhetoric, and, in solidarity with the "caninized" actor, barking ferociously until the "real" dogs retreated.

Presumably, most of us are not mongrel readers. While we acknowledge the thorny problem of the ontology of fictional discourse, in practice we are generally able to recognize the presence of a fictional text by its own combination of external and internal markers: externally the book as a physical object in itself, and the liminary elements that Genette (1987, 7–8) calls the "paratexte" of the work—title, preface, epigraph, etc., and internally by stylistic clues. The latter may be as close to the time-honored "Erase una vez . . ." [Once upon a time . . .] as is the opening sentence of Cervantes's novella, *La ilustre fregona* [The Illustrious Kitchen-Maid]: "En Burgos, ciudad ilustre y famosa, no ha muchos años que en ella vivían dos caballeros principales y ricos" [Cervantes 1990, 297: In the illustrious and famous city of Burgos, not many years ago there lived two principal and rich gentlemen]. Or the clues may appear more subtly and slowly, as in *La fuerza de la sangre* [The Power of Blood]: "Una noche de las calurosas del verano volvían de recrearse del río, en Toledo, un anciano hidalgo, con su mujer, un niño pequeño, una hija de diez y seis años y una criada. La noche era clara; la hora, las once; el camino, solo, y el paso, tardo" [Cervantes 1990, 239: One of those hot summer nights, in Toledo, an elderly gentleman, with his wife, a small boy, a sixteen-year-old daughter and a serving girl, were returning from an outing to the river. The night was clear, the hour, eleven o'clock, the road, deserted, and their pace, slow]. Even in this second case, the special rhythm of the second sentence would alert most readers that they are not perusing a seventeenth-century equivalent of a police report.

If these subtle forms of framing are, in practice, generally sufficient to delimit a fictional text, what, then, are the purpose and function of the much more assertive framing devices used by Boccaccio in the *Decameron* (c.1350), Chaucer in the *Canterbury Tales* (1386–1400) (and their Eastern predecessors), and the many novella writers who followed in that tradition? Why did Cervantes in his *Novelas ejemplares* [Exemplary Stories] (1613) dispense with the frame and why did Lope personalize it in the *Novelas a Marcia Leonarda* [Stories for Marcia Leonarda] (1621–24)?[3] Why did the many Spanish novella writers of the 1620s and 1630s follow the example of Cervantes rather than Boccaccio or Lope? Finally, the question of most interest to me, why did María de Zayas y Sotomayor opt to use a frame tale again? She appears to have written at least eight of the stories of the first volume and to have been preparing them for publication around 1625, when the preferred style was Cervantes's frame-less model. Yet she encloses her collection within a single frame that unites the two volumes, despite the ten-year separation in their publication and the much darker tone of the second volume.

In tackling these questions, I would like to make one more preliminary detour through a recent use of the frame tale, the Rob Reiner film *The Princess Bride*, which I would describe as a romance packaged for postmodern cynics. And very effectively packaged indeed. Any of you who have sons and daughters the approximate age of mine have probably seen at least bits of this film more times than you can count, and my daughter says that at the mere mention of it, her college friends launch into gleeful recitals of their favorite lines. The film opens with the sound of a child's cough, followed by strains of "Take Me Out to the Ball Game" and a view of a Nintendo-style baseball game on a television screen. The young boy playing it is ill and confined to his room, but is less than delighted when his grandfather arrives to visit bearing a present—"a *book*??"—and proposing to read to him the story that his father read to him when he was sick, that he read to the boy's father and will now read to him. The boy is unenthusiastic but when his grandfather assures him that it has lots of sports in it, he says he'll try to stay awake. What the grandfather reads is a classic tale of a poor, gallant hero Westley who defeats an evil prince Humperdink and wins his beautiful ladylove Buttercup, all seasoned generously with humor, magic, and valiantry. At key points in the narrative, the camera cuts back to the boy, now fully engrossed in the tale, but interrupting the reading when the story seems to depart from his ideal paradigm, or when Westley and Buttercup spend too much time kissing.

This cinematographic frame tale contains most of the major elements of classic literary frames. The first is the motif of illness. In Boccaccio's frame, this illness is without—the plague raging through Florence, from which the seven ladies and three gentlemen retreat both physically and psychologically, recounting stories in the safe haven of beautiful gardens in country estates. More often, the sickness is within; in Petrus Alfonsi's twelfth-century *Disciplina clericalis*, a dying Arab transmits his wisdom to his son by telling him a series of stories and proverbs containing moral lessons (Gittes 1991, 59).[4] The pretext for story-telling in María de Zayas's novellas is the illness of the heroine of the frame tale, Lisis, whose friends gather to entertain her and speed her convalescence by telling stories. In Zayas's tale, as in numerous stories in novella collections, the true illness is *doubly* within, for the physically symptoms are the result of *mal de amor* [malady of love]—in the case of Zayas's Lisis, suffering caused by jealousy and disappointment in love, as her beloved don Juan neglects her for her cousin Lisarda. Boccaccio (1982, 2–3) too, in his "Proemio" [Proem] cites his former suffering and frustrated passion and offers his stories as pleasure, counsel, and cure for the "charming ladies" who suffer love's melancholy. Zayas's frame narrative seems, until the very end, to posit two possible remedies for the suffering of unrequited love; on the one hand, Lisis is promising to marry another man, the adoring Don Diego; on the other, the enclosed narrators hammer in the point that their tales are to warn women against the pitfalls of desire and male treachery. Their counsel prevails at the end as the heroine of the frame follows many of the fictional protagonists into the closed, woman's world of the convent. No kissing there.

Another element that Reiner's cinematic frame shares with literary frame tales is that of a physical separation from the everyday world, a separation that permits story-telling. Often the frame underlines the horror and threat of the outside world. Boccaccio describes the physical and social ravages of the plague with gruesome detail, and Marguerite de Navarre's narrators in the *Heptameron* (1559) narrowly escape war, violent bandits, and a roaring flood.[5] Zayas, and later Mariana de Carvajal's *Navidades de Madrid* [Christmas in Madrid] (1663) mark the separation in terms of temperature, contrasting the inner warmth within the icy December temperatures without. In so doing, they link their settings with the folklore tradition of storytelling "alrededor de la lumbre" [around the fire], a tradition also evoked by the very titles of two earlier Spanish novella collections, Timoneda's *El Patrañuelo* [Tall Tales] (1567) and Eslava's *Noches de invierno* [Winter Nights] (1609).[6] I would hardly be original in suggesting that the comfort proffered in the frame settings in companionship and a crackling fire is a physical translation of the psychic or metaphysical warmth, comfort, or cure provided by narrative itself, as it models a meaningful design for human life, for a cold, chaotic existence in which order and purpose are rarely self-evident.

Reiner's grandfather, like the narrators of many frame tales, represents the wise man (or woman) who instructs an inexperienced listener through an entertaining tale. In the eighth-century frame narrative *Panchatantra*, the three doltish young sons of a mighty king learn worldly and political wisdom from the tales of a wise man (Gittes 1991, 9–10); in Don Juan Manuel's *El Conde Lucanor* [Count Lucanor] (1335), the wise old servant Petronio provides the guidance requested by the count in the form of exemplary tales. While the grandfather reads to a boy, Boccaccio, Lope de Vega, and many other writers of novella collections posit a primarily female readership. Zayas's narrators, however, address a mixed audience, both within the frame and as presumed readers of the collection, exhorting women to attend the warnings in the tales, and entreating men to hear or read them with a chivalrous spirit and open mind.

This dialogue with a fictive audience is, of course, one of the primary functions of the frame tale, as Amy R. Williamsen demonstrates in the case of Zayas. Anne Cayuela points out in her study of the liminary apparatus of seventeenth-century Spanish fiction that reading is a communicative act in which one of the parties is absent, and publication in printing made works available to a large and heterogeneous audience. One result is an emphasis in the liminary apparatus on the nature of the *destinatario* [receiver] and on the concrete aspects of the communicative act (Cayuela 1994, 81, 123–24). The prologue, in a kind of act of seduction, creates an image both of the author and of the implied or ideal reader in order to obtain not only a reading, but a particular kind of reading (321–22). Two of our novella authors perform this image-creating function quite literally: Cervantes in the self-portrait he paints in the prologue to his *Novelas ejemplares* [Exemplary Stories], and Lope de Vega, who depicts his fictive listener, Marcia Leonarda, in glowing color. The fully personified communicative act in frame narratives make this image-operated seduction of the reader yet more dramatic, particularly in frames such as those of Marguerite de Navarre and María de Zayas, which involve extensive exchange between fictional narrators and their listeners. This function of the frame is of the utmost importance in Zayas's collection, as we will see.

First, however, I would like to consider two other perspectives on the nature and function of frames, theories that focus more on the other end of the author-to-real-world relation, that of the sociohistorical and ideological context and the author's use or omission of a frame tale. Katherine S. Gittes (1991) provides a fascinating perspective on the relation between cultural structures and frame narratives in her study of an early time period, the development of the tradition from early eastern tales to Chaucer and Christine de Pizan's *Cité des Dames* [The Book of the City of Ladies] (1405). With reiterated apologies for the imprecision of the terms "eastern" and "western,"[7] Gittes draws a fundamental contrast between East and West in the metaphysical conception of the world. The East, rooted in nomadic tribal life, saw the world as open, and appreciated the infinite variety and limitless renewability of life. Early Arabic literary forms, such as the pre-Islamic *qasida*, or ode, and the tenth- and eleventh-century Arabic picaresque, or *maqamat*, have a loose, open-ended, and linear structure, organized not by a unifying theme or idea but by the perspective of the speaker or central character (334–45). Hence, a collection such as the *Thousand Nights and a Night,* the product of a culture that avoids rounding off numbers, but prefers 1001 as meaning a large, indefinite number (33, 46). Gittes traces the western view of a more closed universe back to Greek mathematical principles, to the preference of Pythagoras for geometry over algebra, and for what Gittes describes as

[a] concept of organization, a notion of unity, in which the whole has greater importance than the parts. . . . Pythagoras, voicing what had been implied in Greek thought before his time, stated that the universe is harmonious because all its parts are related to one another mathematically. He thought that mathematical order lay behind the apparently mysterious, arbitrary, and chaotic workings of nature. (Gittes 1991, 24)

This insistence on harmony, unity, and the orderly subordination of the part to the whole underlies the literature, art and architecture, and world view passed on from Greece and Rome to medieval European philosophers. (29)

Medieval Spain served as the bridge over which the frame-tale collection, along with so many other elements of eastern culture, reached the West. The collection of tales known as the *Panchatantra,* much of which seems to have originated in India and the Near East, acquired in its eighth-century Arabic translation an open-ended frame in which a wise man tells stories to educate a king's son who had previously refused instruction (Gittes 1991, 8–20). Augmented and renamed with an Arabic touch, *Kalilah and Dimnah* came to Europe through the Arab conquest. When Alfonso X had it translated in the thirteenth century, it became, according to a recent editor Thomas Irving, the first extensive piece of prose literature in the popular language of Spain and a point of confluence in the streams of Arabic and Spanish civilization (Irving 1980, xi). It also furnished the model for the widely read *Disciplina Clericalis* that the converted Spanish Jew, Petrus Alfonsi, wrote first in Arabic, then translated into Latin. That work, according to Gittes, "ranks above all other works in bridging 'Eastern' and 'Western' narrative traditions and in funneling Arabic content and structure to European medieval vernacular writers (57).[8] The frame narrative tradition that developed thereafter, according to Gittes, bore the continuing tension between open and closed structures, between the attraction of symmetry and the suspense of the indefinite (113). Whereas

the earliest Arabic frame narratives suggest that medieval Arabs perceived the natural world as a world where boundaries and structure, if they exist, are not especially desirable. The later European frame narratives, notably the *Decameron*, the *Confessio* and the *Canterbury Tales* suggest the reverse; that even though the natural world appears disorderly, the medieval Christian longed to see a spark . . . which would give the sensation that underneath the disorder lies a comforting divine harmony, perhaps ordered along Pythagorean lines. The harmony hinted at in these fourteenth-century frame narratives is a harmony which the reader will see and fully comprehend in the afterlife. What looks like disorder on earth is God's order misperceived. (148)

H. H. Wetzel, beginning approximately where Gittes leaves off in time, traces the development of the novella from the late Middle Ages to Cervantes in a more closely deterministic fashion. He relates the presence or absence of a developed narrative frame—as well as the predominance of different types of novellas—to the relative stability or flux in the political and ideological structures of the age. Within the stable order of feudalism and medieval Christianity, collections of *exempla* did not require an elaborated narrative frame, for order was perceived to be supplied by divine providence, whose operation the *exempla* helped to explain allegorically. Says Wetzel:

> It was not by chance that the first European collections of novellas appeared at the end of the thirteenth century in southern and central Italy; in that "anarchic" land, the autonomy of the towns and of their citizens was most advanced, the social order profoundly overturned by the nascent preponderance of the merchant bourgeoisie and orthodox faith heavily buffeted by the revaluation of man, a new consciousness of his own value and the effect of major heretical movements. (1981, 46)

Within this turbulent world, Boccaccio supplied a harmonious fictional order to contain the chaos of reality, the social breakdown brought on by the plague, "a symbolic index of the danger which threatened to dissolve the civic, religious and moral norms of the society" (Wetzel 1981, 47). That Boccaccio felt empowered to supply such an order, and felt the need to do so, Wetzel relates to the sociopolitical order of Florence in his day, in which a commoner such as Boccaccio could participate actively both in the financial and political life of the city, and in which social norms were in flux and civic equilibrium precarious, as the bourgeois "virtues" of a modern economy intermingled with traditional aristocratic codes of conduct. With the refeudalization of the fifteenth and sixteenth centuries, frame narratives were either weakened or omitted by authors who enjoyed no true political power, but were limited to a subordi-

nate role in princely courts (50). For his mid-sixteenth-century collection, Bandello constructed no organizing frame but dedicated
each of his 214 stories to one of a variety of notable figures in the
courtly society he knew. Wetzel relates this practice to Bandello's
dependent position within an Italy whose cities no longer enjoyed
the relative autonomy of Boccaccio's Florence, but were buffeted
by European power contests on Italian soil, and in which the discovery of the New World and the Reformation were transforming
the mental as well as the physical world (53). That Marguerite de
Navarre, on the other hand, constructed a highly elaborated narrative frame within a rigidly hierarchical political structure, Wetzel
attributes to her privileged position, one of true authority as queen
of France, albeit a France torn by religious dissension. Hence the
importance of the lengthy discussions by fully developed frame
personalities who express profound differences of viewpoint (50–
51).[9] And finally, in the declining empire of seventeenth-century
Spain Cervantes, says Wetzel, "made a virtue of the necessity of
renouncing the frame" (54). He exchanged the powerlessness of an
hidalgo (the lowest level of nobility) without even the comfort of a
subordinate position at court "for the empowerment of a gifted artist who constructed fictive reality to his own image and dissolved
the contradictions of reality through well-known literary devices
such as recognitions, found children, etc." (54–55). One might
contest Wetzel's evaluation of Cervantes's renunciation of the
frame in the light of that author's announcement of a future work
that has the sound of a framed novella collection, *Semanas del
jardín* [Weeks in the Garden]. On the other hand, Wetzel might
claim vindication in the fact that such a collection never saw publication.

   If we bring the theories of Gittes and Wetzel to bear on Zayas's
choice of a fully developed frame narrative, the results are contradictory. From the scarce documentation of her life, we can say that
she probably enjoyed a somewhat more secure socioeconomic position than Cervantes, as the daughter of Fernando de Zayas, who was
at one time the majordomo of the count of Lemos and who was
named administrator of an estate of the Order of Santiago in 1638
(Barbeito Carneiro 1986, 165–72). In no way could we argue that
she enjoyed true political authority, as did Marguerite de Navarre.
At best we could claim for her, as she does for herself, a position of
moral authority as self-appointed spokeswoman for women within
an absolutist, resolutely patriarchal Counter-Reformation society
that denied them any legitimate independent agency. By Gittes's
categories, this was an ideologically closed society, one that would

foster the containment of difference, of the chaotic multiplicity of reality, within a strictly controlling frame, but by those of Wetzel, it would make the erection of such a frame impossible for a powerless female. Zayas does not use the frame as a format for true discussion of philosophical difference, as does Marguerite de Navarre, but rather as an arm of philosophical combat in the defense of women. She makes of it, we might say, a "thesis" frame narrative.[10] And it is the effective propagation of this thesis, I would argue, that motivates her use of such a frame.

The frame narrative of Reiner's film modeled for postmodern viewers how a boy moves from playing electronic games to avid attention to a traditional romance. At first, he objects to the "kissing parts" and tells his grandfather to skip them, although his grandpa assures him "Some day you may not mind so much." That "someday" arrives by the end of the story, when he tells his grandfather *not* to skip the description of the sublime final kiss of Westley and Buttercup.

What has changed his mind? The story, of course. Peter Brooks (1985) suggests that narrative accomplishes what is logically unthinkable. Jerome Bruner (1991) seconds this idea and adds several important observations: human beings, from their earliest years, perceive and organize existence through narrative; narrative *constitutes* reality as much as it reflects it; and changes in narrative paradigms may reshape not just plots, but modes of thought.

The Reiner frame shows narrative moving an oedipal boy to acceptance of what for him was previously unthinkable: that the objective of a hero is not just excelling at sports or defeating the evil antagonist, but should include blissful, lasting union with an ideal member of the opposite sex—the traditional plot that however unrealistic, assures the continuation of the species.

Zayas, however, faced a much more formidable logical obstacle. Within the genre of the *novela amorosa* [love story], she seeks to implant the conviction that heterosexual union is *not* the desired goal but a fatal trap for women, and that true happy endings can only be found by sublimating desire for any corporeal male and rejoining the mother in the feminine world of the convent. To accomplish that, she not only tells story after story of the fatal effects of desire, but *models* in her frame narrative the reeducative effect of those stories, as Lisis breaks her engagement to Don Diego and retreats with her mother to the safety of convent walls. Zayas's decision to employ a frame tale, I would propose, is not aesthetically motivated in the need to delimit and organize fictional worlds, but polemically designed to enhance the power of the narrative to transcend the limits of fiction and reorganize her readers' modes of thought.

N<small>OTES</small>

This essay is a slightly expanded version of an address first presented at the Mid-America Conference on Hispanic Literature, Lawrence, Kansas, in September, 1994. A longer consideration of Zayas's technique constitutes the final chapter of my forthcoming book on her stories, *Desiring Readers: María de Zayas Tells Baroque Tales of Love and the Cruelty of Men.*

1. My print attributes this to Georges de La Tour, but according to the catalog of the exhibit of La Tours work in the National Gallery of Art in 1996–97, while the original conception was due to Georges, some art historians believe the execution of the work may be due in large part to his son Etienne. See Conisbee (1996, 124).

2. See Flecniakoska (1975) and Erdocia (1997).

3. Juan de Piña takes Cervantes one step further in a witty, near-abolition of the prologue in his collection, published in 1624. He reduces it to two sentences: "El *Prólogo* se introduze a suma de lo impresso: dilatado, nunca visto de la ociosidad. Las *Novelas exemplares y prodigiosas historias* deste libro dizen la brevedad que afectan, como el *Prólogo*" [1987, 33: The prologue presents itself as a summation of what is printed, postponed, never seen by idle readers. The *Exemplary Novels and Prodigious Stories* of this book, like its prologue, bespeak the brevity to which they aspire). Piña transfers the explanatory and apologetic function of the standard prologue to a complex epilogue.

4. Illness is also a motif in numerous French collections: Philippe de Vigneulles, *Les Cent Nouvelles Nouvelles*; Le Seigneur de Cholires, *Les Après-disnees du Seigneur de Cholires*, and others (Losse 1994, 63). In Mariana de Carvajal's *Navidades de Madrid*, the lady of the house has been confined to the house caring for her ailing, elderly husband and, curiously, it is his death near the Christmas season that makes the story telling possible.

5. As Lyons (1989, 76–8) points out, however, the refuge they take in a Franciscan monastery is, in a moral sense at least, the heart of the danger, as Franciscan monks, both in the frame and enclosed tales, represent the threat of religious hypocrisy. The same could be said of Zayas's frame refuge, for the courtly gathering of men and women revolves around the same lure and threat of amorous desire central to her stories.

6. Eslava (1986) shows the economic effect of love sickness as well; the first tale tells how one of the participants of his frame gathering lost a ship due to the immoderate passion of its young captain.

7. Gittes (1991) cites María Rosa Menocal's study of the insistent repression of the substantial impact in medieval Europe exercised by Arabic culture, both as the source of learning, of literary traditions, of material well-being, and as a negative pole against which theologians and writers like Dante reacted.

8. Menocal (1987, 139–42) argues that Boccaccio scholars have paid too little attention to the importance of the Arabic and Hebrew inspiration and Arabic or Andalusian sources in the *Decameron,* as, for example, the model of scatalogical tales within a didactic frame provided him by Petrus Alfonsis's *Disciplina clericalis.*

9. Wetzel is thus closer to Marcel Tetel's reading (1981) of a fundamental ambiguity, indeed a manichean duality, in the *Heptameron* than to Paula Sommer's assertion of an ascendance (1984) of Protestant faith therein.

10. Montesa Peydró (1981, 351), in his excellent discussion of Zayas's use of the frame, also describes her collection as a whole as an *obra de tesis* [thesis work] (emphasis in the original).

WORKS CITED

Anonymous. 1980. *Kalilah and Dimnah*. Edited by Thomas Irving. Newark, Del.: Juan de la Cuesta.

Bandello, Matteo. 1966. *Le Novelle*. 2 vols. Edited by Francesco Flora. Verona: Arnoldo Mondadori Editore.

Barbeito Carneiro, Isabel. 1986. *Escritoras madrileñas del siglo seventeen: Estudio bibliográfico-crítico*. 2 vols. Ph.D. diss., Universidad Complutense.

Boccaccio, Giovanni. 1982. *Decameron*. Translated by Mark Musa and Peter Bondanella. New York: Mentor Books.

Brooks, Peter. 1985. *Reading for the Plot: Design and Intention in Narrative*. New York: Vintage Books.

Bruner, Jerome. 1991. "The Narrative Construction of Reality." *Critical Inquiry* 18: 1–21.

Carvajal, Mariana de. 1993. *Navidades de Madrid y noches entretenidas, en ocho novelas*. Edited by Catherine Soriano. Madrid: Comunidad de Madrid.

Cayuela, Anne. 1994. *L'Appareil liminaire des libres de fiction en prose, contribution à l'histoire de la lecture en Espagne au XVIIème siècle*. Ph.D. diss., Université Stendhal Grenoble Third.

Cervantes Saavedra, Miguel de. 1990. *Novelas ejemplares*. 6th ed. Edited by Fernando Gutiérrez. Barcelona: Editorial Juventud.

Conisbee, Philip. 1996. *Georges de La Tour and his world*. Catalog of the exhibition at the National Gallery of Art and the Kimbell Art Museum, Fort Worth, 1996–97. New Haven: Yale University Press.

Erdocia, Carolina. 1997. *Hacia una poética de la representación sacramental del Siglo de Oro español: Loas sacramentales de Calderón de la Barca y la celebración del Corpus Christi*. Ph.D. diss., Princeton University.

Eslava, Antonio. 1986. *Noches de invierno*. Edited by Julia Varella Vigal. Pamplona: Institución Príncipe de Viana del Departamento de Educacin y Cultura del Gobierno de Navarra.

Flecniakoska, Jean-Louis. 1975. *La loa*. Madrid: Sociedad General Española de Librería, S.A.

Genette, Gerard. 1987. *Seuils/Gerard Genette*. Paris: Seuil.

Gittes, Katharine S. 1991. *Framing the Canterbury Tales: Chaucer and the Medieval Frame Narrative Tradition*. New York: Greenwood Press.

Losse, Deborah N. 1994. *Sampling the Book: Renaissance Prologues and the French Conteurs*. Lewisburg, Pa.: Bucknell University Press.

Lyons, John D. 1989. *Exemplum: The Rhetoric of Modern France and Italy*. Princeton: Princeton University Press.

Menocal, Mara Rosa. 1987. *The Arabic Role in Medieval Literary History: A Forgotten Heritage*. Philadelphia: University of Pennsylvania Press.

Montesa Peydró, Salvador. 1981. *Texto y contexto en la narrativa de María de Zayas*. Madrid: Dirección General de la Juventud y Promoción Sociocultural.

Navarre, Marguerite de. 1984. *Heptameron*. Translated by Paul A. Chilton. London: Penguin Books.

Pabst, Walter. 1972. *La novela corta en la teoría y en la creación literaria: Notas para la historia de su antinomia en las literaturas románicas*. Translated by Rafael de la Vega. Madrid: Editorial Gredos, S. A.

Piña, Juan de. 1987. *Novelas exemplares y prodigiosas historias*. Edited by Encarnacin Garca de Dini. Verona: Facolt di Lingue e Letterature Straniere, Universit degli Studi di Pisa.

Reiner, Rob, director. 1987. *The Princess Bride*. Screenwriter William Goldman. Castle Rock.

Sullivan, Henry. 1983. *Calderón in the German Lands and the Low Countries: His Reception and Influence, 1654–1980*. Cambridge: Cambridge University Press.

Tetel, Marcel. 1981. *"L'Heptaméron*: Première nouvelle et fonction des devisants." In *La nouvelle française à la Renaissance*, edited by Lionello Sozzi and V. L. Saulnier. Geneva: Editions Slatkine.

Timoneda, Joan. 1986. *El Patrañuelo*. Edited by Jos Romera Castillo. Madrid: Cátedra.

Vega Carpio, Lope de. 1988. *Novelas a Marcia Leonarda*. Edited by Julia Barella. Madrid: Ediciones Jucar.

Wallace, David. 1991. *Giovanni Boccaccio: Decameron*. Cambridge: Cambridge University Press.

Wetzel, H. H. 1981. "Eléments socio-historiques d'un genre littéraire: l'histoire de la nouvelle jusqu'à Cervantès." In *La nouvelle française à la Renaissance*, edited by Lionello Sozzi and V. L. Saulnier. Geneva: Editions Slatkine.

Williamsen, Amy R. 1991. "Engendering Interpretation: The Manipulation of Reader Response in María de Zayas." *Romance Languages Annual* 3: 642–48.

Zayas y Sotomayor, María de. 1983. *[Desengaños amorosos]. Parte segunda del Sarao y entretenimiento honesto*. Edited by Alicia Yllera. Madrid: Cátedra.

———. 1948. *Novelas ejemplares y amorosas*. Edited by Agustín C. de Ameza y Mayo. Madrid: Aldus.

Lasting Laughter: Comic Challenges Posed by Zayas and Castellanos

AMY R. WILLIAMSEN

Years ago (in fact, many more years ago than I care to admit), when I began to work on María de Zayas, I was struck by the lack of critical attention to the humor that graces her work, especially the *Novelas ejemplares y amorosas* [The Enchantments of Love: Amorous and Exemplary Novels].[1] Bearing in mind Adrienne Rich's insightful proclamation that "All silence has a meaning" (1979, 308), I became even more interested in this facet of her texts.[2] In fact, past evaluations of Zayas's literary technique have, for the most part, denied the presence of humor and irony in her prose. Amezúa's pronouncement, "no conocerá el humor ni la ironía porque esos matices no son posibles a su temperamento dinámico y fogoso" [Amezúa 1950, 23: she would not know about humor or irony because these nuances are not possible given her dynamic and fiery temperament], remained virtually unchallenged until the publication of Salvador Montesa's seminal study, *Texto y contexto en María de Zayas* [Text and Context in María de Zayas] in 1981. He affirms that "la insistencia en los aspectos trágicos de las novelas y en el pesimismo que destilan puede hacernos olvidar una faceta interesante en la obra zayesca: el humor" [225: the insistence on the tragic aspects of the novels and the pessimism they exude can lead us to forget an interesting facet of Zayas's work: humor]. Yet, he dedicates only six pages out of four hundred to a consideration of humor. A recent bibliographic search confirmed that, to date, Zayas's humor remains largely uncharted territory.

In an earlier article, I proposed that Zayas employs humor to challenge patriarchal structures. While acknowledging that, as others have noted, the author's feminism might not conform to our current formulations, I suggested that her implicit program anticipated the paradigm formalized by Rosario Castellanos, one of the foremost Mexican feminists of our own era. In this essay, I would like to explore more fully the common threads that link these two apparently disparate figures. Although I would never venture to establish a direct influence, it seems that an examination of the shared characteristics might yield important insights into the role of humor in feminist theory and practice.

Castellanos states that her purpose as a feminist is to explore the myths that govern society's expectations of women and to begin the process of demythification using humor to reveal the absurdities of underlying accepted social conventions. She repeatedly emphasizes the liberating force of humor, affirming that "reírse de algo es la forma más inmediata de colocarse fuera del alcance de ese algo" [1973, 173: to laugh at something is the surest way to place oneself outside its reach]. She identifies three constellations of myths that constrain women: the aesthetic, the intellectual, and the ethical. Many of Castellanos's works serve to "debunk" these myths (Nigro 1980); curiously, the same myths and their absurdities serve as fodder for Zayas as well.

Yet, as Nina M. Scott cogently argues, Castellanos "avoids Manichean oversimplification by underscoring women's complicity" (1973, 24) in the perpetuation of these cultural myths. Zayas also portrays women who perpetuate the oppression of other women as in the case of La inocencia castigada [Innocence Punished] where the sister-in-law participates in the torture of Inés. Nonetheless, many of these examples, especially those involving relationships across class lines, prove troubling since it remains unclear whether the texts question or accept such conduct.

Castellanos's frontal attack on the "beauty system" and its detrimental effect on women is well documented—as Scott convincingly demonstrates, Castellanos underscores that "whereas it is a woman's obligation to be beautiful, standards of beauty and fashion are often dictated by men and ignore factors such as physical comfort or well-being" (Scott 1989, 22). In fact, her humorous assault on fashion whims reveals a darker side to the widespread admiration of small-footed women:

Son feos, se declara, los pies grandes y vigorosos. Pero sirven para caminar, para mantenerse en posición erecta. En un hombre los pies grandes y vigorosos son más que admisibles; son obligatorios. Pero ¿en una mujer? Hasta nuestros más cursis trovadores locales se rinden ante "el pie chiquitito como un alfiletero." Con ese pie . . . no se va a ninguna parte. Que es de lo que se trataba, evidentemente. (1973, 9; qtd. in Scott 22)

[Large, vigorous feet are said to be ugly. But they're good for walking and for maintaining oneself in an upright position. In a man large and vigorous feet are more than acceptable: they are obligatory. But in a woman? Even our most ridiculous local troubadours are smitten by "the foot as dainty as a pincushion." With a foot like that . . . you can't go anywhere. Which is what it was all about, evidently.]

She also exposes the "specular economy" in which a woman's worth is akin to that of "un mueble decorativo que tiene la ventaja de que, además de poder ser mostrado a las visitas, puede ser transportado, para su lucimiento, a fiestas y reuniones" [1974, 27; qtd. in Scott 22: a decorative piece of furniture that has the advantage, apart from being able to be shown off to visitors, of being able to be transported and displayed at parties and gatherings].

Centuries earlier, Zayas also humorously targeted the "specular economy." In "El castigo de la miseria" [The Miser's Reward], often dismissed as a tale influenced by Quevedo's *Buscón*, there is a vital twist.[3] Although the work wickedly depicts Don Marcos's avarice in a markedly Quevedan vein, indicating that because of his excessively frugal diet "se vino a transformar de hombre en espárrago" [1973, 120: he was transformed from a man into an asparagus stalk], it nonetheless departs from the male-inscribed literary model by consistently underscoring the nature of marriage as an economic transaction in which a woman's value is determined not only by her possessions but also by her "beauty." The text leaves no doubt about the commercial aspect of this exchange by referring to the matchmaker as "tercero no sólo de casamientos, sino de todas mercaderías" [124: a go-between not only for marriages but for anything that was up for sale]. Don Marcos is immediately smitten "más del dinero que de la dama" [132: more by the wealth than by the woman], but considers marriage to the supposedly older woman of thirty-six acceptable because of her "youthful" appearance. The process of his "desengaño" [disillusionment] begins when he first sees her unadorned the morning after consummating their union:

pensando hallar en la cama a su mujer, no halló sino una fantasma porque la buena señora mostró las arrugas de la cara por entero, las que les encubría con el afeite . . . porque los cabellos eran pocos y blancos, por la nieve de los muchos inviernos pasados [más cerca de cincuenta y cinco que de treinta y seis]. . . . Los dientes estaban esparcidos por la cama, porque como dixo el príncipe de los poetas, daba perlas de barato, a cuya causa tenía don Marcos uno o dos entre los bigotes, de más de que parecían tejado con escarcha. . . . (148)

[expecting to see his wife there in the bed, but what he saw was a phantom, a deathly ghost. The good woman's face showed each and every

wrinkle she had so carefully covered with makeup, successfully disguis-
ing her years, which surely where closer to fifty-five than thirty-six. . . .
Her hair was thin and gray from the many snowy winters she had lived
through. . . . Her teeth likewise were scattered all over the bed—as the
prince of poets once said "her teeth were like pearls scattered before
swine." Don Marcos even had several caught in his mustache, which
looked like a rooftop sprinkled with hoarfrost. (Boyer 1990, 100)]

Doña Isidora, grabs her displaced bun—her hairpiece, that is—and
retires "al Jordán de su retrete" [1973, 149: to the Jordan (fountain
of youth) of her dressing room] to reassemble herself. Piece by
piece, Zayas's narrative comically deconstructs the societal construction of woman's beauty. The text then underscores that Don
Marcos deserves his fate because of his "miseria" [miserliness],
which led him to be more interested in the bride's material assets
than the bride herself. Doña Isidora is the vehicle for, rather than
the target of, this comic challenge aimed at a society that underval-
ues women.

Moreover, Zayas and Castellanos both forcefully defend wom-
en's intelligence. The oft-cited remarks from Zayas's "Al que ley-
ere" [To Whomsoever May Read This] and many of Castellanos
best known essays persuasively argue that women's socialization,
not a lack of native wit, explains the diminished participation of
women in the intellectual sphere. Yet, perhaps the humor within
their fictional works poses the most effective challenges to the
myths of women's mental inferiority.

In "El prevenido, engañado" [Forewarned but not Forearmed]
the male protagonist, Don Fadrique, views women's intelligence as
"dangerous" and responsible for their deceptions; he discounts his
active participation in their sexual exploits. He opts to marry a
completely innocent, totally naive young girl despite warnings that
ignorance does not guarantee virtue. He falsely informs his new
bride, Gracia, that in married life, the women's nightly "duty" consists of keeping armed watch over her husband. During his first absence, an ardent suitor assures Gracia that he can teach her another
way to fulfill her wifely duty—one she finds much more pleasant.
Unaware that she has engaged in an illicit activity, she excitedly
informs her husband, upon his return, that "another husband" has
helped her discover a more entertaining way to spend their eve-
nings. In the end, Fadrique praises "las discretas que son virtuosas
porque no hay comparación ni estimación para ellas; y si no lo son,
hacen sus cosas con recato y prudencia" [173: discreet women who
are virtuous, saying that they are priceless beyond all thought and,

if they're not virtuous, at least they know how to behave prudently and modestly (Boyer 1990, 152)]. The conclusion ironically undermines Gracia's supposed stupidity:[4] "Entró doña Gracia monja, contenta . . . porque como era boba, fácil halló el consuelo gastando la gruesa hacienda" [173: Doña Gracia became a nun, happy . . . because since she was stupid, she easily found solace spending the huge fortune] that she inherited from her husband. If "el ácido corrosivo de la risa" [laughter's corrosive acid] in the *novela* fails to reveal the absurdity of the dominant view of women's intelligence as "dangerous" and antithetical to moral development, the narrator explicitly identifies the text's purpose: "para que se avisen los ignorantes que condenan la discreción de las mujeres, que donde falta el entendimiento, no puede sobrar la virtud" [173: warning all the ignorant people who condemn discretion in women: there can be no virtue where intelligence is lacking (Boyer 153)]. This novella, the other tales, and the frame narrative unequivocally defend women's intelligence as a necessary, positive force.

The premise of Castellanos's *El eterno femenino* [The Eternal Feminine] is the invention of a device to produce dreams to prevent women from thinking while they sit under the dryer in beauty salons. As we all know, there is nothing more "dangerous" than a woman given time to think. In the second act—often suppressed in production and ignored in the critical tradition[5]—key women from Mexico's history come to life. As they reenact pivotal episodes from their lives according to their own perspectives, they reveal the partial nature of "official history." In one scene, Josefa Ortiz de Domínguez uses her supposed illiteracy and ignorance as a cover for her revolutionary activities as illustrated in the following lines she exchanges with her husband, the *corregidor*:

> Corregidor: ¿Sabes leer?
> Josefa: No, mi señor marido. . . .
> Corregidor: (Al canónigo, triunfante): ¿Lo ve usted? Es sencillísmo. Así no hay manera de que se enteren de nada ni de que propaguen nada . . .
> Josefa: Soy una tonta . . .
> Corregidor: Es tu deber y lo cumples a conciencia . . . (113–14)

> [Magistrate: . . . Can you read?
> Josefa:No, dear husband.
> Magistrate: (To the canon, triumphantly): See what I mean? It's very simple. There's no way they can find out anything or disseminate anything . . .
> Josefa: I'm just stupid . . .
> Magistrate: That's your duty and you do it well . . .]

Later, developments reveal Josefa's role as one of Miguel Hidald-
go's primary accomplices. Act two—often suppressed in production and ignored in the critical tradition—consistently portrays
women's intelligence as a necessary, positive force, just as Zayas
had years before.

The range of ethical myths challenged by these women writers is
daunting; therefore, I will limit my comments to three. First, and
perhaps most surprising, is that each of them questions the traditional concepts of "good" and "evil" by reinscribing the figure of
the devil. In Zayas's "El jardín engañoso" [The Magic Garden],
the devil magnanimously returns the deed for a man's soul. After a
prolonged debate, all the inscribed narratees agree that the devil is
the figure who committed the greatest act of good in the tale. Similarly, in Castellanos's intensely ironic portrayal of Eden at the beginning of the second act, the devil is cast as a political exile who
helps Eve to find a more meaningful existence. Their humorous verbal repartee initiates an irreverent dialogue with tradition that esca-
lates throughout the subsequent scenes.

Secondly, the issue of women's relationships across social
boundaries are explored by both authors. Contemporary critics
often censure Zayas for her unenlightened stance and "reactionary"
ideology that uphold the values of a hierarchical society. Undeniably, her texts repeatedly dismiss women of the "servant classes,"
a fact that leads to debate about whether her works can be read as
consistent with a "feminist" sensibility or not. In turn, Castellanos
challenges the existence of a mythical "sisterhood" that would
eclipse all differences. The historical women of the second act of
El eterno femenino certainly do not bond in a "utopian" manner;
instead, the play highlights a plurality of voices and positionalities.
La Adelita gets angry because Sor Juana "anda disfrazada de es-
pantapájaros, como si la Constitución no existiera" [walks around
disguised as a scarecrow, as if the Constitution didn't exist (Marting and Osiek 1988, 304)]; Josefa becomes upset by the lack of
respect that Adelita demonstrates toward Sor Juana; and Carlota
grows furious at the lack of "etiquette" displayed by the other
women—especially La Malinche—who all ignore "protocol" (86).
In sum, each represents a distinct reality characterized by her race,
ethnicity, social class, and historical circumstances. Castellanos
thus anticipates Dale Bauer's "feminist dialogics," which consists
of "a paradigm which . . . challenges the cultural powers that often
try to force us to contain or restrict the otherness of textual voices"
(1991, 673). At the same time, perhaps Castellanos provides us
with the insight necessary to approach Zayas's problematic treat-

ment of race and class while still recognizing her revolutionary exploration of gender.

By far the most prevalent myths humorously addressed by both authors are those of a sexual nature. This, in itself, disputes a common critical myth. Eustaquio Fernández de Navarrete proclaims that María de Zayas:

> Carecía de la observación y de aquel íntimo conocimiento de las escenas del mundo que sólo puede adquirir un hombre, y de que está privada una señora por el retiro y circunspección en que la obliga a vivir el decoro de su sexo. A éste no le es permitido penetrar . . . nunca en el garito de los tahures ni en el burdel de la cortesana corrompida. (Quoted in Pardo Bazán 1892, 10–11)

> [She was lacking observational experience and that intimate knowledge of the real world that only a man can acquire and that is denied a woman because of the seclusion and circumspection within which the decorum of her sex requires her to live. Woman is never permitted to penetrate . . . either in the gambling-den of the cardsharp or in the bordello of the corrupt courtesan.]

Perhaps, as Pardo Bazán suggests, we can dismiss "la falta de sagacidad que revela su dictamen" [12: the lack of wisdom which his dictum reveals] given the period in which he wrote.[6] However, it seems much more difficult to dismiss the blatant sexism, bordering on the hilarious, in Gershon Legman's declaration in 1975 that "sexual [humor] . . . has all been created by men and . . . there is no place in it for women except as the butt" (217). As recently as 1988, Mulkay asserts that "the domain of humour is a world where the male voice constantly triumphs over that of the female and where women are made to exist and act only as appendages to men's most basic sexual inclinations" (137).

Yet, Zayas's novellas include frequent examples that explode the myth of woman as sexually passive. In "El prevenido, engañado," a noblewoman's insatiable sexual appetite has literally drained her black slave of his vital forces. In a scene tinged with grotesque humor, he implores her to leave him alone: "¡Déxame ya, por Dios! ¿Qué es esto, que aun estando yo acabando la vida me persigues? No basta que tu viciosa condición me tiene como estoy, sino que quieres que cuando ya estoy en el fin de mi de vida, acuda a cumplir tus viciosos apetitos" [149: Leave me alone, for the love of God! How can you pursue me even as I lie dying? Isn't it enough that your lasciviousness has brought me to this end? Even now you want me to satisfy your vicious appetites when I am breathing my last?

(Boyer 1990, 128)]. This episode also inverts the stereotype, especially prevalent in early modern Spain, of the voracious appetite of black men. As Marina Brownlee notes, the tale is definitely not "politically correct." Nonetheless, these problematic textual elements serve to provide intriguing and, at times, disturbing insights into the intersection of gender, race, and class in Zayas's works.

In *El eterno femenino*, Castellanos humorously deflates the myth of female sexual passivity.[7] The scenes between Rosario de la Peña and Manuel Acuña clearly reveal that the poet did not commit suicide because his lover spurned him, but rather because he could not bear to live once she had revealed herself as a subject of sexual desire:

> Manuel: Usted era mi amada ideal, ergo, imposible. . . . Con el paso que acaba usted de dar lo ha destruido todo. Mis más caras ilusiones: las de vivir en un mundo de ensueño en el que tú estarías siempre enamorada y yo siempre satisfecho. (Se paraliza un instante y corre a escribir lo que exclama en voz alta.) ¡Y en medio de nosotros, mi madre como un Dios! (1975, 96)
>
> [Manuel: You were my ideal love, ergo, impossible. . . . With the step you have just taken, you have destroyed everything. My dearest illusions: those of living in a fantasy world in which you would always be in love with me and I would always be satisfied. (He stands still as if paralyzed for an instant and then runs to write what he recites in a loud voice.) And between us, my mother, like a god! (Marting and Osiek 1988, 308)]

The significance of these two examples becomes even more striking when considered in light of Mulkay's admission, after a purportedly exhaustive study of humor, that "although the principle of 'men as objects' can be used to construct sexual humor, I know of no instances where it has actually been employed" (139).

Both authors also offer examples of what might be termed the "manipulated man"—definitely a subcategory of the "man as object" type of sexual humor. In "El desengaño amando, y premio de la virtud" [Disillusionment in Love and Virtue Rewarded], Zayas presents a tale in which a man is so bewitched by a woman that he abandons his wife. Eventually, the wife gains access to a mysterious chamber in the other woman's house where she finds the apparent source of the magic spell her rival has cast to control her husband: "un gallo con una cadena asida de una argolla que tenía a la garganta y . . . luego tenía puesto unos antojos a modo de los de caballo, que le tenían privada la vista" [1973, 224: a rooster with a chain attached to a ring around his throat and . . . he also wore blinders like those horses wear, so that he was unable to see (Boyer 1990, p. 208)]. That her husband be represented by a blind cock reverberates with sexual humor that transcends cultural boundaries; in case the reader might be inclined to gloss over this, the character's reaction serves as a guide "Quedóse Clara viendo esto tan absorta . . . por una parte se reía, por otra se hacía cruces . . . sospechando si acaso en aquel gallo estaban hechos los hechizos de su marido, a cuya causa estaba tan ciego que no la conocía" [224: So astonished and absorbed by this sight was Clara . . . she was both laughing hilariously and crossing herself at the same time. She suspected that most probably the rooster was the charm that bewitched her husband, rendering him so blind that he didn't even recognize her (Boyer 208)].

Perhaps one of the most intricate instances of the "manipulated man" involves Doña Ana and Doña Violante from "El prevenido engañado," who convince Don Fadrique that he must lie with Ana's husband in her stead so that she can enjoy her tryst with his cousin. In elaborate detail, the narrator describes how Don Fadrique, convinced he is sleeping with another man, attempts to elude his partner's amorous advances:

> mas don Fadrique que se vio en tanto peligro, tomó muy paso el brazo del dormido señor, y quitándole de sí se retiró a la esquina de la cama. . . . Apenas se vio libre desto, cuando el engañado marido, extendiendo los pies los fue a juntar con los del temeroso compañero, siendo par él cada acción destas la muerte. En fin, el uno procurando llegarse y el otro apartarse, se pasó la noche. (Zayas 1973, 161)

> [Don Fadridque felt very threatened. As gently as he could, he took the sleeping man's arm and removed it from around his neck and huddled over in a corner of the bed. . . . Don Fadrique had just survived the first test when the deceived husband stretched out his feet and rubbed them against those of his terrified bedmate. Don Fadrique thought each of these contacts was almost like dying. To be brief, the two spent all night long like this, with one trying to snuggle up and the other trying to slither away. (Boyer 1990, 140)]

At dawn's first light, Ana enters to reveal Violante who, laughing all the while, recounts in great detail how she made Fadrique suffer.

In this case, as in others throughout the novella, he is truly the "object" of sexual humor. The tally of his ill-fated romantic liaisons even mentions that in Naples "tuvo una dama que todas las veces que entraba su marido, le hacía parecer una artesa arrimada a una pared" [Zayas 1973, 164: he had a mistress who, every time her husband came home, made him pretend he was a hutch backed up against a wall (Boyer 1990, 143)]. As if imitating a hutch (or a trough) were not sufficient, later he is locked in a chest by a duchess who teases him by revealing his hiding place to her husband as part of an elaborate riddle. In fact, humorous instances of men being enclosed or entrapped by women abound throughout the *Novelas ejemplares*. Each of Don Gáspar's thwarted attempts to rendezvous with Hipólita in "Al fin se paga todo" [Just Desserts] ends in disaster. Once he becomes stuck in the window, "se quedó atravesado en el marco de la ventana por la mitad del cuerpo . . . siendo fuerza a don Gaspar el correr metido en su marco" [245: he got stuck in the frame, halfway in and halfway out . . . don Gaspar had to run quickly away, still stuck firmly inside the windowframe (Boyer 228)]; subsequently, she locks him a trunk to hide him from her husband. Significantly, the ludic tone present in the examples of manipulated men enclosed by women in the *Novelas* contrasts sharply with the tragic one dominant in the cases of hapless women enclosed by men in the *Desengaños*. Perhaps, the carnivalesque spirit, much more evident in the first collection, allows for the inversion of "traditional" sexual roles in which male dominance is questioned.

In *El eterno femenino*, Castellanos incorporates several examples where men are "manipulated" by the women; in the opening of Act Two, Adam is putty in Eve's expert hands. Yet, perhaps even more unsettling is the dialogue between the prostitutes in act three. When the experienced hooker questions the new arrival as to how she ended up in their mutual profession, the latter responds "Pura onda. Desde chiquita me gustaba darle vuelo a la hilacha" [1975, 154: Just for fun. Ever since I was a little girl, I have always liked to paint the town red (Marting and Osiek 337)]. The senior woman silences her, explaining that no matter what, she can never say that because "desanimas a la clientela . . . [A]l cliente lo que le gusta es pensar que te está chingando" [155: you discourage the clientele . . . what he likes to think is that he's screwing you over (Marting and Osiek 337)]. Basically, the novice is indoctrinated in how to manipulate the male clients most effectively by maintaining the illusion that she is incapable of being the subject of desire.

I would contend that the importance of these instances of humor in Zayas and Castellanos transcends their usefulness as a rebuttal to the common assertion that "feminists just don't have a sense of humor" and to the disavowal of women's humor by theorists. They suggest that these constellations of myths—the aesthetic, intellectual, and ethical—can serve as sites of humorous discourse that may facilitate feminist inquiry. Indeed, they reveal a certain connection between generations—perhaps yet another reflection of the bonds between the Baroque and the postmodern explored by Marina Brownlee. However disheartening it may seem that these authors, separated by several centuries, must tackle some of the same obstacles, perhaps we can seek solace in the fact that their humor does provide for liberation since it serves "as a prolonged anarchic assault upon the codes constricting" women (Gagnier 1991, 929). Ultimately, as Kaufman maintains, "Where mainstream humor strives to hurt the weak, to maintain hierarchy and the status quo, feminist humor strives to educate both weak and powerful in order to stimulate change in the direction of equity or justice" (1991, ix). If, as Dale Bauer argues, "because we all internalize the authoritative voice of patriarchy, we must struggle to refashion inherited social discourses" (1991, 672), then Zayas and Castellanos offer powerful examples of how humor can effectively function to recast inherited forms of expression and understanding by challenging culturally transmitted "myths." Undoubtedly, we must laugh to survive, so let us join these writers in their lasting laughter. As we pursue our feminist theory and practice, let us follow Castellanos's worthy dictum: "Accept no dogma that cannot withstand a good joke" (1973, 40).

NOTES

1. Unless otherwise noted, translations are my own. In the case of titles, I maintain those employed in published translations. I thank Vern G. Williamsen for his assistance.

2. I wish to thank Joyce Tolliver and Lisa Vollendorf for their comments on earlier versions of this article.

3. Interestingly, "El castigo" is one of the most frequently anthologized and studied of Zayas's novellas. Perhaps it owes its popularity to its obvious links to Quevedo's tale, or perhaps to its broad-based humor.

4. In many ways, Bakhtin's observations on "stupidity" apply well here. He explains that "Studipity [incomprehension] in the novel is always polemical: it interacts dialogically with an intelligence [a lofty pseudo intelligence] which it polemicizes and whose mask it tears away" (403).

5. It is important to note that in most theatrical presentations this act is eliminated or reduced to the first scene; for a discussion of the impact of this performance tradition, see my "De boca en boca."

6. For a revealing discussion of how Pardo Bazán uses Navarette's criticism of Zayas, see Joyce Tolliver's article on Pardo Bazán and literary / feminist polemics.

7. Significantly, in his study of the humor of El eterno femenino, Juan José Pulido Jiménez only briefly discusses this type of humor.

Works Cited

Amezúa, y Mayo Augustiú G. de, editor. 1950. "Prologue." In María de Zayas y Sotomayor, *Desengaños amorosos*. Madrid: RAE.

Bakhtin, Mikhail. 1981. *The Dialogic Imagination*. Edited by Michael Holquist. Austin: University of Texas Press.

Barreca, Regina. 1992. *New Perspectives on Women and Comedy*. New York: Gordon and Breach.

Bauer, Dale. 1991. "Gender in Bakhtin's Carnival," In *Feminisms: An Anthology of Literary Theory and Criticism*, edited by Robyn Warhol and Diane Price Herndl. New Brunswick, NJ: Rutgers University Press.

Boyer, H. Patsy, translator. 1990. *The Enchantments of Love: Amorous and Exemplary Novels*. By María de Zayas. Berkeley: University of California Press.

Brownlee, Marina S. 1995. "Postmoderism and the Baroque in María de Zayas." In *Cultural Authority in Golden Age Spain*, edited by Marina S. Brownlee and Hans Ulrich Gumbrecht. Baltimore: Johns Hopkins University Press.

Butler, Judith. 1990. *Gender Trouble: Feminism and the Subversion of Identity*. New York: Routledge.

Castellanos, Rosario. 1973. *Mujer que sabe latín*. México: SEP.

––––––. 1974. *El uso de la palabra*. Edited by José Emilio Pacheco and Danubio Torres Fierro. México: Ediciones de Excélsior-Crónicas.

––––––. 1975. *El eterno femenino*. México: Fondo de Cultura.

Fuchs, Esther. 1986. "Humor and Sexism: The Case of the Jewish Joke." In *Jewish Humor*, edited by Avner Ziv. Tel-Aviv: Papyrus.

Gagnier, Regina. 1991. "Between Women: A Cross-Class Analysis of Status and Anarchic Humor." In *Feminisms: An Anthology of Literary Theory and Criticism*, edited by Robyn Warhol and Diane Price Herndl. New Brunswick, NJ: Rutgers University Press.

Ivanov, V. V. 1984. The Semiotic Theory of Carnival as the Inversion of Bipolar Opposites. In *Carnival!* edited by Thomas A. Sebeok. Berlin.

Jacobs, Deborah. 1991. "Critical Imperialism and the Renaissance Drama: The Case of the Roaring Girl." In *Feminism, Bakhtin, and the Dialogic,* edited by Dale M. Bauer and Susan Jaret McKinstry. Albany: State University of New York Press.

Kaufman, Gloria. 1991. *In Stitches: A Patchwork of Feminist Humor*. Bloomington: Indiana University Press.

Legman, Gershon. 1975. *Rationale of the Dirty Joke*. Vol. 2. New York: Grove.

Marting, Diane E., and Betty Tyree Osiek, trans. 1988. The Eternal Feminine. In *A Rosario Castellanos Reader,* edited by Maureen Ahern. Austin: University of Texas Press.

Miller, Martha LaFollette. 1985. "Humor, Power, and the Female Condition in the Poetry of Rosario Castellanos." *Revista / Review Interamericana* 25: 1–4, 61–72.

Montesa, Salvador. 1981. *Texto y contexto en la narrativa de María de Zayas*. Madrid: Ministerio de Cultura.

Morson, Gary Saul, and Caryl Emerson, eds. 1989. *Rethinking Bakthin: Extensions and Challenges*. Evanston: Northwestern University Press.

Moses, Joseph. 1978. "The Comic Compulsion." *Sewanee Review* 86: 84–100.

Mulkay, Michael. 1988. *On Humor: Its Nature and Its Place in Modern Society.* Cambridge: Polity Press.

Nigro, Kirsten F. 1980. "Rosario Castellanos' Debunking of the Eternal Feminine." *Journal of Spanish Studies: Twentieth Century* 8, no. 1–2: 89–102.

Ordóñez, Elizabeth J. 1985. "Woman and Her Text in the Works of María de Zayas and Ana Caro." *Revista de Estudios Hispanos* 19, no. 1: 3–13.

Pardo Bazán, Emilia. 1892. "Breve noticia sobre doña María de Zayas y Sotomayor." *Novelas de doña María de Zayas.* [Biblioteca de la mujer, tomo 3.]. Madrid: Agustín Avrial.

Pulido-Jiménez, Juan José. 1993. "El humor satírico en *El eterno femenino* de Rosario Castellanos." *Revista Canadiense de Estudios Hispánicos* 17, no. 3: 483–94.

Rich, Adrienne. 1979. "Disloyal to Civilization." In *On Lies, Secrets, and Silence.* New York: W. W. Norton and Company.

Scott, Nina M. 1989. "Demythification Through Laughter." *Humor: International Journal of Humor Research* 2, no. 1: 19–30.

Tolliver, Joyce. " 'Mi excelsa compañera Tula (en los Campos Elíseos)': Emilia Pardo Bazán and Literary Feminist Polemics." To appear in *Recovering the Spanish Feminist Tradition,* edited by Lisa Vollendorf.

Vollendorf, Lisa. 1995. "Reading the Body Imperiled: Violence against Women in María de Zayas." *Hispania* 78, no. 2 (May): 272–82.

Welles, Marcia. 1978. "María de Zayas and her *novela cortesana:* A Re-evaluation. *Bulletin of Hispanic Studies* 60: 301–10.

Williamsen, Amy R. "De boca en boca: la dialogia carnavalesca en *El Eterno Femenino.*" Forthcoming.

Zayas, María de. 1973. *Novelas completas.* Edited by María Martínez del Portal. Madrid: Bruguera.

———. 1989. *Tres novelas amorosas y tres desengaños amorosos.* Edited by Alicia Redondo Goicoechea. Madrid: Castalia.

Xavier Villaurrutia as a Neo-Baroque Writer

SALVADOR OROPESA

THE PERTINENCE OF THE TERM NEO-BAROQUE

The influence of the Baroque period on the Mexican avant-garde has been documented by numerous critics. In Mexico, the neo-Baroque comes through Góngora and Sor Juana Inés de la Cruz (1651–95), and the latter's rediscovery thanks to writers like Amado Nervo, Ermilo Abreu Gómez, and Alfonso Reyes. Roberto González Echevarría clarifies the issue of Góngora's rediscovery:

> While it is a commonplace of Spanish literary history to say that the Generation of '27 in Spain looked to Góngora for inspiration, the fact is that the revision that brought about Góngora's rediscovery began in Spanish America with the *modernistas*—José Martí and Rubén Darío in particular—and continued in the writings of the Mexican Alfonso Reyes during the teens. (1993, 195)

Víctor García de la Concha summarizes the whole situation with a wonderful quotation by Miguel de Unamuno: "Rubén didn't come from Paris, but from Góngora" (Echevarría 1993, 69).

Mervyn R. Coke-Enguídanos has explained well the relationship between Rubén Darío and Quevedo, studying Darío's sonnet "La poesía castellana" [Castilian Poetry], where the Nicaraguan assimilates, interprets, and imitates a sonnet using Quevedo's technique (1988, 47–48). Alberto Forcadas closed the controversy concerning the influence of Góngora over Darío (Dámaso Alonso and Emilio Carilla thought this influence to be very weak), following Ricardo Senabre Sempere, who had already demonstrated that Darío knew Góngora's poetry well. Forcadas brought more examples to illustrate the knowledge Darío had of Góngora's poetry and how he influenced Darío. Rex Hauser has also studied the presence of similar metaphors in Góngora and in Darío.

According to Octavio Paz:

59

Somehow, mannerist periods correspond to epochs of crisis. Similarly, there is an obvious if not clearly understood, relation between the emergence of subjectivism and the several expressions of mannerism: baroque, romantic, symbolist, modernist [*vanguardismo*]" (1988, 52).

It is interesting to notice how Paz connects the Baroque and the avant-garde. He perceives them as related, as parallel movements or phenomena. Paz says that this relationship has to be studied, and others have followed his advice. According to Kathleen Ross, the so-called *Barroco de Indias* [New World Baroque] has been analyzed as two different ideologemes. Octavio Paz and Lezama Lima understand this baroque as oxymoronic, therefore symbolic, thus forming a true baroque of the Americas. On the other hand, John Beverley saw it as an imperial baroque of Spanish origin, and he analyzed this baroque using a materialist approach. Ross proposes the following:

> My own investigation is indebted to these materialist and symbolic critiques, but I wish to go beyond the dichotomy that considers them mutually exclusive paradigms. A literary analysis that takes into account findings from history is a path out of this critical dead end. (1993, 5)

Her analysis in *The Baroque Narrative of Carlos de Sigüenza y Góngora: A New World Paradise* (1993) is very successful because she achieves true New Historicism, using history and poststructuralism, including gender studies, to analyze Sigüenza y Góngora.

Octavio Paz in the *Children of the Mire* gave the historical reason for the importance of the Baroque to poets in modern Spanish poetry. According to González Echevarría:

> Paz underscores an unpleasant, yet unavoidable fact: that there are no first-rate romantic poets in Spanish. . . . Without a recent tradition on which to base their search for a poetic language, Hispanic poets had to look back to the Baroque. (1993, 115)

It has to be noticed that there are several characteristics of Baroque literature that would later form part of the avant-garde, the most important one being the dissolution of mimetic language. González Echevarría says:

> Góngora is obscure, but only because his poetics worked at the margins of the Western tradition, at the point where the tradition subverts itself by nurturing forces that negate its mainstream ideology. (197)

González Echevarría had already used Derrida as a theoretical framework in other analysis, that is, studying *La Celestina* or Severo Sarduy's *Cobra*. In this instance, the echoes of Derrida are also clear. Góngora belongs to the group of western writers who challenge the idea of a center in our metaphysical culture and, simultaneously, defy the idealist tradition in language. Salvador Novo, Xavier Villaurrutia, and the rest of the *Contemporáneos* group could identify themselves with this position. As will be explained later, they were working at the margins of Mexican culture, attacked by those who read their literature as outside of the Mexican mainstream and against the *true* concept of nationality (cf. Díaz Arciniega). It cannot be forgotten that the new mainstream created by the Mexican Revolution was firmly established in the mimetic language of realism, the novel of the revolution, and did not want to explore new possibilities to explain, and possibly denounce, the chaos of the revolution. Mimetic language created a fantasy of achievement and revolutionary greatness that was going to be challenged by the avant-garde movement.

González Echevarría continues:

> Góngora's poetry is inclusive rather than exclusive, willing to create and incorporate the new, literally in the forms of neologisms. He is anxious to overturn the tyranny of syntax, making the hiperbaton the most prominent feature of its poetry. (1993, 197)

What connects the Baroque and the avant-garde writers of the *Contemporáneos* group is this idea of inclusiveness. The writers of the Baroque exploited classical literature, they revisited the classics, chose the elements they wanted, and made new cultural artifacts out of them. Decorum did not apply here, because the classical texts could be decontextualized and recycled without showing respect for the originals. What is more, decorum had already been challenged by Garcilaso de la Vega, Góngora, and Quevedo with their use of obscenity in the poetic text (see Navarrete 1995, 199; 236–37). These Baroque writers liked the classics, but were not overwhelmed by them; in other words, they understood and used to their advantage the "greatest hits" approach to classical antiquity aimed at by the Renaissance and the Baroque. This is why Baroque writers put together enjoyment and use of the classics. It was *imitatio*, but of a very particular form, for it included slang, the language of African slaves, popular songs like ballads and dance tunes, obscene tavern songs, nursery rhymes, and the cannibalization of all classical culture. All these cultural artifacts could be used to make literature, putting together high and low brow culture, or what we know today as popular culture. In Leibniz's analysis, the Baroque was the attempt to reconcile the tension built between the rationalism of the Renaissance and the irrational forces of the seventeenth century (Delenze 1993). Paolo Rossi has noticed hundreds of books of the Baroque period refer to the term *novus*. Besides, the New World was being explored, new stars were discovered, and the microscope brought more new worlds to explore, with inevitable consequences:

> The rejection of the exemplarity of classical culture (on which all the humanists had insisted) took on strongly polemical overtones and in many cases (as in these lines of verse by Perrot de la Sale) took the forms of a rejection of classical culture itself:
>
> > De Grec et de Latin, mais point de connaissance
> > On nous munit la teste en notre adolescence.
>
> > [In our adolescence they stuff our heads with Greek and Latin but not with knowledge.] (1995, 278)

It is the same with the Mexican avant-garde writers among the *Contemporáneos*, who were not satisfied with the scientific knowledge of the *Porfiriato*. The dynamism of the United States as an economic and cultural force could not compete in their eyes with the "official" French culture, which was being overwhelmed by the new cultural forms of the United States: poetry, painting, architecture, music, etc., in both, high and pop forms. González Echevarría says:

> Góngora's style is not always "high," nor does he attempt to purge reality of base or heterogeneous elements. Reality did not enter his formula either to be accepted or rejected; its representation did. And here Góngora, like Cervantes and Velázquez, liked to juxtapose received forms of representation—"high" and "low"—critically. Everything can be part of beauty, even that which is not altogether comprehensible, and worse yet, even that which appears to be ugly, grotesque, or monstrous. (1993, 197)

For Novo and Villaurrutia, the discovery of the Baroque model gave them the opportunity to use everything—classical culture as understood by their models: the language of the streets of Mexico City with its *albures* [puns with sexual content] and the language of low class, *nacos*, *merolicos* [charlatans], and *carpas* [stand-up comedians like Cantinflas or Roberto Soto]; Nahuatl; obscenity; the lyrics of popular songs; the quick language of radio, newspapers, and wire news; Aztec culture; American newsreels; and also the trendy words in French and English (even *pachuco*)—to create their own slang. The possibility of using the United States, or Spain, as a literary model—which had been taboo for political reasons—and, also, the French models had been vindicated by *everybody* in the intellectual Latin American world since José Joaquín Rodó and before. Above all, it gave them the opportunity to escape the temptation of converting the revolution into a master narrative. They rejected the possibility of creating a lay religion out of the ideals of the revolution, ideals that they did not share. The Baroque was the model to write free literature in a context of oppression. If the Baroque had redesigned the margins of western literature in the seventeenth century, it could and should do the same in the Mexico of the twenties and thirties.

The last and most important quotation from González Echevarría says:

> This aesthetics of difference is another way of saying that the Baroque incorporates the Other; it plays at being the Other. . . . The Baroque assumes the strangeness of the Other as an awareness of the strangeness of Being. Being is being as monster, at once one and the other, the same and different. . . . An awareness of otherness within oneself, of newness. . . . It is a sense of one's own rarity, of oddity, of distortion. Hence the plurality of New World Culture, its being-in-the-making as something not quite achieved, of something heterogeneous and incomplete, is expressed in the Baroque. (1993, 198–99)

Villaurrutia, like Novo and other writers of the group, was gay in the modern sense of the term: the Baroque was the perfect ideologeme to problematize their gender and their art. Most of the homosexual avant-garde writers of Spain and Hispanic America pioneered the tradition of contemporary gay writing in Spanish. Critics like Paul Julian Smith have already done a timid but queer reading of Góngora, and Lluis Fernández presented the hypothesis of equalizing the neo-Baroque and queerness. (Isn't this the main purpose of Lezama Lima's *Paradiso*?).

The Baroque was the perfect starting point for modern Mexican culture of the twentieth century. The Mexican Revolution of 1910 had closed the nineteenth century, but the young writers realized that the first cultural models created by the revolution belonged to the previous century. Realism, even the *modernista* movement, had become old. Modernity was a gap to be filled, and with their youth, erudition, and boasting they could (re)write modern Mexican culture. They were more than ready to accomplish this task.

An interesting but failed book is *Neo-Baroque: A Sign of the Times* by Omar Calabrese, because the characteristics he perceives in neo-Baroque coincide with what is known nowadays as postmodernism, and as this term is well established today, it does not make sense to change the terminology. John Beverley has offered a fine observation regarding the relationship between the postmodern period and the Baroque. According to him, the similarity between the Baroque period and the postmodern one is in the fact that both are, at the same time, a technology of a power system and the consciousness of the limit of that power (1994, 27).

In his seminal article, "Language and the Body in Francisco de Quevedo," Malcolm K. Read explains the importance of bringing the body to the realm of literature and all the problems implied by this process. Quevedo gave voice to the body and realities like buggery. He brought the anus, feces, farts ("ruiseñor de los putos" [nightingale of the faggots]) to his literature, even if it was to deny or condemn the practice. Quevedo saw, tasted, listened to, smelled, touched, and wrote the body. This also represents a significant influence on gay writers who wanted to bring the body, the gay body, to the *idealistic* realm of poetry (from Croce to Dámaso and Amado Alonso, the main theoricians of literature were implying the truism of idealism as the only possibility). "Nocturno amor" is a fine example of the new writing of the gay body in modern poetry:

> Guardas el nombre de tu cómplice en los ojos
> pero encuentro tus párpados más duros que el silencio
> y antes que compartirlo matarías el goce
> de entregarte en el sueño con los ojos cerrados
> sufro al sentir la dicha con que tu cuerpo busca
> el cuerpo que te vence más que el sueño
> y comparo la fiebre de tus manos
> con mis manos de hielo
> y el temblor de tus sienes con mi pulso perdido
> y el yeso de mis muslos con la piel de los tuyos
> que la sombra corroe con su lepra incurable.
> Ya sé cuál es el sexo de tu boca
> y lo que guarda la avaricia de tu axila
> y maldigo el rumor que inunda el laberinto de tu oreja
> sobre la almohada de espuma
> sobre la dura página de nieve
> No la sangre que huyó de mí como del arco huye la flecha

sino la cólera circula por mis arterias
amarilla de incendio en mitad de la noche
y todas las palabras en la prisión de la boca
y una sed que en el agua del espejo
sacia su sed con una sed idéntica
De que noche despierto a esta desnuda
noche larga y cruel noche que ya no es noche
junto a tu cuerpo más muerto que muerto
que no es tu cuerpo ya sino su hueco . . . (Villarutia 1966, 49–50)

[You keep the name of your accomplice in your eyes / and I find your eyelids harder than silence / and before sharing it you'd be able to kill the pleasure / of surrendering yourself, in a dream with your eyes closed / I suffer when feeling the pleasure you are looking for with your body / the body you are looking for is stronger than sleep / and I compare the fever of your hands / with my icy ones / and your temples are trembling with my lost pulse / and the plaster of my thighs against the skin of your thighs / the shadow is rotting it with its insatiable leprosy. / I already know the sex of your mouth / and what is hiding in the greed of your armpit / and I curse the rumor inundating the labyrinth of your ear / over the foam pillow / over the dark page of snow / This is not the blood that left me like the arrow flees the bow / it is the anger circulating in my arteries / a yellow flame in the middle of the night / and all the words in the prison of my mouth / and a thirst that is in the water of the mirror / quenching it with an identical thirst / During the night I wake up to this naked / long night and cruel night that is not a night anymore / beside your body more dead than dead / it is not your body but its void . . .]

According to my own reading, there are fourteen neo-Baroque poems in Villaurrutia, and I understand other readers can come up with a different list. From *Primeros poemas* [First Poems] can be included "Ya mi súplica es llanto" [My Plea is Now a Cry] and "El viaje sin retorno" [The One-Way Trip]; from *Reflejos* [Reflections] "Poesía" [Poetry] and from *Nostalgia de la muerte* [Nostalgia for Death, 1938] "Nocturno en que nada se oye" [Night in Which Nothing Can Be Heard—a reference to the Santa Teresa title "Nothing Can Be Heard"], "Nocturno amor" [Nocturnal Love], "Nocturno eterno" [Eternal Night], "Nocturno muerto," [Nocturnal Death], "Nocturno de los ángeles" [Night of the Angels], "Cuando la tarde . . ." [When the Afternoon . . .], "Estancias nocturnas" [Nocturnal Stanzas], "Décima muerte" [Death in Décimas (a stanza of ten octosyllabic verses)], "Décimas de nuestro amor" [Stanzas of Our Love], "Deseo" [Desire], and "Soneto del temor a Dios" [Fear of God Sonnet].

RHETORIC AND POETIC LOGIC

The best starting point here are two articles by César Rodríguez Chicharro, who has studied Villaurrutia's use of puns. Rodríguez Chicharro begins juxtaposing two comments: the first one from Pedro de Valencia to Góngora telling him not to please common people (*el vulgo*) with puns, and the other by Alí Chumacero, who thinks Villaurrutia's puns undermine the depth and seriousness of his message (1964, 249). Rodríguez Chicharro uses, among others, the following examples:

> *Góngora:*
> Cruzados hacen cruzados,
> escudos pintan escudos,
> y tahures muy desnudos,
> con dados ganan condados;
> ducados hacen ducados
> y coronas Majestad,
>   !verdad! (1964, 250)

[Money makes honored knights, / gold pieces paint escutcheons, / and gamblers with nothing, / with dice they win counties; / ducats make dukedoms / and crowns majesty, / it's true!]

> *Villaurrutia:*
> En Boston es grave falta
> hablar de ciertas mujeres
> por eso aunque nieva nieve
> mi boca no se atreve
> a decir en voz alta:
> ni Eva ni Hebe. (251)

[In Boston it is a grave offense / to speak of certain women / and thus although it snows snow / my mouth dares / say aloud: / neither Eve nor Hebe.]

> *From Villaurrutia's "Nocturno en que nada se oye":*
> Y con el jugo angustioso de un espejo frente a otro
> cae mi voz
> y mi voz que madura
> y mi voz quemadura
> y mi bosque madura
> y mi voz quema dura. (254)

[And with the anguish of one mirror facing another / falls my voice / and my voice that is maturing / and my scorched voice / and my forest is maturing / and my voice burns hard.]

Rodríguez Chicharro finds in Villaurrutia examples of such Baroque devices as *disemia, paronomasia* [paranomasia, double entendre, heteronym, polypteton], *correlación,* and *paralelismo* [symmetry]. Another trope that is found is that of *calambur* (as when Góngora says, for instance, "a este lopico, lo pico" [I sting this little Lope]). To Rodríguez Chicharro, these poetic elections are, of course, legitimate, while Navarrete reminds us that *paronomasia* can be found in Boscán's translation of *Il Cortegiano* (51), in which Boscán also praises wit (52).

"Sor Juana Inés de la Cruz" is the title of one of the most important lectures compiled in the *Obras* (1991, 773–85), in which Villaurrutia explains why Manuel Touissant, Ermilo Abreu Gómez, and he himself decided to edit Inés's sonnets and the *endechas* : because she is a classic of Mexican letters according to Don Marcelino Menéndez y Pelayo and Karl Vossler; that is, *foreign* critics had declared the importance of this Mexican writer to provide a better and more complete picture of western culture. Villaurrutia describes Sor Juana as a poet of intelligence (wit); he labels her as *conceptista* using Menéndez y Pelayo's terminology. A second characteristic is her *barroquismo*, "tan característico del espíritu mexicano" [so characteristic of the Mexican spirit] (779). According to Villaurrutia, the Baroque is an essential part of Mexican culture. The third characteristic is the most influential for Villaurrutia himself:

[Sor Juana] es, pues, un poeta de la inteligencia, un poeta del concepto, una poetisa de la razón. Si examinan por ejemplo la serie de sus sonetos sobre el amor, encontrarán una clave sobre este tema. Estos sonetos pueden parecer fríos, si es que la inteligencia, que a mí no me parece, admite este término. Pero Sor Juana no es sólo una poetisa de la razón; es también un poeta del sentimiento. Puede en ella predominar lo que llamaba yo en la conferencia pasada el poder lógico de la palabra. (779)

[She is a poet of intelligence, a poet of concepts. She is a female poet of reason. If you examine, for instance, the series of sonnets about love, you will find the key. These sonnets seem cold, if it is possible for the intelligence to be cold. *I do not think so.* But Sor Juana is not just a female poet of reason, she is a poet of feelings. It can be predominant in her poetry what I call the logical power of the word.]

The previous lecture is "Introducción a la poesía mexicana" [764–72: Introduction to Mexican Poetry], a very interesting document for the study of Mexican poetry. In this lesson, Villaurrutia explains the aristocratic component of Mexican literature. Villaurrutia repeats the process followed by Boscán and Garcilaso at the beginning of the government of emperor Carlos I, as explained by Navarrete. What Boscán and Garcilaso did after the Comuneros war was to take away from the *people* the servant poet, poetry, and to create the figure of the courtly poet, the knight who was also a writer of lyric poems. He asserts that Mexico's poetry is not popular like that of Spain, Ireland [*sic*], and Germany. What Villaurrutia is telling us here is that popular forms like the melodramatic *bolero* and the epic ballad (*corridos*) are not going to be allowed by the avant-garde writers to define Mexican literature.

BRIEF ANALYSIS OF "MAR"

One of the most interesting poems by Villaurrutia is "Mar," published posthumously in 1953 (see Forster 1976, 100). It can be assumed that Villaurrutia considered it very personal when he decided not to publish it.

> Te acariciaba, mar, en mi desvelo;
> te soñaba en mi sueño, inesperado;
> te aspiraba en la sombra recatado;
> te oía en el silencio de mi duelo.
> Eras, para mi cuerpo, cielo y suelo;
> símbolo de mi sueño, inexplicado;
> olor para mi sombra, iluminado;
> rumor en el silencio de mi celo.
> Te tuve hirviendo entre mis manos,
> caí despierto en tu profundo río,
> sentí el roce de tus muslos cercanos.
> Y aunque fui tuyo, entre tus brazos frío,
> tu calor y tu aliento fueron vanos:
> cada vez te siento menos mío.

[I caressed you, sea, in my vigil; / I dreamt you in my unexpected dream; / I breathed you in the shadow, quite; / I heard you in the silence of my mourning. / You were my body's sky and ground; / symbol of my unexplained dream; / scent for my well lit shadow; / a rumor in my silent jealousy. / I had you very, very warm between my hands, / I fell, awake, in your deep river, / I felt the close touch of your thighs. / And although I belonged to you, in your cold arms / your warmth and your breath were vain: / every time I feel you, less and less mine.]

According to Forster:

> The careful and extended personification in this poem suggests strongly a symbolic interpretation. The sea might symbolize physical love, in which the poet finds diminishing meaning, or perhaps even poetic inspiration, which becomes progressively more difficult. The sea could even represent the source from which all life comes, and in this way the sonnet becomes a search for metaphysical meaning. (101)

The stormy sea as a metaphor for emotions belongs to the Petrarchan tradition (see Navarrete 1995, 217), and this connection is reinforced by the fact that the form of the poem is the classical sonnet. Garcilaso de la Vega, Lope de Vega, Fernando de Herrera, Luis de Góngora, and Francisco de Quevedo wrote love poems based on the sea metaphor. It is clear, then, that Villaurrutia wanted to insert himself in this tradition; Octavio Paz has noticed how Villaurrutia and his group were preoccupied with the idea of continuity and tradition in literature (1991, 14). The sonnet form and the metaphors used in the sonnet, mainly the *sea* and the antithesis *calor/frío,* emphasize a standard emotion, which Villaurrutia has decided to develop with cliché tropes. The difference, which is also a *différance* in the Derridean sense of the term, is in the queerness of this particular love, especially the last two tercets: line nine can be read as the poet having in his hand the sperm of the lover. The image of the river as a place of erotic encounter is present in Garcilaso's eclogues, and in a poet of the body like Villaurrutia, the thighs as synecdoche of the lover are very important. Line twelve is critical because it puts the poetic voice in a position of passivity as a lover: "fui tuyo," that is, the poet is sodomized by the lover who has cold arms, although this lover with his warmth and his breath tried, vainly, to warm the poet. This last piece of information is not given, but it is inferred from the last line of the sonnet: "every time I feel you, less and less mine." The rhyme between "frío" and "menos mío" is essential, because a logical relationship is established between these two concepts. And, of course, there is a metaphysical dimension: this is not just the eternal fight between lovers, but a forbidden love fiercely attacked by a homophobic society. In the tradition in which Villaurrutia is inserting himself there are homophobic poems written by Cervantes, Quevedo, and Góngora, poets who also included queer moments in their literature.

The poem is based on three concepts: the semiotization of water, shadow / light, and cold / hot. It would be interesting to explore how the use of water by Villaurrutia corresponds to Garcilaso's and his animism, and shadow could be explored in its relationship to San Juan de la Cruz's religious animism, instead of the lay animism of Garcilaso. Let us stay, however, with the cold / hot metaphor. Merlin H. Forster entitled his book on Villaurrutia's poetry *Fire and Ice: the Poetry of Xavier Villaurrutia* (1976), marking with this title that this is the most important metaphor in Villaurrutia's poetry. Forster does not explain the semiotic process of this metaphor, but Eugene Lawrence Moretta has traced its origin:

> The epigraph of the first group of *nocturnos* is a line from the poetry of the English writer Michael Drayton (1563–1631) which reads, "Burned in a sea of ice, and drowned amidst a fire." (1971, chapter 5, page 12)

Moretta goes on to explain how the metaphor appears in other poems and that Elías Nandino, in a study of Villaurrutia, paraphrased the metaphors but did not explain them. Moretta limits himself to displaying the metaphor without deciphering it. But the "fire and ice" poet in Spanish is Fernando de Herrera (1534–97). In Herrera, as in Villaurrutia, the lover is the absolute, and the poetic voice is always aiming to become one with it/him/her. And in Herrera, like in Villaurrutia, this union can be either bliss or death. The fire of the lover melts the ice of the loved one to become one, but this same fire can eliminate the object of desire. This is the poetic logic of Herrera, which is borrowed by Villaurrutia (cf. Rodríguez). The awkwardness of Herrera's lover can help him develop the awkwardness of his own love(r).

FINAL REFLECTIONS

Forster only alludes once to Villaurrutia's homosexuality: "[T]his is a poem ["Nocturno amor"] of homosexual love, incomplete, unrealized, and represented in terms of physical desire" (1976, 125). The key word is, of course, unrealized. This lack of consummation is not in the poem. Forster's platonic reading is mediated by his intention not to taint the poet's reputation. A plausible scenario is that Forster had been asked by the family or Villaurrutia's friends not to touch the subject. In another context, Salvador Novo had asked Frank Dauster not to write about his homosexuality when criticizing his poetry.

Octavio Paz says:

> Mientras Novo hacía una suerte de ostentación de sus inclinaciones sexuales, Xavier defendía su paz privada. No creo que fuese hipocresía. No

se ocultaba y era capaz de hacer frente a la condenación pública. Era discreto lo mismo en la vida real que en la literatura. (1977, 16)

[While Novo always sort of flaunted his sexual leanings, Xavier defended his private life. I do not think it was hypocrisy. He did not hide and was able to cope with public condemnation. He was discreet in real life and in literature.]

Let us put together these words by Paz with what Rosario Villari has to say about the baroque rebel:

What made the figure of the rebel of the baroque age tragic—his eagerness to avoid being branded as a rebel, even in contradiction with his own acts and his own goals; his attempts to connect himself at all costs to a constitutional legality and an established tradition—depended largely on the conviction that rebellion was fated to fail. Although the Protestant reformation suggested that successful revolution was possible, on the more strictly political and social plane failure was the rule. (*Rebel*, 1995, 107)

The poets of the *Contemporáneos* Group, and Xavier Villaurrutia was no exception, were unhappy with the revolution because of the lack of depth in the revolutionary process and at the same time in what is contradictory only in appearance, because of the magnitude of the revolutionary change. In Villaurrutia it is easy to follow this process of love and hate in his poetry and theater. The poet is a rebel as defined by Villari, and the playwright is a more conservative writer, more in the line defended by Maravall in his thesis that baroque culture is "a government culture working in the interests of political stability and public tranquility that managed to impose itself and gain common acceptance, drastically thrusting aside (more than had been true in past times) notions of opposition, protest, or subversion, whether open or clandestine" (1995, 101). Villari disagrees with Maravall, believing that his theory is too radical. Even if this position is correct, one cannot disregard the presence of a culture coming from the institutions of power. It is interesting to notice how writers like Lope de Vega and Xavier Villaurrutia used different genres to take diverse positions, expressing more freedom when using lyric poetry than when using a public space like theater.

Ed Cohen in his article "Who are 'We'? Gay 'Identity' as Political (E)motion (A Theoretical Rumination)" tries to explain what gay identity is, using, reluctantly, the liberal theories of the political theorist C. B. Macpherson. Cohen quotes Macpherson:

seventeenth-century individualism contained [a] central difficulty which lay in its possessive quality. Its possessive quality is found in the conception of the individual as essentially the proprietor of his own person and capacities, owing nothing to society for them. The individual was seen neither as a moral whole, nor as a part of a larger social whole, but as owner of himself. The relation of ownership, having become for more and more men [sic] the critically important relation determining their actual freedom and actual prospect of realizing their full potentialities, was read back into the nature of the individual. (1991, 78)

Rosario Villari, in the introduction to *Baroque Personae*, notices how figures like Giordano Bruno, Galileo Galilei, Francis Bacon, René Descartes, and Baruch Spinoza—and I would add to that list Juan de Mariana (1536–1624), the theoretician of the people's sovereignty, or Diego de Saavedra Fajardo (1584–1648)—have been read as precursors, when in reality they were people of their time, the artificers of the Baroque. Twentieth-century avant-garde writers turned to seventeenth-century individualism because there they found the origin of their ideological premises, individualism in the context of an aristocratic society, in spite of the dominant substantialism of that society. The new dogmatic and authoritarian ideologies of the twentieth century presented their own challenges, and the Baroque provided a good model for overcoming them.

WORKS CITED

Beverley, John. 1994. "Gracián o la sobrevaloración de la literatura (Barroco y postmodernidad)." In *Relecturas del Barroco de Indias*, edited by Mabel Moraña. Hanover, N.H.: del Norte.

Calabrese, Omar. 1992. *Neo-Baroque: A Sign of the Times*. Translated by Charles Lambert. Princeton, N.J.: Princeton University Press.

Cohen, Ed. 1991. "Who are 'We'? Gay 'Identity' as Political (E)motion (A Theoretical Rumination)." In *Inside/Out: Lesbian Theories, Gay Theories*, edited by Diana Fuss. New York: Routledge.

Coke-Enguídanos, Mervyn R. 1988. "Rubén Darío Encounters Quevedo". *Hispanófila* 93: 47–57.

Deleuze, Gilles. 1993. *The Fold: Leibniz and the Baroque* Trans. Tom Conley. Minneapolis: University of Minnesota Press.

Díaz Arciniega, Víctor. 1989. *Querella por la cultura "revolucionaria."* México, D. F.: FCE.

Forcadas, Alberto. 1972. "Más sobre el gongorismo de Rubén Darío." *Papeles de Son Armadans* 66, no. 196: 41–55.

Forster, Merlin H. 1976. *Fire and Ice: the Poetry of Xavier Villaurrutia*. Chapel Hill: University of North Carolina.

González Echevarría, Roberto. 1993. *Celestina's Brood: Continuities of the Ba-*

roque in Spanish and Latin American Literatures. Durham, N.C.: Duke University Press.

Hauser, Rex. 1993. "Settings and Connections: Darío's Poetic *Engarce.*" *Revista canadiense de estudios hispánicos* 17, no. 3: 437–51.

Lluis, Fernández. 1990. "Neobarroco: En la vorágine del pop." *El País Temas* (26 April): 6.

Maravall, José Antonio. 1981. *La cultura del Barroco: Análisis de una estructura histórica.* 2d ed. Barcelona: Ariel.

Moretta, Eugene Lawrence. 1971. *The Poetic Achievement of Xavier Villaurrutia.* Cuernavaca: Centro Intercultural de Documentación.

Navarrete, Ignacio. 1995. *Orphans of Petrarch: Poetry and Theory in the Spanish Renaissance.* Berkeley: University of California Press.

Paz, Octavio. [1974] 1981. *Los hijos del limo: Del Romanticismo a la Vanguardia.* Reprint Barcelona: Seix Barral.

———. [1977] 1991. "Xavier se escribe con equis." In *Antología,* edited by Xavier Villaurrutia. Reprint, Mexico, D. F.: Fondo de cultura económica.

———. 1982. "El reino de la Nueva España." In *Sor Juana Inés de la Cruz o Las trampas de la fe.* Barcelona: Seix Barral.

———. 1988. *Sor Juana, or The Traps of Faith.* Translated by Margaret Sayers Peden. Cambridge, Mass.: Harvard University Press.

Read, Malcolm K. 1984. "Language and Body in Francisco de Quevedo." *Modern Language Notes* 99, no. 2: 235–55.

Rodríguez Chicharro, César. 1964. "Disemia y paronomasia en la poesía de Xavier Villaurrutia." *La palabra y el hombre* (April–June): 249–60.

———. 1966. Correlación y paralelismo en la poesía de Xavier Villaurrutia. *La palabra y el hombre* (January–March): 81–90.

Rodríguez, Juan Carlos. 1974. *Teoría e historia de la producción ideológica: 1. Las primeras literaturas burguesas (siglo sixteen).* Madrid: Akal.

Ross, Kathleen. 1993. *The Baroque Narrative of Carlos de Sigüenza y Góngora: A New World Paradise.* Cambridge: Cambridge University Press.

Rossi, Paolo. 1995. "The Scientist." In *Villari.*

Smith, Paul Julian. 1986. "Barthes, Góngora, and Non-Sense." *PMLA* 101, no. 1: 82–94.

Villari, Rosario. 1995. *Baroque Personae.* Edited by Rosario Villari and translated by Lydia G. Cochrane. Chicago: University of Chicago Press.

———. 1995. "The Rebel." In *Baroque Personae,* edited by Rosario Villari and translated by Lydia G. Cochrane. Chicago: University of Chicago Press.

Villaurrutia, Xavier. [1966] 1991. *Obras.* Edited by Miguel Capistrán, Alí Chumacero, and Luis Mario Schneider. Reprint, México, D. F.: Letras mexicanas.

Through the Looking Glass: Reflections on the Baroque in Luis Buñuel's *The Criminal Life of Archibaldo de la Cruz*

SIDNEY DONNELL

Now that so many years have passed since Luis Buñuel's death in 1983, a retrospective on the filmmaker may represent, especially for younger generations, an introduction to the life and works of one of the pillars of cinema. Even for those who already know his work well, the colossal museum exhibit, entitled "¿Buñuel!: La mirada del siglo" [¿Buñuel!: The Gaze of the Century] invites us to remember a man who has had a tremendous impact on international culture well into the next millennium.[1] Perhaps, Buñuel will be remembered most for his cinematographic incursions into surrealism, including *Un chien andalou* [An Andalusian Dog; 1929] and *L'age d'or* [The Golden Age; 1930]. These particular films today, however, require a detailed familiarity with their respective moments in history, and so, for those trying Buñuel for the first time, the effort may seem too daunting. Even for the more experienced viewer, a seemingly simpler film may be required in order to approach Buñuel's multifaceted life and works with new vigor. François Truffaut commended *Ensayo de un crimen* [Rehearsal of a Crime; 1955], released internationally as *The Criminal Life of Archibaldo de la Cruz*, for its apparent simplicity despite the complexities of the story and cinematographic discourse. Filmed during his long years of exile from Spain, this overtly comic *film noir* met both critical *and* commercial acclaim,[2] and is still particularly adept at introducing or reintroducing a world that is unique in its complicated use of the literary symbols, tropes, aesthetics, and discursive forms of the sixteenth and seventeenth centuries. In this essay, I will highlight how the film develops a Neo-Baroque world that disrupts categorical distinctions between the real and the unreal, between the psychotic and the sane, and between criminality and morality in order to reveal a scathing parody of the Mexican bourgeoisie in the 1950s.

74

Thanks to the recontextualization of the Baroque by scholars such as Alejo Carpentier and Roberto González Echevarría, it has become less cumbersome to conceive of the cultural currents that flow between generations of artists. Today, for example, Buñuel's world may be understood as less surrealist than his beginnings may indicate. In fact, surrealism, according to my understanding of Buñuel, is part of a grander cosmos of intersecting forces in Hispanic culture that includes dramas about class honor, picaresque narratives about criminal infamy, and excessive imagery. This cosmos may, in fact, be divided into parallel universes, one darker than the other. On the darker side, social critique and self-criticism absorb energy and light, occasionally returning them in the form of uneasy laughter. The brighter side is what "Latin" peoples usually call *el barroco*, the Baroque—a cosmos generated from reflections of the sun in the irregular surface of a rough, imperfect pearl. Webster's Dictionary claims that the word "baroque" came into use in English via the French borrowing of the Portuguese word: "*barroco* rough pearl, masc. of *barroca* stony ground," which took the word from the Arabic "*buraq*, pl. of *burqah* pebbly ground." In a speech in 1975, Alejo Carpentier cites the complete inadequacy of dictionaries in defining a spiritual cosmos that is ingrained within the Hispanic world, and he warns against accepting the overgeneralization that the Baroque is a European invention restricted to art in the seventeenth century (1990, 168–70). To this extent, the literary group of 1927, to which many Spanish surrealists ascribed, formed on the three-hundredth birthday of the Baroque poet, Luis de Góngora. In part, this commemorative day was chosen because of many surrealists' great admiration for the poet's audacious use of metaphor. In this regard it seems appropriate that the word "*barroco*" may be a cultural borrowing of a term already based on a metaphor.

The brighter side of the Baroque, however, would be incomprehensibly vacuous without the imperfections of its darker half. Our imperfect minds need some*thing* to grab and hold in order to translate an image, often through the use of metaphor, into human understanding. In general, I find that some of the themes and techniques that accompany the postmodern are often deployed as a means to smooth and round the imperfections on the pearl, and in so doing, void an image of any possible material content or meaning. In this respect, the recent retrospective museum exhibit "¿Buñuel!: La mirada del siglo," tends to depoliticize a lifelong career. With the exception of screening his docudrama, *Las Hurdes* [Land Without Bread; 1933], the displays seem influenced by an aesthetic of the here and now, recasting Buñuel as a postmodernist.

The argument, per se, goes as follows: Buñuel's obsession with particular images—a woman's artificial leg, a cross, a straight-edge razor, an eye—may be more easily attributed to the artistic sensibilities of the time period than a recognizable code of subliminal messages. An image is an image is an image, and Buñuel adores focusing on and repeating a single object over decades. Repetitious images create a visually self-referential language. An image of an object may refer back to previous works of Buñuel's or those of colleagues during his long career. This is a plausible interpretation of the film maker, and in the case of *The Criminal Life*, he certainly packs his ninety-minute film with objects, all potentially intertextual and self-referential in character. Indeed, a close-up of a man's hand holding a straight-edge razor refers back to a similar image in *Un chien andalou*. To this end, almost every film during Buñuel's long career is congested with objects, and the congestion occurs through an accumulation of scenes focusing on a single object that fills the screen, but this does not necessarily mean that his aesthetic is one of "pure" image that is void of other meaning.

It is often said that, despite the visual genre he chose for himself, Buñuel pertains more to the group of surrealist poets, like Federico García Lorca, than to the group of visual artists, like Salvador Dalí.[3] According to Guy Scarpetta, he is more Baroque than surrealist, dark humor and the chance appearance of objects being Buñuel's most, and only, surrealist characteristics (1988, 64). It could be argued that Buñuel is never a strict adherent to any canon, surrealist or otherwise, and this would certainly give his work some postmodernist characteristics. Indeed, he never, even at the height of surrealism's war on the anecdotal, completely rejects the use of narrative in his films:

Là où le surréalisme, au-delà de la simple contestation du réalisme, en vient à suspecter toute forme de récit romanesque, Buñuel, lui, n'hésite pas à définir de façon extrêmement "réaliste" le cadre social de ses fictions (*Le journal d'une femme de chambre*, *Tristana*, *Le charme discret de la bourgeoisie*), et s'inscrit dans une tradition narrative explicite, celle du récit picaresque (*La voie lactée*, *Le fantôme de la liberté*). (Scarpetta 1988, 64)

[In contrast to surrealism, which goes beyond simple refutation of realism to profound suspicion of any form of novelistic convention, Buñuel does not hesitate to define the social context of his fictions in an extremely realistic manner (*Diary of a Chambermaid*, *Tristana*, *The Discreet Charm of the Bourgeoisie*) and to inscribe himself in an explicit narrative tradition—that of the picaresque (*The Milky Way, The Phantom of Liberty*).]

An attempt to confound classification, however, may not be an exclusively postmodern gesture. It may, in fact, be founded as a reaction to political ideology. To reject narrative is also to reject history. In other words, upholding the tenets of surrealism would appear to be a renunciation of other interests of his, including Marxism, a philosophical and political ideology that relies on a critique of history—past, present, and future.[4] Without an ideological grounding in history, he would never have been able to move from *L'age d'or* to the overt social criticism in his docudrama, *Las Hurdes*. In this regard, Buñuel's craft often includes a cynical world, requiring some notion of one's position in history; it is a story that links our present with a before and after.[5]

Understandably then, there are also aspects of picaresque narrative in Buñuel's work, a genre that flourished alongside the Baroque in Spain and Mexico; that is to say, Buñuel never relies solely on the audacious use of metaphor that the surrealists are said to have reclaimed from the Baroque. Buñuel is fascinated by the rougher side of the pearl, and the picaresque, in its loosest form, hinges on the impossibility of individual integrity in a corrupt society. Authors often approach this topic with wry wit or cynicism, ranging from the proto-picaresque novel, *Lazarillo de Tormes* (anonymous 1554), to the scathing philosophical treatise, *El Criticón* (Gracián 1651–57). A similar wit and cynicism occur in many of Buñuel's works, and Truffaut situates Buñuel somewhere in between Renoir's critical optimism and Bergman's nihilism (1975, 272). Regardless of the tone, the telling of some of Buñuel's works are grounded "dans une tradition narrative explicite, celle du récit picaresque (*La voie lactée, Le fantôme de la liberté*)" [Scarpetta 1988, 64: within an explicit narrative tradition—that of picaresque storytelling (*The Milky Way, The Phantom of Liberty*)]. While traditional picaresque narrative is an obvious influence in some films, others like *Nazarín* (1958) or *Viridiana* (1961) are more subtle adaptations, only revealing their heritage through contrast with the picaresque. Specifically, the typical picaro attempts to climb up the social ladder, while the heroes of both these films seek answers by climbing down the same rungs—not unlike some of Critilo's experiences in *El Criticón*. They do not confess their crimes like picaros, but they are judged to be criminals, crushed by the weight of their respective sociohistorical circumstances.

A PICARO WANNA-BE IN THE LAP OF LUXURY

Buñuel's films tend to be about people living on the edge, and his return to international acclaim was overt in this regard. *Los olvidados* [The Young and the Damned; 1950] is a biting portrayal of boys living on the streets of Mexico City. The titular hero of *The Criminal Life of Archibaldo de la Cruz* is clearly a man living on the edge, but he is also glaringly *unlike* the typical narrator–picaro who is born into poverty. The criminal "hero," Archibaldo (Ernesto Alonso), is a child of the bourgeoisie and makes no attempts to change his class position. Archibaldo likes his surroundings—the Neo-Baroque imagery of an almost imperial ostentation. This elite, well-to-do image of Mexico in the 1950s—a "Golden Age" of jet-setters in black, shiny Cadillacs—is a period Carpentier might add to his list of cultures that chose to express themselves through Baroque imagery. According to Carpentier, the Baroque spirit appears during "la culminación, la máxima expresión, el momento de mayor riqueza, de una civilización determinada" [1990, 169: the culmination, the maximum expression, the moment of greatest richness, of a determined civilization]. In Golden Age Spain, however, the picaresque represented the less glamorous side of the social sphere, bringing the Baroque back down to earth. Curiously, Archibaldo is a "picaro wanna-be" who has no need of social climbing, but he fits part of the definition: a first-person narrator who confesses his life of crime, often in a legal setting. The challenge, at least as Archi sees it, is to maintain his class position by committing aesthetically "perfect" crimes, not the "ordinary" picaresque scams and swindles. In other words, Buñuel places his pseudopicaresque hero on the inside of the bourgeoisie, and the social critique may seem more subtle than in films like *Los olvidados*, *Nazarín*, or *Viridiana*.

The film opens with a first-person, voice-over narration about Archi's bourgeois upbringing, a hand literally turning the pages of a photographic history of the Mexican Revolution. Then we see a still-shot of Archibaldo's childhood home as if it were another page in the history of Mexico. Archi explains how his depraved existence is rooted in childhood, but again, his social conditions do not produce a life of petty crime in order to eat and survive, as in the case of the traditional picaro. Indeed, Archibaldo is surrounded by a corrupt society, but it is the white-collar world of those with bourgeois aspirations. The film is almost always humorous, intentionally laughing at snobbery, sometimes by making incursions into the popular wisdom indicative of the picaresque. For example, a pearl of popular wisdom, in the form of a proverb, ironically pops up in an antique shop. When two shopkeepers take Archi's money for a music box that was stolen from his family during the Mexican Revolution, they joke, "Decente y pobre es peor que granuja y rico" [Being decent and poor is worse than being a rogue and rich]. The principles of the individual in a bourgeois society are dulled by greed, and they only manifest themselves through a picaresque or Gracianesque cynicism about a world in which wealth is valued more highly than human decency. As we know from the first-person narrator, the movie is concretely framed by history: Little Archi witnesses what appears to be a world beginning to turn upside-down during the Mexican Revolution, unseating the idle rich and dislodging them from their possessions. Through the reappearance of the music box years later, *we* see that an adult Archi and the bourgeoisie never *really* fell from grace.

The comic *film noir*'s plot is loosely based on a detective novel by Rodolfo Usigli, *Ensayo de un crimen* [Rehearsal of a Crime; 1944], although Buñuel and Eduardo Ugarte changed Usigli's third-person narration to fit the discursive definition of a picaresque narrative. Both the departure from Usigli's novel and the fact that the pseudopicaresque frame tale is in first person, explain the shift in title to *The Criminal Life of Archibaldo de la Cruz* once the movie left Mexico and hit the international market. The new title matches the syntax and content of a typical picaresque title, such as *La vida de Lazarillo de Tormes y de sus fortunas y adversidades* [The Life of Lazarillo de Tormes and of His Blessings and Misfortunes]. More importantly, it signals the fact that adult Archi confesses his life of crime in picaresque fashion. The tale is a retrospective narrative, leaping from childhood to a few weeks prior to the adult's narrating present:

El punto focal de la narración es la memoria y la imaginación del narrador-protagonista. De aquí que, en su historia, queden desdibujadas las fronteras entre lo vivido y lo imaginado, la realidad exterior y la visión subjetiva, el tiempo pasado, el presente y el futuro. Los sucesos se reordenan en su dimensión configural, preñada de significados latentes, iluminada y oscurecida por las pulsiones subconscientes instintivas puestas al desnudo de reprente. (Fuentes 1993, 124)

[The focal point of the narration is the narrator-protagonist's memory and imagination. Thus in his tale remain undrawn the borders between what is lived and what is imagined, exterior reality and subjective vision, past, present, and future. The events reorder themselves in their configural dimension, pregnant with latent meanings, illuminated and obscured by the instinctive subconscious impulses suddenly laid bare.]

Often, too much effort is spent in psychoanalyzing some objects in *The Criminal Life*, when, in fact, objects may be deployed as narrative markers, denoting the pseudopicaresque frame tale. For instance, Archi begins his confession to a nun in a hospital, telling her about his morbid attraction to the corpse of his dead governess during his childhood. When the nun dies there is an inquest, and Archi enters a judge's chambers with a cane. The bulk of Archi's confession takes place here about events closer to adult Archi's present. The scene fades out, and most of the movie consists of episodes in which we witness the narrator–protagonist without the use of the cane. Toward the end of the movie, the narrating present resurfaces, and we see Archi, cane in hand, leaving the judge's chambers. In the last scene of the film, he tosses the object aside while walking in a park. He no longer needs the cane for support, inviting a figurative interpretation about Archi's future, but Buñuel has also made sure we are able to distinguish between Archi's confessional present (with cane) and Archi some weeks in the past (without cane). Once he tosses it aside, the gesture also announces generic closure; that is to say, the film no longer needs the cane to support the telling of the story.

What is so intriguing about *The Criminal Life* is Buñuel's ability to maintain the tension between surreal / Baroque imagery and picaresque narrative—a seemingly postmodern resistance to generic or formal classification. On the one hand, we perceive an economy of floating signifiers, and on the other hand, an historically and politically invested narrative form. As Fuentes suggests above, *The Criminal Life* is more than the straightforward realism typical of a picaresque narration, usually consisting of an introduction in the narrator–protagonist's present, followed by a chronological series of uninterrupted flashbacks from his earliest childhood memories through his adult life, and concluded when the narrator–protagonist's story reaches the present. Archibaldo dwells on memories and *imagination*, a process that emphasizes the subjective reconstruction of events both real and imagined. The mélange of fantasy and reality defines the entire tale as representation, in other words, a form of Baroque abstraction: "La perversion des conventions sociales, des codes de comportement, est littéralement *produite*, chez Buñuel, par la dénaturalisation de la fiction. Ce qui définit le Baroque même" [Scarpetta 1988, 64: The perversion of social conventions, of codes of conduct, is literally *produced*, in Buñuel's world, by the denaturalization of fiction. This is what defines the Baroque itself]. This may appear contradictory to picaresque realism, but such paradoxes are indicative of Buñeul's craft and craftiness. It would seem, at first glance, that Buñuel emphasizes the notion that Foucault echoes years later—representation may reveal itself to be pure representation (1973, 16). However, Buñuel's treatment of representation is, at times, Neo-Baroque.

For instance, Buñuel subtly incorporates mirrors into almost every major scene of *The Criminal Life*. A reflection in a mirror is a representation of reality once-removed. When reflections become part of the story and discourse of a film, they remind us that what we are viewing is already a representation of reality, and that moving photographic images of a reflection in a looking glass is, *at the very least*, a representation of reality twice-removed. In the Baroque, nature (reality) and artifice (representation) were usually thought of as opposing concepts. The latter was often more highly esteemed, tending toward double or multiple reflections, not of nature, but of the human imagination. In other words, abstraction and "pure thought" became goals unto themselves, in part, because some Baroque artists in the seventeenth century had an early understanding of the concepts of alterity and fragmented subjectivity. Many reveled in the contradictions of their own binary systems, such as nature/artifice, and they thought that it was humanly *impossible* to faithfully represent nature because, even on the simplest of religious terms, it is beyond our capacity to understand that which is without beginning or end (Gracián 1984, 3).

Some critics and biographers of Buñuel have tended to cite his intellectual heritage as resting heavily on the writings of the Marquis de Sade, and Archibaldo certainly has a sadistic imagination. Augustín Sánchez Vidal is one critic who mentions the influence of de Sade in *The Criminal Life* (201–2), citing the judge / confessor's response to Archi's self-incriminating accusations: "El pensamiento no delinque" [Thought is not a crime]. Part of the master criminal's charm is his imagination—he never *directly* harms anyone. He is always rehearsing, hence the first title, *Ensayo de un crimen*. His pseudopicaresque confession, signaled by the film's alternate title, *The Criminal Life of Archibaldo de la Cruz*, could be further altered to better fit de Sade's thought: *The Criminal Fantasies of . . . .* Yet even de Sade is too canonical an explanation of Buñuel's comic *film noir*. While most of Archi's so-called crimes are imagined, not actualized, critics tend to forget that the protagonist threatens the nun in the hospital with a straight-edge razor. She inadvertently falls down an elevator shaft when running

away from Archi because she fears for her life. In other words, Buñuel does not let us off the reality hook so easily. Playing with
knives *really is* dangerous. It is no reflection, and, as Archi perceives it, he can no longer save himself from the evil thoughts that
haunt him. Convinced of his own guilt, Archi marches straight to
the inquest and confesses that he is responsible for the nun's murder, and also takes responsibility for the deaths of other women.
Without witnesses to corroborate his story, the Mexican magistrate
releases this bourgeois picaro, the confessional mode serving as a
frame for Archi's first-person retrospective. Amused but not convinced by Archi's confession, the judge decrees that he is only
guilty of an over-active imagination.

LOST IN A MIRROR

Lazarillo de Tormes concludes with the narrator-picaro deluding
himself into believing that, after years of climbing rung-by-rung up
the ladder of success, he has finally arrived. At the end of the tale,
close to the narrating present, he tells us that he is now a town-crier,
and that the position became available through an Archpriest who
did a little string pulling. What Lázaro implies, but does not specifically say, is that he maintains his position by turning a blind eye
to the fact that the Archpriest keeps Lázaro's wife as a concubine.
It is left for us to conclude that Lázaro is a cuckold, everyone in
town knows he is a cuckold, and far from being a success, he is, in
fact, the town fool.

In much the same way, Archibaldo convinces himself that he is a
master criminal—the type that is written about in detective fiction
or portrayed on the motion picture screen. In this regard, Archibaldo's confession at the inquest occupies most of the movie, fad-
ing out to the bizarre events taking place over the few weeks prior
to this picaro wanna-be's narrating present. His tale is a psycho-
drama about a cast of bourgeois players in their Neo-Baroque milieu. Sometimes the story is comic; other times suspenseful. The
adult's story chronologically begins after purchasing a childhood
possession—the long-lost music box for sale in the antique shop;
he takes it to his adult home in Mexico City and plays it in the privacy of his bedroom. As he gazes intently at the beautiful ballerina
spinning on top of the box, the scene begins to fade to a close-up
of the ballerina turning, and the song winding down, an indication
that time has passed. When the ballerina stops, the camera pans to
Archi shaving in the adjacent bathroom. The frame shifts to a frag-

mented image of Archi. While looking over Archi's shoulder, we see a double-reflection of him in the mirrors over his bathroom sink. He is concentrating on his shaving, straight razor in hand. Suddenly, organ music begins to play the same tune that the music box was just playing, but this time in a minor, not major, key. As soon as the music starts, he accidentally cuts himself and starts to feel the cut with his right finger. Then the background organ music helps to link a rapid succession of short takes: a close-up of Archi's right hand, blood streaming down his index finger, followed by more blood streaming down the framed image; smoke (or steam from the sink) and a fade-out, returning to a previous close-up of the governess on the floor of his childhood home as blood pours out of the bullet hole in her neck; more smoke and a fade-out, this time showing the governess's legs and hips again as the same dark liquid streams down the framed image, blocking our view; more smoke and a fade-out, returning to a frontal view of Archi holding his right hand in front of him. Now a servant speaks, the music ends, and the frame shifts to the servant entering the bathroom.

Spooky music, blood, smoke and mirrors all combine, transporting Archi back in time to the evening of his governess's death. Close-ups of her corpse are reminiscent of the dead subjects of Baroque painting, but the objects are not suspended aimlessly in time. They help mark Archi's history, even the moments when he goes over the edge. It is not clear if these are examples of self-induced hypnosis, hallucinations, or walking nightmares, but Archi's disassociative behavior increases in intensity. Later that afternoon on the street outside his love interest's home, Archi meets an *intrigante*, a sort of gold digger named Patricia Terrazas (Rita Macedo). She flirts with him, then taunts him shamelessly, showing off her legs as she enters her boyfriend's Cadillac. Archi walks toward the entrance of the home, but he transforms into a sort of zombie as the warped tune from the music box plays in the background, having graduated into a nightmarish form of carrousel music. The music accompanies the image of Archi walking toward the entrance but falls silent whenever the image shifts to a matronly dame looking down from a window, presumably at Archi. In other words, Archi is the only one who can hear the nightmarish music. It stops once Archi is greeted by the maid and the *grande dame* we saw only moments before, suspiciously named Mrs. Cervantes (Andrea Palma).[6]

Early in the film we learn how comically delusional the protagonist is when we discover that the first woman he begins to stalk, Patricia Terrazas, is deceiving Archi, not the other way around. He follows his prey to an illegal, private casino she conveniently had mentioned to Archi when they met at the entrance of his future fiancée's home. Inside these smoke-filled rooms, an acquaintance asks Archibaldo what he thinks about Patricia. Archi replies, "La asesinaría con mucho gusto" [I would gladly kill her], but within the joking context of two playboys in the know, it appears that Archi is also saying that he would like to seduce her. Moments later, Archi manages to take advantage of a fight between the shapely blonde and her boyfriend, Willy Corduran (José María Linares Rivas), that takes place in a drawing room adjacent to the main gallery. He witnesses their dispute in the reflection of a Baroque, drawing-room mirror—one of many voyeuristic images in the film. They appear to have broken up, and Archi drives her to her apartment, making a brief detour to go home and pick up a straight-edge razor and a pair of gloves.

At this point, Buñuel tosses another Baroque genre into the fray. As I stated earlier, the razor invites us to return to *Un chien andalou*, but it also leads to the bloody instruments of seventeenth-century wife-murder plays. Inside Patricia's apartment, Archi slips into one of his trances while Patricia is in the kitchen, which develops into a flash-forward about how he plans to kill her. When Archi "awakens" from his daydream, he jumps up and hides behind a curtain in order to take her by surprise. He puts a glove on his right hand and takes out the razor. As it just so happens, Willy knocks on the door, Patricia answers it, and Archi has to pocket his razor and glove. What Archi had witnessed in the casino was just another of their tumultuous love-spats. Both lovers knew all along that Willy would appear at the door, and they would make up. They consult "off-stage" in the kitchen, and Patricia says that they will explain everything to Archi: "No lo tenemos necesidad de hacer ninguna comedia" [We don't have to put on an act (a play) for him], although that is what they have been doing all along. They make their grand entrance on stage and reveal that Archi is simply a ruse—helping them throw another log on the flames of their passion, as it were.[7] They begin to kiss, transforming Archi into a sort of voyeur. He leaves out of embarrassment, and Patricia and Willy begin to argue again.

The *comedia* is particularly well known for exploring the limits of love relationships, including those that are seemingly without bounds, as in the case of *loco amor* or *amour fou* [mad love], incest, and adultery. It is not at all far-fetched, therefore, to associate such scenes with diverse plays from Spanish drama, like Lope de Vega's *El castigo sin venganza* [Punishment Without Revenge; 1631],

Pedro Calderón de la Barca's *El médico de su honra* [The Physician of His Honor; 1635], and even parodies of the genre itself, as in the case of Sister Juana Inés de la Cruz's *Los empeños de una casa* [The Trials of a Noble House; 1683]. All were particularly adept at incorporating Baroque imagery, like reflections in a mirror, into dramatic narratives, and Archi's plight is strikingly parallel to that of characters in Lope's work, written toward the end of a very long career when Lope was competing with the younger Calderón. *El castigo sin venganza* is an excellent exploration of telling a story using Baroque imagery, and there is a moral to be learned through the self-destructiveness of living "in one's reflection" (González Echevarría 1993, 80).[8] As in *The Criminal Life*, imagery is *not* simply deployed for imagery's sake.

The next day a policeman pays a call on the would-be assassin and announces that Patricia had killed herself that night after leaving a suicide note addressed to Willy. The police also know Archi had been one of the last people to see her alive. In her apartment, we view a police handwriting expert claim that the note is hers—and case closed.[9] As far as we know, Patricia did commit suicide, but for Archi, the news only confirms his identity as a serial killer. The fact that she died with her throat slit, just the way Archi had imagined, and the fact that the police briefly considered him a potential suspect, are enough to convince Archi that he has recovered his secret boyhood powers. His mother and governess both wove a fairy tale around the little music box "con mucho símbolo vaginal, ¡con perdón de Buñuel!, a quien tanto le disgustaban estas fáciles comparaciones simbólicas" [Fuentes 1993, 126: with much vaginal symbolism, may Buñuel pardon us, (because) he so disliked these facile symbolic comparisons]. He who owns the box has absolute power. In other words, Archi believes that if he wills someone dead, the invisible genie who resides in the magic box will make it happen. Archi lives through and for a powerful reflection from childhood—the shiny music box that once belonged to his mother.

It appears that Archi suffers from an obsessional neurosis, a particular category in which the subject remembers, and reenacts compulsions and obsessive ideas, but at the same time struggles to avoid them. Archi's history is, in fact, a problem with history, called the aporia, recalling and avoiding. Archibaldo is a neurotic who received too much pleasure from the reified element of the childhood event cited earlier (the death of his governess after having wished for it), and his behavior is to avoid what he sees as an end of his desire. In addition, this event was also a childhood trauma, and although trauma is something that escapes symbolization, it keeps recurring in a symbolic form—in Archi's case, various sexually criminal fantasies. Archi's eventual "normalization" would be a symbolic reintegration of the event, but this never seems to occur in the film. Baroque objects and signifiers appear to float around Archi in a never-ending story, but we may also recall that narrative markers, like the cane, remain in order to define the film's telling. The story is grounded in history even if Archi is incapable of comprehending it. In other words, psychosis is Archi's way of excusing himself from having to distinguish between appearance and reality. For the viewers, melodramatic music and smoke and mirrors are only a few of the cinematographic techniques Buñuel uses to portray the fantasies of Archi's "criminal" mind, establishing conventions early in the film with which to distinguish between appearance and reality. For the time being, smoke and mirrors remind us that the murders are all in Archi's imagination.

Throughout the film, Buñuel allows simple dreamlike obsessions to color Archi's waking moments. At times, the director plays with different camera angles in order to represent Archi's childlike gaze. For example, Archi walks into a bar, looks across the room, and sees a woman who looks familiar to him. Our gaze merges with that of Archi, and we see her engulfed in the flames of the punch cups on her table. In other moments, Buñuel also relies on duplicitous speech and simple, everyday sounds to represent the way in which Archi distorts reality through his boyish naïveté. In the same bar, the mysterious woman takes notice of Archi, excuses herself from her group of gringo tourists by telling them she wants to greet her "cousin," approaches him, sits down beside him, and they meet. Lavinia (Miroslava Stern) then horrifies Archi by whistling the haunting tune from his mother's former music box. He calms down when he realizes that she is not privy to his inner secrets. She simply had been looking at the music box in the antique shop before he purchased it. Her "papá" enters the bar, an older man with whom she had visited the antique shop, and she quickly gets up from Archi's table. He asks for some way to get in touch with her again, and she gives him the address of a fashion shop on Insurgentes: "Allí estoy día y noche aunque me tienen bastante arrinconadita" [I am there day and night although they have me in a corner]. She says good-bye and walks over to the older gentleman. They begin to discuss their pending wedding. Then she returns to her *gringuitos* [little gringos] and introduces the older man as her "uncle."

Archi is still a child in a grown man's body, and in this sense, the picaresque never really disappears. Archi is very much like young

Lazarillo, but he has no blind master to guide him. What he lacks is a perceptual apparatus to "read" duplicitous statements and ambiguous situations, that is to say, to "see" beyond the reflections in the mirror. Again, he reacts with surprise the next day when he asks for Lavinia at the dress shop on Insurgentes and learns that no one by her name has ever worked there. Then he notices a mannequin on the shop floor—an identical wax replica of Lavinia, and he understands what she meant by her cryptic statement about working day and night. Without great difficulty, he finds the walking-talking version of Lavinia leaving the artist's workshop in Coyoacán. Archi begins his own game with her, telling her that he is an artist, although we know he is a member of the idle rich, and only makes clay pots as a hobby. He invites her to model for him, and he assures her that his female cousin will be at home. In other words, there will be a chaperon on the premises, and she accepts his invitation. The older man meets her in the square, and she walks toward him and says something that we and Archi cannot hear. Then the shapely model walks off with the older man, all the while making flirtatious gestures toward Archi from a distance. In short, whether visual or auditory, internal or external realities, part of the content of the story is its very telling—and Baroque *lack* thereof.

Young picaros usually become apprentices to abusive masters, and these men teach them how to swindle and scam. Ironically, Archi's school of hard knocks is administered by the very objects of his desire, such as Patricia and Lavinia. In the case of the bosomy model who sometimes likes to play tour guide, Lavinia chooses to keep her appointment with Archi. However, at the precise moment he is about to strangle her, a large group of gringo tourists surprises him by ringing the bell at the street entrance. Before leaving with her group, she confesses and tells Archi she plans to marry the older man she had once called "papá." Shocked but undeterred, Archi's imagination takes over, and the adult continues rehearsing his life of crime, strangling the mannequin and then burning Lavinia in effigy. Even if he were never to attempt to act out his "criminal life," others are plotting around him, and nothing is as it appears to be. In other words, the adult Archibaldo de la Cruz is still as gullible and self-centered as he was when he was a child. In fact, even the woman he wants to marry, the saintly Carlota (Ariadna Welter), has maintained a long-time, secret love affair with a married architect. It turns out that ongoing plans to renovate the family chapel are a pretext for the two to meet. Carlota's mother, Mrs. Cervantes, plays a duplicitously Celestinesque role as intermediary between her daughter, Archi, and his rival. Like the titular heroine and many other characters of *La Celestina* (Rojas, 1499–1514), she is an expert at making up spur-of-the-moment lies and excuses so that Archi will never suspect that he has proposed marriage to a woman who is of questionable virtue.

In one of the more comic moments of the movie, Carlota and Mrs. Cervantes pay a surprise visit to Archi's home. Outside the street door, Carlota explains that she needs her mother there to help legitimize the scene they are about to play out. Seated in his living room, Mrs. Cervantes suggests that Carlota has decided to accept his proposal of marriage, but both women are a couple of con-artists. Carlota wants social legitimacy and respectability, and so she is willing to marry Archi even though she does not love him. Her problem is that she cannot lie and needs her mother to help convince Archi of her sincerity. To this end, they never quite come out and say that Carlota *wants* to marry Archi. When Archi asks her directly, "¿Es posible que haya aceptado ser mi esposa?" [Is it possible that she has consented to be my wife?], Mrs. Cervantes intervenes and bursts into tears, attempting her role as mother about to give away her only daughter. Without waiting for Carlota's reply, both Archi and Carlota move over to comfort Mrs. Cervantes. Her daughter, however, rolls her eyes and tells her, "¡Por Dios, Mamá! Ya sabía que iba a hacer una escena penosa" [For God's sake, Mama! I knew that you were going to make a big scene].

We then see a close-up of Archi consoling Mrs. Cervantes, but we cannot see her. As we hear her respond, Archi's expression indicates that he has noticed something on the floor below him, something that worries him. Then there is a close-up of a high-heel shoe belonging to the life-size mannequin of Lavinia with whom he had just been "rehearsing" moments earlier. We then see Archi's face again, his eyes cutting over to see if the mother-and-daughter act has taken notice of the prop from the previous stage show. The camera sweeps down to the shoe on the floor, and we see Archi discreetly kicking the incriminating object underneath the sofa to hide it from his future bride and mother-in-law. Like the early picaro Lázaro, and the Baroque rogues to follow, Archi deludes himself into thinking that he dupes but is not himself duped by others.

PSYCHOANALYSIS AND CLASS PRIVILEGE

Archi's mental illness permits Buñuel a way of playing with the pseudopicaresque telling of his tale and of placing surreal / baroque images in the service of a critique of the bourgeoisie. The filmmaker, however, also adds another dimension to this dynamic, drawing in the audience. As the plot unfolds, Buñuel no longer adheres to the symbols he had previously used to assist us in distinguishing between appearance and reality, making it increasingly more difficult for us to discern between the two. We begin to understand what Archi's confusion is like, not knowing if he is subject or object, author or character. For a time, Buñuel deprives us of the conventions he had respected within the context of feature-film realism, and we enter the totally conceptual, Neo-Baroque world of Archi's mind. Words and objects seem to have been reascribed arbitrary meaning, and only those inside his mind and fantasies can begin to comprehend their significance. Buñuel's sense of humor relies, in part, on the incongruous, but he replaces comedy for a while with suspense.

To this end, Archi's narrative now takes an epistolary turn in the form of a mysterious, unsigned letter, instructing him to go to the architect's place on the eve of his marriage to Carlota in order to bear witness to his fiancée's infidelity. Archi does what the letter says, lurking behind the garden bushes in his Humphrey Bogart trench coat while the sound of a freight train passes.[10] He moves closer to a picture window, horizontally lined by venetian blinds, and sees Carlota and the architect embracing through it. Looking over Archi's shoulder, we see the venetian blinds close, and the background noise of the passing train stops suddenly, as if controlled by the lever on the venetians. Inside, the viewer realizes that Carlota is trying to tell her lover good-bye forever. Outside, Archi waits and ponders. He is neither actor nor audience for the mini-drama taking place on the other side of the Venetian blinds.

The real drama occurs inside Archi's mind where he rehearses over and over for "real life." Role-play is something the picaro has to learn how to do, shifting careers and identities to suit his life of crime. Through the cinematic tricks of modern narrative, Buñuel also lets us peek at Archibaldo's fantasies with their augmenting distortions. Outside, Archi is engulfed by smoke and nightmarish carrousel music, the former ditty from the music box long ago having transformed itself in his mind. He slumps on a park bench, and we hear his thoughts spoken out loud. If he were to kill Carlota on her way out of the architect's place, he would be judged as a common criminal. If it were the night of their wedding, he would be judged "como a un esposo que ha vengado su honor" [like a husband who has avenged his honor]. So, he decides to play the cuckolded, class-conscious husband at the end of a Calderonian tragedy, carefully selecting the time and place: "Mañana por la noche en la cámara nupcial" [Tomorrow night in the nuptial bed].[11] Once he is married, life imitates art, and a literary genre sets a precedent for murder.

Although this is the mid 1950s, Carlota is like the unlucky, misunderstood wife in a Golden Age honor play. She is, in fact, stuck between a rock and a hard place. If she attempts to make a clean break with the architect without marrying Archi, the bourgeoisie, armed with seventeenth-century Calderonian "high culture," will set itself against her. Now that Archibaldo knows part of the truth and has decided to restore his lost honor, there is little she can do. Her only option would be to maintain her status as the "other woman" to a man whose wife will not give him a divorce, but then the bourgeoisie would condemn her as a picara, using the weapon of the bogusly "low-culture" picaresque tradition. Carlota takes her chances on having Archi believe she is a virgin rather than continue hiding her affair with a married man. Either way, if discovered, she is at the mercy of the class-conscious patriarchy of 1950s Mexico.

For several moments, particularly in relation to Carlota's demise, we do not know for certain whether Archi is dreaming or if there is an actual murder in progress. Once again, the warped tune from the music box and the smoke and mirrors announce one of Archi's waking dreams, but Buñuel suspends their use after a fade-out to Archi and Carlota's wedding night. For a few brief scenes, the relation between story and cinematographic discourse is no longer obvious for the first-time viewer. We are convinced that Archi has a vividly sadistic imagination and bad luck in realizing his fantasies, but then again, why do most of his intended victims keep winding up dead? By the time Carlota dies, Archi believes that he *really is* a great criminal, a tremendous serial killer who deserves to be punished, especially since punishment would authenticate his identity as a criminal. He needs an outside source to corroborate his case and prove that it must be more than coincidence that every time he plans a murder, fate intervenes, and the object of his murderous desire ends up dead. Carlota's murder confirms the secret power the owner of the music box is said to possess, but no one wants to hear Archi's confession. Not the nun. Not the judge. No one. We, however, empathize with Archi and other characters' craziness. Buñuel pulls in the audience, particularly a bourgeois audience, as part of his critique of the bourgeoisie.

"All the world's a stage" and Archi is a mere player, peeking through the venetian blinds. Someone else's hand is on the lever in an alienating *theatro Mundo* worthy of Baltasar Gracián—and it is a world steeped in a material history in which the very squandering of resources calls our attention to the gulf between rich and poor (Gracián 1984, 6). This type of discourse about social inequality is one that Marx echoes centuries later, often articulating it in terms of the alienation of the worker from the means of production. So why is Archi's agency as narrator–protagonist of his adventures constantly challenged and even stolen from him at times? He is, after all, a member of the idle rich, so shouldn't he be safe from such dangers? The answer is rather simple. Archi is vacuous; Buñuel is not. Archibaldo's misadventures permit us the opportunity to realize that both fantasy and reality are moving higher and higher up the social registry. Buñuel, always the staunch satirist and critic of the bourgeoisie, portrays twisted morals that go unquestioned, and are, therefore, indirectly protected through class privilege. Archi's well-heeled contemporaries perceive him as eccentric and sometimes buffoonish, but they always think of him as the perfect gentleman within the parameters of their class. While the music-box fairies may have made him feel powerful as a child, they also bring him adult frustrations, a dynamic Archi may or may not want to resolve, and this is the stagnant, self-satisfied position where Archibaldo and his class find themselves.

In an amusing scene that takes place in the midst of Archi and Carlota's wedding party, a priest, a colonel, and a police commissioner are enjoying polite conversation. The commissioner, the same man who investigated Patricia Terraza's death, confesses that what moves him to tears is a bride at the altar or a national military parade. Buñuel picks these paternal symbols as a way of revealing the "marriage" of church-mediated religion, state bureaucracy, and military patriotism—and the fact that these institutions are pulling strings behind the scenes of a world stage. To this extent, a patriarchal elite also pulls the strings of the police commissioner, the priest, and the colonel. Something or someone is keeping everyone on good behavior, and maintaining the tenets of class privilege. Moments later, Carlota is shot dead by her former lover, but there is no revolution this time, unlike the night Archi's governess died. Regardless of the outcome of this so-called *loco amor*, brides and soldiers are still marching on. In fact, Carlota's story turns out to be a classic wife-murder from her point of view. While it is the most Calderonian episode in the movie, in some ways it is the most banal of Archi's unrealized "crimes."

I have already discussed the importance of mirrors, the music box, and the walking cane, and one may infer the autoerotic implications of a life-size mannequin and Archi's "doll play." Occasionally, however, Buñuel may be throwing us red herrings rather than deep symbols from the preconscious, and not withstanding, many studies have placed great weight on the film's symbolism. For example, much has been said about the grasshopper that Archi observes at the end of the film (some think it is a praying mantis),[12] but it seems tenuous to say that an object appearing once at the end of the movie unlocks all of Archi or Buñuel's secrets. This seems particularly fallacious when objects that repeat over and over are overlooked or ignored, such as the cane Archi uses to point at the grasshopper. For its part, the insect represents Archi's return to simple childhood pleasures: "Por primera vez puedo decir que la vida me parece una cosa sencilla" [For the first time I can say that life seems to me a simple thing]. In all likelihood this is only a fleeting Neo-Baroque image, proving as ephemeral as life itself. It is most certainly a political comment about a man of means and his entire class who float along without any apparent ideology or convictions, poking at insects, stalking the sexual objects of their desire, and imagining how to commit the "perfect sex crime" while preserving an aura of bourgeois respectability. Even in psychoanalytic terms, Archi's only "breakthrough" is to further simplify his childlike life and continue pushing away that which will bring him pleasure. When he hurls the music box in a park lake near the close of the film, Archi distances himself further from the trail of clues leading back to the childhood origins of his criminal pleasures. At the end of the film, many viewers are left with their own aporia about Archi's psychological aporia. François Truffaut mentions that viewers leaving the cinema like the movie about Archi, and they even like Archi, but they do not know whether he actually murdered anyone or not. Some, because of the movie's title, think he did. Others think he is completely harmless (1975, 279). In other words, after one viewing, we are left with a philosophical aporia concerning Archi's psychological aporia about *where* to begin, *what* to do or say, and *how* to go about it.

After Archi throws his music box into a lake, orchestral music announces closure in the movie, but not necessarily in Archibaldo's criminal life. Buñuel actually makes Hollywood convention oddly extraordinary. Apart from melodramatic organ music during the opening credits, this is the first occasion that Buñuel has used feature-film music in the background of *The Criminal Life*, and its intrusion seems simultaneously familiar to the genre and incongruous in this particular movie. The internal codes established during the course of the film have indicated that silence or the music-box ditty accompany realism; the nightmarish organ interpretation of the music box tune signals fantasy. So, a Hollywood-like orchestral arrangement seems strangely out of place. Archi proceeds on his musically accompanied stroll through the park, sees the grasshopper, and accidentally meets Lavinia a little farther down the path. For her part, she announces that her wedding plans fell through: "Además de ser rico y honorable, resultó que era policia honrado y celoso" [Besides being rich and honorable, it turned out that he was a virtuous and jealous policeman]. In other words, she implies that she left her older friend because he was too constraining and jealous, not because she has changed in any significant way. Some argue that Archi is cured of his neuroses and about to embark on a "normal relationship with a mature woman" at the end of the film (Conrad 1978, 337), but even Buñuel claimed the following: "[T]he audience can ask itself, what is going to happen to Lavinia? Archibaldo may kill her an hour later, because nothing really indicates that he has changed" (Buñuel in Colina 1992, 121). The same can be asserted about his pseudopicaresque rival, Lavinia. She may be staging another little play that inadvertently foils his plans. After all, a group of voyeuristic gringo tourists may be waiting for them just behind a tree—or in front of the movie screen. And so, the orchestral arrangement announces conventional closure, indicative of films from Hollywood's Golden Age, but it parodies the content of the story.

Are Archi and his criminal life completely depoliticized and dehistoricized by the conclusion? Buñuel's combination and recombination of genres could lead us to claim that he operates in postmodernist fashion, never embracing any form unproblematically or single-mindedly. Images, however, have a subtle way of referring to narrative structure in Buñuel's work, permitting us the opportunity to explore *why* history matters. As Archi and Lavinia walk arm-in-arm into a celluloid happy ending, the titular hero leaves us with one last gesture, marking the seemingly cinematic frame that surrounds them. Tossing aside his cane becomes a beginning to the end and an end to the beginning. In other words, Buñuel leaves us with a reference to the picaresque narrative framework for his tale.

While absolute closure in the picaresque particularly defies logic because the story appears to end long before the first-person narrator's life has ended, the genre itself is grounded in history and a socioeconomic critique of its period. Don Quixote, an upper-class picaro, asks Ginés de Pasamonte, a lower-class picaro, if he has finished writing the first-person narration about his criminal life: "—¿Cómo puede estar acabado—respondió él—, si aún no está acabada mi vida?' " [Cervantes 1978, 22: How can it be finished, he replied, if my life is not yet over?]. We could say that a conclusive answer seems suspended somewhere on the other side of the looking glass of history—the reflection in a beautifully ornate baroque mirror, contained in the imperfect glitter of Buñuel's celluloid pearl. But then again, all of Buñuel's mirrors in *The Criminal Life of Archibaldo de la Cruz* have the historical and political frames of the bourgeois households where they hang. The music box and its unforgettably cloying little tune—not so much the mirrors and cane—assist us in tracing Archi and the Mexican bourgeoisie's history in the first-half of the twentieth century. With the little music-box ditty spinning around in our heads after viewing the film, we start to realize that Archi—with his child-like innocence sheltered by class privilege—disassociates himself from history and the historical precedent of class struggle set during the Mexican Revolution, especially the night a stray bullet killed his governess.

NOTES

I would like to thank the editors as well as the following people for their valuable assistance: María Luisa Fischer, Carl Good, Roxanne Lalande, Jeff Maskovsky, Matt Ruben, and Pithamber Polsani.

1. The exhibit, entitled "¿Buñuel!: La mirada del siglo," began in Madrid at the Museo Nacional Centro de Arte Reina Sofía and ran from 16 July to 14 October 1996. It then moved to the Museo del Palacio de Bellas Artes in Mexico City, running from 4 December 1996 to 2 March 1997.

2. Pedro Almodóvar uses a televised broadcast of *Ensayo de un crimen* in background sequences of *Carne trémula* [Live Flesh; 1997]. For many younger viewers, this was their first encounter with Buñuel.

3. In his obituary for the film maker, Paul Mayersberg notes the influence of the poets more than the painters (1983, 258). Of course, Buñuel influenced and was influenced by both groups of surrealists. For example, Lorca and Dalí were friends of Buñuel's at the *Institución libre de enseñanza*, and both became friends and rivals at different points of the film maker's life.

4. André Breton, one of the original surrealists, describes his displeasure with Buñuel's political leanings in an unedited text from 1951, printed in *¿Buñuel!: La mirada del siglo* (1996, 35–7).

5. Buñuel mixes, inverts, or otherwise confounds canons and genres, so that critical work identifying him as an exclusively psychoanalytic, surrealist, or Marxist film maker becomes reductive and simplistic. For a Marxist history of Mexican cinema, see García Riera.

6. At first glance, it may seem to be a contradiction, but Buñuel's *The Criminal Life* uses both Baroque and Cervantine currents that run throughout Hispanic culture. For more on Cervantes and Buñuel, please refer to my article, "Quixotic Desire and the Avoidance of Closure in Luis Buñuel's *The Criminal Life of Archibaldo de la Cruz*" *MLN* 114 (1996): 269–96.

7. In passing, Sánchez Vidal says "de nombre Willy Corduran: significativas denominaciones para esta conmovedora historia de *loco amor*" [1984, 200: regard-

ing the name Willy Corduran: significant denominators for this moving story of mad love]. Indeed, Patricia and Willy are possessed by an *amour fou*, and the name "Willy" in English is suggestive of many things, including the expression "willy-nilly" for vacillating behavior and the children's word "willy" for penis. "Corduran" is related to the Spanish word *cordura*, meaning "common sense" or "sanity." At this point in the film, Willy talks "man-to-man" with Archi, and out pops another popular proverb, this time from the mouth of a man who is coded as nouveau riche and too Americanized: "Vale más el engañado que el desconfiado" [Better deceived than suspicious].

8. At the beginning of the third and final act of *El castigo sin venganza*, Aurora, inspired by jealousy, tells a courtier about what she saw in the reflection of a mirror: The duke's son was kissing his young stepmother, that is to say, his father's new wife (2040–20). Her testimony about a *loco amor*, inspired by her own *loco amor* for the son, requires the duke to kill his son and young wife. Ironically, it was the duke's years of lascivious behavior and decision to marry a younger woman that creates a destructive chain of events unleashed by what Aurora saw in the reflection of a mirror.

9. The police commissioner decides to go out for coffee rather than continue the investigation. Nonetheless, besides her suicide note, we witness Patricia tell Archi, "A veces que pienso que no vale la pena seguir viviendo" [Sometimes I think that it's not worth going on living].

10. Sánchez Vidal chooses to describe Archi's detective attire as "gabardina, estilo Bogart" [garbardine, in the Bogart style] (1984, 202).

11. This situation recalls the twisted plot of *Él* [He; Mexico, 1952], especially the protagonist's monstrous transformation once married. The irony is that the husband winds up in a convent at the end of the movie, not the wife.

12. Many critics mention the scene with the insect, including Estève (1963, 192), Truffaut (1975, 279), Mellen (1978, 18–19), Higginbotham (1979, 96), Fuentes (1993, 128).

Works Cited

Almodovar, Pedro (director). 1997. *Carne trémula* [*Live Flesh*]. El Deseo.

Breton, André. 1996. "Desesperada y apasionada." In *¡Buñuel!: La mirada del siglo*, edited by Yasha David. Reprint of unedited text in Spanish, Madrid: Museo Nacional Reina Sofía.

Buñuel, Luis. 1992. *Objects of Desire: Conversations with Luis Buñuel*. Translated by Paul Lenti. New York: Marsilio, 1986. Reprint, originally published as *Luis Buñuel: Prohibido asomarse al interior*. Edited by José de la Colina and Tomás Pérez Turrent. Mexico City: Planeta.

Buñuel, Luis (director and screenplay writer). 1933. *Las Hurdes*. 30 min., black and white, silent film. Madrid: Luis Buñuel and Ramón Acín (producers).

———, and Eduardo Ugarte (screenplay writer). 1955. *Ensayo de un crimen*, or, *The Criminal Life of Archibaldo de la Cruz*. 90 min., black and white. Mexico City: Alfonso Patiño Gómez (producer), Alianza Cinematográfica.

———, and Julio Alejandro (screenplay writer). 1961. *Viridiana*. 90 min., black and white. Madrid / Mexico City: Gustavo Altriste, Pedro Portabella, and Ricardo Muñoz Suay (producers), Uninci, Films 59 (Madrid), Producciones Alatriste (Mexico).

96   SIDNEY DONNELL

————, Julio Alejandro and Emilio Carballido (screenplay writers). 1958. *Nazarín*. 94 min., black and white. Mexico City: Manuel Barbachano Ponce (producer), Producciones Barbachano Ponce.

————, and Luis Alcoriza (screenplay writer). 1950. *Los olvidados*. 80 min., black and white. Mexico City: Oscar Dancigers (producer), Ultramar Films.

————, and Salvador Dalí (screenplay writer). 1930. *L'age d'or*. 63 min., black and white. Paris: The Viscount and Viscountess de Noailles (producers).

————. 1929. *Un chien andalou*. 24 min., black and white, silent film. Paris: Luis Buñuel (producer).

Calderón de la Barca, Pedro. 1962. *No hay burlas con el amor: El médico de su honra*. Madrid: Espasa-Calpe.

Carpentier, Alejo. 1990. "Lo barroco y lo real maravilloso." In *Obras completas de Alejo Carpentier*. Vol. 13 of *Ensayos*. Mexico City: Siglo Veintiuno.

Cervantes Saavedra, Miguel de. 1978. *El ingenioso hidalgo don Quijote de la Mancha*. Vol. 1. Edited by Luis Andrés Murillo. Madrid: Castalia.

Conrad, Randall. 1978. " 'A Magnificent and Dangerous Weapon': The Politics of Luis Buñuel's Late Films." In *The World of Luis Buñuel: Essays in Criticism*. edited by Joan Mellen. New York: Oxford University Press.

Donnell, Sidney E. "Quixotic Desire and the Avoidance of Closure in Luis Buñuel's *The Criminal Life of Archibaldo de la Cruz*." *MLN* 114 (1999): 269–96.

Estève, Marie-Cécile. 1963. Les obsessions d'Archibald de la Cruz. *Études Cinématographiques*, nos. 22–3, Luis Buñuel 2 (spring): 187–92.

Foucault, Michel. 1973. *The Order of Things: An Archaeology of the Human Sciences*. Edited by R. D. Laing. New York: Random House, 1966. Reprint, originally published as *Les mots et les choses*: Paris: Gallimard.

Fuentes, Víctor. 1993. *Buñuel en México: Iluminaciones sobre una pantalla pobre*. Teruel: Instituto de Estudios Turolenses.

García Riera, Emilio. 1969–95. *Historia documental del cine mexicano*. 17 vols. Guadalajara: Universidad de Guadalajara.

González Echevarría, Roberto. 1993. *Celestina's Brood: Continuities of the Baroque in Spanish and Latin American Literatures*. Durham, N.C.: Duke University Press.

Gracián, Baltasar. 1984. *El Criticón*. Edited by Santos Alonso. Madrid: Cátedra.

Higginbotham, Virginia. 1979. *Luis Buñuel*. Boston: Twayne.

Juana Inés de la Cruz, Sister. 1989. *Los empeños de una casa*. Edited by Celsa Carmen García Valdés. Barcelona: Promociones y Publicaciones Universitarias.

Mayersberg, Paul. 1983. The Happy Ending of Luis Buñuel. *Sight and Sound* 4: 248-9.

Mellen, Joan. 1978. An Overview of Buñuel's Career. In *The World of Luis Buñuel: Essays in Criticism*, edited by Joan Mellen. New York: Oxford University Press.

Rojas, Fenando de. 1974. *La Celestina*. Edited by Bruno Mario Damiani. Madrid: Cátedra.

Sánchez Vidal, Agustín. 1984. *Luis Buñuel: Obra cinematográfica*. Madrid: Ediciones J.C.

Scarpetta, Guy. 1988. "Buñuel: surréaliste ou baroque?" *Art Press* 129: 64.

Truffaut, François. 1975. "Buñuel le constructeur." In *Les films de ma vie*, 272–81. Paris: Flammarion.

Usigli, Rodolfo. 1993. *Ensayo de un crimen*. Mexico City: J. Mortiz.

Vega Carpio, Lope de. 1990. *El castigo sin venganza*. Edited by Antonio Carreño. Madrid: Cátedra.

La vida de Lazarillo de Tormes y de sus fortunas y adversidades. 1983. Edited by Joseph V. Ricapito. Madrid: Cátedra.

Webster's Encyclopedic Unabridged Dictionary of the English Language. 1989. New York: Random House.

Abjection's Tapestry: Saint-Amant's Reading of *Don Quixote*

SALVADOR J. FAJARDO

Don Quixote was first known in France through translations of selected episodes such as Nicolas Baudoin's rendition of the intercalated novella, "El curioso impertiente" ["The Tale of Impertinent Curiosity"], "Le Curieux Impertient" (1608), or the episode of Marcela and Grisóstomo, "Le meurtre de la Fidélité, et la Défense de l'Honneur. Où est racontée la triste, et pitoyable avanture du Berger Philidon, et les raisons de la belle et chaste Marcelle accusée de sa mort. Avec un discours de Don Quixote des Armes sur les Lettres" ["The murder of fidelity, and the defense of honor. Which tells of the sad and pitiful adventure of the shepherd Philidon, and the reasons of the beautiful and chaste Marcela accused of his death. With a discourse of Don Quixote's on Arms over Letters"] by an anonymous adapter (1609). The complete first part of the novel was translated in 1614 by César Oudin.[1] Very quickly the *Don Quichotte* became "un livre de lecture courante, que l'on a sous la main, que l'on connait, que l'on cite" [Reynier 78: 1914, a book commonly read, that one has at hand, that one knows, that one quotes]. Part two would be translated in 1618 by François Rosset.

In 1637, as the newly formed Académie Française (founded in 1635 by Richelieu) was preparing its *Dictionary*, Marc Antoine de Gérard, sieur de Saint-Amant (1594–1661), offered his services as a source for the vocabulary of the burlesque and the marginal. The intention of the Académie was to standardize usage, and this act may be seen as an aspect of the increasing hegemonization of society, a process that reaches its ancien régime apex during the *age classique* [classical age] proper, the reign of Louis XIV. In spite of his conversion to Catholicism—he came from a Huguenot family—Saint-Amant was generally considered a *poète libertin* [libertine poet], a reputation that his own admission of loose living and attraction to *la débausché* [debauchery] did nothing to allay. Yet he was attached to important noblemen of the time (Retz, Montmorency)

98

and was admired as a most gifted poet. The friend to whom he addresses the piece that interests us, "La chambre du débauché" ["The Wastrel's Room"], was the marquis de Marigny-Mallernoë, a not inconsiderable personage, and Saint-Amant's tavern companion.

Saint-Amant may have read Oudin's translation of *Don Quixote*, or, since he knew Spanish, he may have read the original. At any event he refers to *Don Quixote* several times in his poetry, namely in "Les Visions" ["The Visions"], probably written around 1623, in the burlesque poem "La Berne" ["The Practical Joke"] of the same year, in "Le Poète crotté" ["The Muddied Poet"] and in "Le Paresseux" ["The Lazy One"], both written around 1626 (*Oeuvres*, vol. 1). All his references are of a burlesque nature, except for Le Paresseux, where the poet compares himself to "un Dom-Quichot en sa morne folie" [a Don Quixote in his dismal madness]. His most substantial and interesting reference to the book, however, is that of the "Ode-Epître" "La chambre du débauché," in which he devotes one hundred lines to the novel.

The ode had been introduced in France by Ronsard and later taken up with enthusiasm by the other members of La Pléiade; Ronsard used the ode form to sing topics of an elevated nature. By the time it reached Saint-Amant, it had shed its strictly classic Anacreontic form of strophe, antistrophe, and epode, which Ronsard himself abandoned with his sixteenth ode. The ode's prosody was now simplified to ten-line stanzas of octosyllables with a rhyme scheme in *ababccdeed*, but was still reserved mainly for important topics. Saint-Amant describes his poem as "This Ode clothed as an Epistle," but maintains this same prosody (Moner, 817–20). As an ode, one would expect it to convey matters of substance. As an epistle, it conforms to the rhetoric of personal address. The epistle, which was frequently reserved for special occasions or matters of a daily nature, allowed for a freer range of expression and for the introduction of the marginal. In fact, since all that remains of the ode form is its prosody, it would be more appropriate to describe the poem as an "Epistle clothed as an Ode." By reversing the terms, Saint-Amant announces immediately the irreverent nature of his discourse and its attack on traditional, highflown, hegemonic form. He also creates for himself an interstitial space that allows such discourse to express a modicum of agency as freedom from preestablished genre positioning and subjected authorial responsibility. The conditions of the poem's writing, as declared in its first strophe, are suggestive:

Plus enfumé qu'un vieux Jambon	Smokier than an old ham
Ny que le bœuf-salé de Pitre,	Or than salt beef from Pitre,
Je te trace avec un charbon	I sketch for you with a coal
Ceste Ode habillée en Epître:	This Ode clothed as an Epistle:
Marigny mon parfait amy	Marigny my perfect friend,
Que mon oeil ne voit qu'à demi	Whom my eye only half sees
Non plus que ce qu'il veut descrire,	No better than what it wants to describe,
Parbieu! tu dois bien admirer,	Sblood! you must truly admire,
Que je tasche a te faire rire	That I try to make you laugh
Quand je ne fay rien que pleurer.	When all I can do is weep.[2]

Another aspect of this "clothing" comes through in the rhyming of "Pitre" and "Epître," which isolates "pître" in the latter term. Pitre is a region in France famous for its smoked ham and with a circumflex on the "i" the word "pître" also means clown, to suggest "clownish Ode."

Some of the details of this first stanza only acquire their full meaning after a second reading. For instance, "enfumé," which literally means "smoked," can also mean drunk.[3] As we learn later, both senses are operant in that the chimney fire will fill the débausché's[4] room with smoke and the speaker's visit concludes with a drinking bout. The smokiness of the room also explains, retroactively, the stanza's last line as weeping not from sorrow but from smoke. Yet the stanza's initial sense, independent of rereading, maintains the double entendre and works rhetorically as an intriguing invitation to read on: "That I try to make you laugh / When all I can do is weep." As well, it is either the smoke or the drinking that would account for "Whom my eye only half sees." All this points from the outset to the double discourse in play—suitable to the double nature of the Ode-Epistle—a double discourse that becomes clear at the end of the poem as we reread, and which is then confirmed by our double, or multiple, reading. The suggestion of circularity is itself already inscribed in the first stanza where the last line's "weep" is explained by the opening line's "smoked." Another detail that acquires meaning as we read on is "I sketch for you with a coal." This indicates that the poem is written in broad strokes, carelessly, and also that it demonstrates a general ekphrastic element. The poem contains within it the further ekphrasis of the *Don Quixote* scenes. This inner ekphrastic moment interrupts the external one (the description of the room) as a series of frames within a frame—in the other traditional sense of ekphrasis as a description that interrupts an action, though here reversed, as a series of depicted actions that interrupt a description, thus maintaining, conceptually, the reversing of categories typical of the burlesque: eight stanzas, the seventh through the fourteenth, the approximately central third of the piece, render a series of scenes/episodes from *Don Quixote I* selected from its first half.

In the second stanza, the speaker wonders how he could have entered a room whose door was so low that a rat "could enter only on its knees" (20); furthermore the room is such that "Even in the heat of the Summer / One finds the month of December" (13–4). We are penetrating a separate, marginal space, difficult of access, where abnormal conditions prevail. It is a space propitious for transformations. This impoverished, abject room is, of course, a synecdochic projection of its owner's, the *débausché's*, inner psychic space, as the space through which Don Quixote moves is a projection of the knight's own psyche. The speaker also makes clear, in parallel fashion, how the scenes from the novel that he perceives on the walls of the room are projections of his own imaginative interior. In the room itself, as across the roads of La Mancha, objects are changed to accommodate inner needs. The *débausché*, as he does violence to his body, center, and origin of his personal world-making, of his signifying practice, does violence to the space and objects around him by transforming their use, therefore their meaning: a basket is both table and stool, the broken case of a lute, all that is left of a previous employment, is both a suitcase and a pillow.

Stanza six introduces the *Don Quixote* scenes:

Comme on voit au soir le Enfans	As one sees children in the evening
Se figurer dedans les nues	Imagine among the clouds
Hommes, Chasteaux, Bois, Elefans,	Men, Castles, Forests, Elephants,
Et mille Chimeres cornues:	And a thousand horned Chimeras:
Ainsi nos yeux dans ces crachats,	Thus our eyes, amid the spittle
Se forgeants à leurs entrechats	Conceiving in their capers
Cent mille sortes de postures,	One hundred thousand poses,
Pensent voir contre la paroy	Think they see upon the wall
Les plus grotesques avantures	The most grotesque adventures
De Dom-Quichote en bel arroy.	Of Don Quixote on beautiful display.

The poet here attends to his own transformative power. The mock-idyllic reference to children's imaginations—apparently devaluing his own inventiveness by comparing it to a child's dream—contrasts with the repulsive description of this surprising tapestry. The transmutation of space is congruent with the expression of poetic decision; in fact, it proclaims the power of language with panache, underlining the very process of transformation as a successful, quixotic entreprise. The poet, like the child, like Don Quixote, can transform the most abject reality into adventure and ornament.

The first scene that takes form through the room's smoke is the scrutiny of Don Quixote's books and their smoky burning. This scene allows the speaker an aside on the mass of worthless books printed in France, which would also provide a splendid bonfire; thus, he pursues the literary topic, now as an attack on useless, sanctioned discourse. The other scenes selected by Saint-Amant highlight movement and transformation in Don Quixote's adventures. After the book burning, the episodes in question are: Don Quixote's attack on the Benedictine Friars (8); the adventure of the windmills (8); the battle of the sheep and its aftermath (18); Sancho's *manteamiento* at the inn (17); Mambrino's helmet (21); Sancho's finding of Cardenio's purse (23); Dulcinea-as-Aldonza sifting grain (31); and the Yanguesans (15). Saint-Amant is not kind to the knight or to Sancho; he calls Don Quixote "Guidon de carnaval," that is, carnival captain, "chevalier de foin" or straw knight, and "nostre fantome," our phantom, while Sancho is a "pauvre sot," poor fool. However, he reserves his unkindest cuts for Dulcinea-as-Aldonza Lorenzo: "Icy mouvant le χρουπιον / Repaire de maint μορπιον / Ses bras font un métier pénible" [125–8: Here moving her butt / Abode of many a crab / Her arms do a difficult task].[5] The topic of grotesque eroticism is pursued in the next stanza dealing with the episode of the Yanguesans where Rocinante "piqué d'un désir paillard, / Veut desrouiller sa vieille dague" ["133–4: stung by a ribald desire, / wants to repolish his old dagger"].

The following strophe is transitional to the continuation of the room's inventory and addresses possible critical readers:

Mais, c'est assez Quichotisé,	But enough Quixotizing,
Et si quelque bourru Critique	And if some churlish Critic
Ne dit aussi tost sottisé,	Does not as soon say chattering,
Je n'entends rien à la pratique:	I know nothing about this business:
Cependant un tel repreneur,	However such a reprover,
Dans la lice du point-d'honneur	In the lists of the point of honor
Pourroit bien gister sans littiere,	Could well lie without a berth,
Et sentir sur son hocqueton	And feel upon his jacquet
Que je suis en cette matiere	That I am in this matter
Tres-asseuré de mon baston.	Most assured of my staff.

The speaker again returns to the ongoing process, warning such readers that he (perhaps like Cervantes?) knows very well what he is about.

The rest of the room's inventory now proceeds: the *débausché* uses a flask as a candle-holder, a chamber pot as a cup, and his sword as a skewer and knife; gaming dice are his arithmetic, cobwebs, his cloth hangings, and so on. In all its abjection the room is a privileged space, generator of change and invention. It is the space of poetic imagination, seen as marginal to sanctioned exchanges and hegemonic practices in general. And the most abject of its productions is the viscous, imagined tapestry of *Don Quixote* scenes, elaborated from expectorations caused by the debauched's *vérole*. *Vérole*, the pox, could be syphilis, as well as any scarring infection: thus, self-disfigurement, itself the visible result of violence to the body, is projected on the wall as a shadowgraph of the psyche onto external space. We recall that the débausché was using a broken lute box as a suitcase and pillow, a suggestion that he may himself have been a poet in more propitious times—or may still be one for that matter—although drinking, gambling, and illness have reduced him to his present state. On the other hand, the speaker, poet, and interpreter of this space, and within it of the abject tapestry, is also showing that *this* poetry originates in abjection. He submits his body as well to the generative enclosure where he will get drunk (the body's preparation and abuse for poetic ends) and sing the health of Marigny, his addressee.

The discourse originating in this space is picaresque and burlesque. It is inseparable from the bodies that produce it, reproduces their plasticity, and is congruent with their self-inflicted violence. But this text is as well an object of desire, in that it negotiates a space wherein some agency may be produced that escapes the preordained subject positions of hegemonic society.[6] In fact, the text begins to construct an autonomous subject. Its burlesque/carnivalesque character and its linking of abject bodies and abject discourse allows it to mediate between classes and classifications.[7]

The speaker himself, who has negated and reduced the vertical (socialized) axis of his body to enter the room, comparing himself implicitly with a rat (vermin, to which all spaces are accessible), is both superior to, and one and the same as, the *débausché*. The self-negating penetration into the space of the abject allows him to produce a discourse free from traditional forms of subjectivity, with the further implication that there is a strong kinship between these practices and these spaces: the practice being not merely marginal (grotesque/picaresque) poetic discourse, but poetic discourse in itself, as an expression of agency in a highly stratified society. The speaker has been clear on this point when in stanza sixteen, for instance, he refers dismissively to those who may condemn *nostre douce vie* [our sweet life], including here his addressee and the *débausché* among those who delight in such sweet life, a life of pleasure, drinking, and, equally, writing poetry. Similarly, in the last stanza he says:

Toutesfois nous ne laissons pas,	However we do not refrain,
Trinquans et briffans comme drôles,	Boozing and feasting like rascals,
D'y faire un aussi bon repas	Of making there as good a meal
Qu'on puisse faire entre deux Poles:	As anywhere between two Poles:
Nous y beuvons à ta santé	There we drink your health
Du meilleur qu'ait jamais vanté	From the best ever to be praised
François Paumier ce grand yvrongne,	By François Paumier that grand drunkard,
Sans nul soucy de l'advenir,	With no concern of what's ahead,
Si ce n'es de revoir ta trongne	Except to see your mug again
Et de vivre en ton souvenir.	And to live on in your memory.

Clearly, Saint-Amant in this poem is embracing the abject, and uses it as a means of poetic invigoration. The conditions of the room as womblike, and his entrance into it suggest a reintegration into the Kristevian presymbolic, semiotic realm that precedes identity formation, that is, social formation of possible subject positions.[8]

According to Kristeva, the abject disturbs identity, system, and order. In this sense, the disturbance is what the poet needs; he portrays it systematically (objects lose their identity in the room) and chooses to further reinforce this power with scenes from a text, *Don Quixote*, where the creative imagination of a burlesque protagonist also has that effect on his reality. Here Saint-Amant recognizes the profound effect that the text can have. Literature, Kristeva (1974, 79) says, introduces "across the symbolic, [the semiotic] which works, crosses it and threatens it." Since both the symbolic and the semiotic, imposing limits upon one another, contribute to the formation of the subject, Saint-Amant proposes a text/experience where the semiotic is reinvoked and reinforced to disturb the subject limitations of the symbolic.

The ekphrasis of *Don Quixote* scenes within the chamber centralizes their importance and renders them emblematic of Saint-Amant's current enterprise. In effect he, as writer, places himself in a position parallel to that of the narrator (or narrators) in *Don Quixote* vis-à-vis the knight, voices both inside and outside the text. The novel contains scenes where the identity of objects has been changed to suit Don Quixote's fantasy and needs, as the poem depicts a space where the identity of objects has been changed to suit its inhabitant's needs. The triangular relationship within the novel, Don Quixote<—>Sancho<—>narrator, is reproduced in the poem as debauched<—>his valet (who comes in with wood that he has stolen in town and is described as "his little thief of a valet")<—>speaker. The further triangulation that includes the reader in *Don Quixote*: narrators<—>text<—>readers is equally reproduced in the poem as speaker<—>text<—>addressee (Marigny-Mallenoë). The composition of *Don Quixote* as a peripeteia with interpolated episodes and encounters along a narrative line is also reproduced in the poem as a description with a further (interpolated) ekphrasis (*Don Quixote*). And precisely this interpolation leads the speaker to assert that he is perfectly aware of what he is doing ("Most assured of [his] staff"). In other words, the interpolation is justified by his craft and his intention, implying that the interpolations in *Don Quixote* (attacked by critics) may also be.

Furthermore, Saint-Amant's use of the burlesque and of abjection as a means to undermine social strictures and his imbrication of *Don Quixote* in this enterprise suggest that he understood this other component of Cervantes's novel. It has become a commonplace of *Don Quixote* criticism to point out how the knight creates havoc along his path. He is comparable to a free radical (in chemical terms) circulating across the tightly structured social spaces of seventeenth century Spain, disturbing boundaries, generating transformations, and cutting across the compact strata of blood and rank. As George Mariscal (1991, 172) points out in *Contradictory Subjects*: "Cervantes's representation of a radically autonomous individual runs head on not only into the traditional constraints of shame and revenge but finally into the twin powers of early Spanish absolutism . . . which work to suppress it." The accession to agency by Don Quixote, strictly refunctioned through the abject and the burlesque, was clearly recognized by Saint-Amant, who inserts it into his own marginal discourse.[9] Upon the abject tapestry on the *débauché's* wall, ekphrasis within ekphrasis, grotesque within grotesque, Don Quixote's world becomes the model against which the chamber reveals its countersocial values and that links them to text production as subversion.

Saint-Amant shows in this poem that he was a most acute reader of *Don Quixote*. He did read it as a funny book—we still do, of course, as it is a funny book—but he also shows a keen awareness of other compositional and ideological aspects of Cervantes's book, such as the implications of the text's orientation to the reader, the structural relationship of interpolations to composition, and the relationship of the burlesque to the subject's autonomy. Thus, he seems a much more sophisticated reader, at least than those who appear in *Don Quixote II*, including Sansón Carrasco. The best readers of *Don Quixote* have often been themselves writers. Saint-Amant, one of the earliest, proves to be among the very best.

NOTES

I want to thank my colleague Carroll Coates for bringing the Saint-Amant poem to my attention.

1. César Oudin had rendered service to Henri de Navarre, the future Henri IV, in various diplomatic undertakings. He was a fervent Hispanist who produced, among other things, a grammar, a collection of proverbs, and a dictionary. In 1597 he became official secretary and interpreter of foreign languages for Henri de Navarre. He died in 1625 (Bardon 1971, 23–4).

2. I translate exclusively for sense.

3. In Hatzfeld and Darmesteter, *Dictionnaire géneral de la langue française: Du commencement du XVIIè siècle jusqu'à nos jours* [General Dictionary of the French Language: From the Beginning of the Seventeenth Century Through Our Times], under *enfumé*, the dictionary's third item reads: "3. *Fig.* Troubler le cerveau par les fumées du vin, l'esprit par les fumées de l'orgueil" [898: To confuse the brain with wine fumes, the spirit with pride's fumes].

4. On *débausche*, the same dictionary reads: "Dérèglement de conduite par excès de table ou par mauvaises moeurs" [627: Dissolute behavior due to excesses at table or evil morals]. On *débausché*: "Qui vit dans la débauche des moeurs. *Par plaisanterie*: Qui s'est détourné de ses occupations ordinaires" [627: One who turned to dissolute morals. In Jest: One who turned from his/her ordinary employment]. This latter sense situates *débausche* in the realm of the marginal, together, if not synonymous, with the writing of poetry. As I indicate later, the *débausche* transforms reality (as does poetry), and objects of daily use; they are *détournés* from their normal employment.

5. It was not uncommon among satirical and "libertin" writers to use Greek characters when writing risqué/obscene words. This also narrows down the text's readership to those "in the know," or in on the joke. The phenomenon is in itself interesting: it presupposes a set of educated readers who will understand the *clin d'oeil* and smile—although one would characterize this as a somewhat sophomoric kind of humor, a *lycée* sort of joke—but it likewise plays up to others who will also understand but may not agree with the writer's implicit stance, by the pretense of a code. Some readers may have seen the linguistic licentiousness displayed by Saint-Amant, here and in other poems, in his free use of regionalisms and of slang as precisely what the Académie would set to rights.

The use of marginal language—and in this instance the words in Greek could be located somewhere around the top of an ascending curve of illicit usage—solicits the complicitness of the reader. There are as well two possible moves implied here: only those educated enough to read Greek are worthy, and capable, of understanding; (this I offer as a mere possibility) I (Saint-Amant) show my respect for our great French language by not debasing it with the printing of such words that, even in this context, may be considered a bit rich. In any case, Saint-Amant was walking on thin ice—ideologically speaking—for most of his life, and was only saved from major problems by his very influential friends.

6. "The process by which the dominant social groups exclude and contain subordinate groups yet at times represent in writing many of the qualities of those groups in a kind of cultural play-acting produces a poetry that voices what is otherwise denied by the dominant culture. . . . What is striking about texts such as these is the overall tone of lighthearted defiance which gently mocks the social powers that have incarcerated the speaker" (Mariscal 1991, 136–7).

7. According to Kristeva, Smith says, "[t]he 'subject' experiences the abject in a way beyond or prior to subject relations . . . it is the mark of the painful difficulty for the 'subject' of being constituted in the semiotic/symbolic dialectic" (1974, 127). Thus the abject beckons and allows the subject to uncover an awareness of agency that precedes its social formation.

8. Saint-Amant in fact makes use of the three central taboos of our culture: food, waste products and sex. The final feast occurs, undisturbed, amid the room's filth and waste, while clandestine sexuality is implied in the *débausché's vérole*.

9. It is true, of course, that we may consider such texts, when addressing their subversive nature, as the productions allowed by the structures of power in order to reconfirm their authority, that their very subversiveness, their negation, implies the overarching authority they rise against. But it is also true that such texts offer subjectivities that manage to achieve at least transitory agency within a society whose thorough hierarchization makes such access increasingly restricted.

WORKS CITED

Bardon, Maurice. 1971. *Don Quichotte en France, 1605–1815*. Vol. 1. New York: Burt Franklin.

Hatzfeld, H., and A. Darmesteter. 1895–1900. *Dictionnaire de la langue Française: Des le début du XVIIè siècle jusqu'a nos jours*. C. Delagrave: Paris.

Kristeva, Julia. 1974. *La Révolution du langage poétique*. Paris: Seuil.

Mariscal, George. 1991. *Contradictory Subjects*. Ithaca: Cornell University Press.

Morier, Henri. 1961. *Dictionnaire de poétique et de rhétorique*. Paris: PUF.

Reynier, G. 1914. *Le Roman réaliste au XVIIè siècle*. Paris: Hachette.

Saint-Amant, Marc Antoine Gérard, sieur de. 1971. *Oeuvres*. Vol. 1. Edited by Jacques Bailbé. Paris: Marcel Didier.

Smith, Paul. 1988. *Discerning the Subject*. Minneapolis: University of Minnesota Press.

Comparative Anatomy: Cervantes's *Don Quixote* and Furetière's *Le Roman bourgeois*

JAMES A. PARR

It is not my purpose here to study the influence of Cervantes on Furetière—nor yet, as Borges might hazard, of Furetière on Cervantes. This is partly because I doubt there is any, in either direction, but also because such studies seem to be in disrepute these days. While it is considered unseemly to speak of the influence one mind may have exerted on another—there is, after all, a suggestion of surreptitious spirituality in all that—it seems acceptable in today's considerably less mindful, more materialist climate to discuss style as an expression of the inexorable functioning of language, while content becomes the inevitable product of class, race, gender, or some such construct that co-opts individuality and limits freedom of thought and expression. Clearly, some influences are acceptable, others are not. I leave the paradox for others to ponder and perhaps resolve.

It seems to me perfectly legitimate to seek out procedural and structural parallels between the two texts at hand, whether or not their elaboration is couched in the current coinage of narratology (e.g., intertextuality, hypertextuality, the disnarrated, etc.), while occasionally highlighting significant differences. A respectable comparative study will surely strive to display examples of both convergence and divergence. And it is always advisable at the outset, naturally, to acknowledge our common debt to Barthes, Kristeva, Todorov, Genette, Prince and co., lest the reader draw that most devastating of all possible inferences: that the writer is innocent of theory!

My procedure will be to comment first on what might be called the gross anatomy of the anatomies at hand, proceeding to an intermediate level of commonalities and differences, coming finally to more minute and detailed considerations. The progression, then, will be from the more general to the more specific. In doing so, I take my cue in part from Furetière himself, who follows a similar progression in the sequence of inventories that concludes part two, as we shall see shortly.

Both *Don Quixote* (*DQ* hereafter) and *Le Roman bourgeois* [The Bourgeois Novel,] (*Rb* hereafter) are products of the seventeenth century. Part I of Cervantes's major work appeared in 1605, Part II in 1615, while Furetière brought out both parts of his *ouvrage comique* [comic work]—so subtitled—in a single volume in 1666. There is greater continuity between Cervantes's two parts than between Furetière's. Indeed, the latter seems to delight in disorienting his reader by asserting complete control over the material and total freedom to do with it what he will; in the words to the reader preceding the *Livre second* [Second Book], that worthy is addressed with a curious mixture of superciliousness and aggressiveness (not unlike the posture of the dramatized author of the prologue to Part II of *DQ*, one might add):

> Si vous vous attendez, Lecteur, que ce livre soit la suite du premier, et qu'il y ait une connexité nécessaire entre eux, vous êtes pris pour dupe. (1981, 167)

> [Reader, if you expect this volume to be a continuation of the first one, and that there be a close connection between them, you have been sadly taken in.][1]

He goes on to advise the reader that his story is neither heroic nor fanciful but is, rather, a sober recounting of sometimes unrelated, even disconnected, events that will require the bookbinder's final touch if unity and proper sequence are to emerge from the mélange:

> Ce sont de petites histoires et aventures arrivées en divers quartiers de la ville [de Paris], qui n'ont rien de commun ensemble, et que je tâche de rapprocher les unes les autres autant qu'il m'est possible. Pour le soin de la liaison, je le laisse à celui qui reliera le livre. Prenez donc cela pour des historiettes séparées, si bon vous semble, et ne demandez point que j'observe ni l'unité des temps ni des lieux, ni que je fasse voir un héros dominant sur toute la pièce. (167)

> [These are occurrences and happenings that have taken place in various parts of the city, which have nothing in common as a group, and which I am attempting to join together as best I can. I leave the final touch in this process to the person who will bind the book. Accept this as a series of disjointed anecdotes, if you will, and don't expect me to observe the unities of time and place, nor that I make the work revolve around a single protagonist.]

Probably we shall never know whether the bookbinder did his duty as anticipated, but there is a curious parallel with the printers of Cervantes's Part I, who are also held responsible for certain sins of omission and commission, specifically Sancho's disappearing and reappearing ass.

The "romantic" rebellion against classical norms evident in the passage just cited is more reminiscent of Lope de Vega than of Cervantes, whose rejection of models centers on more contemporary texts. As something of a classicist, Cervantes would likely have looked askance at the wholesale disparagement of classical norms and, needless to say, he does rely on one central figure throughout both parts of *DQ*, albeit a mock-hero rather than a hero. One might venture that the loosely connected and often disparate adventures related in the 1605 Part I have more in common with Furetière's theory and practice than could be said of the 1615 Part II, for in it one senses an almost palpable concern for unity and a corresponding reluctance to digress.

One additional consideration pertaining to gross anatomy is necessarily the question of genre. The satiric thrust of both works is apparent, although it is more subtle in *DQ*. Some would grant that Cervantes's masterpiece is, superficially, a satire of the books of chivalry that so obsessed the main character but would maintain, nevertheless, that it is more properly read as the first modern novel. I have taken up the issue elsewhere and cannot rehearse the argument here, but, for now, I would say that it is essential to distinguish between parody and satire in this instance (parody is more likely to inform satire than the other way around), and would also point out that the picaresque looms large in the background. *DQ* is arguably an alternative, or countergenre, not just to the romances of chivalry but also to *Lazarillo de Tormes* and *Guzmán de Alfarache*.

Furetière too is responding to kinds of writing he finds less than appealing. In his case, first among these would be the novel itself, as it had begun to develop in the preceding decades. Frequently he will call attention to the fact that he could have extended this or that description or character depiction, but opts instead to suppress that information in the interest of brevity and, also, artistic integrity. Surely he had in mind such absurdities as La Calprenède's *Cléopâtre* of 1647, a stream-of-consciousness narrative that filled twenty-four volumes and four thousand pages, as Jacques Prévot points out in the preface to his standard edition of the *Rb*. Other narrative types that seem to have incurred his disfavor are the pastoral and the heroic adventure story (sometimes the retelling of an epic, in prose), both of which descend from antiquity.

It seems clear, then, that whatever other motivations may have prompted them, both Cervantes and Furetière were led to pen the texts that interest us here in response to what they considered inferior kinds of writing circulating in their respective *moments et milieux* [moments and environments]. Cervantes was able to present a viable alternative, announcing both the realistic and self-conscious forms of the novel, and his effort met with great success. Furetière is witty, but he lacks the fine sense of irony we associate with Cervantes. The Frenchman is caustic and sententious. He seems more interested in dismantling the novel and venting his spleen at Charles Sorel than in creating something new and different. Had it been within his power, he would have nipped the novel in the bud. Prévot claims to see foreshadowings of Balzac and Flaubert in Furetière's negative portrayals of the bourgeoisie, and there is surely some truth in what he says, but that is a fairly minor achievement alongside Cervantes's prescient prose. At the other extreme of Cervantes's spectacular success with *DQ*, Furetière's *Rb* fell flat on its frontispiece.

There is a significant commonality, nevertheless, in the implicit desire to educate the reading public by inculcating a certain skepticism toward the authority of the printed page and also a fairly explicit probing of what it means to be bourgeois, in the case of Furetière, and what it means to belong to the common herd, the *vulgo*, in the case of Cervantes. Don Quixote is seldom more eloquent than when he articulates the unconventional notion that being "common," or sharing the mind-set of the *vulgo*, is not a factor of class but of outlook, and that outlook can sometimes be found even among the nobility:

Y no penséis, señor, que lo llamo aquí vulgo solamente a la gente plebeya y humilde; que todo aquel que no sabe, aunque sea señor y príncipe, puede y debe entrar en número de vulgo. (II:16)

[And please do not think, sir, that by "*vulgo*" I refer only to the lower classes; for anyone who is obtuse (or uninformed), even if he is a lord or a prince, can and should be considered common.]

One of the better studies I have found on the *Rb*, and one that sets out specifically to reassess the work in a more positive light than is usually cast upon it, is by Ulrich Döring. Among other thought-provoking comments, the one following is especially pertinent to the present discussion:

Le but de Furetière n'est pas de se moquer de sa classe sociale, mais de développer un idéal de la personalité qui soit aussi accessible pour un noble que pour un bourgeois. (1986, 418)

[It is not Furetière's objective to poke fun at his social class, but rather to make manifest an ideal type of personality that is accessible to both the nobility and the bourgeoisie.]

Döring argues for a rereading of the *Rb* that would emphasize the constructive, educative dimension of its satire, focusing at the same time on a separation of characters who display the positive quality of autonomy (Angélique and Laurence) versus those who remain mired in the bourgeois mind-set, which is unduly respectful of authority. A proper education is the key to creating the autonomous personality Furetière favors, according to Döring.

Now Charles Sorel had previously published an antinovel of sorts, the *Berger extravagant* (Extravagant/Absurd Shepherd), in which he parodies pastoral romance, so it is not surprising that Furetière should switch locales completely for his own send-up of solemn story-telling, concentrating instead on an urban setting. The attitude displayed by the French academician toward his literary rival is suggestively similar to that of Cervantes toward Lope de Vega. The Spaniard does not go so far as to disguise Lope as a character, as Furetière will do with Sorel in his roman à clef—calling him Charroselles and depicting him as one of the more monstruous denizens of the degraded and "depersonalized" world he inhabits (see Thiher, 1969)—but there are any number of pointedly negative remarks in *DQ* referring to that other Monster of Nature.

Finally, on the matter of genre, the dramatized author of the preface to Furetière's second part makes an extremely insightful observation:

Que si vous y vouliez chercher cette grande regularité que vous n'y trouverez pas, sachez seulement que la faute ne serait pas dans l'ouvrage, mais dans le titre: ne l'appelez plus roman, et il ne vous choquera point, en qualité de récit d'aventures particulières. (1981, 168)

[For if you must seek in it an impressive uniformity that is not to be found there, be aware that the flaw is not in the work but in your terminology: don't call it a novel, and you won't be surprised by its status as a collection of episodes involving various individuals.]

In other words, don't call it a novel and you won't be shocked at the liberties taken with that literary form. The importance of calling things by their right names is implicit. Our expectations of a text are conditioned to a considerable degree by the sense of genre we bring to bear on it. If we approach *DQ* assuming it to be a novel, we will look for—and, miraculously, sometimes find—things it does not offer, such as character development. Would that a disclaimer such as the one quoted above were to be found somewhere in *DQ*! But it did not occur to Cervantes, for his conceptual universe would not allow it. For him, *roman* would have been an alien notion, and novel (*novela*) meant a short story in the Italian manner, a novella. His lexicon offered *historia*, meaning both history and story—and he gets as much mileage from that concept as one could hope for—along with *vida* (used by both saints and pícaros) and *libro* (as in "books of chivalry"). His practice was prodigious, however, even if his theory was limited, and it behooves the modern critic to set certain things right, beginning by calling the literary forms he cultivated by their right names. It may be unrealistic to speak of progress in art, but it is fair to say that there has been progress in the scientific study of art, which, for present purposes, means genology and narratology.

If Furetière offers us an antinovel, Cervantes's contibution is an antiromance primarily, but also an antinovel of a different stripe. This is so because of its implicit confrontation of the picaresque, a nascent form of the novel. Both *DQ* and the *Rb* are predominantly satires, but their targets are not primarily the obvious ones. Furetière fustigates the bourgeoisie, of that there is no doubt, but it seems to me that a larger concern is for literature. Cervantes ostensibly censures literature of several kinds, but, again, he has other fish to fry. If Furetière uses society as a platform from which to make a statement about literature, Cervantes will present as a critique of literature what is, in a broader perspective, a commentary on a sociopolitical agenda. He incarnates that agenda in Don Quixote and his muddle-headed mission, and it is simply the notion that there was once a pristine past, a national sociopolitical golden age, which seventeenth-century society can somehow recapture.

The common concern for literature must be taken seriously in both instances, it seems to me, and it is not my intent to suggest that Cervantes is less than serious in that preoccupation. His concern for literature is so transparent and so ubiquitous that it needs no further elaboration. I merely hope to show that it is nevertheless subordinate to the less obvious one having to do with discrediting the mad quest for a nonexistent, and therefore irretrievable, place of plenitude and plenty back there somewhere in the mists of time.

Furetière's interest in literature is sometimes seen as a negative

one, since he seems to focus primarily on censuring other writers
and kinds of writing. Jean Serroy has maintained, however, that he
belongs to a long line of illustrious writers, from Rabelais to Jules
Romains, who are fascinated by inventories, lists of things, and the
pure materiality of language. This is to give him greater credit than
he deserves, it seems to me. While Rabelais does indeed love lists,
he compiles them with wit and panache; they are scurrilous, scato-
logical, sexual—but, more than anything, they are creative. They
are indeed material in nature, for they tend to relate to the lower
stratum of the material body. Furetière, on the other hand, is a fussy
pedant whose lists betray his legal training and practice, along with
certain stylistic obsessions. There is precious little originality in the
verbose and otiose compilations that conclude Part II. They serve
the dubious design of bringing matters to an end, not with a bang
but a whimper. But to give credit where it is due, there is a certain
logic to the presentation, in that the focus shifts progressively from
larger entities to smaller ones. An inventory of a recently deceased
writer's possessions leads to an inventory of his books, which leads
to a lengthy listing of the chapter headings of one book in particular, a certain "*Somme Dedicatoire*, ou examen general de toutes les
questions qui se peuvent faire touchant la dedicace des livres,
divisée en quatre volumes" [1981, 234: *Dedication Summation*, or
overview of all the questions that can be asked concerning dedica-
tions of books, divided into four tomes]. The list of chapter headings occupies a full ten pages! But there is more. The last chapter
of volume four points to yet another list, this one consisting of suggested payments to authors for composing verse in specified metri-
cal forms or for creating various characters, descriptions, and plot
situations in prose fiction. This new way of assessing the value of a
manuscript would presumably replace the then-current practice of
purchasing it by the sheet or folio.

Now all of these inventories that wrap up Part II are read aloud
by one character for the benefit of his interlocutors. In this regard,
they mirror the reading aloud of other kinds of texts, with which
Part I concludes. And, clearly, there is a parallel with the reading
aloud of "El curioso impertinente" [The Tale of Impertinent Curi-
osity], the Italianate novella interpolated in Part I of *DQ*, by the
village priest for the benefit of his fellow travelers at the inn of Juan
Palomeque. In all these instances, the instability and porosity of the
frame that supposedly sets apart the text—a frame largely provided
by the bookbinder of previous mention—is revealed for what it is:
an arbitrarily drawn line in the sand separating what is inside from
what is outside. We as readers might be said to migrate into the

text to join the audience of fictional characters, while these, in turn, transgress that same boundary to join us, momentarily, on the outside, as they become more "real." In the process, we may begin to question our own privileged status. Derrida's paradoxical pronouncement is pertinent: "Il y a du cadre, mais le cadre n'existe pas" [1978, 93: There is framing, but the frame, as such, is nonexistent]. In other words, there is indeed a perceptible process of framing, but, ultimately, the frame is illusory, whether in painting or in prose. Both Furetière and Cervantes (along with any number of others) anticipate the insight, more in practice than in theory.

The relationship between reality and the representation of reality offered by the two texts cannot be dismissed quite so easily. Cervantes has a series of narrative voices that assure us that what we are reading is *historia verdadera*, fact rather than fiction. In other words, it claims to be a faithful rendering of something that did indeed happen outside the book, in external reality, in real time and space. But we know that he protests too much; we know that we are reading fiction, for the pointers to that protocol are less ambiguous, and more ubiquitous, than those pretending it is true history.

Furetière is a bit more subtle in this instance, but he too makes clear that he expects his reader to suspend disbelief. He presents himself as truthful and sincere ("ce très véritable et très sincère récit" [1981, 167: this very truthful and very sincere account]), and as someone who is making every effort to include all pertinent information, who will, indeed, provide any new information that may come to light in the future ("Que si je puis avoir quelques nouvelles . . . je vous promets, foi de auteur, que je vous en ferai part" [158: For if any new information comes my way . . . I promise you, on my honor as an author, to share it with you]). Just how this conspiratorial pact between author and reader is to be consummated is not at all clear. In any event, it is another *effet de réel* [reality effect] that serves to substantiate truthfulness and sincerity and, thereby, the pretense that this is reality and not a simulacrum. Compare Cide Hamete Benengeli's apparently truthful and sincere disclaimer regarding the extraordinary happenings in the Cave of Montesinos: "Tú, lector, pues eres prudente, juzga lo que te pareciere, que yo no debo ni puedo más" [II:24: You, reader, as a prudent person, draw your own inference, for I am not obliged, nor am I able, to do more].

The reader, or narratee, is frequently apostrophized in both texts, sometimes through asides, other times via direct address. The counterpart of Cide Hamete's overture, cited above, might be the following:

Si ce proverbe est véritable, tel maître tel valet, vous pouvez juger (mon cher lecteur, qu'il y a, ce me semble, longtemps que n'ai apostrophé) quel sera le maître dont vous attendez sans doute que je vous fasse le portrait. (1981, 192)

[If the servant resembles his master, as the saying has it, you can ascertain (my dear reader, since it has been a long time, it seems to me, since I addressed you) what the master must be like, the one you are no doubt expecting me to sketch for you.]

The implicit apology for having neglected the reader is perhaps the most interesting aspect. The narratee envisioned by the text seems invariably to be a social and intellectual peer, someone who can occasionally be addressed ironically, but who will usually be treated with deference and a modicum of respect. The narratees of Cervantes's text have yet to be studied in detail, but it seems reasonable to assume that each identifiable narrator can be matched with a corresponding narratee, whose profile can be inferred from the manner of address, assumptions made in that address, and so forth. The inferred author is quite a different construct, but it can also reasonably be assumed that he, in turn, infers an ideal (and also, perhaps, an educable) reader whose image(s) he has before him as he pens the work. These two varieties of reader can be called the *discretos* and the *vulgo*, or the percipient and naive types. The Furetière one infers from reading his text assumes only one type of reader, the percipient or discreet sort. Unlike Cervantes, he shows little inclination to follow Horace's advice on combining the useful with the sweet by offering instruction in aesthetic distance or related reading strategies.

The device of having texts read aloud within a longer text has been mentioned. And there is evident in all this a common concern for careful composition, although not necessarily for reception. These texts are critiqued (only in the respective Parts I) by one or more of those who have shared the experience of reception, and usually found wanting in some regard. In addition, both authors offer examples of obsessive readers, while pointing to the pernicious effects of this sort of maniacal dedication. The prehistory of Don Quixote, summarized in the first few pages, is precisely that of an obsessive consumer of one particular kind of fiction. Furetière gives us a female character who in certain ways anticipates Madame Bovary and who is seduced into reading by one of her suitors. When the poor Javotte receives a parcel from her admirer, Pancrace, containing the four parts (said here to be in five volumes) of Honoré d'Urfé's *L'Astrée* [Astraea]:

Elle courut à sa chambre, s'enferma a verrou, et se mit à lire jour et nuit avec tant d'ardeur qu'elle en perdait le boire et le manger. (1981, 143)

[She ran to her room, bolted her door, and proceeded to read day and night with such passion that she forsook both food and drink.]

Shades of Don Quixote! Like him, she is also led to imitate the characters about whom she has read. She begins to live literature. The narrator proceeds to offer one of his frequent editorials, this one dealing with the dangers of reading for certain types of people, particularly impressionable young women:

Il arrive la même chose pour la lecture: si elle a été interdite à une fille curieuse, elle s'y jettera à corps perdu, et sera d'autant plus en danger que, prenant les livres sans choix et sans discrétion, elle en pourra trouver quelqu'un qui d'abord lui corrompra l'esprit. Tel entre ceux-là est l'*Astrée*: plus il exprime naturellement les passions amoureuses, et mieux elles s'insinuent dans les jeunes âmes, où il se glisse un venin imperceptible, qui a gagné le coeur avant qu'on puisse avoir pris du contrepoison. Ce n'est pas comme ces autres romans où il n'y a que des amours de princes et de paladins, qui, n'ayant rien de proportionné avec les personnes du commun, ne les touchent point, et ne font point naître d'envie de les imiter. (144)

[The same holds true for reading: if an inquisitive young woman has been denied access to books, she will take to them with a passion, and will be in even greater danger for, drawing upon them indiscriminately, she may well come upon one that will corrupt her mind. *L'Astrée* is just such a book, since, by its very nature, it makes manifest amorous passions, and these readily infiltrate the minds of the young, where an imperceptible poison insinuates itself, overpowering the emotions before an antidote can be administered. It is not like those other novels that recount the loves of nobles and knights, who, being so very different from ordinary folk, have no effect on such readers, and do not foster a desire to emulate them.]

The final sentence might be seen as evidence that Furetière did not know *DQ*, for Alonso Quijano's problem is precisely that he is inspired to imitate persons well above his station, the amorous and adventurous princes and paladins he has read about.

There are other curious similarities and differences between characters in the two works. The brutish Belastre, who is unexpectedly made a judge despite his total lack of qualifications, is remindful of Sancho Panza, the accidental governor of Barataria who, in that capacity, is called on to render several judicial opinions—one of which is decidedly Solomonic. The major difference is that Sancho is wise, witty, and likeable, while Belastre is a dolt who has no redeeming qualities.

The narrative transitions between Sancho on Barataria and Don Quixote at the ducal palace in Part II are mirrored in the *Rb*. Cervantes's narrator will frequently say something like "ello [the background to the fracas with the felines] se dirá a su tiempo, que Sancho Panza nos llama, y el buen concierto de la historia lo pide" [1984, II:48: that matter will be recounted in due course, but Sancho Panza claims our attention, and the proper progression of the story demands it]. Furetière, transitioning from Lucrèce to Nicodème, will make comments like "je veux la laisser [Lucrèce] un peu reposer, car il ne faut pas tant travailler une personne enceinte" [1981, 84: I'll let her rest a bit, for one mustn't make someone who is pregnant work too hard]. Maternity leave, if you will. When it comes time to dispense with Nicodème, we find this less than sentimental send-off:

> Le voilà donc libre pour aller fournir encore la matière de quelque autre histoire de même nature. Mais je ne suis pas assuré qu'il vienne encore paraître sur la scène: il faut maintenant qu'il fasse place à d'autres; et, afin que vous n'en soyez pas étonnés, imaginez-vous qu'il soit ici tué, massacré, ou assassiné par quelque aventure, comme il serait facile de le faire à un auteur peu consciencieux. (147–48)

> [So there he is, free to go provide further material for some other story of the same sort. But I am not sanguine about his reappearance on this stage: he must now give way to others; and, so that you will not be surprised when he fails to reappear, imagine that he has now been killed, massacred, or assassinated by chance, as it would be easy for a less conscientious author to do to him.]

Furetière eschews the easy way out, "character assassination," sending Nicodème in search of new adventures instead, and, possibly, in search of an author. He has effectively been given his walking papers as far as this story is concerned.

A final point of contact within this midrange of similarities and differences centers on negative characterization, that is, on the way narrators present characters on whom little love is lost. One way of doing this is to introduce the question of audience, making clear that the character is foolish and absurd for not taking audience into account. In the *Rb*, Charroselles is a pompous ass who vents his spleen on any occasion, even when his audience is uncomprehending:

Charroselles sourit de cette belle approbation, et insensiblement prit occasion, en parlant de vers, de déclamer contre tous les auteurs qu'il con-
naissait, et il n'y en eut pas un, bon ou mauvais, qui ne passât par sa
critique, sans prendre garde s'il parlait à des personnes capables de cet
entretien. (1981, 219)

[Charroselles smiled at this lovely approbation, and subtly seized the
opportunity, while speaking of poetry, to hold forth against all the authors he knew, and there was not a single one, good or bad, who escaped
his criticism, without taking into account whether he was addressing
those capable of understanding him.]

Don Quixote too makes an inappropriate speech, the one on the
golden age, to an audience of illiterate goatherds (and Sancho),
none of whom has even a glimmer of what he is talking about:

Toda esta larga arenga—que se pudiera muy bien escusar—dijo nuestro
caballero, porque las bellotas que le dieron le trujeron a la memoria la
edad dorada, y antojósele hacer aquel inútil razonamiento a los ca-
breros, que, sin respondelle palabra, embobados y suspensos, le estuvie-
ron escuchando. Sancho asimesmo callaba y comía bellotas, y visitaba
muy a menudo el segundo zaque. . . . (1984, I:11)

[Our knight delivered this entire lengthy harangue—which could very
well have been left unsaid—because the acorns they gave him brought
to mind the golden age, prompting him to make that useless speech to
the goatherds, who, perplexed and amazed, took it all in. Sancho too
kept silent but continued eating acorns, while visiting the second wine-
skin with some regularity. . . .]

The narrator makes clear his disapprobation, describing the perora-
tion as pointless, and observing that it might very well have been
left unsaid. Whether the text-speaker here is Cide Hamete, the second author, or the editorial voice I have called the supernarrator, the
ironic treatment of the main character—established already in the
title itself and maintained through the prologue, festive preliminary
verses, and first eight chapters—undeniably continues unabated.

The final point of contact I would consider takes us into the third
phase, the realm of the minute and often overlooked. It has to do
with the other side of the coin, disnarration rather than narration,
in other words, with what is suppressed, elided, or is so seemingly
inconsequential that it falls below the threshold of narrativity. As I
observed earlier, Furetière frequently suppresses material, ostensibly in the interest of artistic integrity and concern for the reader. A

typical example occurs early on, when it comes time to describe the locale where most of the action will transpire, *la place Maubert*:

> Un autre auteur moins sincère, et qui voulait paraître éloquent, ne manquerait jamais de faire ici un description magnifique de cette place. Il commencerait son éloge par l'origine de son nom; il dirait. . . . (30)

> [Another less forthcoming author, who might like to pass for eloquent, would never miss the chance to present here a magnificent description of this square. He would begin his elegy with the origin of its name; he would say. . . .]

Despite the disclaimer, he proceeds to offer a description of sorts, although perhaps not as detailed as his less-sincere counterparts might have presented. This strategy of closing the front door, only to smuggle in the material by the back door, is reminiscent of Cervantes's technique of "not" describing Don Diego de Miranda's house:

> Aquí pinta el autor todas las circunstancias de la casa de don Diego, pintándonos en ellas lo que contiene una casa de un caballero labrador y rico; pero al traductor desta historia le pareció pasar estas y otras semejantes menudencias en silencio, porque no venían bien con el propósito principal de la historia; la cual más tiene su fuerza en la verdad que en las frías digresiones. (1981, II:18)

> [Here the author describes Don Diego's house in considerable detail, sketching in all the things the home of a well-to-do gentleman farmer contains; but the translator of this story opted to pass over these details in silence, because they did not conform to the main thrust of the story, whose essence lies in its truthfulness, not in tedious digressions.]

Cervantes's strategy is to focalize the scene through the eyes of the main character, letting him make the description that is suppressed at the diegetic level:

> Halló don Quijote ser la casa de don Diego de Miranda ancha como de aldea; las armas, empero, aunque de piedra tosca, encima de la puerta de la calle; la bodega, en el patio; la cueva, en el portal, y muchas tinajas a la redonda. . . . (II:18)

> [Don Quixote found Don Diego de Miranda's home to be a spacious country house; the coat of arms, although made of rough stone, above the main entrance; recently pressed, fermenting wine, in the patio; the cellar, near the entrance, and a quantity of large wine jars all about. . . .]

The recourse to the mimetic as a way of bringing in the description, despite the misgivings of the translator, represents a more subtle strategy than simply telling the reader one thing, then proceeding to do the opposite at the diegetic, or narrative, level.

Much later, in Part Two, Furetière will bring forward a quite different justification for disnarration:

> Si j'étais de ces gens qui se nourrissent de romans, c'est-à-dire qui vivent des livres qu'ils vendent, j'aurais ici une belle occasion de grossir ce volume et de tromper un marchand qui l'achèterait à la feuille. Comme je n'ai pas ce dessein, je veux passer sous silence cette conversation, et vous dire seulement que l'homme le plus complaisant ne prêta jamais une plus longue audience que fit Charroselles. . . . (1981, 175)

> [If I were one of those who puts food on the table by writing novels, that is, someone who lives off the books he sells, I would have here a wonderful opportunity to pad this volume and trick a publisher who would purchase it by the sheet. Since that is not my intent, I shall pass silently over this conversation, and tell you only that the most obliging of men never participated in a more lengthy hearing than did Charroselles. . . .]

Cervantes utilizes other pretexts in order to offer a gamut of variations on disnarration, but let me cite only one, which I consider to be a playful—but at the same time magisterial—conflation of two aspects of the disnarrated, namely the nonnarrated (or elided) and the nonnarratable (consisting of details unworthy of narration):

> Sucedió, pues, que en más de seis días no le sucedió cosa *digna* de ponerse en escritura, al cabo de los cuales, yendo fuera de camino, le tomó la noche entre unas espesas encinas o alcornoques; que en esto no guarda la puntualidad Cide Hamete que en otras cosas suele. (1984, II:60)

> [It turned out, then, that during an entire week nothing worth transcribing happened to him, at which point, having left the highway, night overtook him in a grove of oaks or cork trees; here Cide Hamete is not as attentive to detail as is his custom.]

Hard upon the suppression of the events and conversations of six entire days comes the quibble over the kind of tree providing shelter, as the nonnarrated gives way to the nonnarratable (details so insignificant as to fall below the level of narrativity)—all of this within the confines of a single short paragraph. There is nothing—nor should we expect anything—in Furetière to parallel this amazingly proleptic juxtaposition of the two techniques. Cervantes is writing near the beginning of the seventeenth century; Gerald Prince will detail and assign names to these phenomena near the end of the twentieth century.

At times it behooves the critic also to practice disnarration, passing over a multitude of things that might have been said, both in the interest of brevity and out of concern for his reader. This brief incursion into commonalities and differences is not a study of intertextuality, as it is commonly understood, nor yet of Genette's hypertextuality, although it might be said to partake of the latter to a limited degree (Genette 1982, 16). Rigorously applied, both phenomena posit citing, rewriting, absorbing, or transforming through imitation, none of which are perceptible in Furetière vis-à-vis Cervantes. I would argue that the coincidences are nevertheless noteworthy, while the disparities may be even more so, since they serve to highlight the remarkable achievement that *DQ* represents in European literature. There is, in addition, a larger sense of intertextuality that does come into play, having to do with the generic tradition to which both texts belong, Menippean satire. Both look back, each in its own way, to the venerable tradition of Menippus and his many successors. Of those descendants, it would seem to be Horace's relatively restrained approach that is echoed in *DQ*, while Furetière's more acerbic censures bring to mind the less-engaging, more personalized, frontal attacks of Juvenal. Don Quixote himself distinguishes between the two traditions, and it is as though he foresaw and were describing Furetière's personal attack on Charles Sorel (a.k.a. Charroselles), all the while looking back to the unnamed but readily identifiable Juvenal:

> Riña vuesa merced a su hijo si hiciere sátiras que perjudiquen las honras ajenas, y castíguele, y rómpaselas; pero si hiciere sermones al modo de Horacio, donde reprehenda los vicios en general, como tan elegantemente él lo hizo, alábale; porque lícito es al poeta escribir contra la invidia, y decir en sus versos mal de los invidiosos, y así de otros vicios, con que no señale persona alguna. . . . (1984, II:16)

> [Scold your son if he writes invectives that damage anyone's reputation, and chastise him, and tear them up; but if he writes satires in the manner of Horace, where vice in general is reproached, as he did so elegantly, praise him; because it is proper for poets to condemn envy and speak ill of the envious in their verses, and also of other vices, provided they do not single out any one person. . . .]

I hope I have not set up Furetière as a straw man in order to score points for his Spanish predecessor; Cervantes needs no publicity agent, whereas Furetière's work is sufficient unto itself—it does what it sets out to do, whether or not that agenda meets, then or now, with the widespread approbation of readers. Cervantes situates himself within the Horatian satiric tradition, while Furetière opts for the more splenetic Juvenalian approach. Largely as a consequence of those choices, the *Rb* comes across today as timebound, narrowly focused, and quaint—a slice of bourgeois life for a select minority, unlikely to appeal to a wide spectrum of readers—while *DQ*, originally a pop art production of modest aspirations, continues to seduce both popular and erudite audiences.

NOTES

1. All translations are my own. There are none of the *Rb*, and, although there are two very fine ones of *DQ*, I prefer to render Cervantes's prose in my own words. The two best translations available at the moment are Jarvis's, edited by E. C. Riley (Oxford 1992), and Burton Raffel's (Norton 1995). Riley's edition of Jarvis comes closer to reproducing the tone and tenor of Cervantes's original, albeit in British English, while Raffel's makes the book more accessible to the modern North American reader.

WORKS CITED (AND OTHERS UNCITED)

Bareau, Michel, et al., eds. 1987. *Les contes de Perrault: La contestation et ses limites. Furetière. Actes de Banff-1986.* Tübingen: Papers on Seventeenth-Century French Literature / Biblio 17.

Cervantes Saavedra, Miguel de. 1998. *El ingenioso hidalgo don Quijote de la Mancha.* Edited by Salvador Fajardo and James A. Parr. Asheville, N.C.: Pegasus Press.

Derrida, Jacques. 1978. *La vérité en peinture.* Paris: Flammarion.

Döring, Ulrich. 1987. "De l'autorité à l'autonomie: *Le Roman bourgeois*, roman pédagogique." In *Actes de Banff*, edited by Michel Bareau et al. Tübingen: Papers on Seventeenth-Century French Literature / Biblio 17.

Furetière, Antoine. 1981. *Le Roman bourgeois: Ouvrage comique.* Edited by Jacques Prévot. Paris: Gallimard.

Genette, Gérard. 1982. *Palimpsestes: La littérature au second degré.* Paris: Seuil.

Giardina, Calogéro. 1993. *Narration, burlesque, et langage dans* Le Roman bourgeois *d'Antoine Furetière.* Paris: Archives des lettres modernes.

Parr, James A. 1988. Don Quixote: *An Anatomy of Subversive Discourse.* Newark, Del.: Juan de la Cuesta.

———. 1991. Plato, Cervantes, Derrida: Framing Speaking and Writing in *Don Quixote.* In *On Cervantes: Essays for L. A. Murillo*, edited by James A. Parr. Newark, Del.: Juan de la Cuesta.

———. 1994. Antimodelos narrativos del *Quijote*: Lo desnarrado, innarrado e innarrable. In *Actas: Asociación Internacional de Hispanistas. Irvine*, 1994. Edited by Juan Villegas. Irvine, Cal.: University of California. 5: 134–40.

Prince, Gerald. 1969. "The Disnarrated." *Style* 22: 1–8.

Serroy, Jean. 1969. "Scarron/Furetière inventaire de l'inventaire." *Littératures classiques* 11: 211–9.

Thiher, Roberta J. 1969. "The Depersonalized World of the *Roman bourgeois*." *Romance Notes* 11: 127–9.

Vialet, Michèle. 1987. *Triomphe del'iconoclaste:* Le Roman bourgeois *et les lois de cohérence romanesque*. Tübingen: Papers on Seventeenth-Century French Literature / Biblio 17.

Wine, Kathleen. 1981. "Furetière's *Roman bourgeois*: The Triumph of Process." *L'Esprit Créateur* 19, no. 1: 50–63.

Part III
Subjectivity and Identity

Transgendering the Mystical Voice: Angela de Foligno, San Juan, Santa Teresa, Luisa de Carvajal

ANNE J. CRUZ

The familiar early modern exemplars of lyric poetry, from Petrarch's *rime sparse* to Góngora's Baroque sonnets, ground their poetic voice, what has been called an *énonciation* or speech event, in a fictionality nonetheless dependent on the act of mimesis or representation. Recent studies on Renaissance theories of imitation by Thomas Greene and George Pigman, among others, have taught us that the Renaissance poet understood and practiced *imitatio* as a means of negotiating the unresolved tensions that at once precluded, on the one hand, complete submission to classical authority and, on the other, total demarcation of personal autonomy. Either because critics are continually seduced by the poems' apparent authenticity, however, or tend to privilege Baroque complexity and intentionality over Renaissance lucidity and symmetry, such poets as Garcilaso de la Vega and Francisco de Aldana are repeatedly relegated to the "natural" side of a poetic nature / culture dichotomy in opposition to the Baroque's more "writerly" language.[1]

Yet it is due precisely to the highly cultured artifice of Garcilaso's verses that Daniel Heiple claims to dissociate himself from a host of critics, from Marcelino Menéndez y Pelayo to Rafael Lapesa, by viewing the poet "less as a real lover expressing his unrequited passion and more as a serious thinker struggling with new material and norms of poetic expression" (1994, xi). Heiple's exacting analyses restore rhetorical control to the poet, showing how, in the *Eclogues* especially, the emotion-laden poetic voice is distanced from the disinterested narrator (23). The temporal split between narrator and poetic voice uncovers the lack of unity that is generally masked in lyric poems, where, as Inés Azar reminds us, the "I" of the poet barely disguises the fractured voices of fractured selves: "The speakers . . . appear suspended in their grief, torn between silence

127

and the impersonal, between the pronouns, that will keep the integrity of self but only as a reflexive, redundant 'I,' and all the other words, that will depict the self but only as a displaced fragmented object" (1989, 35).

In his analysis of Garcilaso's sonnet on the myth of Hero and Leander, Eric Graf further exposes the poet's inability to reconcile the female / male dialectic inscribed in the sonnet's hermaphroditic subject and form. The poem, he tells us, "slowly deconstructs the masculine dominance of Leander until we are left only with his dying cry" (1994, 171). Although he remains silent on Hero, Graf conclusively demonstrates that Leander's failure to achieve sexual union in turn negates Platonic reunion, and that both incompletions emblematize the instability of the poetic self. Indeed, the poem ends with a temporal and logical inversion that orchestrates our emotional reaction to the poem by reversing its narrative sequence. We are apprised of the failure of Leander's plea even before Leander desperately entreats the feminine waves (*ondas*) to grant him reprieve from a watery death until after he consummates his love:

> como pudo esforzó su voz cansada,
> y a las ondas habló desta manera,
> (mas nunca fue su voz de ellas oída):
> —Ondas, pues no se escusa que yo muera
> dejadme allá llegar, y a la tornada
> vuestro furor esecutá en mi vida. (Garcilaso 1966, 101)

> [He strove mightily to force his tired voice,
> addressing the waves in the following manner,
> (yet his voice was never heard by them):
> "Oh, waves, since there is no reprieve from death,
> allow me to reach the shore and on my return
> vent your fury upon my life."][2]

The poem's audience is made doubly aware of Leander's poetic voice through his direct speech as well as by its placement out of sequence, that is, after its disregard by the unhearing waves. While the split between the poetic and the narrative voices transmits the lover's—and by extension, the poet's—ontological precariousness, the speech act's function is to give the illusion of subjectivity, to represent a self that, at the moment of pronouncement, has, nevertheless, already ceased to exist.

Yet the lyric's self-engendering strategies also necessarily involve an act of self-gendering. What no one questions, not even Graf, who has teased out the poem's confrontationally gendered rhyme scheme, is that for Garcilaso, as for other Renaissance poets, the lover's "self," regardless of its fragmentation and displacement, reflects the poet's gender. It is as much the poem's sexual verisimilitude—the male poet speaking "naturally" in a masculine poetic voice—as its textual authenticity, in Paul Julian Smith's phrase, its "rhetoric of presence," that invokes immediacy and elicits emotion. The male poet's textual persona depends on the illusion of a masculine corporeality that in turn genders its poetic voice. This phenomenon would seem self-evident, were it not for the fact that some have on occasion chosen to break with the grammar of the "same" to speak in what I term a transgendered voice. By this, I do not mean poems whose feminine voices are ventriloquized by male authors, such as the medieval romance lyrics of the *chansons de femmes*, the Mozarabic *jarchas*, or the Galician *cantigas de amigo*, which, although informed by feminine desire, were most likely composed by male poets.[3] Their authorial anonymity precludes individuation and, since many descend from a popular tradition of women's songs and dances, their female voices are more akin to theatrical dialogue than to lyrical expression.[4] Instead, I am referring here to instances when transgendering occurs in poems written by such religious writers as San Juan de la Cruz, Santa Teresa, and Luisa de Carvajal y Mendoza.

If San Juan de la Cruz's *Canción I: Cántico espiritual's* "Canciones entre el alma y el esposo" [*Spiritual Canticle*, Songs between the Soul and the Bridegroom] articulates both the male and female voices of the two spouses, his *Noche oscura del alma* [*Dark Night of the Soul*] leaves no doubt as to poet-narrator's feminine gender. Yet critical readings have gone no further than to acquiesce to its allegorization of the passive soul seeking purgation.[5] The divide between the man composing the poem and his feminized poetic "other" is accepted and acknowledged as a means of vocalizing religious experience, as a poetic visualization of the *via negativa*.[6] Nevertheless, one would have to ask if, despite his commentaries to this purpose, San Juan meant solely to compose a religious allegory.[7] It is because of those commentaries, and regardless of his intentions, that his poems must also be taken to question the very possibility of representing religious experience through language.

We may concur, therefore, with Luce López Baralt that the *Noche oscura del alma* holds both erotic and mystical significance, expanding its meaning through its connection to Sufism. Or we might agree with Calin-Andrei Mihailescu, who posits that, in following Pseudo-Dionysius the Areopagite and Meister Eckhart, among others, the non-representational qualities of the saint's poetry—its silence and its darkness—reveal his apophatic theology, whose attribution of disimagination in turn leads to non-being.[8] Both approaches, I would argue, nonetheless depend on the notion that San Juan's poem achieves significance precisely by challenging the rational limits imposed by language. Mihailescu states as much: "El lenguaje apofático es una idealidad irrealizable en tanto que lenguaje" [13: As language, apophatic language remains an unachievable ideal]. López Baralt, for her part, asserts that even San Juan's commentaries (*declaraciones*) resemble Sufi glosses in that they demonstrate an "idéntica preocupación por la insuficiencia del lenguaje para traducir la ilimitada Divinidad" [1985, 397: identical concern regarding linguistic insufficiency to translate illimited divinity.]

Whether San Juan attempts to express mysticism's ineffability or ascribe to its experience the characteristics of otherness through the process of "disimagination," there is no doubt but that he forces the poem's linguistic boundaries to their breaking point. Paradoxically, therefore, the poem succeeds in transmitting its meaning not despite, but by means of linguistic rupture.[9] From the syntactical break of the first two stanzas by the exclamatory "Oh dichosa ventura!" [Oh, favoring fortune!] to the semantically transgressive use of the reflexives "quedéme, olvidéme, dejéme" [I left myself, I forgot myself, I abandoned myself] in the last stanza, the poem underscores the poet's need to interrupt, distort and otherwise suspend linguistic order.[10] And from the female-gendered pronoun of the first stanza, "salí sin ser notada" [I stepped outside unnoticed] (Rivers 138) to the last stanza's reference to a male lover, "el rostro recliné sobre el amado" [I leaned my face against my lover], what remains reinscribed in the poetic grammar is its transgressed gender order.[11]

The poem's mystical transcendence is effected through the illogicity of this gender reversal; by emitting the poetic voice from the woman's position, San Juan intends to attain her liminal status. Toril Moi has spoken on female marginality:

> If patriarchy sees women as occupying a marginal position within the symbolic order, then it can construe them as the *limit* or borderline of that order. . . . Women seen as the limit of the symbolic order will in other words share in the disconcerting properties of all frontiers: they will be neither inside nor outside, neither known nor unknown. (1985, 167)

The non-being that Mihailescu assigns to apophasis, then, is also a consequence of the poetic voice's positioning as female and thus recalls the sense of unknowing striven for by mystics. Challenging the unproblematized categories of knowledge and belief, the French psychoanalyst, Jacques Lacan, has labelled masculine knowledge an "irredeemable erring" (1982, 50). For the mystic, therefore, any separation from the godhead perforce incurs the errancy of the word.

As is well known, Lacan observes women's position not as a sexual category, but linguistically as "not all:" "it means that when any speaking being whatever lines up under the banner of women, it is by being constituted as not all that they are placed within the phallic function" (1982, 141). Since the subject cannot exist outside language, but is constituted precisely as a division in language, male and female subjects may place themselves on either side of the phallic division. In a specific allusion to San Juan, Lacan explains the male mystic's appropriation of the feminine function:

> There are men who are just as good as women. It does happen. Despite, I won't say their phallus, despite what encumbers them on that score, they get the idea, they sense that there must be a *jouissance* which goes beyond. That is what we call a mystic. (1982, 147)

San Juan's paronomastic lines "¡oh noche que juntaste / amado con amada, / amada en el amado transformada!" [Oh night that joined / lover to beloved, / the beloved transformed into the lover!] echo the Petrarchan lyrics "l'amante ne l'amato si trasforme" (1951, 157) of the *Triumphus Cupidinis* [*Triumph of Cupid*] often intended to signal the lovers' Neoplatonic union. Yet these lines express the lovers' reciprocity as one of supplementarity, not complementarity. San Juan's transgendered self *enjoys*—that is to say, he experiences *jouissance*, the ecstatic pleasure defined by Lacan as "the moment of sexuality which is always in excess, something over and above the phallic term which is the mark of sexual identity" (1982, 137). The invention of courtly love in the secular lyric tradition confirms to Lacan that "love" between man and woman does not really exist: man repeatedly pursues his unattainable desire. As in the myth of Hero and Leander, the love lyrics of the Petrarchan *Canzoniere* instead negate Neoplatonic union because the "oneness" desired allows no synthesis of symmetrical opposites (1982, 139).[12] For Lacan, women's identification with the male fantasy allows the phallic function to continue; so long as women function as objects, they are denied knowledge of their condition. If men desire only their desire, Lacan explains, then women experience jouissance without being aware of its origin or nature.[13] Exiled from language, women "do not know what they are saying": knowledge is instead attributed to the lover, God or man. Similarly, the mystic who appropriates the woman's position supports the godhead by his jouissance, yet he knows nothing of this experience, which becomes transgendered as feminine desire (1982, 147). To compare the mystic to the woman-function, therefore, is to deny divine existence as well: the mystic functions as the woman in the relations between God and man. For Lacan, however, this does not prove the existence of God: "And since it is there too that the function of the father is inscribed in so far as this is the function to which castration refers, one can see that while this may not make for two Gods, nor does it make for one alone" (1982, 148).

In his analysis of Santa Teresa's writings, Paul Julian Smith (1992, 103) focuses on examples of linguistic instability to illustrate Lacan's "vision of Teresa," not as a fixed or biological entity, but as a function: the mystical text uncovers female subjectivity as a shifting process. Luce Irigaray's term *mystérique* concurs with Lacan, in that mysticism opens a space where the feminine function does not reflect male desire, but relates to an absolute Other.[14] For her, the mystic, no matter how abject, sees herself in the specular reflection of the most feminine of men, Christ. In Irigaray's feminist response to Lacan, her psychoanalyst "master," she stresses that the mystical union is not with God the Father, but with the Son: "At last [the female mystic] has been authorized to remain silent, hidden from prying eyes in the intimacy of this exchange where she sees (herself as) what she will be unable to express" (1992, 200).[15]

Smith's deconstructive reading of St. Teresa's *Vida* [Life] interrogates her resistance to God's mercy, where, unlike Irigaray's ultimate exaltation of the female mystic, "[Teresa] must constantly be reminded of her deficiency and negativity" (1992, 108). Although he emphasizes that the saint's desire "is always mediated by language and her femininity is thus a construct, not an essence" (1992, 109), he cites her allusion to Saint Paul's words as an example of her repeated desire for obliteration: "Que no vivo yo ya, sino que Vos, Criador mío, vivís en mí" [1984, 154: That I no longer live, but that you, my Creator, live in me]. In this statement, Smith notes, "the first person of testimony cedes to the second person of apostrophe" (1992, 109).

Smith believes that the use of the third person in her autobiography's title, *El libro de su vida*, [*The Book of Her Life*] also reflects Teresa's loss of self; the importance of Christ in her visions serves instead to underscore her own image of solitude and affliction.[16] Teresa's "union" with Christ "leads not to satisfaction but to suffering and helplessness" (1992, 111). Yet Smith ignores a crucial

difference that obtains in Teresa's poetry, where her symbolic in-
completeness is provisionally fulfilled through the transgendered
poetic voice with which she professes her experience. While the
Pauline expression cited in her *Vida* states that she no longer lives
since the divinity lives in her, in an otherwise obeisant poem, titled
"Vuestra soy, para Vos nací" [I am yours, for you I was born], the
last line of the last stanza instead shifts the pronoun from *Vos* [you]
to the dative *mí* [me]. In contrast to the phrase cited by Smith, Teresa's poem assures that she lived only through God's living in her:
"Sólo Vos en mí viví" [1984, 503: I lived only through you in me].
If, in the *Vida*, she expresses her obliteration (or complementarity)
in the face of God, through her poem, Teresa indicates the supplementarity of Christ's presence in her.

This shift is similarly evident in another poem, "Si el amor que
me tenéis" [If the love you have for me], where Teresa initiates a
dialogue with no less a poetic voice than God's:

> —Alma, ¿qué quereis de mí?
> —Dios mío, no más que verte.
> —¿Y qué temes más de ti?
> —Lo que más temo es perderte. (1967, 510)
> [Soul, what do you want from me?
> —My God, only to see you.
> —And what do you fear most from yourself?
> —What I fear most is to lose you.]

While divine loss is predicated upon the loss of vision and bound
up with Teresa's visions of Christ's humanity, it is articulated
through divine interrogation. When God asks "And what do you
fear most from yourself?" Teresa's response and the following queries then proceed as a means of self-analysis. It is through divine
communication, through dialogue with God, that Teresa comes to
know herself.

Smith concludes his discussion of Teresa by first echoing Julia
Kristeva's concerns as to the mystic's alterity: is woman's silence
broken only at the cost of denying or disavowing her *jouissance*?
Can Teresa become a speaking subject without sacrificing her irre-
ducible difference? (1992, 112) For Kristeva, who reads the psychotic text through a conflation of truth and the real, (in French, the
vréel, from *vrai* and *réel*), the answer to both questions is indeed
positive, since the hysteric, like the mystic exiled from standard discourse, attempts to obliterate sexual difference and destabilize the
paternal signifier (Smith 1992, 120–21).

On the borders of rational discourse, San Juan and Santa Teresa's mystical poems press language's limits first and foremost by transgendering their poetic voice, by appropriating the provisional state to which the feminine is relegated by the symbolic order. In an excellent article on Santa Teresa's *Interior Castle*, Catherine Connor (Swietlicki) coins the term "femystic" to describe what she calls mysticism's "paradoxical gender identification," since mystical activity was practiced by more women than men (1989, 281). My readings of these poems, on the contrary, have convinced me that we should not ascribe a role gender reversal solely to male mystics. Nor should we accept their own view of themselves as "androgynous," a characteristic that, for Connor, equates feminine mystics with "virile women" (1989, 282, n.17). What I have observed instead is that, while male mystics embrace a female excess or *jouissance* through the feminine poetic voice, female mystics verbalize a uniquely Christocentric position that both transgresses and transcends gender order.

This phenomenon, evinced in Santa Teresa's dialogue-poem with God, may also be seen in the poetry of Luisa de Carvajal y Mendoza (1556–1614), a Spanish noblewoman who travelled to England as a missionary to convert the Anglicans to Catholicism. Unappreciated by modern critics as a religious poet, Carvajal was neither a member of a religious order nor a visionary.[17] In her spiritual poetry, she distances her "self" from the poetic voice, attributing the poems' religious emotions to Silva, her anagrammatic persona (Cruz 1992). Yet her small but impressive poetic collection, written in both cultured and popular style, nevertheless discloses many of the concerns addressed by San Juan and Santa Teresa: the search for the absent lover, inflamed love, transverberation, and *jouissance*.

The following sonnet in particular echoes the eroticized imagery by which sixteenth-century devotional writers often expressed union with God. However, Carvajal goes both our saints one better: through the poem's transgendered voice, she assumes the very voice of Christ at the moment of communion to ensure her own *jouissance*:

> De inmenso amor aqueste abrazo estrecho,
> recibe, Silva, de tu dulce Amado,
> y por la puerta deste diestro lado
> éntrate, palomilla, acá en mi pecho.
> Reposa en el florido y sacro lecho
> y abrázate en amor tan abrasado

que hasta que el fuerte nudo haya apretado,
no sea posible quede satisfecho.
Mira cómo te entrego amiga mía,
todo mi ser y alteza sublimada;
estima aqueste don que amor te ofrece;
Tendrás en mí gloriosa compañía
y entre mis mismos brazos regalada
gozarás lo que nadie no merece. (1965, 438)

[This tight embrace with immense love brimming
accept, Silva, from your sweet lover
and through my right side's opening
enter, little dove, within my breast.
Repose on the sacred, flowering bed
and surround yourself with love so passionate
that not until the deathknot is fully tied
will it ever be wholly satisfied.
See how I surrender to you, my love,
all my being and eminence sublime.
Cherish this gift by love proffered,
You'll find in me such glorious company,
and in my very own arms held tenderly,
You'll enjoy what no one has deserved.]

Paradoxically, by transgendering her voice, Carvajal anticipates and assures herself of the *jouissance* that Lacan attributes to the female gender. The appropriation by Carvajal of Christ's voice, who speaks to her as her lover, places her, in the traditional gender hierarchy, above San Juan, whose own voice becomes feminized when speaking as the beloved. It also expands upon Teresa's position as an interlocutor, in dialogue with the godhead.

The transgendering of the mystical voice as a means of identifying with God is not, however, a phenomenon found exclusively in religious Spanish poetry. It occurs not only in the spiritual lyrics of San Juan, Santa Teresa, and Carvajal, but in the writings of the medieval Italian mystic, Angela de Foligno (ca. 1248–1309). An Umbrian wife and mother, Angela experienced an intense and passionate love of God that led her to profess as a nun in the Third Order of St. Francis. The first part of her *Book*, the *Memorial*, dictated to her Franciscan confessor and spiritual director, grants us insight into the mystic's conversion from a life of wealth and pleasure to one of mortification and penance.[18] Its thirty "steps," narrated over four years to the scribe, relate her inner voyage, from her purification through suffering to intimacy with Jesus, her "suffering God-man" (1993, 24).[19]

Angela de Foligno's writings circulated in Spain in several separate manuscripts, as well as with other religious writings; besides its being published in Catalan, Cardinal Ximénez de Cisneros ordered her *Book* translated into Latin in 1505 and into Castilian in 1510. Juana Mary Arcelús-Ulibarrena, who has traced Angela's writings on the Iberian Peninsula, believes the *Book* required reading for the *infantas* in Castile, Aragon, Navarra, and Portugal.[20] Favored by Iberian royalty and promoted by the Franciscan order, the *Book* played an important role in the development of Spanish mysticism and religious thought. Oscillating between ecstasy and despair, Angela's mystical experiences plunge her into what she calls "horrible darkness" and desolation. Her meditation on the passion often brought on visions of Christ's humanity and divinity that, she complained, were impossible to describe fully (1993, 147). Yet God's presence is revealed through his voice, and through her anointment as a permanent sign of divine love. Angela's modern editor and translator, Paul Lachance, has aptly described her moment of identification with the crucified Christ:

> In this encounter with total despair, one in which body and soul tremble in uncontrollable agony, from the lowest depths there rose to Angela's consciousness the cry of final abandonment, the words of anguish. She wailed and cried out repeatedly: "My son, my son, do not abandon me, my son!" (1993, 68)

Although Lachance cautiously calls the affiliation a "partial" one, his astonishment at Angela's identification with Christ is clearly discernible when glossing her words. Since they address the startlingly transgendered nature of Angela's language, his comments deserve to be quoted in full:

> By the power and the very dialectic of Christ's burning love for her, Angela was allowed to enter the horror of his final agony and abandonment on the cross. It is this deep participation in the test of this final hour that provides meaning and illustrates most powerfully Angela's experience of the profound abyss and abandonment. To be sure, it is a partial identification and participation. . . . Angela could do no more than share something of what happened on the cross, participate in some of its inner drama and torment—even if, in transposing Christ's last words as she did, *she articulated it in terms of identification unique in the history of mystical literature* (1993, 68; my emphasis).

Angela de Foligno's "transposition" of Christ's words succeeds in rendering them her own—a linguistic capacity that, as we have seen, was not unique to her, but repeated and reclaimed by the Spanish religious poets addressed in this essay.

Angela's immense suffering when visualizing Christ's passion—a pain that transforms her into a mute participant—grants her *jouissance* as she is united with God. The sight of the cross awakened in her a love that she describes as her soul set ablaze. The description of her feelings cannot help but remind us of San Juan's embrace with Christ in his *Dark Night* and of Luisa de Carvajal's sonnet, where Christ bids her to enter the wound in his right side:

> I saw and felt that Christ was within me, embracing my soul with the very arm with which he was crucified. . . . At times it seems to my soul that it enters into Christ's side, and this is a source of great joy and delight; it is indeed such a joyful experience to move into Christ's side that in no way can I express it and put words to it (1993, 175–76)

Her vision of herself with the dead body of Christ anticipates Carvajal's union with the Crucified Christ:

> She found herself on the sepulcher with Christ. She said she had first of all kissed Christ's breast—and saw that he lay dead, with his eyes closed—then she kissed his mouth, from which, she added, a delightful fragrance emanated, one impossible to describe. This moment lasted only a short while. Afterward, she placed her cheek on Christ's own and he, in turn, placed his hand on her other cheek, pressing her closely to him. At that moment, Christ's faithful one heard him telling her: "Before I was laid in the sepulcher, I held you this tightly to me." Even though she understood that it was Christ telling her this, nonetheless she saw him lying there with eyes closed, lips motionless, exactly as he was when he lay dead in the sepulcher. Her joy was immense and indescribable. (1993, 182)

Angela's *jouissance*, her celebration in being at one with Christ, comes at the price of his humanity—and her voice. What is replayed here is Christ's passion and death, which she shares by absorbing his last breath. At this point—when, following Smith, we may think that she has abandoned her self to her Creator—it is instructive to recall Julia Kristeva's notion of abjection:

> The mystic's familiarity with abjection is a fount of infinite jouissance. One may stress the masochistic economy of the jouissance only if one points out at once that the Christian mystic far from using it to the benefit of a symbolic or institutional power (as happens with dreams, for instance) displaces it indefinitely within a discourse where the subject

is resorbed (is that a grace?) into communication with the Other and with others. (1982, 127)

Angela's voice is recuperated through her writings; mystical language is, as Irigaray has pronounced, the only place in the history of the West where "woman speaks and acts so publicly" (1992, 191). Like Santa Teresa and Luisa de Carvajal after her, in assuming the voice of the godhead, Angela de Foligno achieves a *jouissance* that, ultimately and inescapably, goes beyond the very same language that precipitates its experience.

NOTES

1. This dichotomy is alluded to by Rivers in his influential 1962 article, "The Pastoral Paradox of Natural Art."

2. Unless otherwise noted, all translations in this essay are my own.

3. Paul Zumthor notes that in the *jarchas*, the attitude of the female voice is that of desire and anticipation; see Frenk, 115–16. See also Gaylord Randel.

4. Alan Deyermond has classified the "woman's voice lyrics," which he considers mimetic works by male poets, according to their position, language, time, mode of expression, and situation. See also Dronke.

5. In interpreting San Juan, Kavanaugh states: "The intervention of God through a purgation that comes about passively, that is not acquired through human effort, is necessary. The human work is simply a preparation for this particular divine action. What the person undergoing the dark night experiences is a painful lack or privation: darkness in the intellect, aridity in the exercise of love in the will, emptiness in the memory of all possessions, and affliction and torment as a consequence and general state. Such persons receive a vivid understanding of their own misery and think they will never escape from it. . . . The effect of all this is the dread-filled experience of being abandoned by God. . . . All these painful experiences as well as the beneficial fruits of the transformation being wroguht are attributable to contemplation. This contemplation is an inpouring of God, a divine loving knowledge, general, without images or concepts, obscure and hidden from the one who receives it, a knowledge that both purifies and illumines. . . . But contemplation itself is not identifiable with dark night, for contemplation may be given in forms that do not produce these purifying effects. In addition, it is worth saying that if this night darkens, it does so only to give light; and if it humiliates it does so only to exalt; and if it impoverishes, it do so only to enrich" (1987, 159–60; my emphasis).

6. The poem's fictional *vía negativa* was the same as that practiced by mystics. According to Kavanaugh, Francisco de Osuna's *Tercer abecedario* influenced both Santa Teresa and San Juan: "Osuna taught that to advance on the path of union, one must practice recollection (recogimiento). . . . By this recollection, Osuna explained, you withdraw from people and noisy places and enter within youself. By it you recollect the exterior person, the senses and bodily members, withdraw into the heart, unite the powers of the soul with the soul's highest part where the image of God is imprinted. Finally, this prayer joins God and the soul, that is, 'the soul participates in the Lord himself and is perfectly recollected in him.' This way of

recollection, also called mental prayer, had to involve one's whole life. . . . Finally, though the practitioners of recollection gave greater importance to recollection, they did not abandon vocal prayer" (Kavanaugh, Intro 11–12).

7. In the case of Dante's *Divine Comedy*, for instance, John Freccero has taught us that our modern secular reading results in the poem's allegorization as a dream vision, thereby robbing it of its credibility and authenticity.

8. Based on God's statement in *Genesis* that he will make man to his image *and* likeness, positive or cataphatic theology corresponds to visionary or ecstatic phenomena, which also emphasize image and likeness, as in the case of Santa Teresa. Negative, or apophatic, theology instead stresses image or likeness, separating the synonyms into difference. For Mihailescu, these two theologies are aligned with the Platonic/Aristotelian opposition (10).

9. By this, I do not mean that San Juan's language is insufficient; see Davis (1993) for an excellent refutation of this traditional view.

10. Although Mihailescu calls previous readings of San Juan's poems orgasmic, I disagree that the *vía negativa* may only be taken as the text's organizing principle, since it also may be followed through the disrupted, non-logical text. Indeed, the moment of union, unmentioned in the interstices of the middle two stanzas, is balanced between the lover's encounter in an empty space ("a donde me esperaba/ . . . /en parte donde nadie parecía" [where he waited for me/ . . . / in a place where no one was present]).

11. Mihailescu's application of disimagination to San Juan's poetry relies on the final disappearance of the image; its analog in *Noche oscura* is the paratactic repetition of the verbs "quedéme, olvidéme, dejéme" until what is left is the "cuidado olvidado."

12. According to Lacan, the male lover is "in love" with his desire: "except that what he takes in is the cause of his desire, the cause I have designated as the objet à. That is the act of love. To make love, as the term indicates, is poetry. Only there is a world between poetry and the act. The act of love is the polymorphous perversion of the male, in the case of the speaking being" (1982, 143).

13. This has led Smith to argue that "Lacan thus denies both the Divinity and biology the authority with which they are often attributed in the sexual relation at the same time as he describes the way in which they serve to support fantasies of that relation" (Smith 1992, 101).

14. Note, however, that some critics charge her with setting up a general category of woman (Smith 1992, 107).

15. Although Irigaray does not mention Teresa by name, her translator, Gillian Gill, footnotes the saint's description of the Transverberation, long considered the most explicitly erotic expression of feminine ecstasy (1992, 201, n.2).

16. Teresa's book, however, has been edited with the title *Libro de la vida* (Book of the Life) by Dámaso Chicharro; see his "Breve historia del manuscrito" (Brief History of the Manuscript, 69–72).

17. Although anthologized in Serrano y Sanz, the *Biblioteca de Autores Españoles* and Boyce and Olivares, and recently edited by García-Nieto Onrubia, Carvajal's poetry has yet to draw the critical attention it deserves.

18. For an explanation of the book's complex origins, its redactional history and its various editions, see Paul Lachance's Introduction to Angela de Foligno, *Complete Works*, 15–19.

19. Lachance notes that Angela's confessor, after taking down nineteen steps, was unable to complete the remaining eleven, and condensed them into seven supplementary steps (1993, 21).

140   ANNE J. CRUZ

20. Arcelús-Ulibarrena refers mainly to Codices 473, 559, and 9,020 of the Biblioteca de Catalunya (now in the Institute d'Estudis Catalans); the Biblioteca Universitaria, Barcelona; and the Biblioteca Nactional, Madrid, respectively. Angela's writings also appear in Chapter 25 of the 1492 *Floreto de Sant Francisco* (Seville, 1492). According to Arcelús-Ulibarrena, Angela's religious precepts, cited in Ubertino da Casale's *Arbor Vitae* and translated by Queen Isabela in 1492, accompanied the Franciscans to the New World (222).

WORKS CITED

Angela of Foligno. 1993. *Complete Works*. Edited and translated by Paul Lachance. New York: Paulist Press.

Arcelús-Ulibarrena, Juana Mary. 1992. "Angela da Foligno nella Penisola Iberica alla fine del Medioevo." In *Angela da Foligno, Terziaria Francescana. Atti del convegno storico nel VII centenario dell'ingresso della beata Angela da Foligno nell'Ordine Francescano Secolare (1291–1991) Foligno, 17–19 novembre 1991*, edited by Enrico Menesto. Spoleto: Centro Italiano di Studi Sull'Alto Medioevo.

Azar, Inés. 1989. "Tradition, Voice and Self in the Love Poetry of Garcilaso." In *Studies in Honor of Elias Rivers*, edited by Bruno M. Damiani and Ruth El Saffar. Potomac, Md.: Scripta Humanistica.

Carvajal y Mendoza, Luisa. 1965. *Epistolario y poesías*. Edited by Camilo José Abad. Vol. 179. Madrid: Biblioteca de Autores Españoles.

———. 1996. *Poesías completas*. Edited by María Luisa García-Nieto Onrubia. Badajoz: Clásicos Extremeños.

Connor (Swietlicki), Catherine. 1989. "Writing 'Femystic' Space: In the Margins of Santa Teresa's *Castillo interior*." *Journal of Hispanic Philology*. 13 (spring): 273–93.

Cruz, Anne J. 1992. "Chains of Desire: Luisa de Carvajal y Mendoza's Poetics of Penance." In *Studies on Hispanic Women Writers in Honor of Georgina Sabat-Rivers*. Edited by Lou Charnon-Deutsh. Madrid: Castalia.

Davis, Elizabeth B. 1993. "The Power of Paradox in the 'Cántico espiritual.' " *Revista de Estudios Hispánicos* 27: 203–23.

Deyermond, Alan. 1986. "Sexual Initiation in the Woman's Voice Court Lyric." In *Courtly Literature: Culture and Context. Selected Papers from the 5th Triennial Congress of the International Courtly Literature Society, Dalfsen, The Netherlands, 9–16 August*. Amsterdam: John Benjamins.

Dronke, Peter. 1984. "Learned Lyric and Popular Ballad in the Early Middle Ages." In *The Medieval Poet and his World*. Roma: Storia e Letteratura.

Frenk, Margit. 1984. *Las jarchas mozárabes y los comienzos de la lírica románica*. Mexico: El Colegio de México.

Garcilaso de la Vega y sus comentaristas. Obras completas del poeta. 1966. Edited by Antonio Gallego Morell. Granada: Universidad de Granada.

Gaylord Randel, Mary. 1982. "The Grammar of Femininity in the Traditional Spanish Lyric." *Revista / Review Interamericana* 12 (spring): 115–24.

Graf, E. C. 1994. "Forcing the Poetic Voice: Garcilaso de la Vega's Sonnet XXIX as a Deconstruction of the Idea of Harmony." *MLN* 109: 163–85.

Greene, Thomas M. 1982. *The Light in Troy: Imitation and Discovery in Renaissance Poetry*. New Haven: Yale University Press.

Heiple, Daniel L. 1994. *Garcilaso de la Vega and the Italian Renaissance*. University Park: Penn State University Press.

Irigaray, Luce. 1992. *Speculum of the Other Woman*. Translated by Gillian Gill. Ithaca: Cornell University Press.

John of the Cross. 1987. *Selected Writings*. Edited by Kieran Kavanaugh, O.C.D. New York: Paulist Press.

Kristeva, Julia. 1982. *The Powers of Horror: An Essay on Abjection*. Translated by Leon S. Roudiez. New York: Columbia University Press.

Lacan, Jacques. See Mitchell, Juliet.

Lachance, Paul. See Angela de Foligno.

López Baralt, Luce. 1985. *San Juan de la Cruz y el Islam: Estudio sobre las filiaciones semíticas de la literatura mística*. Mexico: Colegio de México; Universidad de Puerto Rico.

———. 1998. "San Juan de la Cruz: ¿Poeta del amor divino o poeta del amor humano?" *Actas del XII Congreso de la Asociación Internacional de Hispanistas, Birmingham 1995. Tomo III, Estudios Aureos II*. Edited by Jules Whicker. Birmingham: Department of Hispanic Studies. 18–32.

Mihailescu, Calin-Andrei. Forthcoming. "Desimaginación en fray Juan de la Cruz." *Revista Canadiense de Estudios Hispánicos*.

Mitchell, Juliet, and Jacqueline Rose. 1982. *Feminine Sexuality: Jacques Lacan and the école freudienne*. New York: Norton.

Moi, Toril. 1985. *Sexual / Textual Politics: Feminist Literary Theory*. London and New York: Methuen.

Olivares, Julian, and Elizabeth Boyce. 1993. *Tras el espejo la musa escribe: Lírica femenina de los Siglos de Oro*. Madrid: Siglo Veintiuno.

Petrarca, Francesco. 1951. *Rime, Trionfi, e Poesie Latine*. Edited by F. Neri et al. Milano: Riccardo Ricciardi Editore.

Pigman, George W. 1980. "Versions of Imitation in the Renaissance." *Renaissance Quarterly* 33: 1–32.

Rivers, Elias L. 1962. "The Pastoral Paradox of Natural Art." *MLN* 77: 130–44.

Smith, Paul Julian. 1988. *Writing in the Margin. Spanish Literature of the Golden Age*. Oxford: Clarendon Press.

———. 1992. *Representing the Other: 'Race', Text, and Gender in Spanish and Spanish American Narrative*. Oxford: Clarendon Press.

Teresa de Jesús. 1967. *Obras completas. Edición manual*. Edited by Efrén de la Madre de Dios and Otger Steggink. Madrid: Biblioteca de Autores Cristianos.

———. 1984. *Libro de la vida*. Edited by Dámaso Chicharro. Madrid: Cátedra.

Feminine Transformations of the *Quixote* in Eighteenth-Century England: Lennox's *Female Quixote* and Her Sisters

AMY PAWL

The appearance in 1752 of Charlotte Lennox's *Female Quixote* brought a new figure to the attention of the English reading public: a female literary quixote, Don Quixote in skirts. This figure was to persist over the next half century, emerging recognizably from works such as George Colman's *Polly Honeycombe*, Maria Edgeworth's "Angelina," Jane Austen's *Northanger Abbey*, Tabitha Tenney's *Female Quixotism*, and Eaton Barrett's *The Heroine*. The female quixote, as presented by Lennox, has much in common with the male quixote: her delusions, like Alonso Quixano's, arise from her reading; her attempts to interpret the world in terms of her literary models make her both ridiculous and noble; and her kind, generous nature makes her beloved despite her follies. Thus far, she might be a quixote of either sex. There are, however, special difficulties involved in being a female quixote in a society that limits a woman's access to mobility, autonomy, and self-determination. One of the tasks of this essay will be to demonstrate the surprising ways in which Lennox and other authors overcome these difficulties to create female quixotes who become vehicles for fantasies of female power and importance. Its other task will be to set these successes in context by examining the ways in which female power is redirected, corrected, or undercut by characters who attempt the heroines' seduction or reform.

DON QUIXOTE AND THE FEMALE QUIXOTE

Charlotte Lennox's quixote is, like Cervantes's, above all a devoted reader. The daughter of a wealthy and reclusive Marquis, Arabella immerses herself in her deceased mother's books, mostly

French romances "in very bad translations" that have been placed in her father's library and upon which she forms her ideas of the world (7).[1] Arabella's father dies soon after the novel opens, having lived just long enough to approve Arabella's cousin, Mr. Glanville, as her suitor. Arabella, unsurprisingly, finds paternal fiat to be an insufficiently romantic way of proceeding, expecting rather that a lover of hers should "purchase her with his Sword from a Croud of Rivals; and arrive to the Possession of her Heart by many Years of Service and Fidelity" (27). The rest of the book focuses on this impasse, pitting Arabella's desire to live the life of a heroine against the desire of Mr. Glanville (and his father) to see her restored to reason. As Arabella is independently wealthy, highly intelligent, and convinced of the historical truth of the romances she has read, reforming her is no easy task. A quixote armed with quotations is a formidable opponent, as *Don Quixote*'s priest and barber well know.

Both Arabella and Don Quixote govern their lives according to literary precedent. When Sancho Panza attempts to challenge the wisdom of Don Quixote's vow to lead an ascetic life until he wins himself a new helmet, Don Quixote insists, "I know very well what precedent I am following," thus justifying himself in his own eyes (1950, 82). Similarly, Arabella, when she receives her first love letter (from a secret admirer), "search[es] the Records of her Memory for a Precedent," but "not finding, that any Lady ever opened a Letter from an unknown Lover" (13), she orders the letter returned. Time and again, Don Quixote and Arabella attempt to match their actions to those of their literary heroes and heroines, often citing verse and chapter in their own justification. In addition, they both employ literary precedents in an effort to understand the world and to explain or predict the actions of those around them. Their notions of probability are based on their reading. Both, for example, find it impossible to imagine that a hero would be subject to the laws of his country, simply because such an occurrence has never appeared in their reading. "Where have you ever heard or read of a knight errant being brought before a judge, however many homicides he may have committed?" asks the knight rhetorically (80). Arabella concurs: "The law has no Power over Heroes; they may kill as many Men as they please, without being called to any Account for it" (128).

Most importantly, perhaps, both quixotes use literary precedent as a mechanism to protect their illusions. Much of the pleasure of both books, indeed, comes from observing the ingenuity with which the protagonists sift and twist their literary sources in order to come up with an explanation that accommodates their romantic vision and prevents reality from obtruding itself upon their notice. Don Quixote, as his delusions are more extreme (Arabella may be wrong about a person's motives or status, but she does not go so far as to mistake sheep for soldiers, or windmills for giants), needs a more powerful mechanism to protect them, which he finds in the ever-present actions of his evil enchanter, whose envy leads him to change people's faces and forms. Arabella, for her part, must rely on ever subtler applications of her reading. When she sends the unopened missive back to her secret admirer, Arabella expects to learn "that the Return of his Letter would make her Lover commit some very extravagant Actions" (14), and she quizzes her maid Lucy, the messenger, for a description. Lucy answers (accurately, as the reader knows) that Mr. Hervey, the unknown lover, had kissed the letter several times, because he thought it contained an answer from Arabella. Arabella shows her creative reading ability in the following response:

> Foolish Wench! . . . How can you imagine he had the Temerity to think I should answer his Letter? A Favour, which, though he had spent Years in my Service, would have been infinitely greater than he could have expected. No, Lucy, he kissed the Letter, either because he thought it had been touched at least by my Hands, or to shew the perfect Submission with which he received my Commands. (15)

Thus far Arabella has succeeded in making life conform to romance, but when she expresses aloud her fear (or hope) that the despairing lover will "commit some desperate Outrage against himself" she receives a new hermeneutic challenge in Lucy's unwelcome assurance that "There is no Fear . . . that he will do himself a Mischief; for when he discovered his Mistake, he laughed heartily" (15). This is harder to explain away, but Arabella rises to the occasion, and though it takes her "a little Time to consider of so strange a Phenomenon," she insists that "he laughed because his Reason was disturbed at the sudden Shock he received" (15).

At least this episode involved a real love letter; a later incident in Bath poses a greater threat to Arabella's romantic expectations, as she receives not one but two letters that explicitly deny the "crime" of which she has accused the authors, that of being in love with her. As Arabella believes that "all Letters directed to me must contain Matters of Love and Gallantry" (293), she expects to find declarations of love enclosed. Her surprise and chagrin are evident when her cousin, Miss Glanville, snatches the first letter and reads it aloud, noting with some malice that "Mr. Selvin utterly denies the Crime of loving you" (295). But once again, Arabella is saved by literary precendent. Her "Spirits . . . raised by recollecting an Adventure in her Romance, similar to this" (295), Arabella cites the example of "*Seramenes*; who being in Love with the beautiful *Cleobuline*, Princess of *Corinth*, took all imaginable Pains to conceal his Passion, in order to be near that fair Princess," concluding, "In these Cases therefore, the more resolutely a Man denies his Passion, the more pure and violent it is" (295). As a strategy, this is brilliant; by invoking the double bind of love, in which a lover's silence or denial is as revealing as a declaration, Arabella has ensured that she won't encounter disappointment or enlightenment. Rather like Freud's Dora, Arabella's presumed suitors have no way to say no.

If Arabella and Don Quixote see their beloved romances as sources of power and inspiration, those around them agree—but draw very different conclusions about the matter. Arabella's father, the Marquis, and her suitor, Mr. Glanville, resemble the priest, the barber, the niece, and the housekeeper in *Don Quixote*: all tacitly admit to the power of romance by believing that destruction of the books might be enough to liberate the affected quixote from their influence. In a scene that directly echoes the great book-burning in *Don Quixote*, Arabella's father exclaims, "These foolish books . . . have turned her Brain! Where are they? . . . I'll burn all I can lay my Hands upon" (55). But while Mr. Glanville is capable of "cursing *Statira* and *Orontes* a thousand times, and loading the Authors of those books with all the Imprecations his Rage could suggest" (52), he realizes that he can make a virtue of interceding on this occasion, and so persuades the enraged Marquis to allow him to return Arabella's books to her unharmed.

The real danger to the literary quixote, however, lies not with those who dismiss or fear the literature of romance, but with those whose knowledge of it allows them to co-opt its power. While both Don Quixote and Arabella are capable of an eloquent defense when their beliefs are challenged, they are comparatively defenseless when their predilections appear to be shared. Arabella is taken in by the fine language and romantic gestures of her neighbor and would-be suitor, Sir George. A reader of romances himself, he can suit his style to her expectations, pleasing her with his judicious and elegantly phrased observations on love and beauty. So extreme is his language that her cousins assume he is in jest; Arabella, on the other hand, finds that he "speak[s] very rationally upon these Matters" (144). His interpolated life's history, told to the assembled company on a rainy evening, is taken literally by Arabella, who easily credits his claim to be a dispossessed prince capable of killing five hundred men in armed combat. But like the manipulative Duke and Duchess in the second part of *Don Quixote*, Sir George is more adept at imitating form than at understanding content. His story contains, for him, a fatal flaw—he has unintentionally proven himself to be a faithless lover, and Arabella considers him by rights the property of another woman, the beautiful *Philonice* of his own invention. He has failed to appreciate the sincerity and rigor of Arabella's belief system, which requires eternal constancy, not merely "several Years" (250) spent lamenting the loss of an abducted lady.

On this occasion, the purity of Arabella's devotion to her romance models does offer protection against manipulation, as she is above simple flattery. But Sir George's machinations cause real trouble near the end of the novel, when he hires an actress to impersonate Cynecia, Princess of Gaul, thrown into despair by the cruel treatment of an unfaithful lover. Arabella finds this princess wandering in a garden and lamenting her fate; because "this Adventure" is "more worthy indeed to be styled Adventure than any our Fair Heroine had ever yet met with," and because it is "so conformable to what she had read in Romances" (341), Arabella is completely taken in. When "Cynecia," at Sir George's behest, identifies the unsuspecting Mr. Glanville as her unfaithful lover, Arabella is highly distressed and the peace of the household is destroyed.

Sir George's actions here do resemble in a number of ways those of the Duke and Duchess in *Don Quixote*. Like Sir George, they go to great lengths to stage scenes for their quixote, employing and costuming numerous other persons; like Sir George, they are selfishly motivated. Perhaps most importantly of all, like Sir George, the Duke and the Duchess have usurped the quixote's privilege of creating his or her own visions. The enchanted Dulcinea, the case of the bearded lady-in-waiting, the episode of the lady dead of love and revived—all are assaults on the agency of the quixote; they are asking him to play to their script. Both Don Quixote and Arabella are vulnerable to assaults of this kind, as these and other episodes like them show. But unlike quixotes we will see later in the eighteenth century, both Arabella and the Don maintain their dignity by refusing to compromise their beliefs. Ridiculous as their actions may be, they cannot be tricked into revealing a single self-interested, petty, or sordid motivation for them—which is more than can be said for their persecutors.

This laudable consistency and nobility of character is perhaps the most important similarity between Arabella and Don Quixote. The belief system that has evolved from their romance reading is expressed in a highly admirable personal character. The old knight and the young lady are reliably generous, noble, and honorable. Appeals to their generosity are certain to succeed; attempts at intimidation likely to fail. Both are eager to relieve distress in others, no matter what class of person they encounter. In fact, class confusion is another distinctive trait in both novels: Arabella mistakes jockeys at a race course for "Persons of great distinction" (84), Don Quixote mistakes innkeepers for castellans, and both mistake prostitutes for highborn ladies. The quixote's gaze, while imperfect, is always charitable in its effects.

The nobility of their respective quixotes' characters brings us to a larger structural similarity between *Don Quixote* and the *Female Quixote*: the identically vexed relationship in both texts between parody and satire. Both books begin by mocking a literary genre, chivalric romance, through the creation of a character who exemplifies (and exaggerates, where possible) the salient traits of the genre. But each work rapidly reveals that it has an equal if not greater investment in satire, as the "real world" of the text is paraded before the reader and made to look petty, foolish, and even grotesque, especially as seen through the virtuous and defamiliarizing eye of the quixote. The satiric effects of *Don Quixote* have long been appreciated, and as Susan Staves observes, by the eighteenth century, *Don Quixote* was often seen primarily as a satiric work (1972, 194). In her imitation, Lennox seems to enjoy preserving this aspect of the original. When Arabella, making her first public appearance at an assembly in Bath, invites the appropriately named Mr. Tinsel to tell her the "histories" of the persons passing before her, it is not her expectations but the world's littleness that is mocked when all she hears is "Scandal" (277). Hoping for "a pleasing and rational Amusement," Arabella is rightly disappointed: "far from a Detail of Vices, Follies, and Irregularities, I expected to have heard the Adventures of some illustrious Personages related" (277). Her condemnation, finally, of modern society is sweeping. Of the women, she asks: "What room, I pray you, does a Lady give for high and noble Adventures, who consumes her Days in Dressing, Dancing, listening to Songs, and ranging the Walks with People as thoughtless as herself? How mean and contemptible a Figure must a Life spent in such idle Amusements make in a History?" (279). As for the men, "with figures so feminine, Voices so soft, such tripping Steps, and such unmeaning Gestures" (279), they seem to her more likely to be overpowered in battle than to triumph like heroes of old. In these passages and others like them, Lennox seems to be

offering up a familiar, sincere satire, much like that of Alexander
Pope or Jonathan Swift, which targets the superficiality of modern
society and the frivolous belles and effeminate beaux who inhabit
it.

But the very straightforwardness of the satire complicates the position of the quixote as its vehicle. By using the virtues promulgated
by the romance genre as a way to castigate the failings of the real
world, the authors have given legitimacy to their quixotes' views,
which are presumably themselves the target of authorial mockery.
As parody and satire collide, the reader may be forgiven for being
confused. Which is the work's primary goal: the debunking of a
particular literary form, or the deflation of worldly pretenses and
practices? The result in both cases is the ambiguity for which *Don
Quixote* has long been famous: a central character who is either a
lunatic, a hero, or both.

DULCINEA'S STORY

Similar as they are, however, the old don and the "fair visionary"
are crucially distinguished as the result of their difference in gender. Henry Fielding, writing in the *Covent Garden Journal* in the
year of *The Female Quixote*'s publication, points to sexual difference to explain Cervantes's advantage over Lennox. The superiority of certain parts of the original, he comments, is:

> rather owing to that Advantage, which the Actions of Men give to the
> Writer beyond those of Women, than to any Superiority of Genius. Don
> Quixote is ridiculous in performing Feats of Absurdity himself; Arabe-
> lla can only become so, in provoking and admiring the Absurdities of
> others. (1752, 192)

The difference, then, reduces to kinds of action: men "perform,"
while women "provoke" and "admire." Obviously, the stories
written to accommodate these verbs will be very different ones, and
it is important to note that the distinction is not invented by Fielding, but sustained by the sources. Arabella, after all, does *not* want
to be a female knight. She wants to be a lady out of romance: Clelia,
Julia, and Statira are her heroines, not Britomart or Joan of Arc.
What we have, in a sense, is Dulcinea's story, and what kind of a
narrative model is that? What can a lady do, other than to serve as
an inspiration, to receive the homage and conquests of her knight?

One of the first problems a female quixote who is determined to be ladylike faces is finding any adventures at all. The peripeteia of a male quixote is out of her reach: Arabella simply can't traipse all over the countryside, as Don Quixote and Sancho Panza do. As Sancho says, "An honest maid should still be at home as if she had one leg broken," and the force of the proverb has not abated by the eighteenth century. The first thing that Alonzo Quixano does is to get out of town, deciding to "turn knight errant and travel through the world" (1950, 33). With nothing to hold him back, he "hasten[s] to translate his desires into action" (33). This, in many ways, is at the heart of the female quixote's dilemma: how can one "translate desires into action" when both action itself and the nature of the desires (for independence, importance, agency, sexual gratification) are forbidden?

One of Arabella's solutions is to imagine an enforced and therefore feminine type of mobility, in which confinement and abduction are the keys to adventure and the world. The following exchange illustrates the operation of Arabella's paradoxical approach to the broadening possibilities of abduction: admiring the classical beauties of Bath, Arabella remarks:

> I am certain, that if any Chance should conduct me into *Macedonia*, I would not leave it till I saw the Valley of *Tempe*, so celebrated by all the Poets and Historians.
> Dear Cousin, cried Glanville, who could hardly forbear smiling, what Chance, in the Name of Wonder, should take you into *Turky*, at so great a Distance from your own Country? . . .
> Well, interrupted Sir Charles. . . . But I hope my Niece does not propose to go thither. Not unless I am forcibly carried thither, said Arabella; but I do determine, if that Misfortune should ever happen to me, that I would, if possible, visit the Valley of *Tempe*. (261)

Abduction, because it leaves the woman's consent out of the question, is oddly enough the most respectable way to leave home. Arabella makes use of this strategy throughout the novel. She is continually imagining herself to be the target of abduction plots or rape attempts. This delusion gives her the opportunity not to *act*, which would be unfeminine, but to *react*, which allows her to remain true to her romance models while still generating adventures. Thus her suspicion that Edward the gardener (a nobleman in disguise, she believes) is about to break into her house to carry her off allows her to flee from her home into the surrounding countryside at nightfall, an event which invites further incidents.

Another kind of action seemingly closed to Arabella because of her sex is the purely physical. Not only will she never lift a lance, she will never even be on the receiving end of physical violence. The kind of sadistic abuse visited upon Don Quixote and Sancho Panza has no parallel in Lennox's novel. While Don Quixote is often surrounded by spectators who jeer and cheer as he is pummeled, bloodied, and humiliated, Arabella is almost never aware of even the mildest derision of those around her. Her creator, interestingly, protects her from the consequences of her follies. To a large extent, of course, this difference comes once again from the gender roles of the romance source: ladies are not supposed to engage in physical combat. On the other hand, knights-errant are not supposed to have their noses bloodied by goatherds or to vomit upon their squires. Physical indignities are at least potentially a way to deflate the pretensions of quixotes of either sex, as we will see in the examples of certain female quixotes later in the century. Part of the answer may lie in Lennox's own gender: while male authors like Fielding, Sterne, and Smollett enthusiastically replicate the crude physical slapstick that Cervantes modeled, the mode was obviously not compatible with Augustan ideals of feminine decorum and was hence unsuitable coming from a female pen.[2] But the more important answer may be that Lennox has no desire to deflate Arabella's pretensions and instead is dedicated to buoying them up, to increasing their plausibility in the reader's eyes.

For Arabella makes a far better lady of romance than Don Quixote does a knight. Her creator has endowed her with tremendous advantages: she *is* the daughter of a nobleman, she *is* immensely rich and beautiful, and she *does* live in a castle. Her imagination need only change the world, whereas the lean and aged Don Quixote has the much greater task of reimagining himself. Why has Lennox, in her mockery of romance absurdities, made her character into a genuine romance heroine?

I believe it is because Lennox wishes, for a while, to enjoy and to allow her readers to enjoy an unblemished fantasy of the powers that romance does make available to women. Arabella's beauty, time and again, is the magic charm that prevents her from being ridiculous. When the entire assembly at Bath is poised to mock the two-thousand-year-old fashions of the Princess Julia, in which they have heard Arabella is to appear, their reaction replicates romance instead of repudiating it:

> Scarce had the first tumultuous Whisper escaped the lips of each Individual, when they found themselves awed to Respect by that irresistable Charm in the Person of Arabella, which commanded Reverence and Love from all who beheld her. Her noble Air, the native Dignity in her

Looks, the inexpressible Grace which accompany'd all her Motions, and the consummate Loveliness of her Form, drew the Admiration of the whole Assembly. (272)

This is not parody; this is imitation. While Cervantes's hero falls short of the physical ideal in many ways, Lennox cannot afford to let her heroine do so. In a sense, this makes Lennox's undertaking much more conservative than Cervantes's—but the terms of comparison are not equal. Because of the difference of gender, different standards apply. While a male might be allowed to overcome an unfortunate appearance by virtue of a noble soul, a female's identity has historically been too closely tied to her appearance and to her body for this to be possible. If Lennox wants her heroine to be taken seriously at all, she must preserve her beauty. Over fifty years later, Jane Austen comments on the unfair but potent effect of appearance when she describes the "large fat sighings" of an amply proportioned matron over the memory of her deceased son (1995, 46). Commending her hero for his "self-command" in keeping a straight face in this situation, Austen writes:

Personal size and mental sorrow have certainly no necessary proportions. A large bulky figure has as good a right to be in deep affliction, as the most graceful set of limbs in the world. But, fair or not fair, there are unbecoming conjunctions, which reason will patronize in vain—which taste cannot tolerate—which ridicule will seize. (47)

As we will see, female quixotes whose appearance is ridiculed do not succeed in sustaining any readerly respect.[3] In endowing Arabella with beauty and a graceful set of limbs, Lennox has, perhaps wisely, avoided the unbecoming conjuction of romance ideals and a plain female face.

Arabella's power, however, does not stop with her beauty. Despite the restrictions on her action dictated by romance form and discussed above, Arabella's romances and her romance delusions are indeed sites of female power.[4] To begin with, Arabella concentrates on the actions—whether large or small—that *are* available to her literary heroines. While a lady of romance may seem passive in comparison to her bold and venturesome knight, it turns out that she can command others with nothing more than a slight gesture of her hand. These small actions are made much of in the novel, as those around Arabella learn to read and respond to her "dumb signs" (36). Even larger actions, if undertaken in self-defense, are also permissible, such as Clelia's heroic swimming of the Tiber.

But perhaps more potent than her actions are the romance heroine's words. Arabella is a firm believer in their efficacy: with her words a heroine can command a lover to live or die, banish him from the country, or allow him to hope. At various points in the novel, Arabella acts on these beliefs. When Mr. Glanville is sick (of love, she presumes), she commands him to recover. (Arabella cannot conceive of sickness as anything but a plot device or symptom of love.) Offended at what she sees as Mr. Selvin's presumption, she banishes him from England, much to his surprise. In short, Arabella has taken literally the conventions of courtly romance, a form attractive to women precisely because it seems to place them in a position of importance. Arabella repeatedly refers to women as "that Sex which merits all your Admiration and Reverence" (107), and men are expected to show "obedience" to her and "submission" to her commands. Viewed from this angle, it is no wonder that romance is appealing—it seems to depict a utopian gynocracy.

These, then, are Arabella's assumptions. But do they translate into power in the world of the novel? The answer is, initially, yes. Arabella's success is evident on two levels. Interpersonally and socially, she is in control: her uncle and cousin continually seek to accommodate her. They defer to her, they respect her privacy, they respect her preferences. In a telling exchange early in the novel, Arabella has asked her uncle and cousin to leave her to herself. Her uncle, who has only just met her, is inclined to be offended at her abrupt request, but "Mr. Glanville, who knew nothing pleased his Cousin so much as paying an exact Obedience to her Commands, rose up immediately; and, bowing respectfully to her, asked his Father, If he should attend him into the Garden" (63). Mr. Glanville is already, one is tempted to say, well trained. Arabella's preference for being obeyed is presented as if it were anomalous, simply the result of her romance fixation—but in actuality, who wouldn't be pleased at having an "exact obedience" paid to his or her commands? In simple household terms, Arabella is a winner.

Arabella also succeeds on another level by getting others to enact her romance fantasies for her. Glanville is the primary victim of her success: he does (twice) take up his sword for her, and he does suffer a protracted and anxious period of courtship, which stands in pointed contrast to his initial, complacent marriage proposal. As Margaret Doody points out, Glanville quickly learns to read Arabella's hand gestures, allowing them to function as she intends (1989, xxv). We are certain that Glanville has been deeply affected by Arabella when we catch him speaking her language to himself (81). Arabella's maid Lucy is another apt pupil, who, although she mangles her mistress's fine language in a manner reminiscent of Sancho Panza, takes her precepts to heart and is soon able to jump to conclusions as quickly as Arabella can. However it is measured, Arabella's power is considerable.

Considerable, but not without an end. For Arabella's power is in an important sense negated by her reform at the end of the novel. The reform brackets her power, disavowing it and setting it to one side. Arabella's repudiation of her romance delusions, like Don Quixote's, is made from a sick bed; unlike Don Quixote, Arabella recovers, and marries. By giving her heroine a conventionally happy ending, a romance ending in fact, Lennox does a great deal to discredit the subversive powers Arabella has embodied. They were not, it seems, so important after all, if she can give them up and still live. Don Quixote, in contrast, has the advantage here: death lends an unmistakable éclat to his reform; the loss of his romance ideals is nearly coterminous with the loss of his life and character. Certainly the other characters experience it that way, and Sanson Carrasco and Sancho Panza strive to convince the knight to resume his chivalric beliefs, the latter with tears and with a moving final speech that paints the beauties of the quixotic life. In contrast, the death of Arabella's ideals has no mourners—not even the faithful Lucy. The reader who regrets their passing has no representative in the text. The female quixote, restored to her proper place in the social hierarchy, has dwindled into a wife; the male quixote has grown into an icon.

ARABELLA AND HER SISTER QUIXOTES

The female quixotes who follow Arabella are in one important respect a new breed: they are reading not antique romances but the latest and most popular of literary genres—the novel. In his review of Lennox's novel, Fielding notes the belatedness of Lennox's critique, commenting that "the Humour of Romance, which is principally ridiculed in the Work," is "not at present greatly in fashion in this Kingdom" (1752, 193–4). George Colman's *Polly Honeycombe*, a comic play subtitled "A Dramatick Novel of One Act," draws attention to this shift in taste on the part of the reading public:

> Hither, in days of yore, from Spain or France,
> Came a dread Sorceress; her name, ROMANCE.
> . . . .

This fiend to quell, his sword *Cervantes* drew.
A trusty Spanish Blade, *Toledo* true
. . . .
But now, the dear delight of later years,
The younger Sister of ROMANCE appears:
Less solemn is her air, her drift the same,
And NOVEL her enchanting, charming name.

The genealogy Colman establishes is clear. The novel, while not identical to the romance, *is* closely related. Lennox's audience was no doubt easily able to extend her satire of the misguided romance reader to include novel readers as well. Because the novel's "drift [is] the same," the novel-reading quixote has much in common with the romance-reading quixote. Both expect adventures, admirers, coincidences, noble or sentimental friendships, and a happy ending. But the novel-reading quixote must adhere to the new standards of realism that her genre embraces: she must not expect her heroes to mow down their enemies by the hundreds, and if she is abducted (which is still likely), it will be by an ordinary baronet and not a prince or a giant. The verisimilar is now valued above the marvellous by readers, as many contemporary writers were to note.[5]

The female quixotes that populate the second half of the eighteenth and early part of the nineteenth century are an amusing, and in some ways heterogeneous, lot. Colman's *Polly Honeycombe* (1760) presents a stage version of the quixote, a merchant's daughter whose novel reading makes her reject the properous and pompous Mr. Ledger, a suitor proposed by her father, in favor of the poetically inclined Mr. Scribble. The tone of the play is light and the moral inconclusive: the irrepressible Polly escapes marriage altogether, her father is thrown into impotent confusion, and the play concludes with an ironic encomium on the virtues of novels. Maria Edgeworth's novella "Angelina" (1801) targets the sentimental novel specifically, and is unique in focusing on the heroine's desire for a female friend. Having begun a correspondence with "Araminta," the author of a popular novel, Angelina is persuaded to run away to "Angelina's Bower," a rustic cottage whose picturesque charms are soon discovered to be no compensation for "the want of double refined sugar, of green tea, and Mocha coffee" (23). The want of refinement in Araminta, however, turns out to be a greater obstacle to the consummation of their sentimental friendship, and Angelina returns home chastened, under the care of a female relative who advises her to read *The Female Quixote*. Jane Austen's *Northanger Abbey* (in manuscript form by the 1790s), as the title suggests, pokes fun at the Gothic novels that were all the rage in the closing decade of the century. Since such works were essentially novels of sentiment repackaged to include Gothic architecture and wild natural scenery, the conventions Austen ridicules are more broadly those of her sentimental predecessors. Her heroine, Catherine Morland, is intentionally constructed to undo what Austen saw as the artificial and unnatural virtues of a novel heroine: Catherine is not particularly pretty (although she gets prettier), she does not excel in the usual feminine accomplishments, such as painting and piano-playing, and she does not write sonnets. But despite her imperfections and her penchant for the writings of Ann Radcliffe, Catherine does have a kind heart and a good nature, and her creator rewards her with that most conventional of romantic endings, marriage to the worthy hero.

The final two female quixotes I will consider are treated less sympathetically by their authors. Tabitha Tenney's Dorcasina, the heroine of an American novel entitled *Female Quixotism* (1801), undergoes repeated humiliation at the hands of fortune hunters who seek to take advantage of her delusions, and ends up unmarried and alone, condemning romance novels as the *radix malorum* of her life but unable to take pleasure in any other kind of writing. Similarly, although Eaton Stannard Barrett's Cherubina (*The Heroine*, 1813) is married off happily at the end of the novel, her adventures with fortune hunters and other characters real and unreal have been extremely prejudicial to her character and dignity. In addition, they have also had serious negative consequences for innocent bystanders: it is with Cherubina's approval that her father is incarcerated in a madhouse, for example. The heroines' names are further symptomatic of the authors' attitudes. While Arabella and Angelina have elegant ones which indicate that the characters are, at least on one level, suited to being heroines, Dorcasina and Cherubina have invented their own names, rejecting the unromantic plainness of Dorcas Sheldon and Cherry Wilkinson; the result is that the reader is reminded of the heroines' absurdity and pretension several times per paragraph, or as often as the names appear.

All the female quixotes after Arabella share the basic quixotic traits: they read too much, and their reading has skewed their perceptions and expectations of the world. But with the exception of Catherine Morland in *Northanger Abbey*, I believe that these quixotes are presented as being both more culpable and more vulnerable than Arabella. In general, the effects of their willful misreadings are messier and more compromising to heroinely dignity. One figure in particular seems to sum up the new danger to the novel-reading quixote: the lower-class, silver-tongued fortune hunter, who serves as the focus for social and authorial anxieties that were carefully separated in *The Female Quixote*. Class confusion, the self-serving manipulation of the language of romance, and the heroine's own sexual vulnerability are all treated in Lennox's novel, but they do not converge significantly. Edward is a gardener, not a prince—but since he has never tried, by any speech or action, to convince Arabella otherwise, the confusion over rank is all on her side and poses little threat. Sir George, who does try to manipulate Arabella by speaking in the language of her books, is well and truly upper class himself. And finally, if as some critics have suggested, Arabella is secretly attracted to Edward or others of the suitors she invents, her strict romance code requires her to expect twenty years of courtship before she grants so much as a kiss—so her virtue is never really in danger. In contrast, almost all of the other heroines come very close to marrying a lower-class imposter, whose talent for romantic speech and whose near success indicts the heroine by providing evidence of her unruly desires. Polly Honeycombe attempts to run off with the eloquent Mr. Scribble, who turns out not to be "a gentleman" but rather a mere "attorney's clerk," nephew to Polly's nurse. One of Dorcasina's first suitors is an ex-highwayman and "artful adventurer" (1801, 27) who persuades Dorcasina that he is "a perfect Sir Charles Grandison" (28) by playing the flute, speaking of love and novels, and casting "languishing glances upon Dorcasina, from his fine black eyes" (27). He addresses her as "my goddess" and "my angel" (31), working upon her so successfully that "she could scarcely refrain from throwing herself into his arms, and confessing a mutual flame" (35). Cherubina is taken in by the actor Abraham Grundy who, after he learns that she has ten thousand pounds at her disposal, "admits" that he is really Lord Altamont Mortimer Montmorenci, and swears to become her protector, later borrowing twenty-five pounds from her to pay his landlady. Even Edgeworth's Angelina fits this pattern, for although the "suitor" in question is female, she has lured Angelina away from her home by writing her romantic letters about the domestic bliss they will enjoy in a retired country cottage. The lower-class status of the heroine's "unknown friend" is in a sense the story's punchline: after a prolonged search for the "aimiable Araminta," Angelina takes one look at the gross, bourbon-swilling "Miss Hodges," and realizes the error of her ways. In all of these instances, the reading of novels exposes the women to very real dangers from people of a lower class, who correctly read the heroines' improper desires in order to take advantage of them.

Dorcasina and Cherubina pay for their transgressions physically, as both are subjected to the kind of "comic" abuse usually reserved for male quixotes. Early in the novel, Dorcasina is chased by a pack of boys who strip off her bonnet and handkerchief, ripping her gown and forcing her to leave her shoes in the mud (1801, 60). Later, covering her grey hair with a wig and cantering off for a ride in the company of her newest suitor "with the air and spirit of a girl of eighteen" (256), Dorcasina finds herself the center of attention when her wig blows off, leaving her to ride through town bald, "her head undecked even by a single hair" (257). The wig, for its part, undergoes further trauma, involving a hog, some mud, and more of those mischevious local boys. Cherubina is similarly mistreated on more than one occasion. Her account of the melee in a milliner's shop is typical: "I was attempting to rush from the shop, when I found my spangled muslin barbarously seized by the woman, who tore it to pieces in the struggle; and, pulling off the bonnet, gave me a horrid slap in the face" (1813, 41).

However ridiculous Lennox's Arabella may seem at times, it is impossible to imagine her on the receiving end of a slap, or in any kind of proximity to a hog. This is, I think, evidence of her creator's genuine endorsement of Arabella's goals and principles as extracted from her readings, an endorsement wholly lacking in the literature which follows her. Arabella is the only character who, Don Quixote-like, derives significant power from her literary sources, her madness, and her imitative oratory. Later female quixotes are more unambiguously discredited, if not by physical assault then by the implication that novel reading makes women immodest, and makes them so deperate for male attention that they welcome it even from lower-class men. Catherine Morland in *Northanger Abbey* is in some ways an exception to this rule, but in spite of the affection with which her author treats her, she is lovable despite her reading rather than because of it. *Northanger Abbey* does not abuse its quixote, but neither does it value her for her literary leanings. In contrast to Arabella, whose uncle thinks that she could have made a great figure in Parliament had she been a man (311), Catherine is not unusually intelligent, and there is no suggestion that her reading provides a consistent, alternate code of behavior as Arabella's does. Catherine's own simple character—not the rules of romance, as in Lennox's novel—provides the point of view from which the author satirizes the follies of society.

Arabella, then, is the female quixote closest to Don Quixote not only in time but also in spirit. Susan Staves, in "Don Quixote in

Eighteenth-Century England," claims that during the eighteenth century, Don Quixote became increasingly more heroic:

> At first we see Don Quixote as a buffoon, a madman who belongs in a farce. Then ambiguities creep in, and we have a Don Quixote who is still ridiculous, still a buffoon, but who, at the same time, is beginning to look strangely noble, even saintly. Then, finally, toward the end of the century we begin to glimpse the romantic Don Quixote, an idealistic and noble hero. (1972, 193)

I find this persuasive with regard to male quixotes, but for female quixotes, the opposite is true. Lennox's Arabella, appearing in 1752, marks the high point of heroism for female quixotes. Despite her conservative ending, Lennox has taken her heroine seriously, producing a blend of comedy and heroism that resembles the ambiguity of Cervantes's original more closely than anything that follows. After Lennox, the female quixote becomes a straightforward figure of fun, deployed by her author to suit a much simpler moral and rhetorical agenda. If, as contemporary commentators feared, novel reading might lead women astray, the female quixote could always be used as a scarecrow to frighten women away from the fertile fields of romance and back onto the straight and narrow paths of duty and virtue.

NOTES

1. All citations of Lennox will be to the 1989 Oxford University Press edition.

2. The two authors who do subject their quixotes to physical abuse, Tenney and Barrett, are an American woman and an Irish male, respectively. No English female author uses her quixote in such a way.

3. Tabitha Tenney's quixote is a good example of the opposite strategy. Tenney wishes to discredit her character and does so in great part by means of her appearance. Ironically, by the end of the novel Tenney's character is most like Cervantes's in that she has been allowed to age. But instead of admiring her for striving to overcome her physical shortcomings, we are encouraged to ridicule her for continuing to believe that she is romantically attractive.

4. Craft provides a good account of the operation of Arabella's power. See also Spacks (1988, 533) on Arabella's desire for power.

5. Lennox herself is of course on one level opposing the realism of her novel to the implausibility of romance. Critics who address the intersections of romance, the novel, and the fictional in Lennox's work include Langbauer and Ross. Horace Walpole is one contemporary who complains that because of the modern preference for realism, "the great resources of fancy have been dammed up, by a strict adherence to common life" (1966, 21).

Works Cited

Austen, Jane. 1995. *Persuasion*. New York: Norton.

Barrett, Eaton Stannard. 1813. *The Heroine*. London: Henry Colburn.

Cervantes Saavedra, Miguel de. 1950. *The Adventures of Don Quixote*. London: Penguin.

Colman, George. 1760. *Polly Honeycombe: A Dramatick Novel of One Act*. London: T. Beckett and T. Davies.

Craft, Catherine. 1991. "Reworking Male Models: Aphra Behn's *Fair Vow-Breaker*, Eliza Haywood's *Fantomina*, and Charlotte Lennox's *Female Quixote*." *Modern Language Review* 86: 821–38.

Doody, Margaret. 1989. Introduction to *The Female Quixote*, by Charlotte Lenrox. Oxford: Oxford University Press.

Edgeworth, Maria. 1832. "Angelina, or, L'Amie Inconnue." In *Tales and Novels*. Vol. 3. London: Baldwin and Cradock.

Fielding, Henry. 1752. *The Covent Garden Journal*. Edited by Ioan Williams. No. 24 of *The Criticism of Henry Fielding*. New York:

Langbauer, Laurie. 1990. "Diverting Romance: Charlotte Lennox's *The Female Quixote*." In *Women and Romance: The Consolations of Gender in the English Novel*, Ithaca: Cornell University Press.

Lennox, Charlotte. 1989. *The Female Quixote*. Oxford: Oxford University Press.

Ross, Deborah. 1991. "*The Female Quixote*: A Realistic Fairy Tale." In *The Excellence of Falsehood*. Lexington: University of Kentucky Press.

Spacks, Patricia Meyer. 1988. " 'The Subtle Sophistry of Desire': Dr. Johnson and the *Female Quixote*," *MP* 85: 532–42.

Staves, Susan. 1972. Don Quixote in Eighteenth-Century England. *Comparative Literature* 24: 193–215.

Tenney, Tabitha. 1801. *Female Quixotism*. Boston: I. Thomas and E. T. Andrews.

Walpole, Horace. 1966. *The Castle of Otranto*. New York: Dover.

Comedia Contributions to a
Molière Masterpiece

THOMAS P. FINN

The enormous theatrical productions of Spain and France in the early and mid-seventeenth century provide numerous examples of characters who assume other identities by manipulating widespread beliefs, rumor, and even attire, and in so doing, they explore and expand the otherwise restrictive societal criteria for identity. The mercurial, complex, and resilient characters of the Spanish *comedia*—whose existence as such challenges society's power to impose upon them static, simplistic identity criteria—find their counterparts in the French dramatic world, whose characters ardently seek to create their own subjectivity.

Despite the dissimilarity in plot between Tirso de Molina's *Don Gil de las calzas verdes* [Don Gil of the Green Breeches, 1615] and Molière's *Le Bourgeois gentilhomme* [The Bourgeois Gentleman, 1670], the denouement of each play suggests a society willing to give some kind of concession to an individual imaginary identity, whether that concession be ardent manifestations that such an identity really exists or the appearance of belief in the imaginary persona.[1] The role of the *maestros* [teachers] in Finea's transformation in Lope de Vega's *La dama boba* [The Lady Nitwit] is also important not only as a point of comparison with M. Jourdain's *maîtres*, but also as an introduction to the notion of changing identity through a knowledge of arts that manifests itself primarily in physical appearances. Thus it is clear that the impact of the seventeenth-century Spanish *comedia* in Molière's work went far beyond the borrowing of some character traits or basic plots. Although it is the contention of this study that traces of the Spanish theatrical tradition permeate *Le Bourgeois gentilhomme*, it should be stated that there is little evidence to support the notion of a single *comedia* that served as Molière's model for this play.[2]

This essay will study the underlying belief shared by both protagonists that they have the right and ability to construct their own identity instead of passively accepting that assigned to them by society. Recent studies have revised the traditional view of the early modern hero/heroine as an individual forced to conform to the role society has prescribed for him/her (Diez-Borque 1976, 107; Reichenberger 1959, 309), contending that identity is a much more mutable phenomenon:

> human identity is more constituted than constitutive; constituted by, for example, the preexisting structures of language and ideology, and by the material conditions of human existence. Thus is the subject decentered, and subjectivity revealed as . . . not the antithesis of social process but its focus. (Dollimore 1986, 54)

George Mariscal calls this "move toward individuation" a "dangerous undecidable" (1991, 95) while Catherine Connor (Swietlicki) affirms that "the *comedia* sustains and contains the status quo" as it "simultaneously subverts the very structures on which its existence depends." (1994, 45). Both Tirso's Juana and Molière's M. Jourdain attempt to control the dynamic equilibrium between individual and society, usurping the collectivity's traditional right to create, distribute, and confirm the identities of its members. In addition, they try to force society to accept their new personas as valid.

The main difference between the Spanish and French traditions is one of belief. Like many Spanish protagonists, Juana does not believe in the persona she projects. The *comedia* seems to view subjectivity as a game, a conscious exercise of wit and deception that may be adopted or discarded at the will of those playing. In contrast, Molière's theatre depicts characters who believe in their improbable identities and want others to believe in them, too. M. Jourdain is the incarnation of Foucault's Baroque character who reverses everything, recognizing strangers while not knowing friends, unknowingly wearing a mask while he believes he is unmasking others, believing things are what they are not (1966, 63). M. Jourdain's subjectivity, then, is not just a game, but rather a serious struggle during which he risks facing the tragic realization that he may not be capable of actualizing his new persona without winning a significant concession from the collectivity.

To this end, M. Jourdain discovers a medium in which appearances are given special emphasis and the possibilities of transforming and expanding one's identity are greatly increased. He turns his life into theater, that magical place where disbelief is suspended and the normal limits of human existence are pushed back. This is evident in act two, where the tailors fit him for a new suit:

Dès lors, [the tailors' ballet], ce «gentilhomme» se révèle au spectateur, de manière toute cinétique, comme un bourgeois incurablement rigide qui, dans le sens littéral aussi bien que dans le sens péjoratif de l'expression française, «se donne en spectacle.» (Brody 1968, 315)

[From that point, (the tailor's ballet), this "gentleman" reveals himself to the spectator, in a completely kinetic way, as an incurably rigid bourgeois who, in the literal as well as pejorative sense of the French expression, "makes a spectacle of himself."]

This spectacle is infectious, spawning a stage-like world of potentialities yet to be realized. Indeed M. Jourdain certainly believes that a nobleman already exists within him and that all his noble persona lacks is an accurate imitation of the actions of the "gens de qualité" [people of quality]. Consequently he mimicks the nobility in an effort to gain the world's admiration (Defaux 1980, 281).

For this reason he is disinterested in any skill that he cannot show off or that has no immediate applicability. He declines the offer of the "maître de philosophe" to teach him logic, ethics, and physics, opting instead for a spelling lesson (during which M. Jourdain thoroughly enjoys the exaggerated pronunciation of vowels) and a tutoring session to help him write a love letter to the "marquise." He also learns the terms "prose" and "poetry," which are valuable to M. Jourdain, not because he is ignorant of the difference between the two (he has known the difference for years without being aware of the terms), but rather because it is demonstrable, albeit useless, knowledge that he may flaunt before others. M. Jourdain must attract attention, must be seen, heard and well known in his community because it is in conjunction with and/or in defiance of his community that he will construct his new persona. Consequently, he spends much of the play trying to imitate the noble arts of music, dance, fencing, gastronomy, and even courtship. But because he has not been instructed from birth in these areas, he must hire teachers ("maîtres") so he may learn them.

A similar attempt at identity transformation is undertaken in Lope de Vega's *La dama boba* (1613). Finea, the title character, is forced by her father to learn the alphabet and practice dance so that she may develop external graces that more closely correspond to her noble birth, thus increasing her prospects for marriage. Finea does not seem very gifted in these areas and so greatly exasperates the reading "maestro" that he resigns his position despite the handsome salary paid by Finea's father. Exhausted by the constant lessons, Finea makes a comment that gets to the heart of the question of education for the sake of appearances:

¡y todo es nada! (1427)

[and it's all nothing!]

In a sense, Finea is correct, for her father intends to provide just enough instruction so that she may give the impression of an educated and refined lady, worthy of her social rank and a noble husband. But Finea is interested in more than just the superficial signs of a woman of the upper class:

> Finea aspira a aprender a leer los libros más difíciles; ahora bien, no quiere leer meramente al pie de la letra, sino desde un puesto de lectora que le permita tener acceso a múltiples niveles de significación que el discurso lingüístico puede generar. (Carrión 1991, 241)

> [Finea aspires to learn to read the most difficult books; now, she does not merely wish to read literal meanings, but rather from a reader's position which allows her access to the multiple levels of meaning that linguistic discourse can generate.]

Once in love, Finea is not satisfied with the mere façade of an upper-class lady. While her new thirst for knowledge may not be beyond the bounds of an educated seventeenth-century Spanish woman (Howe 1990, 155), Finea aims to exceed the charm of her sister, Nise, who is originally considered the more elegant and cultivated of the two. By the end of the play—which covers a period of about two months—Finea not only has acquired literacy, but a facility with words allowing her to manipulate their multiple meanings and buy her enough time to find a way to marry the man she loves. The ability to see and utilize linguistic subtleties seems to be the yardstick by which her mutation of identity is measured:

> *bobería* is manifested above all as a failure to grasp symbolic language. . . . Transformed by love, Finea will manifest her new-found *ingenio* on a verbal level through the clever manipulation of language. (Surtz 1981, 163)

Exactly the reverse is true of M. Jourdain. Whereas Finea learns and profits from her penetration into the more sophisticated nuances of language, this bourgeois seeks only to show off his acquired merchandise and knowledge for public consumption in the hopes that he will convince the community that he belongs in its upper echelons. M. Jourdain is in line with the long-standing *comedia* tradition of equating noble identity with noble appearance and noble reputation, (e.g., García of *La verdad sospechosa* [Truth Suspected]). Unlike Finea who undergoes a significant personal metamorphosis, M. Jourdain concentrates his efforts solely on the external manifestations of his supposedly noble persona. To this end, he tries to influence what others say about him and how they see him. He insists that the "maître de musique" [music teacher] and the "maître à danser" [dance instructor] remain until his tailor arrives so they may see him in his new suit in the style of "les gens de qualité" [1. 2: people of quality]; he tells his valets to follow behind him during his promenade through the city "afin qu'on voie bien que vous êtes à moi" [3. 1: so they see that you belong to me]; he explains to his wife the benefit of having others notice the Count Dorante frequenting their home; and he is of course thrilled to be the center of attention at the ceremony where he receives the empty title of "Mamamouchi." M. Jourdain believes the only difference between himself and the nobility is their reputations in the community, and how they are perceived by the rest of society. He accepts the premise that noble reputation is acquired through external manifestations and so seeks to imitate them in order to achieve noble identity.

Ironically for M. Jourdain, his exaggerated and inaccurate emulation of the nobility is indeed the natural expression of his bourgeois identity. Whereas the protagonist believes he is communicating what he considers to be his true noble identity, his actions are, in reality, only more evidence that he cannot escape from the ostentatious consumerism that characterize many of Molière's bourgeois. M. Jourdain makes no conscious effort to trick anyone. His project is executed in good faith, for he truly believes he is participating in the ordinary activities of the nobility. Nonetheless, in a very real sense, it is more difficult for M. Jourdain to distinguish himself from the bourgeoisie than it is for him to imitate the upper classes. M. Jourdain's behavior cannot help but belie the persona that only he sees as an undeniable reality. In society's eyes, his actions bring him closer to the bourgeoisie from which he wants to set himself apart.

Imitation and differentiation are crucial themes in this play. Even the various "maîtres" try to prove their superiority over their rivals, thus establishing within the work a method that M. Jourdain himself will follow. For example, the "maître de philosophie" tries to elevate his stature by pointing out how one must set himself apart from the rest of society:

Ce n'est pas de vaine gloire et de condition que les hommes doivent disputer entre eux; et ce qui nous distingue parfaitement les uns des autres, c'est la sagesse et la vertu. (2.3.3)

[It is not for vain glory and rank that men should fight amongst themselves; what distinguishes us from others is wisdom and virtue.]

He, of course, quickly betrays his own observation by falling into the same argument that preceded his arrival, bickering with the other "maîtres" over which art form is more important.

It is clear that if M. Jourdain is to be successful in assimilating himself into one segment of society, he certainly must distance himself from another:

Il essaie de se transformer en «homme de qualité» pour se distinguer du commun bourgeois (homme riche mais sans intelligence, dérisoirement ignorant et malhabile). (Mishriky 1982, 18)

[He tries to transform himself into a "man of quality" in order to distinguish himself from the common bourgeois (a rich man but without intelligence, ridiculously ignorant and unskilled).]

The protagonist needs to establish a difference between himself and those he considers beneath him. This is evident when M. Jourdain becomes upset with his tailor upon noticing that the latter has made a suit for himself out of the same material used for his own suit. It is further demonstrated in the previously mentioned scene in which M. Jourdain tries to explain to his wife his newly learned distinction between prose and verse and becomes a source of serious concern when he refuses Cléonte's request to marry his daughter because he is not a "gentilhomme." He not only becomes more firm in his refusal despite his wife's objections, he seems to enjoy the conflict since it emphasizes the difference between his supposed noble stature and the inferior rank of his wife:

Voilà bien les sentiments d'un petit esprit, de vouloir demeurer toujours dans la bassesse. (3. 12)

[Those are indeed the opinions of a small mind, wanting always to remain in lowliness.]

M. Jourdain, then, is dependent not only on reputation in general to assure his imaginary identity, but specifically on a negative reputation among the bourgeoisie. He sees distancing himself from his bourgeois surroundings and integrating himself into the nobility as one and the same thing. The further he mimics the comportment and dress of the upper classes, the more he becomes the object of scorn for his family and servants. This ridicule, however, far from making him see that he is at best a poor imitator of aristocratic ways, only reassures him of his ascendancy and his family's low social status that, for M. Jourdain, prevents them from fully understanding him. Thus the derision he endures from the bourgeoisie only reassures M. Jourdain that buying societal recognition is the correct path to follow. M. Jourdain's goal is not to persuade the community to verify his noble birth or any inward grace, but rather to coax the collectivity into acknowledging his outward appearances of nobility, even though he cannot fathom the idea that such acknowledgment might be a ruse:

> Only the superficial aspects of nobility are of concern to Monsieur Jourdain, for he cannot grasp that being and seeming are not the same thing. Naïvely he assumes that others are also unable to distinguish between counterfeit façades and essential traits. (Gaines 1984, 157)

It is not really a question, then, of the protagonist's conscious rejection of what others consider to be authentic identity, for he seems unaware that another definition of identity exists. Consequently, he does not seek to convert his community, but rather, to buy its cooperation. For M. Jourdain, it is a publicity problem. He believes that if he purchases enough things that make him visible, he will receive the acknowledgment he has deserved all along. In his mind, the "Mamamouchi" ceremony is the unmistakable sign that his plan has come to fruition.

While this ritual may have had a similar prototype in the *comedia*,[3] my interest lies with those characters who convince their community of the veracity of an imaginary persona—a notion embodied in the protagonist of Tirso's *Don Gil de las calzas verdes*. Indeed, it is Juana's gift for generating multiple and believable personas that remains constant in this otherwise unpredictable and intricate *comedia*.[4]

The title character is, of course, Juana in disguise, her assumed identity a part of her scheme to force Martín to fulfill his promise of marriage. During the course of her masquerade, she convinces virtually everyone that Gil is a real person. Not only do they believe Juana's portrayal of Gil, but Inés falls in love with Gil, as does her friend Clara. Furthermore, Don Juan (a rival for Inés's hand) and Martín become jealous of Gil's romantic overtures toward Inés. Tirso's comic genius and the community's faith in the existence of Gil reach their peak at the end of the play when, for various reasons, there are at least four characters who try to pass themselves off as Gil.

All of this goes beyond the traditional quid pro quo of mistaken identity. Juana's disguises and ruses can be construed not so much as an inquiry into the validity of the traditional criteria for individual identity, but rather as a serious challenge to society's ability to control said criteria. Indeed, it is Juana's unique skill at manipulating the diverse elements of identity that allows her to create and channel the emotions and suspicions that drive the members of her community (Ly 1984, 183). She is able, then, to recreate herself as well as to create an identity whose authenticity the collectivity will not only rush to acknowledge, but will ultimately imitate.

Juana succeeds in producing a persona out of her own remarkable ingenuity and astuteness, yet she is nonetheless aware that she needs society's cooperation. Appearances may prompt the community to recognize and authenticate a particular identity without investigating the individual's motivations for putting forth such appearances, but the collectivity must have a reason for such collaboration. It is society's need to believe in this imaginary persona that Juana exploits and that allows her to conjure up a new state of things:

> [Juana crea una] misteriosa seudo-realidad en que se embrollan los otros personajes gracias a su avaricia, sus celos, su deseo de hallar un esposo galán o una mujer rica, y sus propias decepciones unos de otros. (Varey 1989, 367)

> [(Juana creates a) mysterious pseudo-reality in which the other characters embroil themselves due to their avarice, their jealousy, their desire to find a handsome man or rich woman, and their own deceptions of one another.]

Juana is then using society's own weaknesses against itself. She does not change the criteria for identity, but wrests control over it from the collectivity and uses it to her own advantage. Juana exploits the vulnerabilities of society and not only convinces it of a false identity, but actually forces the collectivity to submit itself to her own machinations and, in the process, to accept her version of what is true and what is false. Turning back to Molière's work, M. Jourdain would like to pick up where Juana leaves off. As successful as Juana is in her endeavor, it is important not to lose sight of the reason she undertakes such a project:

> La realidad nueva no fue creada para evadirse, sino como medio para alcanzar una meta. Por sus varios papeles, trucos y distorsión de la verdad, Juana crea un laberinto más que desagradable para Martín. Esto le

devuelve al mundo de la realidad. Lograda su meta, Juana abandona su personalidad múltiple. (Hesse 1981, 271)

[The new reality was not created as an escape, rather as a means to a goal. Through her various roles, tricks, and distortion of the truth, Juana creates a more than unpleasant maze for Martín. This returns him to the real world. Her goal achieved, Juana abandons her multiple personalities.]

While the temporary nature of Juana's plan may not constitute a full-scale indictment of society's authority to decide identity, it does provide the blueprint for M. Jourdain's attempt to impose indefinitely his imaginary persona on his community. To that end he spares no expense, not only to acquire noble accoutrements, but also to buy a permanent aura that heightens his attempts to create a new reality. Lessons and new clothes are but two of his high-priced commodities:

the expenses involved in acquiring a noble mistress are massive: 18,000 livres to Dorante to serve as go-between . . . a costly diamond, feasts, serenades, and entertainment. Jourdain's road to noble privilege runs through the means of personal relations purchased with his family's patrimony. (Gaines 1984, 159)

This is no temporary project with a short-term goal. M. Jourdain is far too business-conscious (remember his quick addition, without pen or paper, of Dorante's debt in 3. 4) to spend his money for a new status of which he will quickly dispose after he tires of it.

This is why it makes sense to him to pay heavily for appellations which he believes will bring him enduring recognition of his noble identity, although they are in reality void of meaning or substance. He pays handsomely and reacts joyously each time his valet addresses him as "Mon gentilhomme . . . Monseigneur . . . [and] Votre Grandeur" (2. 5). Being generous in return for lofty forms of address establishes in his mind the logic of a process in which one purchases noble attire as a sort of public announcement of membership in the upper classes. This announcement, in turn, gives rise to the empty titles of dignity seen above. In essence, this is what M. Jourdain hopes for throughout the play—public recognition of a title he possesses,[5] even though it never enters his mind that this cognomen is meaningless to the rest of society. That the community might not believe in his imaginary persona is beyond the realm of possibility for M. Jourdain as long as he has the community's obedience.

The "Mamamouchi" ceremony of the final act is of course the materialization of this compliance. The collectivity finally concedes defeat not to the authenticity of M. Jourdain's noble persona, but rather to the impossibility of derailing his individual imaginary identity. Indeed, he is so certain of his identity, he continues to see his wife as the stubborn one:

> Vous venez toujours mêler vos extravagances à toutes choses; et il n'y a pas moyen de vous apprendre à être raisonnable. (5. 6)

> [You always come along and mix your foolishness into everything; and there is no way to teach you to be reasonable.]

M. Jourdain's enduring struggle to wrest this concession from society does more than make us laugh at an obvious and ridiculous impostor. Although he is never a serious threat to society's fabric, the result of M. Jourdain's project is that he exposes the collectivity's reliance on precarious criteria for the creation and distribution of identity as well as its impotence when it comes to correcting the outrageous behavior of its members. Neither ridicule nor reasonable discourse have any effect on M. Jourdain. Even Cléonte, the "honnête homme" par excellence of the work, makes no headway when he explains to the protagonist that, although he (Cléonte) is not of noble lineage, merit makes him worthy to marry Lucille. Cléonte is, thus, forced to play by M. Jourdain's rules to win his daughter's hand. But the young man's disguise as the son of the "Grand Turc" has some very serious ramifications. The fact that he must hide his real identity only reinforces the futility of the individual's struggle against a society which extols appearances and respects vacuous titles (Mishriky 1982, 149).

M. Jourdain is certainly not aware of Cléonte's ruse, and it is impossible to predict how he would react if he were aware of the trick. Yet it is important to remember that Cléonte is only being practical and M. Jourdain is only being consistent. Despite Cléonte's dislike for society's preference of appearances over identity, he finds he must say what the reluctant father wants to hear (or more accurately, show him want he wants to see) in order to marry the one he loves. As for M. Jourdain, the title of "Grand Turc" convinces him that he is marrying off his daughter to someone of noble rank.

Imaginary identity (for M. Jourdain) and role-playing (for all the others) help the characters to break the impasse. M. Jourdain's community is unable to shake his myopic view of himself and the bourgeois is equally incapable of convincing the collectivity of his noble identity. Something has to give, as Covielle, the valet who organizes the whole masquerade of the "Mamamouchi" ceremony, explains to Mme. Jourdain:

> ne voyez-vous pas bien que tout ceci n'est fait que pour nous ajuster aux visions de votre mari; que nous l'abusons sous ce déguisement, et que c'est Cléonte lui-même qui est le fils du Grand Turc? (5. 6)

> [don't you see that this is only to accommodate hallucinations of your husband; we are tricking him with this disguise, and it's Cléonte himself who is the son of the Grand Turk?]

In the end, the unrelenting conviction of one man denies the collectivity's right to determine identity and its prerogative to punish those who would challenge such an authority. *La dama boba* may have provided a pedagogical method for identity transformation and *Don Gil de las calzas verdes* may have allowed a glimpse at an individual overpowering her community, but M. Jourdain is unique in that he obtains a societal concession without deceit. At no time does his community actually believe he is truly of noble lineage, yet it remains incapable of converting him and is too weak to expel him. The prominence of role-playing in the play (which eventually governs everyone's behavior) indicates society has lost the authority it reserved for itself to be the final arbiter of identity. To break the stalemate between itself and an unyielding individual, society must relinquish this favored position. It is by no means an unconditional surrender, but rather a compromise. M. Jourdain is satisfied (at least temporarily) with the recognition he receives and society neutralizes the immediate threat to the marriage of two young lovers.

EXTENDING THE MOMENT

M. Jourdain is the culmination of many French characters (e.g., Molière's Arnolphe and Alceste) in that he represents the individual who cannot conquer society. Yet he surpasses the others by fighting it to a stalemate, forcing the entire community to play a role, to pretend to adopt the individual's point of view. This is a dramatic departure from the interplay of the individual and society in many *comedias*, where the individual promoting an imaginary identity is made to relinquish role-playing at the end of the work—such as the title-character of Tirso's *Marta la piadosa* [Martha the Pious]—or surrenders the mask like Juana in *Don Gil de las calzas verdes*.

French comedy hypothesizes on what would happen if this moment of illusion, seemingly evoked into existence with such ease in the *comedia*, was extended to a lifetime. Juana poses this "what if?" question by actualizing false identities and making others believe them, if only temporarily. Her will to succeed with her ruse not only completes the task at hand but also reveals the diverse spectrum of identity possibilities. The temporary nature of such imposture is obviously no hindrance to Molière's notion that such role-playing could be expanded and integrated into some of his more complex characters as well as into a buffoon such as M. Jourdain. Nevertheless, Molière, ever aware of the awesome power of the collectivity, instills his protagonist with a deep and durable resilience in order to show the constant, and sometimes painfully slow, progress of the subject as s/he resists society's efforts to dictate identity. It would seem that "extending the moment" leads to a truce between the individual and society rather than to a clear victory in the struggle for the right to create and determine "authentic" identity.

Yet, north and south of the Pyrenees, the truce is unstable. If French comedy of the era does not complete, but rather pushes forward the identity experiments undertaken by Spanish playwrights in the first half of the seventeenth century, then two elements key to the advancement of the subject are revealed: the will and the weapons. Whereas French comedy supplies the stubborn character who tirelessly resists the efforts of society to convert her/him, it lacks the Spanish weapons—the numerous ways a *comedia* character tricks and dupes the community. Thus the Spanish and French notions of subjectivity do not differ so much as they complement each other and when combined, will be a formidable opponent of any society that seeks to control them.

NOTES

1. For a more in-depth study of the role of music and dance in these works, see my article, "The Weapons of Spectacle: Song, Dance, and Imaginary Identity in *Don Gil de las calzas verdes* and *Le Bourgeois gentilhomme*" in the electronic journal *Laberinto*.

2. There is an *entremés* (a short skit usually put on between acts of a featured play) by Moreto that resembles Molière's basic plot, but it is not at all certain that the French playwright even knew of its existence (Huszár 1907, 241). It seems undeniable, however, that Molière had more than a passing knowledge of Moreto's *El desdén con el desdén* [Spite for Spite, 1654] during the composition of *La Princesse d'Elide* (1664).

3. Huszár mentions Lope's *La boba para otros y la discreta para sí* [A Fool for

Others, The Astute One for Herself] and Rojas's *El desafío de Carlos Quinto* [The Challenge of Charles V] as possible models for Molière (1907, 243).

4. Hesse affirms that "it contains, perhaps, the most involved plot in Golden Age drama" (1962, 389).

5. In reality, the protagonist's journey could be described as going from one empty title to another. With the exception of his wife, all the main characters have a first name, whereas the hero is known simply as "Monsieur Jourdain." This is very rare in Molière's theatre in general.

WORKS CITED

Brody, Jules. 1968. "Esthétique et société chez Molière." In *Dramaturgie et société*, edited by Jean Jacquot, Elie Konigson, and Marcel Oddon. Paris: Centre National de la Recherche Scientifique.

Carrión, María. 1991. "La función poética del 'almario:' La Alquimia y los procesos de figuración de lectura y escritura en *La dama boba* de Lope de Vega." *Bulletin of the Comediantes* 43: 239–57.

Connor (Swietlicki), Catherine. 1994. "Postmodernism Avant la lettre: The Case of Early Modern Spanish Theater." *Gestos: Teoría y práctica del teatro hispánico* 17: 43–59.

Defaux, Gérard. 1980. *Molière, ou les métamorphoses du comique: la comédie morale au triomphe de la folie*. Lexington, Ky.: French Forum.

Diez-Borque, José María. 1976. *Sociología de la comedia española del siglo XVII*. Madrid: Cátedra.

Dollimore, Jonathan. 1986. "Subjectivity, Sexuality, and Transgression: The Jacobean Connection." In *Renaissance Drama: New Series Seventeen*, edited by Mary Beth Rose. Evanston, Ill.: Northwestern University Press.

Finn, Thomas P. "The Weapons of Spectacle: Song, Dance, and Imaginary Identity in *Don Gil de las calzas verdes* and *Le Bourgeois gentilhomme*." *Laberinto* 2, no. 1 (1988): http://www.utsa.edu/academics/cofah/laberinto.

Foucault, Michel. 1966. *Les Mots et les choses*. Paris: Gallimard.

Gaines, James F. 1984. *Social Structures in Molière's Theater*. Columbus: Ohio State University Press.

Hesse, Everett. 1962. "The Nature of the Complexity in Tirso's *Don Gil.*" *Hispania* 45: 389–94.

———. 1981. "Estudio psico-literario del «doble» en cinco *comedia*s de Tirso de Molina." *Homenaje a Tirso*. Madrid: Revista «Estudios».

Howe, Elizabeth. 1990. "The Education of Diana in A. Moreto's *El desdén con el desdén.*" *Romanische Forschungen* 102: 149–62.

Huszár, Guillaume. 1907. *Molière et l'Espagne*. Paris: Librairie Honoré Champion.

Lope de Vega, Félix. 1977. *La dama boba*. Edited by Francisco Tolsada. Zaragoza: Clásicos Ebro.

Ly, Nadine. 1984. "Don Gil." *Le Personnage en question: Actes du quatrième colloque du S. E. L*. Toulouse: Université de Toulouse-Le Mirail.

Mariscal, George. 1991. *Contradictory Subjects: Quevedo, Cervantes, and Seventeenth-Century Spanish Culture*. Ithaca: Cornell University Press.

Mishriky, Salwa. 1982. *Le Costume de déguisement et la théâtralité de l'apparence dans* Le Bourgeois gentilhomme. Paris: La Pensée Universelle.

Molière, Jean-Baptiste. 1962. *Oeuvres complètes.* Edited by Pierre-Aimé Touchard. Paris: Seuil.

Reichenberger, Arnold. 1959. "The Uniqueness of the *Comedia.*" *Hispanic Review* 27: 303–16.

Surtz, Ronald. 1981. "Daughter of Night, Daughter of Light: The Imagery of Finea's Transformation in *La dama boba.*" *Bulletin of the Comediantes* 33: 161–7.

Varey, J. E. 1989. "Doña Juana, personaje de *Don Gil de las calzas verdes*, de Tirso de Molina." In *Studies in Honor of Bruce W. Wardropper*, edited by Diane Fox, Harry Sieber, and Robert Ter Horst. Newark, N.J.: Juan de la Cuesta.

The Unheimlich Maneuver: *La dama duende* and *The Comedy of Errors*

WILLIAM R. BLUE

Shakespeare, it seems we have always been told, developed rounded characters, delved into their personalities, and explored their psyches. Golden Age dramatists, A. A. Parker unhesitatingly declared, had other interests and spent little time and effort in developing character: "The generic characteristic of Spanish drama is, of course, the fact that it is essentially a drama of action and not of characterization. It does not set out to portray rounded and complete characters" (1957, 3). But when Shakespearean critics look at *The Comedy of Errors*, one might think that A. A. Parker had been whispering in their ears. "At times," J. Dennis Huston writes, summarizing critical responses, "Shakespeare does not even differentiate between characters: the two Dromios really are interchangeable. He never allows his characters any substantial complexity. In a sense the characters serve as props in this play; the playwright gives them, like puppets, a few defining and unchangeable features—some of them interchangeable—and then he moves his characters mechanically about as he wills" (1981, 14–5). But in recent years, critics have seen the play, the characters, and the notion of character and conflict in another light that illuminates the personalities better and shows a depth to their problems (see Huston, Freedman, and Wells). Likewise, in Golden Age theater criticism, more interest has been taken along similar lines of investigation. In what follows, I will look at *La dama duende* [The Phantom Lady] alongside of and through *The Comedy of Errors* and recent criticism on that play to touch on points of similarity, to examine the characters, and to explore farce and the uncanny in Calderón's comedy.

Both plays begin with sad circumstances for some of the characters. In *The Comedy of Errors*, Egeon, looking for his lost sons, lands in Ephesus. Unbeknownst to him a conflict has arisen between Ephesus and Syracuse—where Egeon was a merchant—and

174

because of the political climate, he is arrested and condemned to death. He then recounts the sad story of his life, including the narrative of a shipwreck, separation among the company of one infant son and one small servant from his wife and the twin of the son and the servant. After passing over an eighteen-year gap, he tells of his son's desire to seek out his mother and brother, his departure with the servant, and the now five-year separation from him during which time he, Egeon, too has roamed the earth searching for his lost family.

In *La dama duende*, we collect the threads of Angela's recent life. She recounts her narrow escape from an unauthorized visit to the plaza, her banishment from her rooms in her brother's house, and her virtual incarceration. She has, sometime before the play begins, married a man and left with him to set up her own household and lead her own life. We learn via her brother Luis's servant that her husband had held an administrative governmental post in a port and that he died owing a debt to the king. She has returned to Madrid to deal with that debt but must live in her brother's home, in mourning clothes, in secret, and guarded constantly. Such a "life," Angela says, is more a living death.

If in *The Comedy of Errors* Egeon imposes a tragic cast over the narrative of his life up to now and over the beginning of the play, the curious confusion of details as well as the gaps in his story might well make the audience wonder just how accurate his version is and just how much his conception of his present circumstances colors his point of view (see Huston 1981, 21–23). Likewise, in Angela's narrative of her life, she leaves out more than she puts in. For instance, we have no idea of how her marriage came about, how long she was married, how deep her feelings ran for her deceased husband, how happy she might have been, how she lived, how much freedom she enjoyed or servitude she endured, nor of what role she might have played in her present financial difficulties. Her narrative of past events is similarly colored by her conception of her present circumstances and living arrangements—in debt, in her brother's home, under his control once again, in widow's weeds, having just escaped recognition by her younger brother in a place and situation where she ought not to have been, "imprisoned" and chafing under her present estrangement from her own rooms. Where both narratives converge, despite their obvious differences, is on the "discontinuity of human experience" (Huston, 23), a pattern initiated in Calderón's play under the guise of mistiming by Cosme's opening speech:

Por una hora que fuera
antes Píramo a la fuente,
no hallara a su Tisbe muerta,
y las moras no mancharan,
porque dicen los poetas
que con arrope de moras
se escribió aquella tragedia.
Por una hora que tardara
Tarquino, hallara a Lucrecia
recogida (238a)

[If Pyramus had reached the fountain
an hour earlier, he wouldn't
have discovered Thisbe dead there.
But the berries didn't leave a stain,
you know, for according to
the poets that tragedy
was written with blackberry juice.
If Tarquin had delayed an hour,
Lucretia would have found seclusion (219)]

as well as by Manuel's breathless introduction to the veiled lady (Angela).

In the Duke of Ephesus's discontinuous reactions to Egeon's narrative: "The enmity and discord which of late / Sprung from the rancorous outrage of your Duke / To merchants . . . / Excludes all pity from our threatening looks" (1.1. 5–7) versus "Nay, forward, old man; do not break off so, / For we may pity, though not pardon thee" (1.1. 97–98); "Merchant of Syracusa, plead no more " (1.1. 3) versus "Nay, forward, old man, do not break off so" (1.1. 97); "I am not partial to infringe our laws" (1.1. 4) versus "My soul would sue as advocate for thee" (1.1. 146) along with the delay of execution, the ransom, and the future discovery of friends in Ephesus contain the seeds of Egeon's redemption. So too in the first scenes of *La dama duende* does the promised discovery or rediscovery of the veiled woman's true identity, the timely / untimely arrival of Manuel, and the sword fight that ends in family recognition and obligation promise to turn imminent tragedy into felicitous comedy. But though the promise of discovery and salvation exists from the outset, chaos, confusion, and contradiction are what the characters experience throughout, as discontinuity disrupts standard relationships and even the "basic facts of nature, apparently overthrowing the very laws which govern the movement of things in space and time" (Huston 1981, 26).

In both *The Comedy of Errors* and *La dama duende*, many of the strange happenings the characters experience are attributed to fairies or witches: "Sure, these are but imaginary wiles, / And Lapland sorcerers inhabit here" (4.3. 10–11); "Thou art, as you are all, a sorceress" (4.3. 66); "Duendecillo, duendecillo, / quienquiera que seas o fueres . . ." [248a: Goblin, ghost, or sprite, whatever / you are or happen to be . . . (243)]; "Válgame el Cielo! Ya es / esto sobrenatural" [260a: God help me, but this / is really supernatural! (274)]. Attributions to the supernatural are part of the search for meaning, for explanation, that runs throughout both plays, and, at the end, both seem to find the sought-for coherence. In *The Comedy of Errors*, Emilia comes on stage with Antipholus and Dromio of Syracuse to clarify the mysteries, and in *La dama duende*, Angela confesses to Manuel her relationship to Juan and Luis. And yet such a "solution," though part and parcel of comedy's essential thrust, is no guarantor of continuity into the future. In a similar fashion, the reversibility of character/audience relations within both plays may make the audiences:

> aware that they must shortly surrender their perspective of godlike superiority and enter a world where they themselves are characters. In this world, too, they may, like the characters of the play, be assailed by apparently discontinuous experience whose meaning cannot be discovered without revelation. (Huston 1981, 28)

The ends of both plays are simultaneously extravagantly discontinuous in their sudden revelations and miraculously coherent as the seeds sown in the first scenes suddenly blossom. Both plays raise questions of order and chaos as they ask us and the characters how to forge meaning out of misrecognitions: "missed opportunities, mistakes, forgettings, losses . . . misjudgments" (Huston 1981, 29). How do we order the fragments of experience and time into a unified narrative?

Almost all of Manuel's attempts to say who or what the phantom lady is fail. Most of Luis's assumptions about others are likewise inoperative, and the same could be said frequently for Juan and Angela. But not only are the characters estranged from each other in *La dama duende*, as they surely are in *The Comedy of Errors*, but also from themselves. Manuel is the serious future governor and *El caballero de La dama duende* [The Knight of the Phantom Lady]; Juan is the serious guardian of his and his sister's honor and the daring gallant, menace to Beatriz's and her father's honor, as she tells him:

> Disgustada con mi padre
> vengo: la culpa tuvisteis;
> pues aunque el galán no sabe,
> sabe que por el balcón
> hablé anoche . . . (251a)

> [It's true I've come because my father
> is displeased with me. But you
> must take the blame for that.
> For when he learned I'd spoken
> at my balcony last night
> to some gentleman (not knowing
> the gentleman was you) . . . (251)]

Angela is the veiled flirt and the imprisoned widow; Luis is the precipitous lover/avenger and the dependent, unlucky, and bitter second son. Each of these characters splits or doubles adopting one mask in one situation, another mask in another. In *The Comedy of Errors*, Shakespeare twinned the Antipholus and Dromio grouping and gave them the same name. Such division in both plays seems, nonetheless, to be healed in the final scenes, as mentioned above. Angela, even earlier, tries to close the gaps when she explains to Manuel who she is in an attempt to rein in his flights of imagistic fantasy:

> No soy alba, pues la risa
> me falta en contento tanto;
> ni aurora, pues que mi llanto
> de mi dolor no os avisa
> Y así os ruego que digáis
> señor Don Manuel, de mí,
> que una mujer soy y fui. (264a)

> [Do not compare me to the dawn
> whose fixed smile I do not share,
> for I am not frequently so blissful.
> Nor am I like the early morning
> light in shedding pearly tears;
> I hope you have not found me weeping.
> In sum, my dear Don Manuel,
> the only thing I'd have you say
> of me is that I've always been
> and am a woman. (283–4)]

The stability seemingly reached here and at the end of the play implies, as Freedman states of similar scenes in *The Comedy of Er-*

rors, that the play "is not simply about the physical division and reunion of a family but about the psychic division and integration of the personality" (1991, 92). And, in *La dama duende*, "mujer" is an unstable identity holding together in tension the angel/devil, widow/whore splits that run through the play. Moreover, since both plays project a future for the characters beyond the final curtain, and since both plays make much of splits, time, and timing, the final scenes and projected futures continue the notion of further splits in the new state that await the characters. In *La dama duende*, one must wonder how Angela will handle her second marriage and how Manuel will deal with the woman he has just promised to marry and with the unknown woman whose portrait and love letters he carries around in his luggage. As in the case of the divided characters in *La dama duende*, a division partially stressed in Manuel's last aside, "Hidras parecen las desdichas mías / al renacer de sus cenizas frías" [271b–272a: All my troubles seem to rise up / Hydra-headed from dead ashes. (303)], so too in *The Comedy of Errors*:

> the use of twins undermines the possibility of self-presence by suggesting that identity is a matter of two who can never be one; being is a function of splitting and attempting to recuperate that loss in future splits. Identity is re-presented as grounded in yet prevented by repression and always haunted by the inevitability of the return of the repressed. (Freedman, 103)

To this point and to the title of my essay I shall return in the final pages.

But first, a brief and perhaps seemingly unrelated excursus through some notions of farce. Shakespearean critics have not been shy about applying the term farce to *The Comedy of Errors* (see Stanley Wells 1994, introduction to *The Comedy of Errors*), but to my knowledge, no one has suggested that the term is applicable to *La dama duende*. In farce, the pace is fast, there is a mood of unreality and improbability, complications accumulate, secrets are uncovered, characters enter and leave suddenly, some characters are subjected to beatings, and "anything can happen next, and probably will" (*The Readers* etc., "Farce"), and all of this is designed to produce laughter. Central to many farces is marriage and the family. While the family may well be sacred to many for "the development of humanity [and] because the proper psychological development of an individual can only occur within the warm circle of the nuclear family" (unattributed but quoted by Eric Bentley 1964, 225), the family "is also the seedbed of neurosis, vice, and crime" (Bentley, 226) as any glance at a newspaper today can surely tell us. Farce highlights family neuroses and laughs at its foundations, at extramarital relations, and at marriage, hence the close association between the term farce and bedroom. In *La dama duende*, Luis is about as neurotic as they come, while marriage, courtship, and widowhood come in for some sharp knocks. This is exemplified by Manuel's laughable fidelity to the unknown woman whose portrait he carries and by Angela's status as grieving widow.

There is violence in farce, but no one really gets hurt. Cosme is pushed by Luis, falls in a mudhole, has his money stolen, is bopped on the head by Isabel, and is threatened by nearly everyone, but everyone laughs at his pain. The Dromios receive several drubbings and once more everyone laughs—everyone, that is, but the ones on the receiving end of the violence.

Farce is madcap but it is not totally unrealistic since "it brings together the direct and wild fantasies and the everyday drab realities" (Bentley 1964, 241). As in *The Comedy of Errors*, so too in *La dama duende*, worries about travel, accommodations, duties and responsibilities, and particularly about money and debt are constant. Cosme worries about his money and its value (see Greer, Blue 1996, 157–68); in *The Comedy of Errors*, Egeon will literally die unless he can find a way to raise a thousand marks, "Try all the friends thou hast in Ephesus; / Beg thou or borrow to make up the sum, / And live" (1.1. 153–55). Concerns about the well-being of family members, their future, and their honor and status can be found in both plays that are, as Bentley states, grounded in the worldly.

Behind farce's first madcap face lurks another graver one, a more dangerous one. Farce establishes a dialogue "between aggression and flippancy, between hostility and lightness of heart" (Bentley 1964, 244). From the outset of both plays, the audience knows a secret that is withheld from most of the characters: in *The Comedy of Errors*, the two sets of twins and their presence in Ephesus, in *La dama duende*, Angela's identity, her many roles, the secret passageway between her and Manuel's chambers, and the two doors to the house. So for the audience, all the accidents, mistakes, blunders, misrecognitions, and mysteries are clear as day and hilarious. For the characters, particularly the two sets of twins and Manuel and Cosme, this is a nightmare:

> The pace and insanity of farce create an atmosphere onstage that approximates the conditions of a dream world or, rather, of a nightmare;

the terrors of humiliation—of being, say, unable to remember the simple answer to a leading question; of being found in a stranger's bedroom without pants on; of being taken for a notorious criminal or a lunatic with not a scrap of evidence to support one's identity—such typical dream fears are familiar to audiences. As they recognize them, consciously or unconsciously, they laugh: they are relieved witnesses of somebody else's nightmare. (*The Reader's* etc., "Farce")

When Manuel arrives in Madrid, he thinks he knows what the future holds for him: reunion with his old chum Juan, a pleasant time, visits to the palace, honor, appointment to a government post, and possibly the continuance and finalization of his love relation with the lady of the letters. But instead, he is accosted by a veiled lady and attacked and wounded by a man who turns out to be Juan's younger brother, Luis. Then, this mysterious woman somehow enters his room, leaves him notes and gifts, and suddenly shows up one night like a ghost. She then invites him, blindfolded, to her home where she entertains him, then suddenly hides him in a back room after another man knocks on her door. When he hears a voice in the room and a candle is lit, the other voice turns out to be that of his own servant, Cosme, and he finds himself suddenly and inexplicably, magically transported back to his own quarters in Juan's house. Yet despite all this, Manuel insists on most occasions that there are rational explanations for all. Cosme's fears of the supernatural, Manuel attributes to wine or superstition:

> Vete de aquí, que estás borracho (245b)
>
> [All right, then—off with you.
> You're drunk! (237)]
>
> No hay duendes?
>   Nadie los vio (249b)
>
> [Did you ever hear of sprites?
> No one's ever seen them. (248)]
>
> Diré que aquesta persona,
> que con arte y con ingenio
> entra y sale de aquí, esta noche
> estaba encerrada dentro
> que, para poder salir,
> te mató la luz, y luego
> me dejó a mí el azafate,
> y se me ha escapado huyendo (256a)

[All I can say is that the person
who makes it his business to get in
and out of this room was somehow
shut in here tonight, and to find
his way out, doused your light,
left me this basket, and escaped. (263–64)]

But yet while insisting on a reasonable explanation, as though he
had seen or experienced or read about something like this before,
he still cannot explain it, "no sé / ni qué tengo de dudar / ni qué
tengo de creer" [262b: who knows, / who knows if I could any
longer / separate credulity from doubt (280)]. Speaking about *The
Comedy of Errors*, Barbara Freedman seems also to capture some
essential feelings about farce and *La dama duende*:

> farce shows human beings unable to cope with or adapt to their environ-
> ments. Instincts that are designed to help us survive are not only de-
> pendable but often rigidly mechanical. When these "purposive vital
> functions" are perceived as dysfunctional, automatic, irrational, and
> perilously inflexible, then the farcical vision comes into focus. That
> farce should take the ego as its object, just as objects were once taken
> for the ego, makes sense from this eccentric standpoint. (1991, 108)

The ego, far from being a stable, present unity, is perhaps best
understood as a process that attempts to bind together into signification the traces of past, present, and future experiences, attitudes,
and beliefs. In *La dama duende*, Manuel is a character desperately
trying to sort what is real and what is unreal, to figure out who the
mystery woman is and what her relationship is to him and others.
Generally, Manuel is confused, but at one point he is plainly terrified:

> ¡Válgame el Cielo! ¿Ya es
> esto sobrenatural . . . De mármol soy! . . . ¡Válgame el Cielo!
> ¿Qué es esto?
> Hidras, a mi parecer,
> son los prodigios, pues de uno
> nacen mil. ¡Cielos! ¿Qué haré? . . .
> Y calzado
> de prisión de hielo el pie,
> tengo el cabello erizado,
> y cada suspiro es
> para mi pecho un puñal,
> para mi cuello un cordel (260a/b)

[God help me, but this
is really supernatural! . . . I'm petrified! . . . God in Heaven,
what am I to make of this?
Wonders seem to spring up
Hydra-headed all about me.
What in the world shall I do? . . . I feel as though
my feet were bound in icy chains,
my hair, standing on its ends,
and every breath I draw,
like a dagger thrust straight
to the heart, or like a rope
tightened round my throat. (274–76)].

But at the same instant, Manuel recognizes in this potentially diabolical figure the image, and "image" because he still does not
know what it is, of a beautiful woman, "Imagen es / de la más rara
beldad, / que el soberano pincel / ha obrado" [260b: The hand of
God / has never drawn a creature / half so beautiful before (275)].
He approaches this "Angel, demonio o mujer" [261a: Angel,
woman, or devil (276)] and seizes it, thereby showing his intent to
reveal, define, and fix. On several different occasions, he describes
his situation as "novedad" [249a: unheard of], "duda" [254a:
doubt], "confusión" [254a: confusion], "sobrenatural" [260a: su-
pernatural], "asombro" [261a: surprising], and "fantástica" [262b:
fantastic], and describes his reactions as "admiración" [260a:
amazement] or madness, "perder el juicio" (266b). Manuel's situation and his descriptions all point to the experience of the uncanny.

The uncanny "is that class of frightening which leads back to
what is known of old and long familiar" (Freud 1995, 220). In his
enlightening yet disjointed essay on the uncanny, *unheimlich*, Freud
establishes some of its constituent elements: the double, duplica-
tion, "ego splitting, and the recurrence of traits, characters, destin-
ies" (Weber 1973, 1105–6), repetition, anxiety, and doubt. When
Freud investigates the meaning of the word unheimlich, he finds
that it is contained in the connotative and denotative meanings of
its apparent opposite, *heimlich* [homely] (see Freud 1995, 220–26).
The uncanny, *unheimlich*, even linguistically, leads back to what
is long familiar, *heimlich*. Freud established the links between the
uncanny, anxiety, and the castration complex, links far too ranging
to enter here. Castration, briefly however, is not reducible to any
real event:

it marks the moment of discovery when the subject is confronted with
the object of its desire as being almost nothing, but not quite. . . . [It]

involves a structuring of experience that far transcends the realm of the individual psyche. . . . Castration thus structures the future identity and experience of the subject, by confronting it with its unconscious desire as a violent and yet constitutive difference. (Weber, 1112).

Manuel arrives in Madrid at one of those transitional moments in life. He has been a student and would probably have lived the raucous life of the denizens of the university town. He has been a soldier and endured the hardships, fears, and glories of the military campaign. He has spent his early years, that is to say, as a typical male of his rank in the company of other men like himself. He even has a lady he has been courting. But now his life is changing as he moves from the field to the court, "su Majestad / con este gobierno premia / mis servicios" [240a: to accept / His Majesty's preferment / for service to the Crown (220–21)]. In Madrid, suddenly confronted by a veiled woman demanding his help, he leaps to her aid, good soldier that he is, and defends her honor to the point of fighting another man. For his efforts, he is wounded. Cosme, at least, thinks Manuel's actions are ridiculous and uncalled for, "¡Que bien merecido tiene / mi amo lo que se lleva, / porque no se meta a ser / Don Quijote de la legua!" [241a: It serves my master / right for playing Don Quixote / to every passing Dulcinea! (225)]. By that remark, Cosme calls attention to the disjunction between what Manuel should be and what he does.

The uncanny is bound up with a crisis of perception and phenomenality, but concomitantly with a mortal danger to the subject, to the "integrity" of its body and thus to its very identity. . . . [The] uncanny is thus bound up with subjective emotions, and upon an affective scale it can even be situated with some precision: it is not simply a form of anxiety, but is located between dread, terror, and panic on the one side, and uneasiness and anticipation on the other. (Weber 1973, 1131–32)

Manuel could not really see the woman he defended, he does not really know what to do next; he slips back and forth between his career aims and his desire; he slides back and forth between his duty and his debt to Juan and Luis and his curiosity about and interest in the unknown woman who so easily enters and leaves his room in his friend's house; he slips from terror to logic. All of this leads to anxiety, or perhaps proceeds from and is a part of the anxiety he feels at this critical transitional point in his life. The uncanny involves a crisis of perception and "the defence against this crisis . . . a defence which is ambivalent and which expresses itself in the compulsive curiosity . . . [is] to penetrate, discover and ultimately to conserve the integrity of perception" (Weber, 1132–33).

Manuel's desire to get to the bottom of this mystery explains his constant attempts to define the mysterious woman, and to fix her once and for all. By identifying the object of his curiosity, if not desire, by stabilizing her, Manuel would then be able to define her relationship to Luis and to Juan, and then her relationship to himself. In that way, he could, to some degree, anchor himself as well. For Manuel must search for what he is and what he will be by going back to and then beyond the roles he once played, the curious, adventuresome, and daring student / soldier, that Cosme, at least, sees now as ridiculous.

In the final scenes, Angela asks Manuel for his help in similar yet different ways from the first scene. Initially, she requests, "amparad a una mujer / que a valerse de vos llega " [239a: defend a woman urgently / in need of your protection (221)], but in the last scene she asks, "que me valgas, me ayudes y me ampares" [271b: to save me, comfort and protect me (303)]. Besides the change from *vos* to *tú*, she has finally revealed her identity and her relation to Juan and Luis. Manuel must now decide what he will do, who and what he will be. He debates with himself whether to respond violently as he did in the first act, "si pretendo / librarla y con mi sangre la defiende, / remitiendo a mi acero su disculpa, / es ya mayor mi culpa" [271b: if I try / to free her and defend her / with my blood, or let my sword / underscore her innocence, / I thereby compound my guilt (303)], or whether to just abandon her to her fate, telling Luis that she is responsible for the whole mess, "Pues querer disculparme con culpalla, / es decir que ella tiene / la culpa," [271b: If I plead my innocence / by implicating her, then that's / to say she was the guilty one (303)]. But he will do neither, for what matters to him now is responsibility and living up to his obligations, and it is for that reason that he steps forth to marry Angela with what sounds like a tepid if not a tasteless proposal, "Y para cumplir mejor / con la obligación jurada, / a tu hermana doy la mano" [272b: Further, / in fulfillment of my sworn vow, / I now take your sister's hand (303)].

As events and characters repeat themselves, with differences, as mistakes, mistimings, and misrecognitions recur, as characters "construct hypotheses to account for others' strange, inconsistent behavior," (Huston 1981, 15) and as characters spin through the outlandish experiences the plays put them in, they offer explanations that, though mistaken, are more plausible than the real answers. They experience the uncanny while the audience, from its knowledgeable and distanced position, experiences farce. For most of the plays' durations we witness in the characters from both plays "the impossibility of self-presence, yet derive identity from this awareness" (Freedman 1991, 110). Both plays invite us to think on the characters' constructions and thereby on our own, for like them,

> we no sooner assert the unity of identity than unconscious splits prolif-
> erate and doubles appear; we no sooner loosen ego boundaries and open
> ourselves up to different points of view than the mind organizes, privi-
> leges, represses. (Freedman, 111)

Both plays stage "splitting, projection, denial, and repression as they haunt our quest for meaning" (Freedman, 111). And both dramatists have chosen moments of crisis in the characters' lives when the search for the other is also a search for the self. The melding of the familiar and the strange, both terms that inhere in *heimlich*, is a maneuver that shows the search for identity that is emphasized at transitional moments in everyone's life. And, depending on the point of view, such moments and such searches can be hilarious or terrifying, farcical or tragic, *heimlich* or *unheimlich*.

NOTES

1. With the exception of single words, all translations of *La dama duende* cite Edwin Honig's English rendering, *The Phantom Lady*.

WORKS CITED

Bentley, Eric. 1964. *The Life of the Drama*. New York: Atheneum.

Blue, William R. 1996. *Spanish Comedies and Historical Contexts in the 1620s*. University Park: Pennsylvania State University Press.

Calderón de la Barca, Pedro. 1973. *La dama duende*. In *Obras completas*. Vol. 2, edited by Angel Valbuena Briones. Madrid: Aguilar.

———. 1961. *The Phantom Lady*. In *Calderón de la Barca: Four Plays*, translated by Edwin Honig. New York: Hill and Wang.

Cixous, Hélène. 1976. "Fiction and Its Phantoms: A Reading of Freud's 'Das Unheimlich'." *New Literary History* 7: 525–48.

Freedman, Barbara. 1991. *Staging the Gaze: Postmodernism, Psychoanalysis, and Shakespearean Comedy*. Ithaca: Cornell University Press.

Freud, Sigmund. 1955. "The Uncanny." In *Standard Edition*. Vol. 17, edited by James Strachey. London: Hogarth Press.

Greer, Margaret. "The (Self) Representation of Control in *La dama duende*." Unpublished.

Huston, J. Dennis. 1981. *Shakespeare's Comedies of Play*. New York: Columbia University Press.

Parker, A. A. 1957. *The Approach to the Spanish Drama of the Golden Age*. London: Hispanic and Luso Brazilian Councils.

The Reader's Encyclopedia of World Drama, 1969. s.v. "farce."

Shakespeare, William. 1984. *The Comedy of Errors*. Edited by Stanley Wells. Middlesex: Penguin Books.

———. *The Comedy of Errors*. 1992. The Arden Edition. Edited by R. A. Foakes. London: Routledge.

Weber, Samuel. 1973. The Sideshow, or, Remarks on a Canny Moment. *MLN* 88: 1102–33.

Wells, Stanley. 1994. "Introduction." *The Comedy of Errors*. Middlesex: Penguin Books.

Part IV
The Discourse of Politics

Rethinking Cervantine Utopias:
Some No (Good) Places in Renaissance England and Spain

DIANA DE ARMAS WILSON

"A map of the world that does not include Utopia is not worth glancing at."
—Oscar Wilde

This essay, which takes as its point of departure José Antonio Mar-avall's "utopianization" of Cervantes, focuses on the New World aspects of that utopian strain. Where Maravall sees Spain's domestic and metropolitan preoccupations as shaping the utopian elements in *Don Quixote*, I see the Spanish colonial achievement as a more impressive model and point of reference for Cervantes's conceptualization of space. Where Maravall displays an intransigence about moving beyond the binary dialectic of utopia/counteruto-pia—a dialectic advertised in the title of his book, *Utopía y contrautopía en el "Quijote"* [Utopia and Counterutopia in the "Quixote"][1]—I see Cervantes's transactions with space as less Manichaean, his locations of culture as less parochial, and his political or moral biases as less transparent. Although Cervantes represents various "eutopias" and "heterotopias" in his novels, this essay concludes by glancing at two of his "dystopias": Insula Barataria and Isla Bárbara.[2] Writing contemporaneously with Joseph Hall's *Mundus Alter et Idem* (1605), perhaps the first early-modern instance of satirical dystopias, Cervantes creates two imaginary worlds that vividly allegorize the New World. If "something of *this* world is always recognizable in utopias," as Steven Hutchinson rightly claims (1987, 181),[3] the world that readers recognize in Cervantes's utopography has been imaginatively displaced to Spain's empire in the Indies.

To do justice to early-modern writings in the utopian genre requires a comparatist's perspective. Given that the genre originated in England, that it posited a fantastic region in South America, and that it dispatched Greek-speaking Portuguese explorers to that ul-

191

tramarine no-place, early-modern utopias invite reflection in a cross-national context. Because Thomas More's title gave the word Greek word "utopia" (Latin, *nusquama*) to literature, his work is considered by all accounts the foundational generic text. Although no Spanish translations of the *Utopia* (1516) were published until Gerónimo de Medinilla's Castilian edition surfaced in 1637, More's original Latin version was widely disseminated among Spanish humanists until its appearance in the 1583 Index of the Inquisition. This textualized utopia triggered, across the sixteenth century, what Maravall variously debunks as "utopian attitudes," "utopian philosophy," or "utopian political thought."

Trying to explain the derivation of such utopian attitudes in England, Quevedo later wrote that More "vivió en tiempo y reino que le fue forzoso para reprender el gobierno que padecía, fingir el convenientes" ["lived in a time and in a kingdom in which, in order to reprove the oppressive government, he was obliged to imagine a suitable one"] (cited by Maravall 1976, 245; 1991, 184). This Spanish interpretation of the origins of an English text makes readers wonder if More was singular in living under an "oppressive government." Working toward an expanded contextualization of Cervantine utopian attitudes within the changing discipline of comparative literature, I wish to explore in what follows some of the cultural relations between the English genre of the utopia and Spanish "utopian" thinking during the sixteenth century. Spain itself did not produce any systematic utopian text during its Golden Age: the first Spanish literary blueprint for a model society emerged circa 1682, when the anonymous *Descripción de la Sinapia, península en la tierra austral* was written.[4] This belated utopian text raises its own set of questions about why Spain produced no literary utopia during the early-modern period, but these belong to a different study.

Maravall considers the chief characteristic of utopias to be a "negación de la realidad" [denial of reality] (1976, 237; 1991, 178).[5] The stress on this privative quality leads him to read *Don Quixote* as both a reflection and a critique of utopianism—which he regards as "false" and "escapist." Maravall's censorious attitude here seems oddly affiliated with that of the English poet and Puritan John Milton who, in his *Areopagitica*, censured any notions of escapism from the "world of evil" into which God had placed us unavoidably: "to sequester out of the world into Atlantic and Utopian polities, which never can be drawn into use, will not mend our condition" (1957, 732–3). Although I agree with Maravall that the enterprise inspiring Don Quixote is "netamente política" ["clearly political"] (1976, 203; 1991, 157), my own reading, as what follows will show, finds value in those Atlantic and Utopian polities that Maravall, like Milton, regards as escapist.

More's *Utopia* helped to produce a utopian "boom" not only in Europe but also in the New World. The text, as Maravall allows, was "leída, citada, aplicada a instituciones que se organizan en la vida real, por gobernantes y evangelizadores en Indias" ["read, quoted, and applied to real-life institutions by governors and proselytizers in America"] (1976, 239; 1991, 179). Sixteenth-century utopian experiments on the American mainland are well known. One could cite the Erasmian labors of the Franciscan friar, Juan de Zumárraga, who set out for Mexico in the vanguard of evangelizers "en defensa de los indios contra la codicia de los colonizadores" ["in defense of the Indians against the greed of the colonizers"] (Bataillon 1950, 819). Well known, too—although often dismissed as fiascos or failures—are the Lascasian communities of Cumaná in today's Venezuela (1520–21) and Vera Paz in Guatemala (1545–60). Along the same utopian lines may be counted the Jesuit missions in South America referred to as *reducciones*,[6] which were founded in 1610, squarely between the writings of Part One and Part Two of *Don Quixote*. These "reductions"—scattered through today's Paraguay, Uruguay, Brazil, and Argentina, with two missionaries serving up to some six thousand Indians—are generally regarded as the most successful of the experimental utopias attempted in the New World.

But it is Vasco de Quiroga's mid-sixteenth-century experiments that serve as a visible link between More's *Utopia* and Cervantes's *Don Quixote*. As the future bishop of Michoacán and founder of the pueblo-hospitals of Santa Fe—evangelical townships for the Indians of Mexico and Michoacán—Vasco de Quiroga was directly inspired by Thomas More's *Utopia*.[7] As in More's Utopian community, the pueblo-hospitals of Santa Fe were based on an agricultural economy with a six-hour workday and much leisure time for religious development. In a passage in *Información en derecho* that anticipates Don Quixote's discourse on the Golden Age, Vasco de Quiroga perceives the New World inhabitants as living in a Golden Age, even as the inhabitants of Europe had fallen from it, having coming "a parar en esta edad de hierro" ["to a halt in this age of iron"] (cited in Bataillon 820).

Whether or not this kind of poetic speech is considered irrational or even dismissed as lunacy, there is no need to debase the heroic attempts on the part of such pioneering religious figures as Vasco de Quiroga to try to organize different economies in the New World. The historian J. H. Elliott allows that "reports from

America, whether of Indians living as innocent beings in a state of nature or as members of ordered polities like Inca Peru with its network of paved highways and its impressive stone buildings, excited the European imagination," and that this excitement, moreover, "was reflected in an important utopian literature" (1995, 394). The New World even generated or revived expectations among Sephardic Jews that tended to express themselves in utopian experiments. What these New World experiments disclosed, above all, was a new vision of the possibilities of space: "America had given Europe space, in the widest sense of that word—space to dominate, space in which to experiment, and space to transform according to its wishes" (Elliott, 406).

Such attempts to organize real world utopias by the oppressed peoples of the Old World may be regarded neutrally, if not benignly, as in this passage by Harry Levin: "America, the land of Europe's futurity, provided a fertile soil for the largest number of earnest endeavors to put utopian theory into practice" (1972, 190). Maravall, however, regards such "earnest endeavors" as irrational. *And he wants Cervantes to regard it that way too.* Allowing that the youthful Cervantes had participated in the utopianism that distinguished the reign of Charles V, Maravall insists that these utopian ideas, in time, "se le vinieron abajo" ["fell apart on him"] (1976, 237; 1991, 147). Political utopianism, especially as manifested during the Caroline imperial phase by certain Spanish thinkers opposed to the new precapitalist spirit, provided the mature Cervantes, in Maravall's view, a position he could demolish across *Don Quixote*.

A Manichaean discourse on utopias and counterutopias constitutes the ideological fulcrum upon which Maravall's Cervantes invents "la primera gran novela del mundo moderno" ["the first great novel of the modern world"], a text that, if read properly, can acquire "un sentido transparente y total" ["a transparent and total meaning"] (1976, 21; 1991, 26). Although I reject these totalizing pretensions, as well as the notion that Cervantes deploys an activist hero to ridicule utopian visions, I celebrate Maravall's attempt to enlighten the mentality of Cervantes's age through a rich culture of citation. The distinctive nature of Maravall's contribution to Spanish historiography has been articulated by Wlad Godzich and Nicholas Spadaccini in an elegant study that acknowledges the "fuzzy notion" of the French term *mentalités* (1994, 60). The more programmatic aspects of Maravall's reading may be fueled by his chosen historical approach: "one of the inherent problems in the history of *mentalités*," as J. H. Elliott notes in a different context, "is that it tends to take for granted the existence of an intellectual or cultural coherence which is rarely to be found" (1995, 401). Taken for granted in Maravall's study is a coherence in the class values of the lower nobility, a coherence which Cervantes's novels themselves call into question. The class values of the self-exiled Antonio in the *Persiles*, for example, who comes from a long line of hidalgos by the name of Villaseñor, are a far cry from those of Don Antonio Moreno in *Don Quixote*, the owner of an Enchanted Head and excessive amounts of leisure time, although both characters may be said to belong to the same strata of Spanish society.

Seeing the lower nobility as bound by a false utopianism that screams for caricature, Maravall never wavers on the issue of intentionality. That Cervantes aimed to debunk this utopianism is documented, for Maravall, by Don Quixote's rejection of three entities: administrative bureaucracies, early-modern methods of warfare, and the new monetary economies. Concerning this last, although it is true that Don Quixote rejects such economies, his anachronistic attitudes to money are not strictly utopian. Or at least they are much funnier, less social, and less moral than the attitudes remarked in such strictly literary utopias as More's and Campanella's, which inveigh against greed—against the European *aurea fames*. Don Quixote's monetary attitudes would seem more nostalgic than utopian: he refuses to give his consent of attention to the new mobile wealth because it has replaced the traditional feudal rewards of land or kingdoms, what we now call "real estate."

The issue of Don Quixote's rejection of modern methods of warfare—of standing armies and gunpowder [armas de fuego]—is more complex. Cervantes's hero makes very clear his retrograde attitudes toward gunpowder during his well-known speech on arms versus learning, where he looks back, with characteristic yearning, to warfare as practiced in the classical Golden Age: "Bien hayan aquellos benditos siglos que carecieron de la espantable furia de aquestos endemoniados instrumentos de la artillería, a cuyo inventor tengo para mi que en el infierno se le está dando el premio du su diabólica invención . . ." ["Those were indeed blessed times which knew nothing of demoniacal cannonading's ghastly fury, the inventor of which must be in Hell, receiving his due reward for so fiendish an invention"] (1973, 470–71; 1999, 263). Not all readers, however, consider Don Quixote ridiculous for deploring the gunpowder that served, according to some of Cervantes's own contemporaries, as "un instrumento de la Providencia" ["an instrument of Providence"] for the conquest and colonization of America (1976, 136; 1991, 109). Don Quixote's rejection of firearms for their technical and "diabolical" superiority may also be read as Cervantes's covert rejection of the providentialist view of, among other enterprises, the Spanish conquest of America, whose native populations were decisively overwhelmed by what Don Quixote rightly calls the "fiendish" invention of the cannon.

In his heated rejection of firearms, Don Quixote would seem to be tilting slightly toward Erasmian pacifism. Whether or not the famous trilogy of Erasmus, Vives, and More incorrectly understood the basic premises of the state system, as Maravall claims (1976, 55; 1991, 75), their writings helped European humanism to develop an expansive conscience for social reform. Humanism, as manifested in More's *Utopia*, was a new method of looking at man, at all classes of mankind, as Raphael Hythlodaeus's famous attack on enclosure and its dire social results documents: "Whichever way it's done, out the poor creatures have to go, men and women, husbands and wives, widows and orphans, mothers and tiny children. . . . Out they have to go from the homes that they know so well, and they can't find anywhere else to live" (1992, 47). Finding a *place* to live, in other words, even an imaginary place, is one of the staples of utopian discourse. The humanist method was not only hospitable to utopias but also, as More's text documents, to a dialogic exchange on the earthly value of such imaginal sites. Like More, Cervantes manifests the kind of dialogic imagination that engenders both utopias and novels. I would endorse Javier Herrero's vision of Cervantes's continued affinity for the radical humanism founded by Erasmus, whom Herrero sees as a socially revolutionary character, as well as for the utopian discourse that Erasmus' disciples, More and Vives, developed from this humanism (1983, 22–33).

Apart from this trio of radical humanists, later collaborators of Charles V such as Guevara or Las Casas would, in their turn, dream up the kind of ideal governments that Maravall also regards as failures. In order to debunk these utopian polities, Maravall posits a reactionary Cervantes, a man who wrote to halt the diffusion of a kind of thought that signified for a large sector of Spanish society "un refugio de escape" ["an escapist refuge"] (1976, 11; 1991, 19). But I am not persuaded that Cervantes created "la figura inadecuada y ridícula de Don Quijote, héroe de todos los fracasos" [the "inappropriate and ridiculous figure of *Don Quixote*, hero of all failures"] in order to rectify escapism (Maravall 1976, 63; 1991, 71). Inadequate and ridiculous as Don Quixote may be, he remains for many readers a lovable and sympathetic caricature precisely because, as Thomas Greene notes, "his will for a world made new" is "so mov-

ingly inflexible" (1968, 264). And this will for remaking the world
stretches to promoting an ideology of virtue over blood: "la virtud
vale por sí sola lo que la sangre no vale" ["virtue possesses an inherent worth that blood does not have"] (1978, 358; 1999, 580).
Such a prescient ideology—strategically reiterated by that "hero of
all failures"—may have itself seemed utopian to many of Cervantes's contemporaries.

MARAVALL'S CERVANTES

Ever since More coined the term "utopia," it has signified a vast
number of different literary "no-places." We can safely say that
Maravall uses the term "utopian" to label projects regarded not
merely as unfeasible but also as *undesireable*. In this he recalls a
practice of the American Tories in the 1770s, as recently documented by Judith N. Shklar. We can also say—and Maravall *does*
say it in his prologue—that his notion of utopia is used loosely, that
it has no strict generic value: "el *Quijote* no es propiamente una
utopía, sino que ésta se halla desarrollada a lo largo del relato, para
descrédito de los que a ella se aferraban" ["the *Quixote* is not a
utopia *strictly speaking* but . . . its author makes use of the idea of
a utopia throughout the narrative in order to discredit those who
cling to such a concept" (1976, 10; 1991, 17). Among those cling-
ers Maravall includes the "utopian writer" Antonio de Guevara, the
bishop of Mondoñedo, and one of Charles V's Spanish collaborators, who makes a brief but memorable appearance in the prologue
to *Don Quixote*, part one. It is well known that Guevara shared the
same antipathy to the *libros de caballerías* that prop up *Don Quixote*, but whether he and Cervantes are of the same mind on, say,
the dangers of utopias is another story. And we can only speculate
about Cervantes's response to Guevara's condemnation of forces of
conquest in El villano en el Danubio. Maravall, however, regards
Don Quixote as "verdadero anti-Guevara" ["a genuine anti-Guevara treatise"] (1976, 10; 1991, 18). Apart from Guevara, another
typical representative of such an utopian ideology is Bartolomé de
Las Casas, whose "utopias of reconstruction" would give way to
the pathetic "utopias of evasion" that Cervantes supposedly aimed
to discredit (1991, 31).[8]

Maravall's Cervantes, then, is not a bona fide utopist: he does not
write a utopia, but only makes use of the idea of a utopia in his
novel. Some theoretical confusion follows: on the one hand, the
novel is an ideal literary genre for depicting a utopia; on the other

hand, the novel is itself created out of a utopia: "Si un Las Casas
había ido al otro lado el Atlántico a buscar unos hombres nuevos,
Cervantes los busca en la creación literaria (y al concebir así una
utopía crea un género literario también nuevo: la novela moderna"
["While Las Casas crossed the Atlantic to discover new men, Cervantes sought them in literary creation, *and by conceiving a utopia
he also created a new literary genre, the modern novel*"] (1976,
242; 1991, 182; emphasis mine). These creative acts are becoming
murky, what with Cervantes pictured as conceiving, *although not
writing*, a utopia. At one point in Maravall's argument, Cervantes's
text even becomes—in the hybrid style of the *baciyelmo*—a "nov-
ela-utopía" ["novel-utopia"] (1976, 209; 1991, 161). This mixed
entity is in the tradition of Menéndez y Pelayo, who called More's
Utopia "una novela utópica" (1905–1915, 1:392).[9]

THE REPEATING ISLAND

Let me attempt a fuller description (or topothesia, to invoke the
handy Renaissance trope) of the various locations, all of them difficult to access, imagined for utopias. Although they may be situated, as Steven Hutchinson reminds us, "on some distant island,
valley, or mountaintop, in the Amazon basin, the Far East, Ethiopia,
or the other side of the world, on the moon or other celestial bodies,
inside the earth or a sea monster, or in the remote past or future"
(1987, 172), Cervantes appears to favor for his dystopias a phantom
island, indeed, a "repeating island."[10] In Maravall's attempts to describe Cervantes's creative processes, he does, in fact, invoke a
convertible island: "Cervantes toma la idea de la ínsula, por una
parte . . . de la literatura caballeresca . . . y, por otra parte, lo trueca
después en el medio de que se sirve el método utópico" ["on the
one hand Cervantes takes the idea of the island as a reward for his
squire from chivalric literature" and "on the other hand he later
turns it into the typical medium of utopian literature"] (1976, 247;
1991, 186). We move from chivalric to utopian literature via the
device of an island, the "typical medium" of utopias. This is a
smart move, given that utopian writers usually gravitate toward islands, which permit them, as Hans Freyer explains in *Die politische
Insel*, "to make their ideal societies to a greater or lesser degree
closed and static (at least in relative terms), with a system of control
strongly limiting the presence of foreigners" (1936, 185).

While negotiating the generic waters around that "idea of the island," however, Cervantes would surely have noticed that in

More's *Utopia*—the paradigmatic text that influenced both sixteenth-century Spanish thinking *and* Maravall's argument—the island is "discovered" by Iberian explorers: the main protagonist of More's text, the Portuguese mariner Raphael Hythlodaeus, explicitly sails to South America with Amerigo Vespucci on the last three of his four voyages to a "nowhere" located "somewhere south of the Equator." What follows is Robert M. Adams's translation from More's Latin:

> Being eager to see the world, [Raphael] left to his brothers the patrimony to which he was entitled at home (he is a native of Portugal), and took service with Amerigo Vespucci. He accompanied Vespucci on the last three of his four voyages, accounts of which are now common reading everywhere; but on the last voyage, he did not return home with the commander. After much persuasion and expostulation he got Amerigo's permission to be one of the twenty-four men who were left in a fort at the farthest point of the last voyage. (1992, 5)

That "fort"—which Vespucci had described in his *Four Voyages*, first published in *Cosmographiae Introductio* (St. Dié, 1507)—has since been identified as Cabo Frío, located in Brazil, north of Rio de Janeiro.

In the later English utopia that More's text seeded—Bacon's *New Atlantis* (1624)—the group of explorers who sail into the Pacific from Peru all speak "in the Spanish tongue" (1981, 211). And although the rulers of Bacon's insular culture are tetralingual humanists, the description of their whole technological utopia is supposedly given to the narrator in Spanish. Although written in English, the fiction of Bacon's *New Atlantis*, in short, is that everyone is speaking Spanish. For all its mechanicalism, the *New Atlantis* may be read as a posthumanist English parody of the Spanish *Crónicas de Indias*. Published in 1623, a few years after Cervantes's death, Bacon does not influence—he reflects—Spanish utopian thinking. Nor does he depict, as Maravall would have it, a purely invented social organization "sin contenido positivo de realidad, al parecer" ["without any apparent relation to reality"] (1976, 238; 1991, 178). Although Cervantes did not read the *New Atlantis*, as a Spaniard he was certainly familiar with the chronicles of conquest that Bacon chose to parody. Indeed, Cervantes may himself be parodying, as what follows will show, selected incidents from the historiography of discovery. Although Maravall equates the existence of knights-errant in Don Quixote's imagination with "los pobladores de 'Utopía,' (y) de la 'Nueva Atlántida" ["the residents of

Utopia, [and] of the New Atlantis"] (1976, 69; 1991, 62), he never seems to consider these "residents" as New World peoples.

To stop and rehearse our argument, then: Maravall allows that it was "ante todo, el factor del descubrimiento y colonización del continente americano" ["above all, the discovery and colonization of the American continent"] that opened the doors of Utopia (1976, 26; 1991, 30–31). He even allows that those doors were generically English doors (More's doors). If Spanish utopian thinking was influenced by More's *Utopia*—a text that "feigns" Iberian encounters in America[11]—then why does Maravall's Cervantes caricature everything *but* these encounters? Why is it that America merits only some half-dozen passing references in a purported study of utopias?[12] Why is Maravall's study so self-referential? Why do his insular reflections remain, in short, so peninsular?

As early as 1964, J. H. Elliott recognized that "no serious historian of Spain could afford to exclude from the reckoning the transatlantic dimension of the Spanish past" (1995, 391). We need to rethink not only Maravall's exclusion but also the *ínsula* he so presciently used as a bridge between genres, if not between continents. As all Hispanists know, the *ínsula* features as a feudal gift exchange in chivalric literature (as in *Ínsula Triste, Ínsula Sagitaria,* or *Ínsula Fuerte*). It also operates as a characteristic device of closure and stasis in English utopian literature, whose two most famous islands are located somewhere (and therefore "nowhere") in the Atlantic and the Pacific, respectively. In Cervantes's two novels, imagined islands abound. *Don Quixote* refers to *ínsulas* over sixty times. It also depicts, in the very heart of Aragón, the landlocked "ínsula de Barataria," a name that would centuries later be borrowed by the first settlers of Louisiana, to christen a swamp forest across the Mississippi from New Orleans (Grummond 1961, 3). This is not a gratuitous borrowing of a Cervantine place-name "in which legends of mastery, physical force, and economic power are remembered," as Elizabeth Anne Wolf argues in an essay documenting the history of " 'white' creolization" in Louisiana:

> the governorship of Barataria is the contrivance of an idle aristocracy, a duke and a duchess, who amuse themselves with their power to deceive and abuse (starvation; physical assaults). In the stories told of Jean Lafitte, Barataria—the Gulf area which includes Grande Terre, Grand Isle and Chênière Caminada—is the home and safehouse where pirated/privateered gold, jewels and human beings who will be sold as slaves are secured (n.d., n. 21 and n. 22).

Pirates, jewels, and human beings sold into slavery are also prominent features of Cervantes's *Persiles*, specifically on Isla Bárbara, the dystopia located at the novel's threshold and serving as its theoretical overture. This island is a place situated "nowhere" in the North Sea but whose "cannibal culture" makes it suspiciously American. Besides calling into question Maravall's astonishing claim that the characters in the *Persiles* are all Spaniards,[13] the many insular cultures described in the *Persiles*—Iceland, Friesland, Gothland, Hibernia—show how Cervantes was drawn, across his last writings, to the topos of a "repeating island."

THE COUNTER ISLAND

In Maravall's scheme, Cervantes first turns the chivalric genre into "a magnificent method for the expression of utopian thought"—a method communicating "the idea of a perfection that is to be desired." This idea of perfection—"to show what must be demanded of a true knight and what must be corrected in those who do not live up to this high ideal" (1991, 188)—must seem strangely inert to postmodern readers. Maravall's Cervantes then turns that same knightly paradigm "upside down" to a "counterutopia," variously defined as the opposite of an ideal state (1991, 180–82), "a utopia in reverse" (1991, 193), or a utopia that contradicts "the falsification of the utopian ideal that Don Quixote himself represents" (1991, 18).[14] That "counterutopia" is Barataria—"the point at which Cervantes's utopia culminates." By using "cruel humor" to make the reader regard the utopian project as impossible, Maravall's Cervantes then shows his reader "la dramática inadequación" ["the dramatic inadequacy"] of the knight as social model" (1976, 252; 1991, 189). The dystopia of Barataria—a paradoxically landlocked insular "nowhere"—discloses, to my thinking, much more than the social inadequacies of knighthood.

Let's look more closely at this *ínsula*. The novel's first allusion to it occurs together with its first invocation of Sancho, that "pobre villano" [poor villager] seduced into Don Quixote's service by the knight's promise to win "alguna ínsula y le dejase a él por gobernador della" ["some island and leave him there as its governor"] (1973, 1.7). Sancho's desire for an ínsula increases as Don Quixote discourses on his desire to gain "perpetuo nombre y fama en todo lo descubierto de la tierra" ["eternal reputation and fame throughout the known world"] (1973, 303; 1999, 150). Because Don Quixote imagines himself "ya coronado por el valor de su brazo, por lo menos, del imperio de Trapisonda" ["already crowned through the valor of his arm, at the very least, of the empire of Trebizond]

(1973, 75; 1999, 15), he is in a position to make such a grandiose promise. The promise itself functions as a parody of a feudal topos found in the books of chivalry: in *Amadís*, for example, the protagonist made his squire count of Ínsula Firme. Parody is classically defined as dealing with strictly literary norms: it is precisely through the metalinguistic uses of the preformed language of chivalry that we recognize *Don Quixote* as a parodic text. But parody can also serve as a medium for the transmission of satire: the terminological confusion between parody and satire actually stands as a sign of their interaction, even their cooperation (Rose 1979, 47). Chivalric parody here works as a vehicle for, among other things, a satire of the conquistadores, who were far more likely to be made governors than counts of ínsulas. Three of the five articles in the "Capitulaciones de Sante Fé"[15] —the charter of Admiral Columbus adopted by the Catholic Kings on 17 April 1492—mention islands: "todas aquellas yslas"; "todas las dichas tyerras firmes y yslas"; "las dichas yslas." Like Sancho a century later, Columbus wished to be made "governador general"["Governor General"] over these still undiscovered "noplaces" (Columbus 1989, 423–4). His own later gift of the island of "Bella Saonese" to Michele da Cuneo— which anticipated innumerable other American "gifts" of this territorial kind—is as operative a subtext in *Don Quixote* as Amadís's gift of "Ínsula Firme" to his squire.

Isla Barataria, the kingdom over which Sancho, as the dupe of the dukes, is finally installed as governor is a highly complex space.[16] Joseph Jones claims that modern readers "need a compass to help them navigate the treacherous waters" surrounding what he calls, in an indispensable study, the "Baratarian Archipelago" (1999, p. 146). The waters would seem to become less treacherous when the focus remains on Sancho instead of the nature of the place he is governing. An instructive example of such a peninsular focus, to mention only one, is Walter Reed's portrait of Sancho as an "upwardly mobile squire" yielding to the "thoroughly middle-class" goal of social status in his desire for a governorship. Reed even claims, not outrageously, that "the rise of the novel" is "embodied in Sancho and the governorship plot" (1994, 267–70). But other enterprises are also embodied in this plot. Setting out for his governorship, Sancho, unlike Don Quixote, does not scorn the profit motive, as his letter to Teresa shows: *"voy con grandísimo deseo de hacer dineros porque me han dicho que todos los gobernadores nuevos van con este mesmo deseo"* [*I'm really anxious to get started because I want to make a lot of money, which is how ... all new governors begin*] (1973, 322; 1999, 554). Such a desire applied most pertinently to governors in the New World, and when Sancho finally gets what he wants, his troubles begin. His very own friend and neighbor, Tomás Cecial, masquerading as the Knight of the Wood's squire, tries to warn Sancho about the perils of his desire:

> a causa que los gobiernos insulanos no son todos de buena data. Algunos hay torcidos, algunos pobres, algunos malencónicos, y, finalmente, el más erguido y buen dispuesto trae consigo una pesada carga de pensamientos y de incomodidades, que pone sobre sus hombros el desdichado que le cupo en suerte.

> because governorships of islands aren't always what they're cracked up to be. Some of them are bent out of shape, and some are just plain poor, and some are dismal, and, to sum it all up, the ones that stand tallest and look the best bring you a heavy load of problems and worries, and the man unlucky enough to bear them gets beaten to the ground (1973, 128–29; 1999, 422).

This is a prescient description of Sancho's later sham governorship, which parodies, among other things, the "dismal" experiences chronicled by countless governors in Spain's colonies.

Chronicling a series of desperate New World gubernatorial experiences, for example, V. S. Naipaul, in his *Loss of El Dorado*, cites the hardships of Governor Diego de Escobar with hostile indigenous peoples, sickness, and hunger on the island of Trinidad. Writing to the metropolis for help, Escobar claimed that his governorship had become "like a joke," that nobody in the world had ever had to endure "such hard luck or such labours": "I haven't been paid my salary. The enemy have robbed me four times since I have been here. I walk about barefooted and virtually naked. The whole thing is incredible" (1969, 115). Like Sancho's emaciated private life as governor of Barataria, New World governors were often obliged to suffer hunger, and sometimes even reduced to eating grass. As Naipaul documents it in his history of Trinidad's colonial past, a transnational history constructed from both Spanish and English chronicles "the time came when no one wanted to be governor" (116). Candidates who were nominated by the Council of the Indies would regularly excuse themselves. In the light of these "real world" governors of Spain's overseas colonies, in short, Sancho's defection seems normative. It also seems satirical. Unlike the island in Shakespeare's *Tempest*—Insula Barataria can never be accused of being "complicit with colonialism" (Cohen 1995, 273). The passages in *Don Quixote* on *ínsulas*—promised, desired, granted, and renounced—reprove not only the medieval institution of chivalry codified in the *libros de caballerías*, but also its Renaissance operations in America, where chivalry rode again, perhaps for the last time.

The issue of satire in Cervantes, especially in its interaction with parody, deserves much more than the passing glance I can give it here. In his 1615 "Prologue to the Reader" of *Don Quixote*, part two, Cervantes pointedly thanks Alonso Fernández de Avellanada, the pseudo-author of a continuation of *Don Quixote*, for saying that his novels "son más satíricas que ejemplares" [are more satirical than exemplary] (1973, 34). Despite some harsh words for satire throughout his writings, Cervantes was not always allergic, as the above remark shows, to being classified as a satirist. James A. Parr, who argues that *Don Quixote* is first and foremost a satire—"a mennipean *satura* in the best homiletic tradition of Horace" (1988, xv)—rightly reminds us that satires are not self-referential but point instead at some possible target in the real world, outside the text. Parr himself identifies three objects of satire in *Don Quixote*: bad readers, abuse of leisure time, and—perhaps taking a page from Maravall—utopian evasionism (xvi). I agree with all but the last, and would suggest another object of satire in its place.

The Colonial Island

As codified in England by More's *Utopia*, the utopian genre is a literary response to the forces of Iberian overseas discovery. In Maravall, however, the utopian genre remains at home. Admittedly reading *Don Quixote* in order "to better understand" the Spanish society of Cervantes's age (1991, 35), Maravall sees Cervantes's object of satire as the medieval model of chivalry, with little attention paid to the discourses of "ocean chivalry" (to borrow William Prescott's phrase for what the *conquistadores* were doing in the New World). I celebrate Maravall for having installed the utopia as a pivotal subtext of Cervantes's novel. But I question his need to have Cervantes satirize humanist currents of social reform—the utopian discourses of Erasmist reformers—when more imperial abuses were there, ripe for political and social satire.

Raúl Porras Barrenechea's remark in 1955 that Cervantes wrote "una sátira benévola del conquistador de ínsulas o Indias" ["a benevolent satire of the conquistador of ínsulas or Indies"] (1955, 238) may have initiated a shift, both in time and space, of targets for Cervantine satire. Two recent critics see Don Quixote, respectively, as "a comic incarnation" of "the *conquistador* mentality of Golden Age Spain" (Skinner 1987, 54) and as a "divinely inspired conqueror" through whom "Cervantes tries to grapple with what is great and what is insane about Spanish imperialism" (Higuera 1995, 1–2).[17] It was perhaps predictable that a colonial Don Quixote would surface in our age, when postcolonial modes of cultural representation have become a "master" discourse, taking his place in a rich assortment of Don Quixotes who range from the comic to the psychotic. No matter which version of Don Quixote future readers might wish to endorse, the book that contains him will continue to represent itself as a reproval of the books of chivalry. Earlier attacks on the chivalric ideal had been issued by Ramon Lull, the Arcipreste de Hita, López de Ayala, Don Juan Manuel, Alfonso de Palencia, and Diego de Valera (Maravall 1991, 64–5). The reproval of chivalry in *Don Quixote* may be read in various ways: as a wish to dismantle the outdated artistic forms of the romantic medieval chivalric tradition, as a wish to destroy the malingering chivalric codifications of Spain's waning imperialist culture, or as both.

Cervantes himself experienced the tragic wages of this culture when, after five years of captivity in Algiers, he returned home to a nation that ignored the needs of even its most heroic veterans. Cervantes's plight as a veteran had been adumbrated over sixty years earlier in More's *Utopia*. Confronting a smug English lawyer at Cardinal Morton's dinner party, Raphael Hythlodaeus sarcastically invokes, if only to dismiss, the case of the disabled soldier:

> We may disregard for the moment the cripples who come home from foreign and civil wars, as lately from the Cornish battle and before that from your wars with France. These men, wounded in the service of king and country, are too badly crippled to follow their old trades, and too old to learn new ones. But since wars occur only from time to time, let us, I say, disregard these men. (1992, 10)

Also wounded in the service of a king and a country that did little for its veterans (we may substitute Lepanto for the above "Cornish battle"), the crippled Cervantes would have surely aligned himself with the concerns of a humanism that, despite its putative "denial of reality," had tried to force Europe to remodel, both at home and abroad, its corrupt political institutions. Sketches of that remodeling project reappear in various Cervantine dystopias, in geographies of the mind that gesture—sometimes comically, always violently—toward the New World.

Notes

1. Although published in 1976, Maravall's book is actually a reelaboration dating back to 1948.

2. I use "heterotopias" not in Foucault's sense of real world "other places" like cemeteries or prisons or brothels (1986), but rather in a sense closer to Gianni Vattimo's heterotopia as a site of multiplicity (1992, 69), or to Tobin Siebers's sense of it as a community based on the inclusion of differences (1994, 20). Negley and Patrick coined the term "dystopia" in 1952 (298).

3. In an essay that brilliantly sketches out "a new orientation for utopian studies," Hutchinson reminds us that dystopias, like eutopias, "differ from other utopias only in the degree to which the criteria of good/bad and desirable/undesirable predominate. Otherwise the same kinds of imaginative processes are involved in making them and the same kinds of interpretative processes are involved in understanding them" (1987, 179).

4. Cro discovered, edited, and published the anonymous edition of Sinapia, a utopia never mentioned in Maravall. See Cro's "New World in Spanish Utopianism" (1979). See also his "Classical Antiquity" (1994) essay.

5. Citations from Maravall's *Utopia and Counterutopia* are parenthetically documented, with pages from the original Spanish followed by pages from the English translation.

6. Kupperman reminds us that the original meaning of "to reduce,". obsolete after the seventeenth century, was "to restore, especially to a belief, and it carried the implication of bringing back from error" (1995, 10).

7. On Vasco de Quiroga's adoption of passages from More, see Zavala's *La utopía de Tomás Moro* [Thomas More's Utopia].

8. See also Maravall's "Utopía y primitivismo en Las Casas" (Utopia and Primitivism in Las Casas).

9. Menéndez y Pelayo was comparing, in this context, More's *Utopia* to Inca Garcilaso's *Comentarios reales*: "los Comentarios reales no son texto histórico; son una novela utópica, como la de Tomás Moro" [1:392: The *Comentarios reales* is not a historical text; it is a utopian novel, like that of Thomas More].

10. This phrase consciously echoes Rojo-Benítez's *The Repeating Island*.

11. More is celebrated, in Sidney's *Defense of Poetry*, as the "poet" of the Utopia, in the sense of a writer given to "feigning."

12. On America, see Maravall 1991, 90, 132, 133, 155, 156, 179.

13. In the closing pages of his study, Maravall notes "the emergence of the utopian element . . . in a brief episode of the *Persiles*" (1991, 188). But which episode is never identified. For an elegant and generative reading, albeit different from my own, of the *Persiles* as "the novelist's utopia," see Baena.

14. In Guillén's well-known descriptions of literature as system, he hypothesizes, within each system, a dialectic of genre and countergenre: the first insinuating and connoting the opposite of itself as both a potential and a need (1970, 8, 135ff.). Claiming that each era possesses its own distinctive system of genres, Guillén stresses that a study of a given system will provide an anatomy of both the ideologies and the therapies of a society.

15. I thank Michael Gerli for calling my attention to this reference.

16. For mention of Barataria in *Don Quixote*, part two, see chapters 32, 45, 47, 49, 51, and 53.

17. For Higuera, artists like Cervantes "are a precious resource for political theorists" (1995, 3); "Anglophone critics ignore the political dimension in DQ" (3);

Don Quixote's "imperial hopes are always on his mind" (3); and Cervantes "was acutely aware" of the striking flourishing, in the sixteenth century, of "natural law theories in international relations" (4).

WORKS CITED

Bacon, Francis. 1981. *New Atlantis.* In *Famous Utopias of the Renaissance*, edited by Frederic R. White. Putney, Vt.: Hendricks House.

Baena, Julio. 1988. "*Los trabajos de Persiles y Sigismunda*: la utopía del novelista." *Cervantes* 8, no. 2 (Fall).

Bataillon, Marcel. 1950. *Erasmo y España: Estudios sobre la historia espiritual del siglo xvi.* Translated by Antonio Alatorre. México: Fondo de Cultura Económica.

Cervantes Saavedra, Miguel de. 1973. *El ingenioso hidalgo Don Quijote de la Mancha.* 2 vols., edited by Luis Andrés Murillo. Madrid: Clásicos Castalia.

———. 1999. *The History of that Ingenious Gentleman Don Quijote de la Mancha.* Norton Critical Edition. Translated by Burton Raffel. Ed. Diana de Armas Wilson. New York: Norton.

Cohen, Walter. 1995. "The Discourse of Empire in the Renaissance." In *Cultural Authority in Golden Age Spain*, edited by Marina S. Brownlee and Hans Ulrich Gumbrecht. Baltimore: Johns Hopkins University Press.

Columbus, Christopher. 1989. "Capitulación del Almirante Colón, 1492." In *1492–1992: Re/Discovering Colonial Writing*, edited by René Jara and Nicholas Spadaccini. Hispanic Issues. Minneapolis: Prisma Institute.

Cro, Stelio. 1994. "Classical Antiquity, America, and the Myth of the Noble Savage." In *The Classical Tradition and the Americas.* Vol. 1, edited by Wolfgang Haase and Meyer Reinhold. Berlin: Walter de Gruyter.

———. 1979. "The New World in Spanish Utopianism." *Alternative Futures* 2, no. 3 (summer): 39–53.

Elliott, J. H. 1995. "The Old World and the New Revisited." In *America in European Consciousness: 1493–1750*, edited by Karen Ordahl Kupperman. Chapel Hill: University of North Carolina Press.

Foucault, Michel. 1986. "Of Other Spaces." *Diacritics* 16 (Spring): 22–27.

Freyer, Hans. 1936. *Die politische Insel: Eine Geschicte der Utopien von Plato bis zur Gegenwart.* Leipzig: Bibliographisches institut ag.

Godzich, Wlad, with Nicholas Spadaccini. 1994. "The Changing Face of History." In *The Culture of Literacy.* Cambridge, MA: Harvard University Press, 55–71.

Greene, Thomas. 1968. "The Flexibility of the Self in Renaissance Literature." In *The Disciplines of Criticism*, edited by Peter Lemetz, Thomas Greene and Lowry Nelson, Jr. New Haven: Yale University Press.

Grummond, Jane Lucas de. 1961. *The Baratarians and the Battle of New Orleans.* Baton Rouge: Louisiana State University Press.

Guillén, Claudio. 1970. *Literature as System.* Princeton: Princeton University Press.

Higuera, Henry. 1995. *Eros and Empire: Politics and Christianity in "Don Quixote."* Lanham, Md.: Rowman and Littlefield.

Herrero, Javier. 1983. "More and Vives: Christian Radical Thought in the Renaissance." *Spain: Church-State Relations*. Chicago: Loyola University Press.

Hutchinson, Steven. 1987. "Mapping Utopias." *Modern Philology* 85, no. 2 (November): 170–85.

Jones, Joseph. 1999. "The Baratarian Archipelago." In *"Ingeniosa Invención": Essays on Golden Age Spanish Literature for Geoffrey L. Stagg in Honor of His Eightieth Birthday,* edited by Ellen M. Anderson and Amy R. Williamsen. Newark, Del.: Juan de la Cuesta Press.

Kupperman, Karen Ordahl, ed. 1995. Introduction to *America in European Consciousness: 1493–1750*, by Karen Ordahl Kupperman. Chapel Hill: University of North Carolina Press.

Levin, Harry. 1972. *The Myth of the Golden Age in the Renaissance*. New York: Oxford University Press.

Maravall, José Antonio. 1974. "Utopía y primitivismo en Las Casas." *Revista de Occidente* 141 (December): 311–88.

———. 1976. *Utopía y contrautopía en el "Quijote."* Santiago de Compostela: Editorial Pico Sacro.

———. 1991. *Utopia and Counterutopia in the "Quixote."* Translated by Robert W. Felkel. Detroit: Wayne State University Press.

Menéndez y Pelayo, Marcelino. 1905–1915. *Orígenes de la novela.* 4 vols. Madrid: Bally-Balliere.

Milton, John. 1957. *John Milton: Complete Poems and Major Prose.* Edited by Merrit Y. Hughes. New York: Macmillan.

More, Sir Thomas. 1992. *Utopia.* Translated and edited by Robert M. Adams. Norton Critical Edition. New York: W. W. Norton.

Naipaul, V. S. 1969. *The Loss of El Dorado: A History.* Middlesex, U.K.: Penguin.

Negley, Glenn, and J. Max Patrick, eds. 1952. *The Quest for Utopia: An Anthology of Imaginary Societies*. New York: H. Schuman.

Parr, James A. 1988. *Don Quixote: An Anatomy of Subversive Discourse.* Newark, Del.: Juan de la Cuesta.

Porras Barrenechea, Raúl. 1955. *El Inca Garcilaso en Montilla (1561–1614).* Lima: Editorial San Marcos.

Quevedo, Francisco de. 1790. "Noticia, juicio, y recomendación de la *Utopía* de Tomás Moro." Prologue to the Spanish translation of More's *Utopia.* 2d ed. Madrid: Aznar.

Reed, Walter. 1994. "Don Quixote: The Birth, Rise, and Death of the Novel." *Indiana Journal of Hispanic Literatures* 5 (fall): 263–78.

Rojo-Benítez, Antonio. 1992. *The Repeating Island: The Caribbean and the Postmodern Perspective.* Translated by James E. Maraniss. Durham, N.C.: Duke University Press.

Rose, Margaret A. 1979. *Parody // Meta-Fiction.* London: Croom Helm.

Shklar, Judith N. 1994. "What is the Use of Utopia?" *Heterotopia: Postmodern Utopia and the Body Politic.* Edited by Tobin Siebers. Ann Arbor: University of Michigan Press.

Siebers, Tobin. 1994. "Introduction" to *Heterotopia: Postmodern Utopia and the Body Politic.* Ann Arbor: University of Michigan Press.

Skinner, John. 1987. "*Don Quixote* in Eighteenth-Century England." *Cervantes* 7, no. 1 (spring): 45–57.

Vattimo, Gianni. 1992. *The Transparent Society*. Translated by David Webb. Baltimore: Johns Hopkins, UP.

Wolf, Elizabeth. " 'The Cardinal Tenet of the Now Familiar Myth': A History of 'White' Creolization in Kate Chopin's *The Awakening*." Unpublished.

Zavala, Silvio. 1965. *La utopía de Tomás Moro en la Nueva España: Recuerdo de Vasco de Quiroga*. Mexico: Porrúa.

Power Grabbing and Court Opportunism: From Spain to France

PERRY GETHNER

When, in April of 1665, Molière's company gave the premiere of Marie-Catherine Desjardins's *Le Favori* [The Royal Favorite], audiences were struck by the tragicomedy's realistic depiction of court life. This realism was pushed to *mise en abyme* with the command performance of *Le Favori* for king and court at Versailles two months later.[1] However, the main theme, namely the downfall of the prime minister Moncade, though set in Barcelona, was potentially explosive, since it called to mind the disgrace of Louis XIV's finance minister, Fouquet, in 1661, followed by a sensational trial that occurred in 1664. But if the play could have been viewed as a criticism of the king, why was Louis not offended and why did he permit a staging of it at Versailles? The probable reasons are that Desjardins based it on a Spanish play, which would curry favor with the Spanish-born queen, and that the protagonist, Moncade, is a "favori" (a prime minister with sweeping powers), rather than just one of a team of ministers, as Fouquet was. Nonetheless, her appropriation of a Spanish source in order to reflect on the current political situation in France reveals a surprising amount about differences, both in dramatic conventions and in real life, between these two countries that were experiencing their golden ages at roughly the same time, but had been almost constantly at war.

How much the French author knew about Spanish drama or politics remains something of a mystery. There is no evidence that she could read Spanish, and no French translation of the play that was clearly her source, Tirso de Molina's *El Amor y el amistad* [Love and Friendship], was ever published. It is likely, though proof is lacking, that she received a manuscript translation or a synopsis from friends or from the Spanish troupe based in Paris in the 1660s.[2]

Tirso's *El Amor y el amistad*, written in 1621 and first published in 1634, is apparently set in the twelfth century, at a time when

Spain was still divided between Cataluña and Aragon, and the political situation is chaotic. Prior to the start of the play, Don Hugo, count of Barcelona, quarreled with his younger brother, Don Ramón, and banished him. Hugo, being childless, thereupon made the king of France his heir. But, as chance would have it, the count had a falling out with the French king and reinstated his brother, whereupon Hugo suddenly died! In Act I, the exiled Ramón returns to become the new ruler. His control of Barcelona remains uncertain, however; to bolster his position, he enters into negotiations to marry the heiress of the kingdom of Aragon. In addition, he is greatly beholden to his cousin, Don Guillén de Moncada, the only nobleman to support him when he was out of favor. His first act as count is to name Guillén his *privado* [royal favorite]. The problem is that both Ramón and Guillén are young men with absolutely no political experience and apparently no core of supporters in the realm. They were not groomed to rule and seem to be improvising their policies as they go along. Moreover, the basic concept of unquestioning loyalty to the ruler has been called into question, since Guillén's outspoken support of the banished Ramón and his heroic defiance of Hugo, going so far as to announce that he would raise an army to defend himself if the count attacked him first, make it clear that, for him at least, loyalty to one's friend takes precedence over loyalty to one's monarch.

In *Le Favori* the political situation is altogether different. The ruler is called the king of Barcelona, probably so as not to confuse a French audience unfamiliar with Spanish history, but also to emphasize the parallels with the France of the author's day. This king has been on the throne for a considerable time, and Moncade has been his prime minister for ten years. There are no challenges of any kind to the king's authority, though we hear vague allusions to past "disturbances" that Moncade succeeded in quelling. Some of these may have been internal insurrections, but the most recent one was certainly a foreign war, since Moncade came to the aid of Prince Clotaire of a neighboring kingdom. In fact, it is presumably Moncade's ability as a general that has made him indispensable. His friend Alvar bluntly states: "Votre bras fut toujours l'appui de sa couronne" [1.1.66: Your arm has always been his crown's support]. It should be added that, even when some of the characters come to believe that the king has turned into a tyrant, no one ever considers revolt; the sole option they deem feasible is to escape from his powerful clutches by fleeing to the provinces.

Desjardins never specifies how old the king is and how much power he really wields. One obvious consideration is the fact that the king has left military matters totally to his minister. Should we suppose that the king did so because he was not of age? This would mean that he is much younger than Moncade, who presumably assumed his position during the ruler's minority. If so, there is a direct parallel to the position of Mazarin during the minority of Louis XIV. In support of this hypothesis is the king's apparent lack of a wife and children. On the other hand, we could suppose that the king is much older than Moncade and too old for military command. His statement that he has been more of a father than a king to Lindamire, the heroine of the play (5.5.1334), suggests that he may have adopted her as his ward following the death of her parents, in which case he could hardly be a very young man. Similarly, why would Elvire, the beautiful coquette who craves the constant admiration of the court, set her sights on the minister and not the king, if the latter were an eligible bachelor? In any case, the king, who behaves with great dignity and moral authority, never feels embarrassed about his continued need for his minister's services.

The fact that Moncade came to prominence as a military commander signals a curious difference between Spanish and French drama in the seventeenth century. French playwrights rarely show weak kings whose prime ministers do the actual ruling, even though in real life two prime ministers, Cardinals Richelieu and Mazarin, wielded nearly absolute power. (Of course, neither one of them ever fell from favor, which was hardly the case of their Spanish counterparts.) Dramatic conflicts between kings and subordinates tend to be set in times of war when the rulers, though considering themselves absolute, cannot lead their armies and require the services of brilliant generals to keep them on the throne. In tragicomedies (most notably Corneille's *Le Cid*) the two parties reach a harmonious resolution, but in tragedies the clash usually ends with the death of the general and the imminent overthrow of the king. *Le Favori* is one of the very few plays dealing with the relations between rulers and prime ministers in peace time. It should be added that in French serious drama of the period kings are more likely to have advisors with little or no official standing (captains of the guard, high priests, former tutors), and often there are multiple advisors capable of offering conflicting opinions. Even designated prime ministers never seem to question the kings' absolute authority. One need only compare how Haman is treated in tragedies based on the Biblical book of Esther. The insecure and frightened Aman of Racine's *Esther* (1689) is a far cry from the overweening and bombastic protagonists of Rivaudeau's *Aman* (1561) or of Montchrestien's play of the same name (1601).[3]

Curiously, the term *favori* in the sense of "prime minister" seems not to have entered the French language until the early years of the seventeenth century, and does not figure in plays until the time of Corneille. Even then it appears only sporadically, most often in works based on Spanish *comedias*, and the minister's precise functions are left rather vague. Indeed, one of the more revealing differences between the protagonists in the two plays is that Guillén, immediately upon his appointment, becomes the official conduit for dispensing patronage, whereas his French counterpart apparently lacks this power; instead, Moncade seems to get stuck with the dirty work of day-to-day operations. Perhaps Desjardins arranged matters this way because the French monarchy had already established a complex network of bureaucracies, which showed greater interest in merit than in noble birth and tried to reduce corruption. Even in the domain of the arts, patronage was increasingly regulated by royal academies. By the time of Louis XIV, the monarch was insisting on subordinate status for ministers and was careful to keep from being upstaged by them.

If all-powerful prime ministers were rare on the French stage in the seventeenth century, the Spanish stage featured them with great regularity. In part, this is because Spain saw a sizable number of such ministers in real life, especially during the reigns of Philip III and Philip IV, and sudden downfalls of favorites were not uncommon. The event that seems to have stirred the public imagination and triggered the popularity of this theme on the stage was the disgrace and public execution of fallen minister Rodrigo Calderón in 1618. The *privado* thus came to be viewed as a legitimate tragic hero, whether he happened to be guilty (typically of excessive pride or of conspiracy), or innocent (a victim of persecution by unscrupulous enemies).[4]

Tirso, of course, is using this tradition for tragicomic effect, since the downfall in *El Amor y el amistad* is simulated, and the audience is let into the secret from the start. The downfall is likewise implausible, since it would make no political sense for the Count to disgrace the only nobleman in the realm who has proven his loyalty in the face of extreme danger, and it would be even more illogical to dismiss the favorite only a few days after his appointment. It is probably not a coincidence that the characters who remain loyal to Guillén after his apparent disgrace were also loyal to him before he attained exalted rank; those who waited until his ascension to declare themselves his friends will not stand by him for even a week.

The most important trait that Spanish dramatists associate with the *privado*, however, is arrogance: he is obsessed with his power, prestige, and future reputation. Even if he is a just and moral person, he tends toward self-righteousness. In the case of Guillén, he seems to enjoy the power of bestowing estates and honors upon various courtiers, whose future loyalty he believes he is buying. He also feels unduly possessive about the people closest to him. No sooner has he conceived his first suspicions that his beloved Estela is unfaithful than he rudely denounces her, forgetting how a proper nobleman ought to behave toward a lady, and similarly forgetting that Estela is not even engaged to him (1.3).[5]

Arguably the greatest sign of his arrogance is his request that the Count participate in a charade designed to put Estela and his best friend, Don Grao, to the test. The Count is to pretend to disgrace Guillén, deprive him of his position and estates, and even put him in prison—but just for a few days, until the effects on the other people become apparent. Guillén seems not at all reluctant to co-opt his monarch into a scheme unrelated to state functions and aimed at resolving problems in his private life, nor does it bother him that he is making the Count engage in deceits and lies. In a later play, *Cautela contra cautela* [Deception Against Deception], Tirso would reuse the device of a king's pretending to disgrace the *privado*, but this time for serious reasons of state. The king has learned that there are traitors lurking in his court, and his intent is to use his minister as a double agent to identify and foil the conspirators. In *El Amor*, however, no one is plotting against the ruler, and the charade has no real political ramifications.[6]

Because Guillén feels a great sense of power by crafting the script for the play-within-a-play, he quickly becomes unnerved when scenes fail to go according to plan. To compound his distress, the Count, as he increasingly takes the initiative, appears to take delight in making Guillén squirm. One of the charade's unintended consequences is that all of the noblemen whom the minister showered with benefits only days before turn against him, and will not even try to save him from the scaffold. The two ladies who have been competing for his attention, the Count's cousins Doña Vitoria and Doña Gracia, likewise abandon him. The unmasking even extends to Guillén's servants: one proves to be fanatically loyal, whereas the other immediately deserts his service and visits the now penniless minister in prison only to demand his wages.

Even when the results of the deception are positive, they do not occur precisely as planned. Thus, when the Count interviews Estela, with Guillén hidden in the room, he far exceeds his instructions, which were to urge Estela to desert the disgraced minister. To the utter surprise of the other characters, the Count proposes to marry the young noblewoman himself. Presumably, the Count has tired of merely playing a role in a script written by someone else, and decides to assume authorial status for himself. Guillén, unable to control himself, rushes forward and denounces them both for their treachery. At this point the outraged Estela, who has been unswervingly loyal to Guillén, explodes in a rage and vows to shun all men henceforth and enter a convent. It will take considerable effort to calm her down and persuade her to marry Guillén, after all. In true Baroque fashion, those characters who try to make all the world into a stage are punished for their presumption; the metatheatrical enterprise is notoriously hard to control, and it is liable to backfire in the most unexpected ways. Just as Tirso, in better known plays such as *El Condenado por desconfiado* [Damned for Despair], shows the folly and peril of trying to achieve absolute certainty about one's destiny in the hereafter, he indicates here that attempts to achieve total control over the present moment are both ethically problematic and doomed to failure.

One of the most surprising changes between Tirso's play and Desjardins's involves the planning and execution of the charade. In the French version it is the king who devises the scheme by himself, and no one, including the audience, realizes that the disgrace is simulated until the end of the play. Moncade, who is as free from arrogance as any moralist could wish, would never imagine he had the right to put other people to the test. It would never occur to him to drag the king into his personal affairs or ask him to participate in a deception. In fact, during his first-act interview with the king, Moncade insists that it would be a serious lack of respect to make a monarch one's confidant (v. 308), and it takes an express command to make him reveal what has been troubling him. His problem appears to be a radical loss of self-confidence, the fear that he deserves neither his rank nor the affection and esteem of others.

Another change, perhaps dictated by the complex code of dramatic decorum, or *bienséances*, is that in the French play the king never actually tells an untruth.[7] Desjardins presumably knew how roundly Corneille had been condemned for having the king in *Le Cid* (1637) tell a white lie to Chimène in order to determine whether she still loves Rodrigue. The monarch in *Le Favori* never accuses Moncade of any wrongdoing and never actually strips him of his titles and position. His responses to other characters are often ambiguous or evasive, but there are no outright lies. He does not even give the unjust orders in person; instead, he sends Carlos, the captain of the guards, to announce to Moncade that he must leave Barcelona by the morrow and retire to his country estates. The most unjust action of all, Moncade's arrest, is not even shown on stage, occurring just prior to Act V.

The moment that produces the most confusion for the reader or spectator is the king's outburst at the end of Act I. When the king complains that Moncade has hurt his feelings by letting love take precedence over friendship, is this genuine anger, or is it the beginning of the charade, which the king has devised on the spot? Or is it perhaps a temporary expression of frustration that his relationship with Moncade is not as open and harmonious as he had wished, to be followed (off stage) by calmer deliberation, leading up to the devising of the charade? The playwright never tells us, thus shrouding the origin of the deception in mystery. However, that very mystery reinforces the message of her play, since, as the king himself declares at the end, "nul ne voit bien clair dans le coeur d'un monarque" [5.7.1430: no one clearly views a monarch's heart]. Absolutist doctrine, as expounded in the drama, accords the king the power to read the hearts of others (an ability resembling that of God) while his own heart remains inscrutable to his subjects. Attempts to manipulate a monarch are dangerous and, as in Tirso's play, doomed to failure. On the other hand, if the monarch manipulates other people in the interests of justice and proper governance, his actions are deemed totally legitimate.

Desjardins's play raises a number of moral issues in the context of the charade. The charge of tyranny is raised in two related contexts: the king arrests an innocent man for no stated reason and without any kind of trial, and he interferes with courtiers' private lives by dictating who they may or may not love.[8] But how does one respond to such manifest injustice, given that no one ever challenges the doctrine of absolute monarchy? The opportunists Clotaire and Elvire, who reject all traditional moral principles, see no contradiction in asserting that justice does not apply to kings. As Clotaire openly declares, once the king has declared Moncade to be guilty, a loyal subject has the duty to believe that Moncade has committed every crime imaginable (5.4.1271–83). Absolutism requires blind acceptance of the king's word on every subject, and courtiers are forbidden to think for themselves, let alone stand up to the king and challenge his actions. Lindamire and Alvar, who dare to do just that, assert that a king's power is limited by the principles of justice and equity. Lindamire further argues that kings have no right to compel the emotions of love and hatred. With the revelation that the king's injustice was merely a charade, the endorsement of Lindamire and Alvar's views becomes explicit.

Ultimately, the differences in the way the two playwrights depict monarchy relate to the types of courts that prevailed at the time they were writing and to their personal attitudes toward the king and his ministers. Tirso was thoroughly dissatisfied with the then-prime minister, the Count-Duke of Olivares, and with the way that the ministers of the previous regime had been purged.[9] Although attacks against the government are less conspicuous than in some of Tirso's other plays, the fact that the courtiers in this play are shown as inexperienced or corrupt or foolish, while the ruler refuses to engage in any of the day-to-day operations of governance, hardly suggests an endorsement of the contemporary situation. The fact that the first two titles that the new Count bestows on Guillén are "conde de Ampurias" and "duque de Girona" (1.7) may well have been intended to encourage the audience to draw parallels between the play and real life.

Desjardins, on the other hand, strongly approved of Louis XIV and of the way he had seized control of the government upon the death of Mazarin. Admittedly, her finances were precarious, and it was vital for her to praise the king and to create good relations with those royal ministers with the power to grant pensions to writers, but there is no indication that she privately disagreed with the views presented in her play. Moreover, although she wanted to depict her monarch and his prime minister in the most favorable light, she felt free to satirize the rest of the court, albeit rather gently. As I have argued elsewhere, Desjardins was very quick to perceive the shallow but elegant subservience that characterized the new breed of courtiers that flourished in the recently completed palace at Versailles.[10] She also understood the serious ramifications of the decline of the heroic values associated with the traditional aristocracy. The play's happy ending endorses the need to link leadership and *générosité* (a complex heroic code involving extreme courage, integrity and magnanimity),[11] but it also suggests, in a manner more comic than sinister, that the new generation of nobles will reject the old values and possibly lead the country away from the path of greatness.[12]

Notes

1. It was, by the way, the first work by a woman playwright to be so honored. Desjardins, who would not begin signing her works as Mme de Villedieu until 1668, was also the first woman to get her plays staged by professional actors in Paris. For more on the background of this play, see my edition of it in my 1993 collection. English translations are taken from my own translation of *Le Favori* in my 1994 anthology. The definitive study of her life and works is that of Cuénin

(1979). The best overall study in English, though superseded by Cuénin's book, is Morrissette's.

2. Surprisingly, I have found no previous full-length comparative study of *Le Favori* and its source. Ernest Martinenche (1900), whose book on French adaptations of Spanish comedias in the seventeenth century is still useful, dismissed Desjardins in less than a page. His view was basically that, since Tirso's play is brilliant, every change made to it must be an aesthetic disaster. However, I see no reason to denigrate one play at the expense of the other; both possess great merit but have very different aims.

3. For studies of royal ministers and advisors in French drama of this period (though not dealing with the type of situation examined here), see Baudin (1971) and Truchet (1981).

4. For a historical overview of the tradition of *privado* plays in Spain, see Mac-Curdy (1978). See also Leicester Bradner (1971).

5. All references to *El amor y el amistad* will cite act and scene numbers.

6. For further discussion of this play, see Kennedy's 1968–72 essay and chapter four of Oriel (1992) ("Dangerous Scripts in Tirso's *Cautela contra cautela*").

7. For this complex set of conventions, the standard sources are Bray (1927) and Scherer (1950).

8. Certain political theorists of the seventeenth century did in fact affirm the king's right to dictate (or forbid) the marriage choices of his subjects. See Couton (1963) and Traer (1980).

9. See, notably, Metford (1959), Kennedy (1980), and Wiltrout (1984).

10. See my "Love, Self-love and the Court in *Le Favori*."

11. On the concept of *générosité*, see, most notably, Bénichou (1948) and Stegmann (1968).

12. A version of this paper was read at the MLA convention in 1996. I would like to express my gratitude to my colleague, Christopher B. Weimer, for his invaluable assistance.

WORKS CITED

Baudin, Maurice. 1938. "The King's Minister in Seventeenth-Century French Drama." *MLN* 54: 94–105.

Bénichou, Paul. 1948. *Morales du grand siècle*. Paris: Gallimard.

Bradner, Leicester. 1971. "The Theme of *Privanza* in Spanish and English Drama 1590–1625." In *Homenaje a William L. Fichter*. Madrid: Castalia.

Bray, René. 1927. *La Formation de la doctrine classique en France*. Paris: Nizet.

Couton, Georges. 1963. "Le Mariage d'Hippolyte et d'Aricie ou Racine entre Pausanias et le droit canon." *Revue des sciences humaines* 3: 305–15.

Cuénin, Micheline. 1979. *Roman et société sous Louis XIV: Madame de Villedieu (Marie-Catherine Desjardins) (1640–1683)*. Lille: Université de Lille and Paris: Honoré Champion.

Gethner, Perry. 1987. "Love, Self-love and the Court in *Le Favori*." In *Actes de Wake Forest*, edited by Milorad R. Margitic and Byron R. Wells. Tübingen: Biblio 17.

———, ed. 1993. *Femmes dramaturges en France (1650–1750) Pièces choisies*. Tübingen: Biblio 17.

————, ed. and trans. 1994. *The Lunatic Lover and Other Plays by French Women of the Seventeenth and Eighteenth Centuries*. Portsmouth, N.H.: Heinemann.

Kennedy, Ruth L. 1968–72. "Tirso's 'Cautela contra Cautela': Its Authenticity in his Theatre and its Importance." *Revista de Archivos Bibliotecas y Museos* 75: 325–53.

————. 1980. "Has Tirso Satirized the Conde-Duque de Olivares in Nineucio of *Tanto es lo de más como lo de menos*?" In *Medieval, Renaissance, and Folklore Studies in Honor of John Esten Keller*, edited by Joseph R. Jones. Newark, Del.: Juan de la Cuesta.

MacCurdy, Raymond R. 1978. *The Tragic Fall: Don Alvaro de Luna and Other Favorites in Spanish Golden Age Drama*. Chapel Hill: University of North Carolina Press.

Martinenche, Ernest. 1900. *La Comedia espagnole en France de Hardy à Racine*. Paris: Hachette.

Metford, J. C. J. 1959. "Tirso de Molina and the Conde-Duque de Olivares." *Bulletin of Hispanic Studies* 36: 15–27.

Molina, Tirso de (Fray Gabriel Téllez). 1968. *El amor y el* amistad. In Obras *Dramaticas Completas*, edited by Blanca de Los Ríos. Madrid: Aguilar.

Morrissette, Bruce A. 1947. *The Life and Works of Marie-Catherine Desjardins (Madame de Villedieu) (1632–1683)*. New Studies, no. 17. St. Louis: Washington University Studies.

Oriel, Charles. 1992. *Writing and Inscription in Golden Age Drama*. West Lafayette, Ind.: Purdue University Press.

Scherer, Jacques. 1950. *La Dramaturgie classique en France*. Paris: Nizet.

Stegmann, André. 1968. *L'Héroïsme cornélien, genèse et signification*. 2 vols. Paris: A. Colin.

Traer, James F. 1980. *Marriage and the Family in Eighteenth-Century France*. Ithaca: Cornell University Press..

Truchet, Jacques, ed. 1981. *Recherches de thématique théâtrale: l'exemple des conseillers des rois dans la tragédie classique*. Etudes Littéraires Françaises 8. Tübingen: Gunter Narr and Paris: Jean-Michel Place.

Wiltrout, Ann E. 1984. "Tirso's Veiled Vindication of a Deposed Privado." *Romance Notes* 25, no. 2:181–4.

Eros and Atheism: Providential Ideology in the Don Juan Plays of Tirso de Molina and Thomas Shadwell

BARBARA A. SIMERKA

Although the traditional idea that early modern literature was a faithful defender of the *political* status quo has been discredited in recent years, representations of *religious* discourses have received much less attention. In this paper, I will utilize the recent insights of historians of religion in order to identify oppositional theologies—skepticism or atheism—in Tirso de Molina's *El burlador de Sevilla* [The Trickster of Seville], and in the adaptation of this play by the British playwright Shadwell. In order to argue for an oppositional *reception* of religious ideology in these plays, I will use Raymond William's (1977) concept of discursive plurality and "epochal analysis" in order to provide a materialist sociology of reception. Finally, I will also seek to demonstrate that there is an important connection between ideology and aesthetics in these plays. For, it is in part through the metadramatic "laying bare" of dramatic conventions concerning providential deliverance that these plays are able to subvert the representation of the intervention of supernatural powers as a force for dispensing justice—thus undermining the moral message upon which so much criticism has focused. Julia Kristeva (1987, 191) has argued that the spectacular merger of text and music in the opera *Don Giovanni* created the first oppositional version of the Don Juan theme; although she is correct in linking spectacle and opposition, she underestimates the theatrical resources of the early modern stage.

Raymond Williams's conception of cultural complexity is crucial to a revisioning of the relationship between orthodoxy and subversion. Williams asserts that monolithic views of history often fail to recognize the significance of competing discourses within a period and tend to grant signification only to the expression of the dominant voice (1977, 121). Williams argues for a more comprehensive "epochal analysis" that valorizes emergent and oppositional voices (122). The recognition of heterodox cultural practices is also relevant to a revisioning of early modern reader/audience response: rather than seeking to establish a univocal reaction to orthodox or transgressive elements in the texts, I would argue that reception, like production, is significantly influenced by the competition among discourses. Hans Robert Jauss, Stanley Fish, and Wolfgang Iser have developed influential notions of reader response, but they focus on the previous textual experiences that make up the reader's "horizon of expectations" (Jauss 1974, 18) or "repertoire," (Iser 1978, 205) and posit a monolithic reading experience. By introducing epochal analysis into the study of how responses to cultural phenomena vary, it is possible to historicize the horizon or repertoire of the respondent, and to include the significant *non*literary discourses in circulation. Fish's notion of an "interpretive community" can also be reformulated, to take into consideration the spectator's "ideological community." (1980, 338–46) A materialist theory of reception[1] will thus permit the analysis of the oppositional as well as affirmative responses available to the early modern reader or spectator. Since the orthodox reception of these plays is already well documented, my analysis of the early modern Don Juan corpus will focus on heterodox possibilities.

The emergence of rationalism as the cornerstone of modernity has important roots in the reemergence of philosophical skepticism in the sixteenth century. Latin translations of the Pyrrhonian skeptic, Sextus Empiricus, were published as early as 1520. His classic text, *Outlines of Pyrrhonism*, was available throughout Europe by the 1560s, and was widely read. Basil Willey (1967) describes Renaissance skepticism as an important turning point in human history, part of the general movement to seek out scientific explanations for phenomena as a replacement for "the necessity of reverencing what was not understood," as well as to feel comfortable with the discoveries of Galileo and Copernicus. For Willey, this new epistemology is the "hallmark of the modern spirit" (39). Richard Popkin (1979, xv) explains that the basic tenet of Pyrrhonian skepticism, the most influential form of skepticism in the sixteenth century, is the rejection of Academic skepticism's belief that nothing at all can be known for certain because of the unreliability of sensory perception, and the resultant impossibility of establishing reliable criteria for judgment. Pyrrhonists emphasize the cultivation of an *attitude*, rather than the development of an epistemological statement. This attitude consists of an ability for "opposing evidence, both pro and con, on any question about what was non-evident, so that one would suspend judgement" (Popkin 1979, XV) on questions of truth and knowledge. The Pyrrhonic skeptical attitude entails reservations concerning the establishment of criteria for judgment, rather than an outright denial of any valid criterion. Popkins's groundbreaking study, *The History of Skepticism from Erasmus to Spinoza*, amply demonstrates the importance of skepticism for early modern England and France. Although Spain did not produce as much skeptical writing as other western European nations, Maureen Ihrie (1982, 20–3) identifies a strong skeptical current in the works of J. L. Vives and in those of Pedro de Valencia, the royal historian to Philip III, and in *Don Quixote*. In addition, Henry Sullivan (1976), Barbara Mujica (1992), and Anthony Cascardi (1986) have demonstrated evidence of skeptical attitudes in other early modern Spanish texts.

The questioning of the validity of miracles as proof of divine intervention is an essential component of this skeptical attitude. Erasmus, Vives, and Hume are prominent among the skeptics who doubted supernatural intervention. Lucien Goldmann's *The Hidden God* (1959) documents the increasing doubts concerning an active personal deity among seventeenth century thinkers. This doubt can be seen in the trademark refrain "tan largo me lo fiáis" [I'll worry about that later][2] of the Spanish hero. The British Don John is even more skeptical; his frequently repeated declarations that miracles are merely natural phenomena that "fools" cannot explain and that "nothing happens but by nature" can be seen in the context of early modern philosophical and religious debates concerning divine participation in human affairs.

These Don Juan plays also stage ideas associated with atheism or unbelief. In the introduction of their anthology, *Atheism from the Reformation to the Enlightenment*, Michael Hunter and David Wooton observe that it is difficult to pinpoint atheism or unbelief during the early modern period. One of the primary reasons is the orthodox reception of writings suggesting alternative belief systems at that point in time; there was a tendency to conflate all ideas which "downplayed the role of revelations and an active personal deity" (1992, 2) under the heading of atheism, in order to discredit any form of questioning of the status quo. Michael Buckley (1987, 10) points out that one of the most common definitions of an atheist is a person who does not believe in divine intervention. In part because of this conflation of terms, the dominant trend among progressive mid-twentieth-century religious historians such as Lucien Febvre has been to assert that premodern atheism was entirely a construct of orthodox thinkers of the period, used to persecute any challenge to their authority. Thus, it came to be considered reactionary, a sort of complicity with the oppressors of the earlier period, for contemporary academics to assert the existence of unbelief prior to the eighteenth century (Wooton, 27–33).

An obstacle to full understanding of religious heterodoxy and atheism in early modern Spain and Italy is that documents of unbelief are often the product of investigations conducted by the Inquisition, and thus suspect for obvious reasons (Wooton 1992, 30, Edwards 1988, 3–4). However, David Wooton, William Christian, and John Edwards are among the scholars who have shown that a "judicious" use of Inquisition documents can provide important information on heterodox ideas. Like antiatheist treatises, the accusations raised by the Inquisitions point, not toward specific examples of nonconformity, but toward the counterhegemonic ideas feared by orthodox thinkers.

Another obstacle to the identification of early modern expressions of unbelief is the extreme persecution suffered by those who openly subverted official dogma, which resulted in the need to express unbelief in an evasive manner. In Spain and Italy, the existence of the Inquisition as an official organization dedicated to the punishment of all dissent is particularly significant. Wooton cites Paolo Sarpi's *Istoria del Concilio di Trento* [History of the Council of Trent], Vico's *Scienza nuova* [New Science], John Toland's "Of the Esoteric and Exoteric Philosophy," and Pierre Charron's *De la sagesse* [Of Wisdom] as examples of early-seventeenth-century texts which devote considerable space to commentaries about how to interpret their works. According to Wooton, these reflections were actually instructions on how to read "between the lines" in order to find the oppositional messages that lay beneath the surface of the apparently conventional works (1992, 34–40). David Berman (1988, 63) also cites "esoteric techniques" as a form of "camouflage" for counterhegemonic beliefs, and identifies another mode for circulation of these beliefs: texts in which the defenses of Christianity are much weaker and shorter than the descriptions of the oppositional ideology. The early modern Don Juan plays offer a literary variation of these techniques, for, as I will show, the character who performs and voices defiance of religious norms is far more attractive and convincing than the forces that seek to contain him. This is particularly true for the spectator or reader already familiar with the technique of looking for camouflaged oppositional ideas.

The seventeenth century also witnessed a proliferation of antiatheist texts that, in their zeal to defeat this heresy, had to give voice to the opposing discourse. David Berman (1988) points to the importance of the controversy surrounding Hobbes's *Leviathan*, in which the detractors of disbelief succeeded in publicizing irreligious sentiments far more openly than the (supposedly) unorthodox text itself. Alan Charles Kors (1990, 266) also notes the importance of seventeenth-century French debates between Cartesians and Aristotelians as a vehicle for the spread of irreligious ideas. One element of this competition concerned the issue of the "best" way to prove the existence if God and thus to disprove atheist ideas. Ironically, the successful attempts of each school to reject the validity of the other's arguments against atheism actually served to affirm atheism! (Kors 1990, 267). Likewise, the Inquisitions, which featured public condemnations of "heretics," functioned as a source for information concerning unorthodox beliefs. Thus, ironically, many forms of repression served to publicize the very forms of unbelief they sought to silence. Despite the recent increase in interest in early modern unbelief there have been no studies of theological writings in Spain comparable to those of Kors or Berman. The conventional wisdom concerning post-Tridentine Spain has been that there could not have been any significant dissemination of oppositional religious ideas. However, Henry Kamen (1985, 86) argues that Spain was not as isolated as historians have supposed; he points to the extensive travel to Italy and the Netherlands, which were hotbeds of subversive ideas, by Spanish soldiers in the Imperial army as one significant source of oppostional ideas. Kamen writes that there is also evidence of a significant clandestine commerce in banned books as another major factor in the transmission of forbidden or foreign ideas. The few studies that have investigated possibilities for an emergent discourse of unbelief have found affirmative evidence; the most complete study is John Edwards's (1988) examination of the *Book of Declarations* from the Soria diocese Inquisition.

One prominent feature of antiatheist writings is the depiction of the unbeliever as immoral; it was not until late in the nineteenth century that nonbelievers succeeded in gaining acceptance for a new definition of atheism in which doubt is not automatically associated with lewd behaviour (Buckley 1987, 10). The depiction of the debauched atheist was due, in part, to the strong belief that only a person who feared God's judgement would want to deny the existence of a divinity (Buckley, 45; Berman 1988, 36; Kors 1990, 23–36). The most common atheist archetype vilified in seventeenth-century French religious tracts is the aristocratic libertine (Kors 36). The connection between sexual misconduct and irreligion in Spain is implicit in the Inquisition's persecution of fornication as a behavioral manifestation of spiritual insufficiency (Haliczer 1990, 291; Kamen 1985, 202). The speeches made by the Don Juan figures themselves concerning religious matters are actually one of the least important components of my argument. The issue of the protagonist's voiced belief or unbelief is relevant only in the sense that *reception* of the "desacralized" world that the play offers at several different levels—overt and covert, visual and thematic as well as linguistic—may be effected by spectator interpretation of the religious views of the respective Don Juans (Riggs 1996, 9). Of course, the Spanish Don Juan never disavows Christianity; his oft-repeated "tan largo me lo fiáis" [I'll worry about that later] indicates that he merely wishes to put off practicing the tenets of his faith. The British Don John and his two acolytes repeatedly affirm their belief that the highest law is that of nature and the senses, and that conventional religion is "idle talk . . . to keep the rabble in awe" (act two).

An examination of the implicit debate between the Don Juan figures, whose lives are a series of skeptical/atheist performances, and their would-be censors, reveals that these plays strongly resemble the antiatheist tracts that make heterodox ideas appear more attractive than the dominant discourse. Critics have offered a plethora of explanations for the powerful attraction of this figure; James Mandrell (1992, 13) has dedicated a book to the study of how and why "Don Juan exercises such seductive power in literary and socio-cultural domains." The negative representation of the entire court is an essential element in Tirso's representation of an attractive atheist (in the sense that the early modern period identified illicit sexual behavior as a sign of atheism) who is more agreeable to spectators than the pious but hypocritical assembly of faithless fiancés and unscrupulous aristocrats. The representatives of terrestrial theocratic patriarchy, the king and Don Juan's father and uncle, are rendered as both ridiculous by virtue of the succession of failures to control one minor headstrong aristocrat and immoral by virtue of their constant efforts to shield Don Juan from legitimate punishment because of his family connections. The ultimate example of patriarchal powerlessness is the king's order to kill Don Juan, which comes *after* the statue has already accomplished the task. The corruption of morals brought about by *privados* is particularly evident in that the king, moved once again by his minister's pleas, is about to rescind the death sentence when Catalinón arrives to narrate his "suceso notable" [3.2829: amazing news].

Shadwell's protagonist asserts the belief that those who are publicly pious "have in reserve private delicious sins" (act one). Shadwell also emphasizes the abuse of aristocratic privilege; Don John is able to evade arrest and imprisonment on several occasions because fellow noblemen intercede for him with the magistrates or give him advance warning so that he can flee. However, the most powerful weapon in Shadwell's demystification of religious orthodoxy is hyperbole. Don John and his fellow atheists seduce and abandon a woman in nearly every scene; they commit incest, kill their own fathers to have access to their inheritances, and burn down convents in order to rape nuns. This implausible list of dirty deeds can thus be seen as a parody of the antiatheist tracts.

The decadence of the aristocratic worlds that the Don Juan figures inhabit is well documented;[3] however, I believe this element takes on a new significance when the court is viewed as the hegemonic voice in a covert debate between orthodox religion and unbelief. In addition, it is significant that in both plays the unsophisticated valets are chosen as the primary mouthpieces of religious orthodoxy.

Don Juan's mastery of language is another key component in his ability to "convince" characters and spectators. This is not to say that Don Juan overtly uses language to advocate atheism or skepticism, but rather that in a theatrical performance a character who uses language well obtains a sort of power—particularly in seventeenth-century Spain, where spectators went to *hear* a play. Even as he takes his first breaths after nearly drowning, Don Juan manages to enchant a self-declared *mujer esquiva* with his *conceptismos*, such as "del infierno del mar / salgo a vuestro claro cielo" [1. 586–7: I escape from a hellish sea into your heavenly presence] and "hay de amar a mar/ una letra solamente" [1. 595–6: just one letter distinguishes sea from love] and assuages Tisbea's concerns about a mixed marriage by insisting "amor es rey / que iguala con justa ley / la seda con el sayal" [1. 932–34: love has its own laws, which do not discriminate between silk and sackcloth]. After obtaining the information necessary to enter Ana's house from her own fiancé, Don Juan brags wittily, "el toro me echó la capa" [2. 1555: the bull handed over the cape to me]. One of the most compelling examples is when Don Juan becomes Aminta's husband merely by declaring it to be so; he answers the bewildered query "¿quién lo ha tratado?" [3. 2018: Who has contracted it (the marriage)?] with "mi dicha" [3. 2019: my word / my happiness], a word that is the past participle of "*decir*" as well as a noun indicating good fortune. Don Juan's ability to engage in small talk with the newly resuscitated statue is also remarkable, as is the fluidity with which he describes the fear that froze his heart—but not his tongue! (3. 2464). Even in his final moments, the doomed man is able to think—and speak—on his feet, hastening to assure the statue "a tu hija no ofendí" [3. 2761: I did not violate your daughter]. Although Everett Hesse (1995) has identified the many instances of performative speech on the part of Don Juan, Hesse's article does not explore the implications of the trickster's speech acts. Shoshona Felman's (1983) study of Molière's adaptation analyzes the central conflict in the play as a battle between two types of performative speech: Don Juan's promises of marriage and his enemies' threats of retribution (26). Throughout *El burlador*, Don Juan repeatedly manipulates performative declarations such as "juro" [I swear] and "prometo" [I promise] in order to obtain sexual favors, with the full knowledge that he will never supply the referent—a marriage ceremony; part of his power derives from receiving the benefits of those speech acts before he has concretized them. By contrast, the sincere threats of the other characters about "Dios" and "la muerte" turn out to be empty signifiers. Don Juan's victims are rendered powerless because their speech acts produce no consequences until the appearance of the statua-ex-machina, whose plausibility, I will argue below, is seriously compromised.

Like the women in Tirso's text, Shadwell's Leonora refers repeatedly to the strong impression Don John made with his "fervent vows" of impending marriage (act one). In keeping with Shadwell's penchant for hyperbole, when Don John is confronted by six of the women he has married and abandoned, all demanding that he announce which one is his true spouse, he declares that he is indeed married to one of them, but that private matters prevent him from making an announcement until the morrow, enabling him, like Molière's protagonist, to maximize the values both of speech and of silence. In addition, the two sidekicks that Shadwell provides for Don John are proof of the libertine's abilities as a proselytizer; they refer to him as the "oracle" whose explanations of the world "dispell'd the fumes which once clouded our Brains" (act one). This observation temporarily blurs the line between stage and audience, as these two characters describe themselves as spectators won over by Don John's verbal performance. In this instance, metalinguistic and metadramatic commentary join forces, inducing the theatergoer to analyze his or her own reception of Don John's unorthodox gospel.

An exploration of the relationship between metaartistic practices and skepticism or unbelief will provide the context for the final section of this article. I will focus on the laying bare of the devices of dramatic convention in these plays. The result of this form of metaart is a shift of the spectator's focus, from what Timothy Reiss (1971, 130) terms "the dramatic illusion," to a scrutiny of theatrical norms—such as the role of the *deus-ex-machina*, and last minute anagnorisis. Maureen Ihrie correctly posits a link between meta- artistic technique and skepticism; where the philosophical text advises the reservation of judgment, because of the difficulty in establishing appropriate criteria, the self-conscious text raises the problem of judgment with reference to its own status (38).

The parodic representation of divine intervention, via the statue-ex-machina, is typical of the elaborate metaart in these plays. Tirso himself was aware of the threat posed by the representation of "far-fetched miracles," and the growing popularity of elaborate stage machinery, writing that the genuinely pious messages of many plays are "submerged" under the avalanche of theatrical novelties so prevalent in the *corrales* (Sullivan 1976, 87). The combination of serious Christian mythology and stage machinery associated with entertainment rather than enlightenment thus problematizes the moral messages delivered by the supernatural figures. It is likely that early productions of *The Libertine* provoked similar complaints, for in the preface to the published text, Shadwell assures the reader that this play is "rather an useful moral than an incouragement [*sic*] to vice."

Metatheatrical elements dominate the final scenes of the plays. In both plays, Don Juan appears nonchalant about the appearance of the statue at his dinner table. This attempt to treat the supernatural as an ordinary occurrence heightens its effect on the audience. The servants provide the more conventional reaction to a supernatural phenomenon: Shadwell's Jacomo cannot pour the wine because he is shaking violently. Likewise, Tirso's Catalinón trembles visibly, and asks the statue the type of stereotypical questions concerning the afterlife that provoke laughter and invite the audience to feel superior to his naïve, medieval view of life and death. His last question, "¿prémiase allá la poesía?" [3. 2360: do they revere literature there?] is blatantly self-referential. This scene provides a significant example of the connection between metaart and skepticism: the laying bare of the devices of the representation of religious dogma foregrounds dramatic convention and at the same time reveals the inadequacy of human knowledge. Throughout the statue's visit, the audience is distracted from the conservative implications of his mission by the shift in perception elicited by the scene's self-conscious staging of the otherworldly guest.

The English audiences were treated to even more supernatural "machine play" scenes. In *The Libertine,* the animated statue is the last in a series of supernatural figures. As early as the final scene of act two, the spectator is treated to the appearance of the ghost of Don John's father. With his typical sangfroid, the unrepentant son declares that the ghost is a product of nature, just like his own behavior, and that neither takes precedence over the other. In the shipwreck that opens act three, Shadwell adds a legion of flying devils who prevent the sailors from extinguishing the fire that endangers the boat, and a thunderbolt that knocks Don John off his feet. The undaunted protagonist takes advantage of the panic among the captain and crew in order to commandeer the only lifeboat for himself and his friends. Shadwell's statue enlivens the scene in Don John's dining room by summoning red devils as proof of "the powers of hell;" however, the host asserts that "fools call unusual things miracles when they cannot explain them," so that the impact of the metaphysical phenomenon is immediately diluted (act four). In these two scenes, the spectator is lead to identify with the skepticism of Don John, because theatrical conventions concerning "machine plays" did not allow for the treatment of serious subject matter.

When the *burlador* arrives at the tomb, with Catalinón as his comic sidekick, Tirso indulges the audience's taste for the macabre with the delightfully grotesque banquet the statue offers. In this context, Don Juan's moment of recognition is almost comical in its inadequacy; he begs, "deja que llame / quien me confiese y absuelva" [3. 2766–7: allow me to call someone to hear my confession and absolve me] only after trying—for once without success—to talk his way out of the situation. Here, self-referentiality and skepticism are united in the laying bare of the convention of anagnorisis as a plot device, undermining the dogma of timely recognition of one's sins as a redemptive force.

Shadwell deflates the final banquet scene even before it begins. Act Five opens with the servant Jacomo dressed in borrowed armor, practicing his inept swordsmanship as preparation for the coming encounter. The statue acts as a sort of stage manager, bringing forth a cast of ghosts of several of Don John's murder victims to compel him to repent and seek salvation. Next, a choir of devils is summoned to sing a description of the "flames of sulphur, eternal darkness, eternal chaos" that await the unrepentant sinner (Act Five). Then, the audience and Don John are treated to a spectacle of loud thunder and splitting earth as the two friends are punished for their sins. Finally, the still-unrepentant libertine is taken into hell by the choir of devils, with thunder and lightening and "a cloud of fire" (Act Five). Shadwell gives the servant the final words of demystification; after pronouncing the orthodox "thus perish all those men who defy heaven" (Act 5) and exiting the stage, Jacomo returns with a metatheatrical epilogue. He describes a danger far more grave than the eternal condemnation that the actors who stage this play will face—not from any divinity, but from the religious zealots who "make solemn leagues and covenants against plays" (Epilogue). The juxtaposition of an implausible staging of divine retribution followed by a self-referential critique of the orthodox thinkers who condemn drama as immoral serves to ridicule both Don John's condemnation and also contemporary hegemonic discourses concerning the evils of the theatrical experience. As a result, the spectator who is receptive to unorthodox theology could extract an oppositional moral relevant to analysis of both Don John's life and Restoration English society.

In both versions, this scene is the culmination of the play's use of *admiratio,* "machine play" technology, and metaartistry. As the audience delights in the spectacle of smoke, fire, stage machinery, and the anticlimactic scenes that follow the Don Juans' deaths, it is uncertain that the statue's moral message could have much of an impact, or that the audience would see this event as plausible proof of providential intervention. For both the original spectator and the contemporary critic, these plays offer a representation of divine intervention in human affairs that dramatizes a wide variety of religious and philosophical discourses. Even for those who choose to interpret the final encounter with the statue as ultimately affirmative of the status quo, the representation of the discursive competition should nevertheless be considered meaningful, and potentially transgressive, for as Jonathan Dollimore (1986, 72) points out, a dramatic representation of containment "may also constitute the terms of a challenge to the dominant ideology." By illuminating one component of the polyphonic nature of the representation of divine intervention in early-modern Don Juan dramas, this essay seeks to contribute to the growing body of studies that validate and valorize the presence of multiple discourses of power and ideology in early modern texts.

NOTES

This article is a revised version of my study of providential ideology in *El burlador de Sevilla,* which appeared in *Gestos* 23 (April 1997).

1. See my *Gestos* article for a much more detailed exploration of materialism and reception theory.

2. All translations from the Spanish are mine; I have chosen to emphasize the connotations rather than the literal meanings.

3. For critical analysis of this theme in *El burlador de Sevilla*, see Ayala 1961; Hesse 1995; Varey 1979; Wade 1979; Parr 1994, introduction. For *The Libertine*, see Tasch 1989; Kaufman 1986; Novak 1977.

WORKS CITED

Ayala, Francisco. 1961. "Burla, burlando. . . ." *Asomante*, 17, no. 2: 7–15.

Berman, David. 1988. *A History of Atheism in Britain*. New York: Croom Helm.

Buckley, Michael. 1987. *At the Origins of Modern Atheism*. New Haven: Yale University Press.

Cascardi, Anthony J. 1986. *The Bounds of Reason: Cervantes, Dostoevsky, Flaubert*. New York: Columbia University Press.

Christian, William A. 1981. *Local Religion in Sixteenth-Century Spain*. Princeton: Princeton University Press.

Dollimore, Jonathan. 1986. "Subjectivity, Sexuality, and Transgression: The Jacobean Connection." *Renaissance Drama* 17: 53–82.

Edwards, John. 1988. "Religious Faith and Doubt in Late Medieval Spain: Soria Circa 1450–1500." *Past and Present* 120 (August): 3–25.

Felman, Shoshana. 1983. *The Literary Speech Act: Don Juan with J. L. Austin, or Seduction in Two Languages*. Translated by C. Porter. Ithaca: Cornell University Press.

Fish, Stanley. 1980. *Is There a Text in This Class?* Cambridge: Harvard University Press.

Goldmann, Lucien. 1959. *The Hidden God*. Paris: Gallimard.

Haliczer, Stephen. 1990. *Inquisition and Society in the Kingdom of Valencia, 1478–1834*. Berkeley: University of California Press.

———, Ed. 1987. *Inquisition and Society in Early Modern Europe*. Totowa, N. J.: Barnes and Noble.

Hesse, Everett. 1995. "Gender and the Discourse of Decay in El burlador de Sevilla." *Bulletin of the Comediantes* 47, no. 2: 155–63.

Holub, Robert. 1984. *Reception Theory: A Critical Introduction*. New York: Methuen.

Hornby, Richard. 1986. *Drama, Metadrama, and Perception*. Cranbury: Associated University Presses.

Hunter, Michael, and David Wooton, editors. 1992. *Atheism from the Renaissance to the Enlightenment*. New York: Oxford University Press.

Ihrie, Maureen. 1982. *Skepticism in Cervantes*. London: Tamesis.

Iser, Wolfgang. 1978. *The Implied Reader: Patterns of Communication in Prose Fiction from Bunyan to Beckett*. Baltimore: Johns Hopkins University Press.

Jauss, Hans Robert. 1974. "Literary History as a Challenge to Literary Theory." In *New Directions in Literary History*, edited by Ralph Cohen. Baltimore: Johns Hopkins University Press.

Kamen, Henry Arthur Francis. 1985. *Inquisition and Society in Spain in the Sixteenth and Seventeenth Centuries*. Bloomington: Indiana University Press.

Kaufman, Anthony. 1986. "The Shadow of the Burlador: Don Juan on the Continent and in England." In *Comedy from Shakespeare to Sheridan: Change and Continuity in the English and European Dramatic Tradition*, edited with introduction by A. R. Braunmuller and J. C. Bulman and forward by Maynard Mack. Newark: University of Delaware Press.

Kors, Alan Charles. 1990. *Atheism in France, 1650—1729*. Vol. 1. Princeton: Princeton University Press.

Kristeva, Julia. 1987. *Tales of Love*. New York : Columbia University Press.

Mandrell, James. 1992. *Don Juan and the Point of Honor*. University Park: Pennsylvania State University Press.

Molina, Tirso de. 1994. *El burlador de Sevilla*. Ed. James A. Parr. Binghamton, New York: *State University of New York Center for Medieval and Early Renaissance Studies*.

Mujica, Barbara. 1992. "Cervantes' Use of Skepticism in *El retablo de las maravillas*." In *Looking at the* Comedia *in the Year of the Quincentennial*, edited by Barbara Mujica, Sharon Voros, and Matthew D. Stroud. Lanham: University Press of America.

Novak, Maximillian E. 1977. "Margery Pinchwife's 'London Desease': Restoration Comedy and the Libertine Offensive of the 1670s." Studies in the Literary Imagination 10, no. 1:1–23.

Parr, James A., ed. 1994. *El burlador de Sevilla*. With an introduction by James A. Parr. Binghamton: *State University of New York Center for Medieval and Early Renaissance Studies*.

Popkin, Richard. 1979. *The History of Skepticism from Erasmus to Spinoza*. Berkeley: University of California Press.

———. 1987. "The 'Incurable' Skepticism of Henry More, Blaise Pascal, and Soren Kierkegaard." In *Skepticism from the Renaissance to the Enlightenment*, edited by Richard Popkin and Charles Schmidt. Wiesbaden: In Kommission bei O. Harrassowitz.

———. 1992. "Jewish Anti-Christian Argument as a Source for Irreligion from the Seventeenth to the Nineteenth Centuries." In Hunter and Wooton, editors.

Reiss, Timothy J. 1971. *Toward Dramatic Illusion: Theatrical Technique and Meaning from Hardy to Horace*. New Haven: Yale University Press.

Riggs, Larry W. 1996. "Don Juan: The Subject of Modernity." *L'Esprit Créateur* 36.1 (Spring):7–20.

Shadwell, Thomas. 1968. *The Complete Works of Thomas Shadwell*. New York: B. Blom.

Simerka, Barbara A. 1997. Early Modern "Skepticism and Unbelief and the Demystification of Providential Ideology in *El burlador de Sevilla*." Gestos 23 (April):38–66.

Sullivan, Henry. 1976. *Tirso de Molina and the Drama of the Counter-Reformation*. Amsterdam: Rodopi.

Tasch, Peter A. 1989. "The Beggar's Opera and The Libertine." *Notes and Queries* 36, no. 1 (Mar.):234–52.

Varey, J. E. 1979. "Social Criticism in *El burlador de Sevilla*." *Theatre Research International* 2: 197–221.

Wade, Gerald E. 1979. "The Character of Tirso's Don Juan." *Bulletin of the Comediantes* 31, no. 3: 3–42.

Willey, Basil. 1967. *The Seventeenth Century Background: Studies in the Thought of the Age in Relation to Poetry and Religion* New York: Columbia University Press.

Williams, Raymond. 1977. *Marxism and Literature*. Oxford: Oxford University Press.

Wooton, David. "New Histories of Atheism." In Hunter and Wooton, editors, 13–53.

The Politics of Adaptation:
Fuenteovejuna in Pinochet's Chile
CHRISTOPHER B. WEIMER

In February of 1601, followers of the earl of Essex paid a group
of London actors to perform Shakespeare's *Richard II*, seeking to
encourage popular support for the nobleman's ultimately unsuc-
cessful attempt to overthrow Queen Elizabeth I with the drama's
depiction of a British ruler's deposition and execution. Elizabeth,
realizing that the conspirators intended audiences to identify her
with the play's unfortunate protagonist, personally denounced the
performances and ensured that all published versions of Shakespeare's tragedy during her lifetime would omit the scene in which
Richard is forced to abdicate in favor of a usurper, a scene that
memorably exposes the fragility and ephemerality of a power more
often constituted as divinely bestowed, immutable, and absolute.[1]
The queen needed no graduate seminars to understand that theatrical performance can be a profoundly political act in numerous
senses of that adjective, although modern students of drama have
indeed benefitted from the work of New Historicists, Cultural Mate-
rialists, and other scholars who have re(dis)covered or at least re-
emphasized this aspect of theater.[2] Nor is Elizabeth I's acuity
unique, for history—the history of power contested, gained, and
lost—provides numerous examples of playwrights and political
figures from the past who were notably cognizant of theater's potential impact and utility. The ancient Athenian founders of drama
frequently addressed current political issues in their works: Aeschy-
lus opposed alliances with Sparta in *The Persians*, Euripides used
The Trojan Women to denounce the horror and degradation of war,
and Sophocles made Theseus in *Oedipus at Colonus* a prescriptive
exemplar of just rulership (Aylen 1985, 65–73). In Golden Age
Spain, the Count-Duke of Olivares created Felipe IV's court theater
to glorify both monarch and monarchy, even as he inadvertently
provided astute dramatists such as Calderón the opportunity to address significant political questions (Brown and Elliott 1980; Greer

1991). And during the years of military dictatorship in modern-day Chile, the popular playwright Isidora Aguirre repeatedly, albeit often subtly, challenged the *junta* with a variety of works, among them her adaptation for student audiences of Lope de Vega's *Fuenteovejuna* [Sheep's Well],[3] a reworking that actively denounces tyranny and praises those who resist it. The purpose of this study is to explore Aguirre's revision (in both senses of the word) of Lope's *comedia* by focusing on the possible political significance of what she retains from the original text, what she eliminates, and what she adds.[4]

Questions concerning the nature and impact of politically subversive theater under repressive governments are rarely simple. The case of Chile is a particularly compelling one, for it was a progressive and democratic nation prior to the onset of the internal political strife that resulted in the 11 September 1973 military coup d'état that toppled the Allende regime and installed a *junta* headed by General Augusto Pinochet Ugarte. Opinions concerning the military government's effect on artistic production in Chile have varied. In 1978, Robert J. Alexander wrote of a "cultural blight" inflicted on Chile by the dictatorship and asserted: "A cloud of conformity and coercion now hangs over Chilean cultural and intellectual life. If this change persists, Chile will have ceased permanently to be one of the world's great centers of intellectual freedom and creation" (1978, 394). In direct contrast to this pessimistic assessment, however, Arturo C. Flores contends that the coup instead politicized Chilean theatrical discourse in the years that followed:

> El golpe militar sirve de catalizador para que el quehacer teatral vuelva a su esencia educativo-moral y a reafirmar su índole social. Es este último elemento el que conlleva el aspecto ideológico que, en el caso del teatro chileno después de 1973, se opone abiertamente a la ideología represiva denunciando los valores m[a]ntenidos por el oficialismo. (1991, 124)

> [The military coup serves as a catalyst for theater to return to its educational and moral essence and to reaffirm its social role. Upon this last element stands the ideological dimension that, in the case of Chilean theater after 1973, openly opposes repressive ideology, denouncing the values maintained by the leadership.]

The subject of this essay, Isidora Aguirre, agrees with Flores's assessment: "Because theater is an ideal medium for criticizing society, playwrights working during the period of the dictatorship would regularly voice the attitude of protest among the citizens" (1994, 85).

Aguirre's belief that theater can indeed possess a political dimension and make an impact upon the spectators' consciousnesses has shaped her writing throughout a career that began long before the coup and that has continued to thrive since the reinstallation of a civilian government.[5] Although perhaps best known for writing the libretto to the wildly popular musical comedy *La pérgola de las flores* [The Flower Market, 1960], she is also renowned for her overtly political dramas, in which she has addressed themes including the exploitation and oppression of the poor (*Los papeleros* [The Ragpickers], 1963; *Los que van quedando en el camino* [Those Who Fall by the Wayside], 1969), colonialism (*Lautaro*, 1982), and the murder of the *desaparecidos* (*Retablo de Yumbel* [Altarpiece of Yumbel], 1987).[6] Still another part of her output during the years of military rule was the reworking of canonical texts, including works by Sophocles, Machiavelli, Molière, Shakespeare, and Lope de Vega, for Chilean student audiences. By no means does Aguirre avoid political questions in these adaptations, which she terms *versiones libres* [free translations]. Indeed, she has openly declared with regard to her reworkings of *Oedipus Rex*, *Richard III*, *Lazarillo de Tormes*, and *Fuenteovejuna*: "In all cases, I emphasized what could be taken as a protest against the dictatorship" (1994, 85).

Such reworkings offer a paradigm of the interpretative process performed whenever inhabitants of one point in time and space approach a text that originated in another. As George Steiner remarks in his study of translation, "every act of understanding is itself involved in history, in a relativity of perspective" (1975, 249). Moreover, Charles Ganelin's study of nineteenth-century *refundiciones* [reworkings] of *comedias* argues persuasively that reworkings of earlier texts can be far more than a case of *vino añejo en odres nuevos* [old wine in new bottles], for "it is one thing to create a new container, yet another to bridge the distance" between the sociocultural context of a play's inception and the context in which it is subsequently regenerated (1994, 19). Of this process Ganelin writes:

> a reworking becomes the by-product of a collusion between authors regardless of the time and geography that separate them. The horizons of later writers open to the past through allusion so that the product of the "original" creator may collude with another creative mind to enable bridge-building between the *materia prima* and the "copy" . . . the reworker fills in historical gaps, another way of defining hermeneutical

bridge-building, to let the old "thought" live on, to show that "thought" is received by him from the context of his horizons, and to pass on the old "thought," now modified, to the spectators, who in turn will incorporate the new experience into their horizons. (15)

This process can serve a variety of ends, including political ones; for example, in her analysis of a controversial Los Angeles Theater Center Staging of *La vida es sueño*, a production that drew parallels between the situations of Segismundo and Rodney King, Barbara Simerka demonstrates the ideological potential of modern adaptations of *comedias*. This is precisely what occurs in Aguirre's *versiones libres* of earlier stage works. She reshapes those texts in accord with her own poetics, which result inevitably from her subjectivity as a woman, as an inhabitant of Latin America as well as of the twentieth century, and—in the case of those works written between 1973 and 1990, including her Fuenteovejuna—as a citizen of a formerly progressive democracy now under military dictatorship. To study Aguirre's Fuenteovejuna from a strictly "literary" perspective would ignore these factors, and it is such readings of Latin American theater that lead Juan Villegas to deplore the common critical inclination to "deshistorizar los textos y sacarlos de su contextualidad social, histórico y teatral" [1984, 7: dehistoricize the texts and remove them from their social, historical, and theatrical contexts.]

Aguirre begins her Fuenteovejuna with a spoken prologue and a song performed by all the actors in the company. The Brechtian opening, entirely original to Aguirre's text, makes clear the didactic intent of her adaptation under the guise of introducing her student audiences, presumably unacquainted with Spanish classical theater, to the work they are about to witness.[7] With this prologue Aguirre establishes beyond any doubt the specific relevance of her Fuenteovejuna to the students in attendance and their families, to all contemporary Chileans. The prologue begins with a key metaphor: that of a journey, the journey of the imagination through time and space about to be experienced by the actors and their audience. The actors proclaim: "Aquí estamos, los actores, embarcados no en una barca, sino en un autor de genio, y de ingenio, el gran Lope de Vega, para invitaros a visitar tiempos de otrora. Será un viaje largo y breve. Breve por el contar de Lope, y larguísimo por cuanto atraviesa siglos" [1: Here we are, the actors, borne not by a boat, but by an author of genius and ingenuity, the great Lope de Vega, to invite you to visit the past. The journey will be both long and short. Short due to Lope's tale, and long due to the centuries to be crossed].

This reference to Lope's canonical place in Hispanic literature might well have served to legitimize Aguirre's choice of subject matter and to forestall possible censorship. The audience's theatrical destination, however, is far from incidental: "Venid pues, hasta la España legendaria de Fernando de Aragón e Isabel de Castilla, los muy católicos reyes . . . los mismos que auspiciaron otro larguísimo viaje, en ruta inversa, el de las tres carabelas de Colón" [1: Come then to the legendary Spain of Fernando of Aragon and Isabel of Castile, the very Catholic monarchs . . . the same monarchs who launched another lengthy voyage, following the reverse route, that of Columbus's three ships]. Just as Columbus led the Spaniards across the ocean to the New World, Aguirre leads her Chilean actors and spectators back to Spain—in search not of gold and slaves, but of a tale in which they might recognize their own political situation. The text constitutes their journey as one taken toward modern Latin America's origins in the public's own collective and national past.

Having defined the audience's destination as an actual temporal and geographic point, Aguirre next asserts the historical basis of Lope's *comedia*, and by extension, that of her own play:

> —Y antes de abrir de par en par las compuertas del tiempo os digo que lo que aquí ocurre no es fantasía, sino un hecho real. Un suceso, algo que ocurrió en esta villa.
> —Lo toma Lope de una[s] crónicas -viejas ya en su tiempo de un siglo- en las que se cuenta que el "Comendador Mayor de Calatrava, don Fernán Gómez, tenía residencia y vasallos en Fuenteovejuna; y que hizo tantos y tan enormes agravios a los vecinos, que ellos determinaron de un solo consentimiento y voluntad ¡alzarse contra él y matarle." (1)

> [—And before opening wide the floodgates of time, I tell you that what will happen here is not fantasy, but rather a real deed. An event, something that occurred in this town.
> —Lope takes it from chronicles, already a century old in his day, in which it is recounted that the "Grand Commander of Calatrava, Don Fernán Gómez, had estates and vassals in Fuenteovejuna; and that he committed so many and such great crimes against the people that they determined, by common consent and will, to rise against him and kill him."]

As all scholars of *Fuenteovejuna* know, the historical accuracy of this play is debatable at best. Lope chose to rely largely upon Rades y Andrada's *Crónica de las tres órdenes*, which was neither the most reliable nor the only source (Aníbal 1934, 698–703). None of Lope's sources, in addition, could have furnished him with the particulars of the Comendador's abuses of his feudal authority in Fuenteovejuna; even Rades's account emphasizes the villagers' political and economic grievances against the Comendador over his treatment of the women (Aníbal 660; Ruggiero 1995, 12–13), while the figures of Laurencia, Frondoso, Mengo, and the other peasants are nothing more than Lope's inventions to dramatize the events related so briefly in Rades's chronicle. Moreover, Aguirre herself departs from Lope's dramatization in her *versión libre*, eliminating, for example, the Maestre and the Comendador's servant Ortuño from the cast and changing the *alcalde* [mayor, village elder] Alonso to Doña Alonsa, a deceased elder's widow and "una mujer principal" [an important lady] who seems to share with Esteban the responsibility for governing the town. Although both playwrights' departures from their respective sources might well problematize the question of historical accuracy, Aguirre's prologue ignores any such questions, instead quoting the famous passage from Rades describing the villagers' revolt and assuring the audience that what they are about to witness is "un hecho real," "un suceso, algo que ocurrió." Not only does this assertion emphasize the veracity of the action depicted onstage, it might well also have served to further protect Aguirre from any official disapproval; she likewise resorted to strict reliance on court documents and newspaper accounts in order to avoid censorship while denouncing the Pinochet regime's political murders in *Retablo de Yumbel* (1994, 85–86).

With the play to follow now firmly rooted in historical reality, Aguirre next urges her young spectators not to see this play as a reenactment of events out of the dusty and distant past, but instead as timeless in its truth; the actors say of the characters they will assume: "Quizá en ellos reconoceréis al pueblo de hoy, de ayer, ¡de siempre!" [2: Perhaps in them you will recognize the people of today, of yesterday, of every era!]. With this final exhortation, the purpose of the prologue becomes apparent: to constitute Aguirre's *versión libre* of *Fuenteovejuna* as a form of documentary theater in which true events are depicted onstage in a manner explicitly relevant to the spectators. Just as Essex's followers hoped to sway public sentiment by staging events taken from British history, Aguirre's actors declare that they will reenact with factual accuracy an actual rebellion drawn from the public's own historical heritage that will reflect contemporary Chilean reality.

As we have already noted, the process of textual adaptation must depend upon the act of textual interpretation. In the prologue, Aguirre declares one central aspect of her perspective on the source

comedia when the actors instruct the audience, "Lope qui[s]o que
el verdadero personaje de su *Fuenteovejuna* fuese el pueblo" [2:
Lope wanted the true protagonist of his *Fuenteovejuna* to be the
people]. The vast accumulated commentary on Lope's play includes many works of scholarship endorsing this interpretation but
by no means offers unanimous critical agreement on the question.
Indeed, the intersection of the play's two plots on the figure of the
Comendador has suggested to more than one critic that the nobleman might in fact be *Fuenteovejuna*'s true protagonist.[8] Aguirre's
text, in contrast, demonstrates little ambiguity with regard to this
question. In addition to making her preliminary declaration of the
pueblo's central role, Aguirre, as we shall see, later deemphasizes
and eliminates many of the features of Lope's text that support such
a reading; her Fuenteovejuna is the story of the eponymous village
alone. The song that immediately follows the prologue and serves
as a bridge to the action reinforces this interpretation; sung by the
company to a popular Asturian melody, it summarizes the events to
be represented onstage:

> Fuenteovejuna se inicia
> para contar con acierto
> que se gana la justicia
> al ponerse de concierto.
> Gente de Fuenteovejuna
> con su ejemplo determina
> que al estar todos a una
> la injusticia se castiga.
> ¡A bailar y cantar los amores
> no queremos al Comendadore!
> ¡Castigad los tiranos señores
> que aquí los que valen son los labradores! (2)

> [Fuenteovejuna begins,
> in order to show successfully
> that justice is won
> by uniting together.
> The people of Fuenteovejuna
> with their example demonstrate
> that by acting as one
> injustice is punished.
> Let us sing and dance in praise of love,
> we love not the Comendador!
> Punish the tyrants,
> for those who matter here are the peasants!]

This song reiterates the unity of the villagers in their rejection of injustice and tyranny; the final two lines verge on an exhortation to modern audiences to rise up against their own *tiranos señores*—who, although not explicitly identified by Aguirre, could only be the military dictators of Chile.

Once the actors assume their roles and the action begins, Aguirre's departures from Lope become immediately apparent. The first scene of her *versión libre*, while corresponding to the encounter between Lope's Comendador and Maestre and conveying much of the same information to the audience, is quite distinct from its source. In the *comedia* it takes place at the Maestre's palace, where the Comendador has come to manipulate the younger aristocrat into attacking Fernando and Isabela's forces in Ciudad Real; in Aguirre's text, it takes place at the Comendador's manor house in Fuenteovejuna, and Rodrigo Téllez Girón is not even a character in this version. Instead, the Comendador had previously sent his servant Flores to the Maestre in order to provoke him into action, and in this first scene Flores reports the success of his mission to his master, who then hurries away to join the Maestre in battle. Most significantly, the *refundición* greatly shortens and simplifies the lengthy political exposition found in Lope. Aguirre's revision of this scene serves several purposes. By relocating the action and eliminating the figure of the Maestre, she immediately centers the drama in the village of Fuenteovejuna and emphasizes the power and influence of the Comendador, who can ignite a rebellion against Fernando and Isabela without even leaving his estates. The changes in the nobleman's persuasive tactics do much to strip that rebellion of any possible justification. Lope's Comendador, as we know, exerts more than one kind of pressure on the youthful Maestre in order to win him over; his arguments include an explanation of the conflicting claims to authority of Isabela and Juana la Beltraneja and of the political advantage to be gained through the active support of Juana and her husband, Alfonso of Portugal (vv. 90–116).[9] In Aguirre's version, the Comendador's arguments are much less sophisticated. He mentions neither Juana la Beltraneja nor her claim to the throne, and also omits any appeals to the youthful Maestre's concern for his honor and reputation. He instead simply frightens the Maestre with the potential political and economic dangers posed both by Alfonso's struggle with the *Reyes Católicos* for the crown and by the power the victor will wield: "lo que vuestros parientes ganaron en combate y que por herencia os corresponde . . . ¡otros codician!" [3: that which your ancestors won in combat and is your legacy . . . others crave!]. By foregrounding the aristocratic military orders' resistance to centralized authority, minimizing questions of royal succession, and eliminating the astute psychological manipulations of Lope's Comendador, Aguirre successfully establishes a parallel between the Spanish Order of Calatrava's actions and the Chilean military's rebellion against the legitimate civilian government.

With this parallel in place, Aguirre is able to render with essential fidelity the Comendador's abuses of his authority as recounted by Lope, thus offering her audience throughout the work repeated opportunities to extend the connection between the tyrannical nobleman and the equally tyrannical Chilean military authorities. After the Comendador's pursuit of Laurencia fails with both the girl herself and with her father, Esteban, the nobleman seeks to forestall the growth of any collective hostility toward him by dispersing the villagers: "En mi ausencia los villanos querrían hacer sus corrillos. ¡Cada cual a su casa!" [14: In my absence the peasants will talk and plot. Everyone go home!]. Such a ban on public assembly is a common feature of martial law and a tactic frequently employed by military governments anxious to eliminate organized resistance, including the Chilean *junta* (Alexander 1978, 344). The relevance of the scene in which Mengo unsuccessfully attempts to defend Jacinta from the Comendador and his soldiers seems equally apparent. Commanding the soldiers to strip Mengo, tie him to a tree, and whip him for his defiance, the nobleman then informs Jacinta that a fate even worse than she had anticipated awaits her: "No para mí, sino para el ejército has de ser" [17: You will not belong to me, but instead to the troops]. This combination of brutal violence and gang rape immediately evokes the Chilean military's most flagrant abuses of power, as does the Comendador's disruption of Frondoso and Laurencia's wedding. Not only does he arrest Frondoso, rationalizing his detention with the gravity of Frondoso's alleged offense to the Order of Calatrava, and seize Laurencia with the intention of raping her, but the Comendador also orders the *alcalde*, Esteban, beaten with his own staff of office. The symbolic value of this final offense in Lope's *comedia* cannot be underestimated; both Herrero (1970–71, 179–80) and Carter (1977, 325) note that Fernán Gómez de Guzmán destroys the legal and sociopolitical order represented by the *alcalde*'s staff when he wrests it from the village elder's hands and assaults him with it. In Aguirre's Fuenteovejuna, the same symbolism is present, but with still more contemporary relevance: the Comendador, emblematic of Chile's rebellious military, subjects civil law and order to the oppressive, coercive authority that derives from superior force and the willingness to employ it violently.

Such abuses of power on Fernán Gómez de Guzmán's part clearly justify the villagers' ultimate revolt against his tyranny. Aguirre closely follows Lope in both her depiction of the rebellion itself and of the subsequent investigation and interrogation commanded by the *Reyes Católicos*; the Chilean playwright's peasants ultimately escape punishment in the same way as their Lopean counterparts. However, the conclusion of Aguirre's drama has little to do ideologically with that offered by Lope de Vega. Lope's ending, in which the *Reyes Católicos* pardon the Maestre's treason and take the village of Fuenteovejuna under their own protection, has presented some scholars and producers with ideological difficulties; many of those drawn to the play's depiction of popular rebellion against tyranny are uncomfortable with its ultimate endorsement of absolute monarchy. As William R. Blue asserts, Lope's *comedia* "draws from nostalgic popular beliefs" in his idealized evocation of Fernando and Isabela, especially in this final scene:

> It is the myth of the Reyes Católicos, the myth of the utopian state. In his play, these mythical monarchs unify their ravaged country through the practical politics of punishing wrongdoers, chastising the wayward, forgiving the errant, restoring tranquility, and holding the reins right in their hands. The dominant political term in this play is monarchy, personal, powerful, active. (Blue 1991, 31)

This aspect of the text has in fact led some theatrical interpreters to eliminate the king and queen entirely or at the very least to omit their final appearance onstage.[10] Aguirre's approach is more subtle. The playwright pays lip service to the figures of Fernando and Isabela, but throughout her Fuenteovejuna, she repeatedly subverts Lope's laudatory and prescriptive depiction of monarchy. Stylistically recalling the time-honored contrast between courtly artificiality and rural simplicity, only in the play's court scenes does the playwright retain the versification that she discards in favor of prose throughout the remainder of the work. This device distances Fernando and Isabela from both their afflicted subjects and from the public, whose identification with the villagers is enhanced by the commonality of a shared discourse, especially in contrast to the formal, stylized proclamations of the *Reyes Católicos*. Aguirre further differentiates the court scenes from those taking place in Fuenteovejuna with the use of a Brechtian *Relator* [Narrator] who, as the following example illustrates, accompanies the stage action with an ongoing commentary, including physical stage directions, descriptions of the monarchs' emotional reactions, and narrative dialogue attributions preceding and / or following the characters' lines:

Relator	Luego que atenta lo escucha
	triste exclama la reina:
Reina	"Un nuevo adversario lucha
	por disputa de encomienda." (10)

[Narr.	Upon listening to him attentively
	the queen exclaims sadly:
Queen	"A new adversary joins
	the struggle over sovereignty."]

This device likewise creates an implicit opposition between the scenes taking place in Fuenteovejuna, which are presented without any such Brechtian commentary, and those taking place at court; the former are represented with an emotional immediacy while the latter are in effect narrated and thereby placed at a distance from the spectator.

Moreover, this distance produces neither respect nor admiration for Fernando and Isabela. Unlike the other characters in Aguirre's Fuenteovejuna, including the villagers and the Comendador Fernán Gómez de Guzmán, the *Reyes Católicos* are not performed naturalistically. The playwright's stage directions for their first appearance leave little doubt concerning the subversive portrait painted by this *refundición*: "*Música de corte: traen unos escaños y sobre ellos trepan dos, actor y actriz, con largo ropaje y máscaras vistosas para los Reyes Católicos. . . . Rey y Reina serán grandes muñecos que accionan y se inclinan al hablar, un poco reyes de naipe*" [9: *Court music: benches are carried in and upon them climb an actor and actress with long robes and colorful masks to play the Catholic Monarchs. . . . The king and queen will be large puppets that gesticulate and lean forward when speaking, a bit like kings and queens on playing cards*]. These two figures resemble more characters from the *commedia dell'arte* than they do any *comedia* monarchs, even the most fallible or ineffective. They certainly have little to do with their counterparts in Lope, and their onstage representation as *muñecos* may well function as ironic commentary on Lope's manipulation of these historical figures.

Fernando and Isabela's second appearance onstage, in which they learn of the comendador's murder, is represented in the same way: the rulers as *muñecos* or *reyes de naipe*, following the *Relator*'s stage directions and speaking in verse. Their third and final appearance, however, is even more daring and theatrically complex. This corresponds to Lope's final scene, in which the peasants appear in front of the *Reyes* and receive their grudging pardon. Aguirre makes this scene doubly remote: the *Relator* returns to the stage to present the action, which in fact consists of Frondoso, Laurencia, Mengo, and the other main characters recreating their audience with the *Reyes Católicos* for the benefit of their fellow Fuenteoveju-nans who remained behind in the village. They openly move the *muñecones "como marionetas"* [34: like marionettes] and speak the rulers' lines for them; later in the scene, Laurencia goes so far as to don Isabela's robes and mask in order to impersonate the queen. Not only does this treatment deprive the *Reyes Católicos* of whatever grandeur they might possess in Lope's *comedia*, it also visually grants control of the situation onstage to the villagers rather than to their nominal rulers. Fernando and Isabela quite literally become puppets in the hands of their lowliest subjects. This device serves to emphasize an ambiguous element of Lope's text: the rulers' effective impotence at a politically hazardous moment when confronted with the villagers' unity, with their refusal to respond to the *juez*'s demands with anything but "Fuenteovejuna lo hizo" [Fuenteovejuna did it]. Aguirre quotes Fernando's often-debated verdict, repeated here by the *alcalde*, Esteban, almost directly from Lope's text:

> Pues no puede averiguarse
> el suceso por escrito
> aunque fue grave delito
> por fuerza ha de perdonarse. (36; Lope, vv. 2442–45)

> [Since what occurred cannot
> be determined in writing,
> although the offense was grave
> it must be pardoned.]

Aguirre's stage directions note that these lines should be immediately repeated in song by the company, and this exultation might well express the villagers' joy at having outwitted their rulers and forcing them to leave the murder of a noble unpunished. It is quite clear in either version, after all, that this pardon results not from the monarchs' sympathy for the villagers' sufferings under Fernán Gómez de Guzmán, but from their inability to identify any specific malefactors whose punishment might serve as an "ejemplo de las gentes" [29: example for the people]. Aguirre's representation of Fernando and Isabela thus ultimately diminishes the symbolic role played by Lope's *Reyes Católicos* and enhances the *pueblo*'s status as the play's protagonist.

Indeed, the closing scene of the play focuses on Fuenteovejuna alone. Rodrigo Téllez Girón's surrender to Fernando and Isabela has disappeared from Aguirre's reworking, which concludes the national subplot after the *Reyes Católicos'* forces retake Ciudad Real. In addition, Aguirre, unlike Lope, does not end her play with the royal pardon and Frondoso's brief closing lines to the audience. After the tale of the royal audience and pardon has been recounted, the villagers resume Frondoso and Laurencia's nuptuals. The significance of this decision cannot be underestimated. For Lope, the restoration of harmony and order is best symbolized and represented by a spoken edict on the part of King Fernando; for Aguirre, that restoration is better embodied by the triumph of Frondoso and Laurencia's love and by Fuenteovejuna's collective participation in their union. The idyllic rural utopia disrupted by Fernán Gómez's crimes now celebrates the deliverance brought about through their own courage and unity, returning to the song featured in the prologue with new words:

> Fuenteovejuna termina
> y os prueba con acierto
> que se gana la justicia
> al ponerse de concierto.
> ¡A bailar y cantar los amores
> don la gente de campo y labranza!
> ¡que al librarse del Comendadore
> quedó llena de paz y esperanza!
> A bailar y cantar los amores
> que no tenemos ya Comendadores
> pues aquí no mandad tiranos señores
> que los [que] aquí mandan son los labradores. (37)

> [Fuenteovejuna ends
> and successfully shows you
> that justice is won
> by uniting together.
> Let us sing and dance in praise of love
> enjoyed by the people who labor in the fields!
> Upon freeing themselves from the Comendador
> they ended up full of peace and hope!
> Let us sing and dance in praise of love,
> for we no longer have Comendadores.
> Tyrants, do not give orders here,
> for those who rule here are the peasants.]

In conclusion, this study has sought to illuminate the dynamics shaping Isidora Aguirre's *versión libre* of *Fuenteovejuna*. The political circumstances of its conception and its author's own sense of political commitment made Lope's *comedia* an appropriate and fertile source; as we have seen, much of the original text offered relevant commentary on Chilean life under the military dictatorship of Augusto Pinochet Ugarte. Aguirre, however, chose to rework the *comedia* as well, making changes that rendered its political relevance more apparent and subverting its monarchical ideology. The final product harshly condemned the tyranny inflicted upon the people of Chile even as it sought to persuade them that liberation and justice were theirs for the taking.

NOTES

1. For details concerning these performances and their aftermath, consult Ure's introduction to Richard II (1961, lvii–lxi). Rackin (1990, 118–9) and Montrose (1996) offer provocative analyses of the political questions involved.

2. Countless such studies now exist, especially in the Shakespearean field. Among them I would recommend those listed in the bibliography by Cox (1989), Dollimore (1993), Dollimore and Sinfield (1994), Greenblatt (1988), Montrose (1996), Mullaney (1995), Orgel (1975), Rackin (1990), and Wikander (1986). Though fewer scholars approach the *comedia* from these perspectives, Greer's analysis of Calderón's court plays (1991) is a rewarding one.

3. All translations, including those of Lope's original text, Aguirre's reworking, and any critical commentary, are mine.

4. I am indebted to Isidora Aguirre for providing me with a copy of her Fuenteovejuna, which, to the best of my knowledge, remains unpublished at the time of this writing. All references to the play cite this manuscript by page.

5. As events of the 1990s have shown, little guarantee exists that the Chilean military will accept without question the civilian government's authority, especially when that authority is invoked against the military's autonomy (Rosenberg 1995). Aguirre contends that the civilian government's all-too-apparent vulnerability has paradoxically stifled the political theater that thrived during Chile's years of dictatorship: "The theater of protest, however, was interrupted when democracy returned in 1990: People were afraid to protest the errors the new system might make. The old incentive—having absolute certainty that denunciation was an important task—simply wasn't there any longer" (1994, 86).

6. Worthwhile studies of Aguirre's other works include those by Balboa Echeverría (1992), Bissett (1984), Dölz Blackburn (1991), Flores (1991), and González (1985).

7. Consult Bissett (1984) for further discussion of Brecht's importance in Aguirre's theater and that of many of her fellow Latin American playwrights.

8. Dixon and Ruggiero both favor this interpretation, while Kirschner makes a strong case for the "collective protagonist" interpretation. See also Hall (1974) on the connection between the play's two plots.

9. For one analysis of these pressures, see my Girardian study of the play (1996, 169–73).

10. The latter departure from Lope's text was for many years standard practice in Soviet Russia, for example, while Lorca's adaptation of the play for La Barraca

248   CHRISTOPHER B. WEIMER

certainly employed this device and may have omitted the *Reyes Católicos* altogether (Kirschner 1979, 19–22).

WORKS CITED

Aguirre, Isidora. 1994. "Chilean Theater 1973–1993: The Playwrights Speak." *Review: Latin American Literature and Arts* 49 (fall): 84–9.

———. Fuenteovejuna. No. 011786 (57,088–91). Dirección de Bibliotecas, Archivos y Museos, Departamento de Derechos Intelectuales. Santiago, Chile.

Alexander, Robert J. 1978. *The Tragedy of Chile*. Westport: Greenwood.

Aníbal, Claude E. 1934. "The Historical Elements of Lope de Vega's *Fuente Ovejuna*." *PMLA* 49: 657–718.

Aylen, Leo. 1985. *The Greek Theater*. Rutherford: Farleigh Dickinson University Press.

Balboa Echeverría, Miriam. 1992. "Historia y representación en Chile: La voz de Isidora Aguirre." In *Actas del X Congreso de la Asociación Internacional de Hispanistas*, edited by Antonio Vilanova. Barcelona: PPU.

Bissett, Judith Ishmael. 1984. "Delivering the Message: *Gestus* and Aguirre's *Los papeleros*." *Latin American Theatre Review* 17, no. 2: 31–7.

Blue, William R. 1991. "The Politics of Lope's *Fuenteovejuna*." *Hispanic Review* 59: 295–315.

Brown, Jonathan, and J. H. Elliott. 1980. *A Palace for a King: The Buen Retiro and the Court of Philip IV*. New Haven: Yale University Press.

Carter, Robin. 1977. "*Fuenteovejuna* and Tyranny: Some Problems of Linking Drama with Political Theory." *Forum for Modern Language Studies* 13: 313–35.

Cox, John D. 1989. *Shakespeare and the Dramaturgy of Power*. Princeton: Princeton University Press.

Dixon, Victor. 1989. Introduction to *Fuenteovejuna*, by Lope de Vega. Warminster: Aris and Phillips.

Dollimore, Jonathan. 1993. *Radical Tragedy: Religion, Ideology, and Power in the Drama of Shakespeare and his Contemporaries*. Durham, N.C.: Duke University Press.

Dollimore, Jonathan, and Alan Sinfield, eds. 1994. *Political Shakespeare: Essays in Cultural Materialism*. 2d ed. Ithaca: Cornell University Press.

Dölz Blackburn, Inés. 1991. "La historia en dos obras de teatro chileno contemporáneo." *Confluencia* 6, no. 2: 17–24.

Flores, Arturo C. 1991. "Teatro testimonial: *Retablo de Yumbel* de Isidora Aguirre." *Hispanic Journal* 12, no. 1: 123–32.

Ganelin, Charles. 1994. *Rewriting Theater: The Comedia and the Nineteenth-Century Refundición*. Lewisburg, Pa.: Bucknell University Press.

González, Patricia E. 1985. "Isidora Aguirre y la reconstrucción de la historia en *Lautaro*." *Latin American Theater Review* 19, no. 1: 13–8.

Greenblatt, Stephen. 1988. *Shakespearean Negotiations: The Circulation of Social Energy in Renaissance England*. Berkeley: University of California Press.

Greer, Margaret Rich. 1991. *The Play of Power: Mythological Court Dramas of Calderón de la Barca*. Princeton: Princeton University Press.

Hall, J. B. 1974. "Theme and Structure in Lope's *Fuenteovejuna*." *Forum for Modern Language Studies* 10: 57–66.

Herrero, Javier. 1970–71. "The New Monarchy: A Structural Reinterpretation of *Fuenteovejuna*." *Revista Hispánica Moderna* 36: 173–85.

Kirschner, Teresa. 1979. *El protagonista colectivo en Fuenteovejuna*. Salamanca: Ediciones Universidad de Salamanca.

Montrose, Louis. 1996. *The Purpose of Playing: Shakespeare and the Cultural Politics of the Elizabethan Theatre*. Chicago: Chicago University Press.

Mullaney, Steven. 1995. *The Place of the Stage: License, Play, and Power in Renaissance England*. Ann Arbor: Michigan University Press.

Orgel, Stephen. 1975. *The Illusion of Power: Political Theater in the English Renaissance*. Berkeley: University of California Press.

Rackin, Phyllis. 1990. *Stages of History: Shakespeare's English Chronicles*. Ithaca: Cornell University Press.

Rosenberg, Tina. 1995. "Force is Forever." *The New York Times Magazine* 24 September, 44–9.

Ruggiero, Michael J. 1995. "Fernán Gómez de Guzmán, Protagonist of *Fuenteovejuna*." *Bulletin of the Comediantes* 47, no. 1: 5–19.

Simerka, Barbara. 1993. "A Postmodern Adaptation of *La vida es sueño*." In *Looking At The Comedia In The Year of the Quincentennial*, edited by Barbara Mujica, Sharon D. Voros and Matthew Stroud. New York: University Press of America.

Steiner, George. 1975. *After Babel: Aspects of Language and Translation*. New York: Oxford University Press.

Ure, Peter. 1961. Introduction to *Richard II*, by William Shakespeare. 5th ed. London: Methuen.

Vega, Lope de. 1991. *Fuente Ovejuna*. 12th ed. Edited by Juan María Marín. Madrid: Cátedra.

Villegas, Juan. 1984. "El discurso dramático-teatral latinoamericano y el discurso crítico: algunas reflexiones estratégicas." *Latin American Theatre Review* 18, no. 1: 5–12.

Weimer, Christopher B. 1996. "Desire, Crisis, and Violence in *Fuenteovejuna*: A Girardian Perspective." In *El arte nuevo de estudiar comedias: Spanish Golden Age Drama and Literary Theory*, edited by Barbara A. Simerka. Lewisburg Pa.: Bucknell University Press.

Wikander, Matthew H. 1986. *The Play of Truth and State: Historical Drama from Shakespeare to Brecht*. Baltimore: Johns Hopkins University Press.

Numancia as Ganymede: Conquest and Continence in Giulio Romano, Cervantes, and Rojas Zorrilla

FREDERICK A. DE ARMAS

Readers and audiences acquainted with the classical flavor, economy, monumentality, and tragic energy of Cervantes's *La Numancia* would find Rojas Zorrilla's two-part imitation, *Numancia cercada* [*Numancia Besieged*] and *Numancia destruida* [*Numancia Destroyed*] a radical departure from the model. These later plays revel in abundance, excess, and diversity, diluting the tragic impact while relying on wonder and *admiratio*. Instead of focusing on a single *agon*, the conflict between the city and the Roman army led by Scipio, Rojas Zorrilla's *comedias* overwhelm by their "monstrous" structure and amaze by their bizarre turns of plot and by the characters' disguises. Cross-dressing, something that is absent from Cervantes's *Numancia*, proliferates in Rojas Zorrilla's plays, becoming a metonym for dramatic turns, transgressive sexuality, and metamorphosis. And metamorphosis itself is an essential metonym, as Leonard Barkan explains, "for the classical civilization that gave it birth" (1986, 18).

Rojas Zorrilla's "Baroque" dramas[1] further point to the ancient world through the use of Renaissance paintings and tapestries that evoke a past that it is anxious to resuscitate. While Cervantes had constructed a theater of memory imitating and refashioning the images and structures of the sixteen frescoes and other decorations found in the *stanze* of Raphael at the Vatican, which he must have visited while serving as secretary for Cardinal Acquaviva in Rome around 1569–70,[2] Rojas Zorrilla activates the memory of Cervantes's pictorial pre-texts by pressing upon the reader / spectator competing images from Giulio Romano. The Hall of Constantine, the last of the four *stanze* that Popes Julius II and Leo X commissioned Raphael to decorate, was actually executed by his assistants, and particularly by Giulio. This essay will show that while Cervantes

250

foregrounds one of the stanza's frescoes, Rojas suppresses it in order to priviledge other works by this Roman artist. By displaying the riches of Giulio Romano, by evoking the artist's works in Mantua, Rojas Zorrilla may well be reminding his audience that Spain's loss of Mantua was as much a political as an artistic catastrophe.[3]

The Apparition of the Cross to Constantine[4] takes place outside of Rome, the day before Constantine's battle with Maxentius for possession of the city. The parallels with the scenes that surround Scipio's harangue to his soldiers in Cervantes's tragedy are striking. I will only point to a few.[5] Both Constantine and Cipión are Roman leaders who wish to impart the necessary valor to their troops to win a battle. Both stand above the soldiers in order to deliver their *allocutio* [harangue]. While Constantine speaks from a pedestal, Cipión "se sube sobre una peña que estará allí" [41: he climbs on a rock that will be there]. Cervantes's explicit stage directions evince his desire to replicate visually upon the stage this feature found in Giulio Romano's painting. The Roman soldiers in Romano's painting, although frozen in the stillness of the fresco, can be seen as rushing forward to hear their leader. In the play, the *allocutio* is delivered immediately after an order is given to the soldiers to come forward.

The Vatican fresco represents in the background the river Tiber, which flanks the city of Rome. In Cervantes's play, the river Duero appears on stage and recounts how it flanks the city of Numancia. Lacking the ability to stage a river, Cervantes uses personification, borrowing the technique from epic authors such as Virgil who characterized the Tiber as a river god. In his allocution in *La Numancia*, the Roman general chastises the troops for having abandoned themselves to the pleasures of Venus and Bacchus. These gods, he claims, are antithetical to the pursuits of the god of war, Mars: "En blandas camas, entre juego y vino / hállase mal el trabajoso Marte" [vv. 153–54: "In soft beds, among gaming and wine, the strenuous Mars is uncomfortable"].[6] Romano's painting, as *poesía muda* [mute poetry], cannot give us the words of Constantine's allocution. And yet, I believe that Cipión's injunctions derive from the Vatican fresco. Daniel L. Heiple reminds us that Renaissance painters and theorists reversed the Horatian notion of *ut pictura poesis* in order to show that painting was like poetry. One way in which a painting could "speak" was through the use of "allegorical figures or mythological figures that could be juxtaposed in a variety of meaningful combinations and postures. These figures already contained deeper meanings, and their new context provided further reflections on possible meanings for the painting" (Heiple 1994, 368).[7]

Giulio Romano and Assistants, *The Apparition of the Cross to Constantine*. (Logge, Vatican Palace. Photo: Alinari/Art Resource, NY)

A viewer can begin to find the answer to what Constantine may be saying to his troops in the emperor's gesture. As Sylvia Ferino Pagden has argued (1989, 86), he may be looking and pointing to the right. Following his gesture, the viewer's gaze would eventually collide with the edge of the tapestry. Here we discover the virtue of *Moderatio* [Moderation] next to Pope Clement I. George Hersey accurately describes her: "One breast is revealed and her thick blond hair, set with pearls, is artfully arranged. The wine jug at her feet is borrowed from the iconography of a sister virtue, Temperance, who stands for moderation in drinking" (1993, 165). The discarded wine jug and the emphasis on the pearls of abeyance are echoed in Cipión's harangue when he argues that victory cannot come as long as his soldiers are "con Venus y con Baco entretenidos" [v. 123 occupied with Venus and Bacchus].

While in Cervantes's *La Numancia* Scipio's harangue to the soldiers is derived from Giulio Romano's fresco at the Vatican *stanze*, Rojas Zorrilla turns away from the previous play and the Vatican fresco by having Scipio prepare an edict for his soldiers (56–57).[8] Cervantes's vividly visual scene is replaced by a text written in prose, which cleverly circumvents the necessity of imitating one of the more forceful moments in Cervantes's tragedy. The prose text not only absents the Cervantine scene and the Italian fresco, but also the figure of Scipio. By transforming an allocution into a written edict, the Roman general is thrice absent: his physical body is missing; it is supplanted by writing, something that cannot be questioned and is thus dead; and finally the edict is in prose, eschewing the personal eloquence necessary for persuasion.

Scipio's absence may represent his powerlessness in Rojas's play—and may even be paradoxically related to his representation as a Hercules killing the Hydra. As the Roman general volunteers for conquest, he clearly equates Numancia with the monstrous that must be defeated for the sake of civilization and empire (vv. 131–40). For Scipio, Spain is truly the hydra, and Numancia its last head:

> España, que ya imitaba
> la lernea venenosa,
> multiplicando cabezas
> siempre que alguna le cortan,
> ya está vencida, ya teme
> vuestro poder. Esta sola
> cabeza, Numancia fiera,
> ha quedado. (vv. 161–9).

[Spain, who imitated the poisonous hydra, growing multiple heads as one is chopped off, is now defeated, now fears your power. Only one head, fierce Numancia, remains.]

Although the hydra was often represented pictorially during the Renaissance,[9] it is interesting to note that Giulio Romano executed a *Hercules and the Hydra* for the Sala dei Cavalli [Hall of Horses], in the Palazzo del Tè in Mantua—and Rojas may have been inspired by this and other Mantuan mythological paintings by Giulio. This should come as no surprise, since much of the Palazzo was decorated for Charles V's visit there, and thus follows a Habsburg program (Hartt 1958, 157–58; Tanner 1993, 116). As Cristina Gutiérrez Cortines Corral asserts: "Giulio Romano fue el artista que mejor dio forma a la imagen imperial. . . . Recordemos que el artista romano fue quien se encargó de diseñar todo el programa escenográfico de las entradas y recibimientos realizados en Mantua en 1530 con motivo de la visita regia" [1989, 170: Giulio Romano was the artist who best shaped the imperial image. . . . Let us remember that the Roman artist took charge of designing the whole program of entries and receptions that took place in Mantua in 1530 due to the imperial visit]. Although to our knowledge Rojas never traveled to Italy, he could have known of Giulio's efforts in portraying Spanish imperial rule through accounts of Charles's Mantuan celebrations; through Vasari's descriptions in his *Lives of the Artists*; through travelers's descriptions, such as the one provided to the emperor at Vienna by Cesario Antiquario (Simon 1988, 196); and through the many *estampas* or prints of famous Italian paintings that circulated in Spain during the Golden Age. Such was the fame of Giulio's Mantuan works that plays such as Aretino's *Stablemaster* and Shakespeare's *Winter's Tale* allude to his frescoes. More importantly, notices of Mantua's artistic riches must have been circulating in Madrid at the time of the Mantuan war of succession starting in 1628. Indeed, the play may well have been written when Spanish influence over the duchy was on the wane or when Spain was close to losing it to the French.[10]

Hercules had often been appropriated by the developers of Spanish monarchical mythology as one of the founders of its dynasty (Tate 1954, 1ff.). The mythical reversal in Rojas's play (where

Francisco de Zurbarán, *Hercules Killing the Hydra of Lerna.* **(Museo del Prado, Madrid. Photo: Scala/Art Resource, NY)**

Scipio—the enemy of Numancia/Spain—becomes Hercules) is particularly significant if we place *Numancia cercada* in its historical context. Although Rojas Zorrilla's *comedia* presents as its central conflict the siege of the Celtiberian city by the overwhelming forces of Rome, I would argue that the Spanish audience of the time would *not* have automatically identified themselves with the besieged city.[11] After all, they, like the Romans, had become a great empire, thinking of the Other as barbarous.[12] If Scipio is Hercules, then he is at the source of Spanish imperial power.[13] Indeed, Zurbarán was commissioned to paint the labors of Hercules for the Buen Retiro in 1635.[14] These paintings were linked to the feats of Philip IV (Brown and Elliott 1980, 160). It is possible, then, to conceive of the Roman general as Philip, a king who many viewed as the last chance for Spanish imperialism to prevail. If Scipio can be identified with Philip, then his lack of communication with his troops, his absence, may well point to the barrier that slowly grew between the Spanish king who tended to leave affairs of state to his *privado* [favorite minister], the conde-duque de Olivares, and his people. By silencing the Cervantine harangue, then, Rojas Zorrilla is not only avoiding one of the strongest moments of his predecessor, but he is also pointing to tensions within his own empire.

Even though the battlefield in *Numancia cercada* rages with cries of war, it is the amorous skirmishes that drive the action, culminating with the unexpected arrival of Retógenes, leader of the Numantians, to the Roman general's tent, seeking his bride. Scipio's judgment is the climactic moment of the third act.[15] This scene bears striking resemblance to another work by Giulio Romano. We are thus confronted by a *clinamen*, or veering away from a key moment in Cervantes's portrayal of Scipio as a warrior (his harangue—which imitates Giulio's *Apparition*) in order to foreground a different work by Raphael's disciple. Bloom, drawing on Lucretius, shows how atoms "swerve ever so little from their course" (1973, 44) and describes how a poet's "revisionary swerves" operate to mitigate the anxiety of influence (44). Rojas Zorrilla's text also swerves, engaging in an act of creative correction. While applauding Cervantes's pictorial pre-text, Rojas shows that another such drawing is preferable.

Scipio's Continence is one of seven tapestries in Philip II's set of Scipio's histories (Domínguez 1991, 69) and thus Rojas Zorrilla could have been acquainted with it.[16] It is based on the story of a beautiful woman prisoner who reveals to the grandfather of Scipio that she is engaged to the Celtiberian prince, Allucius. Instead of taking her for himself, Scipio returns her to her lover.[17] A curiously similar situation can be found in Rojas's play. Here, the Numantian leader, Retógenes, comes to the Roman camp to claim his beloved Florinda from the Roman general. Retógenes warns Scipio of Florinda's almost blinding beauty: "no te ciegue su hermosura" [v. 2290: don't be blinded by her beauty]. As she appears, Scipio acknowledges "que es divina. Es su rostro soberano" [vv. 2336–37: that she is divine. Her face is unsurpassed]. But he is able to contain his passion, affirming: "tengo el alma divina / aunque vive en cuerpo humano" [vv. 2344–45: I have a divine soul even though it lives is a human body]. In Giulio Romano's tapestry, Scipio also shows his continence by averting his glance from the beautiful woman and looking directly at the man to whom he is returning the prisoner. The play swerves from the model by having Scipio look at Florinda as he directly addresses her, pointing to Retógenes: "Aquí está, bella Florinda, / tu esposo" [vv. 2350–51: Here is your husband, beautiful Florinda]. Thus, Rojas Zorrilla draws a Scipio who is even more formidable than the one in the tapestry, one whose gaze is direct, being able to deflect personal desire. In the tapestry, instead of accepting the treasures brought in ransom by her parents, the Roman general gives these riches to Allucius. The play replicates this action, showing both Scipio's generosity and the use of woman as object of exchange (vv. 2362–65).

Contrasting with Scipio's continence in Giulio Romano's tapestry, the *putti* of the frame engage in playful embraces and in sexual exploration. The tapestry thus banishes the lust of Venus to the margins so that the valor of Mars can shine through. The margins serve to encase a center that cannot prevent pleasure from thriving all around. The same holds true for Rojas Zorrilla's *Numancia* plays. Although the Roman general's decree and continence serve as examples of ways in which to banish Venus and Bacchus, these gods revel in the margins, playfully instilling desire all around the central action of the siege. The Numantian *gracioso* Tronco takes on the guise of Bacchus (v. 2661) as he pretends to be an inebriated Roman so as not to be questioned by the enemy, while confusion reigns due to the rivalries between Florinda's suitors. As in Botticelli's *Mars and Venus*, where the female deity is able to tame the god of war (as the *putti* play with his weapons), the siege of Numancia is tamed by desire as Florinda, a woman whose name is related to Flora, the deity ruling over the flowers of spring,[18] becomes a *Venus armata* [armed Venus] enslaving both Numantians and Romans in the snares of passion. Scipio's laws and Scipio's continence have failed to control the chaos of desire. Roman civilization cannot triumph over the power of eros. The play is thus a clear re-

Sandro Botticelli, Mars, Venus, and Satyrs. (National Gallery, London. Photo: Alinari/Art Resource, NY)

flection of the new Spanish empire where Philip IV, a new Scipio, cannot contain desire through legislation—through the *Junta de reformación* [Council of Reform] (1621) and the *Junta grande de reformación* [Great Council of Reform] (1622), which were unable to contain excesses in dress and desire.[19] Indeed, the returning of the dowry in both painting and play can be seen as the *Junta's* attempt to stop dowries from rising. As for Scipio's example of continence, this is something the Spanish king does not follow.[20] The permeability of margins thus becomes central to both tapestry and plays—love is war and war is desire—and Spain contains but cannot contain (suppress) either. The country's impotence thus leads Rojas to problematize the very basis for Spanish civilization.

The opposition between civilization and desire led Freud to assert that "it is impossible to overlook the extent to which civilization is built upon the renunciation of instinct, how much it presupposes precisely the non-satisfaction (by suppression, repression or some other means?) of powerful instincts" (1961, 52). Turning to what he terms the modern world (which would include Golden Age Spain) he decries the extreme interference with sexual freedom:

> But heterosexual genital love, which has remained exempt from outlawry, is itself restricted by further limitations, in the shape of insistence upon legitimacy and monogamy. Present-day civilization makes it plain that it will only permit sexual relationships on the basis of a solitary, indisoluble bond between one man and one woman, and that it does not like sexuality as a source of pleasure in its own right and is only prepared to tolerate it because there is so far no substitute for it as a means of propagating the human race. (1961, 60)

By exploring different forms of sexual desire, and by showing that imperial wars have much to do with this desire, Rojas is engaging in a questioning of the forces of conquest and continence proclaimed by Scipio.

The siege of a walled city, castle, or fortification has often been compared to the wooing and "conquest" of a woman, and vice versa. In the ballad of "Abenámar y el rey don Juan" ["Abenamar and King Don Juan"] the king claims he would wed the city, but she answers that she is already married to a moor. From Christine de Pizan's *Le livre des trois vertus*[21] [The Book of Three Virtues] to Fernando de Rojas's *Celestina*, the opposite equation is pervasive. As Helen Solterer asserts: "This figure of the female body as military fortification is so endemic that most medieval works assess it from the outside alone—as a façade to scale, a construction to besiege and overwhelm. The only perspective is that of the aggressor" (Salter 1995, 107). Man's wooing of woman is often based on trickery and thus recalls Odysseus's guile. The Trojan horse is nothing more than the phallic representation of the conquest of an unwilling woman. No wonder Celestina refers to Melibea as Troya (Rojas 1974, 123), and when Tisbea is deceived and abandoned in *El burlador de Sevilla* [The Trickster of Seville] she sees herself as a burning Troy (Tirso de Molina 1991, vv. 993–99). Imperial schemes are thus closely related to ruses of desire where the male seeks to obtain the *object* of his desires by any means. Thus, Scipio cannot banish Venus from his camp since his imperial desire is not so different from contentions over Florinda. Indeed, the Roman general is not very different from Odysseus. He will win his woman/city through guile—through a siege that will weaken the desired enemy before the walls of the Other can be shattered.

But Rojas Zorrilla introduces a rather disconcerting element into this equation of imperialism and patriarchy versus resisting city and woman. Cayo Mario promises not to return to Rome until the walls of Numancia have been breached and a bird installed within "el ave / que hurtó el paje de copa / de Júpiter [vv. 243–47: the bird who stole Jupiter's cupbearer]. The bird in question is, of course, the eagle, symbol of Rome's empire, which must abide within Numancia, signifying the city's capitulation. At first glance, this is but one more image of penetration and conquest. But in contrast to other myths in the play whose characters are clearly and repeatedly named (Venus, Bacchus, Hercules, Diana), here we have an epithetic circumlocution to refer to Jupiter's beloved. What is hidden is a name that dares not speak its love.[22] Michelangelo's *Rape of Ganymede*, painted for the young nobleman Tommasso Cavallieri is, according to Barkan "so deeply woven into Michelangelo's poetic and imagistic oeuvre as to play a significant role for him and for the Renaissance" (1991, 79). For the Renaissance, Ganymede represented both an image of Neoplatonic transcendent desire and a type of eros that was associated with classical civilization, and that poignantly revealed the gap between the ancients and the early moderns.[23] For, while the pagan pantheon could envision its primary male god abducting a male youth, Christian western Europe denied as much the plurality of gods as the plurality of orientation in sexual matters. Its one God was denied any form of sexual pleasure, while harsh penalties were imposed on males engaged in same-sex relations.

Although the most common narrative concerning Ganymede has Jupiter transforming himself into an eagle in order to abduct the

Michelangelo, *Ganymede*. (Courtesy of the Fogg Art Museum, Harvard University Art Museums, Gifts for Special Uses Fund. Photo: Photographic Services)

youth, there are a number of versions that claim that this deity sent his eagle in order to bring Ganymede to the heavens. Interestingly, the passage from Rojas eschews what, for Leonard Barkan, is the primary metonym for the ancients, metamorphosis (1986, 18), in this case the transformation of Jupiter into an eagle. Metamorphosis was often linked to sexual desire. Barkan asserts that "stories of metamorphosis are stories of pursuit, of travel, of unfamiliar and alien loves" (1986, 14). Rojas Zorrilla's *Numancia* plays certainly concern themselves with pursuit and travel. The unfamiliar and alien loves in these *comedias* include not only those between Numantians and Romans, Ganymede and Jupiter, but must also take into account Scipio's desire for the exotic Celtiberian city. Rojas's *Numancia* plays thus revel in metamorphosis, which can be found in at least four forms: as mythical allusion such as Florinda in the guise of a *Venus armata*, Tronco in the guise of Bacchus, and Scipio and Retógenes as Hercules; disguise of origin, as Scipio's appearance "a la española vestido" [2: v. 2: dressed in Spanish style] in order to lovingly and cunningly gaze upon the walls of Numancia so as to "rendir y sujetar" [2: v. 22: to conquer and subject]; cross-dressing as in Artemisa's disguise as a man, an "hermoso Narciso" [2: v. 240: handsome Narcissus] so as to enter the Roman camp and be next to her beloved King Jugarta; and (4) mythical cross-dressing, as when Florinda calls herself a new Jupiter, becoming a male god who sends metaphorical bolts of lightning upon the invading Romans (vv. 623–25).

The constant transgression of dress and deities creates a certain unease, as the structures of gender, religion, and empire are destabilized. Retógenes is jealous of a woman (Artemisa) dressed as a Roman male page, while his bride Florinda is jealous of this page, knowing that "he" is a woman. And where is Jupiter to be found? Is he embodied in the eagles of the Roman army or in the body of the Numantian *Venus armata* [Armed Venus], Florinda, who scatters thunderbolts? By granting authority to the ancients through this battle for the appropriation of myth, Rojas's *Numancia* plays not only render tribute to what Barkan has called the "counterreligion of paganism" (1986, 18), but also allow other marginalized aspects of ancient culture to seep into textuality. At the center of the many metamorphic questions stands the unnamed Ganymede. Jupiter in the play may be appropriated by males and females, by Romans and Numantians. But the god does not partake of the other metamorphosis, the transformation into an eagle. Instead, he waits in heaven for Ganymede. Why does a text replete with metonyms for the classical civilization resist this transformation?

Certainly, the gap brought about by Ganymede's unnamed presence leads an audience to question the myths of origins that dictate what is sexually accepted within a society.[24] To understand Ganymede's shadowy presence we must look once again at Giulio Romano, since, according to James M. Saslow, he drew this figure more than any other Renaissance artist.[25] Although chosen for the central medallion at the Camerino dei Falconi [Hall of Falcons] in the Palazzo Ducale in Mantua, today Ganymede can hardly be seen, being badly damaged.[26] A drawing based on this painting shows him lifted to heavens by the eagle, which is Jupiter's typical metamorphosis for this myth. As Saslow states, "The handsome nude youth, holding both ewer and bowl, is manifestly an object of erotic desire: his genitals are promiently displayed by his parted legs, and he twists his head to meet the kiss of the eagle's beak" (1986, 138). Jupiter's passion for Ganymede and the god's metamorphosis has its source in Ovid (10.155–61).

But there is a second Ganymede, one who serves to question the myth of origins of an empire. According to Thomas M. Greene, allusion carries with it "the simulacrum of context." It points "to only one of many geneological lines" as when Virgil alludes to Homer. Although "the unconfessed geneological line may prove to be as nourishing as the visible," it must not "obscure the special status of that root the work privileges by its self-constructed myth of origins" (1982, 19). Rojas's allusion points to Virgil, which thus becomes a textual myth of origins that in turn serves as the model for the construction of the myth of origins of empire. As Barkan reminds us: "At the opening of the *Aeneid*, the boy is revealed to be a pivotal cause of the Trojan War" (1991, 19). Virgil's poem opens with Juno's hatred of Troy. It is based in part on the fact that the city's descendants will destroy her cherished Carthage. But war is once again tied to amorous conquests: "deep in her heart lie stored the judgement of Paris and her slighted beauty's wrong, her hatred of the race,[27] and the honors paid to ravished Ganymede" (1978, 1.26–28). Elsewhere in the *Aeneid* we are told that Jupiter sends his eagle and awaits him in heaven. We thus see the ascending Ganymede in the frontispiece of the illustrated *Aeneid* by Sebastian Brandt of 1502 (Saslow 1986, 114). In the Sala di Troia [Hall of Troy], at the Ducal Palace in Mantua, we discover Giulio Romano's Virgilian version of Ganymede.[28] Here, there are four large and four smaller frescoes depicting the saga of the Trojan war, starting with the *Judgement of Paris* and ending with *The Trojan Horse* (Hartt 1958, 181).[29] "Strangest of all," according to Hartt is "the scene in the center of the vault" (1958, 181).[30] Here, Venus swoons, since she has become aware that the Trojans have lost the war. On either side of her are Juno, patroness of the Greeks, and the Trojan Ganymede. By touching Venus's garment, Ganymede signfies that he partakes of her suffering at this defeat. His impassive features and bared torso challenge Juno and seem to say that even though this war is lost, he is still at the right hand of god and the future is on his side. Venus's swooning beauty together with the abducted youth's impassive grace lead Jupiter (if the painting indeed follows the Virgilian text) to predict that Venus's son, Aeneas, will found Rome—which will in turn destroy Carthage (Saslow 1986, 138; Virgil 1978, 1.229–96).

Thus, the fall of Troy has, since ancient times, been subtly linked to the rape of Ganymede. City and youth are taken through an act of *sapientia* [cunning].[31] In *Numancia destruida*, Scipio explicitly calls himself a new Odysseus. Like the ancient hero who cunningly created the Trojan horse, Scipio will use guile to conquer Numancia: "Por esto cantó de Ulises / el divino Homero tanto" [2: 1659–60: This is why the divine Homer sung so much of Ulysses]. The fall of Troy, then, can be equated with the fall of Numancia—and the taking of a female city with the rape of Ganymede. But, the

Giulio Romano, *Venus Swooning in the Arms of Jupiter.* (Palazzo Ducale, Mantua. Photo: Alinari/Art Resource, NY)

descendants of Troy will go on to found Rome. And, a Roman
Scipio is now emulating the Greek "enemy." Who, then, represents
the Spanish empire in the play? Greece, Troy, Rome, or Numancia?
The obvious answer is the latter, but the conflation of imperial de-
sires problematizes the question. And the equation Scipio—
Hercules—Jupiter lends credence to a Spain-Rome linkage.

In *Numancia destruida*, the eagle (the Roman army) does enter
the city, but only after the one surviving child commits suicide. Is
this child Ganymede and does he represent Numancia, the desired
object of the conquerors? After all, unlike Bariato in Cervantes's
tragedy, he is un-named. He, like Ganymede in Rojas Zorrilla, is
nameless. The imperial bird has sought him out, but Rojas's child
prefers death to surrender. It seems as if both the imperial and sexual aims of the conqueror have been frustrated—that Juno has won
the play. And yet, the child does ascend at the end of the work—he
is elevated on the wings of fame.[32] Let us recall that the new Spanish empire prophesied in Rojas's work will be ruled by the three
Habsburg Philips who are often associated with Jupiter. Is the Tro-
jan/Numantian Ganymede then resting in the arms of a new empire
(Rome/Spain)?

In creating a myth of origins for the Spanish empire, Rojas Zorrilla's *Numancia* plays enrich and problematize the Cervantine
tragic vision by conflating sexual and imperial desires. Ancient images of *raptus* are part of Rojas Zorrilla's swerve from his Cervantine precursor, leading us to wonder if Jupiter's eagle can represent
Rojas Zorrrilla's plunder of the riches of Cervantes and Romano.
But *raptus* in its Neoplatonic sense implies a going beyond, as in
Correggio's *Rape of Ganymede*, also painted for Federico Gonzaga
in Mantua and given as a gift to Charles V.[33] Rojas seeks to refigure
his play as a new Ganymede, as a new way of presenting the imperial message. And that message has to do with myth (the making of
the Romans and the Habsburgs), margins (the place of desire, the
placement of Spain), metamorphoses (the construction of gender,
the many names of passion) and the transcendence of Otherness, so
that Ganymede may be able to gaze at a myriad of Jupiters whether
Roman, Numantian, or Spanish, whether disguised as eagles or as
Venuses, without suspicion or guile, but as a worthy and caring
member of an assembly of the gods.

NOTES

1. In the transformation from collective to individual tragedy that Raymond R.
MacCurdy has detected in Rojas Zorrilla's two-part elaboration of Cervantes's

Correggio, *The Abduction of Ganymede*. **(Kunsthistorisches Museum, Vienna. Photo: Erich Lessing/Art Resource, NY)**

play (1960, 100ff.), the character of Retógenes, leader of the besieged city, is viewed by this critic as: "a baroque approximation of the classical tragic hero, and Rojas's Numantia plays are largely this hero's personal tragedy" (1968, 65).

2. For a study of *La Numancia* as a theater of memory see my *Cervantes, Raphael, and the Classics*.

3. The Mantuan war of succession, fought between Spain and France, began in 1628 (Elliott 1986, 337ff.). The play seems to have been written around 1630. By then, Mantua had fallen under French influence.

4. While *The Battle of the Milvian Bridge* follows closely Raphael's sketches, Giulio Romano intervenes radically in *The Apparition of the Cross* and is fully in charge of the *Baptism* and *The Donation of Constantine* (Pagden 1989, 85–88).

5. For a more complete discussion see de Armas, *Cervantes, Raphael, and the Classics*.

6. Although such a speech is not recorded in Ambrosio Morales's *Corónica*, nor in his sources Appian of Alexandria and Aeneus Florus, Morales does record that Scipio found a cowardly and ineffective army, and attributed their decline to vices such as lust (1791, 4, 28). In Appian, Scipio, "having heard that it was full of idleness, discord, and luxury, and well knowing that he could never overcome the enemy unless he should first bring his own men under strict discipline" (1962, 271) sought to train them properly.

7. Through a highly developed sense of syncretism, the "truth" of these pagan mysteries were often Christian truths, which led to hybridization. For example: "Renaissance art produced many images of Venus which resemble a Madonna or a Magdalene" (Wind 1968, 24).

8. All references to *Numancia cercada* will simply list the verse numbers. When refering to passages in prose, the pages will be given. References to *Numancia destruida* will include a "2" before the verse numbers.

9. This image may recall many of the depictions of Hercules's destruction of this monster by Italian painters such as Andrea Mantegna, Baldassare Peruzzi, Raphael, and Giulio Romano, works Cervantes would have seen. Peruzzi painted a ceiling fresco on the subject in the Sala di Galatea at the Villa Farnesina in Rome, which Cervantes would surely have seen since he was inspired by Galatea for his own pastoral novel (Dudley 1995, 32–3). Mantegna's work is a ceiling fresco at the Palazzo Ducale in Mantua, where many of Giulio Romano's frescoes were exhibited. Raphael's work on Hercules is "known only from 4 extant drawings" including *Hercules and the Hydra* (Reid 1993, vol. 1, 550).

10. MacCurdy notes that these *Numancia* plays "figure in the repertory of an unidentified theatrical company, a repertory consisting of twenty-six plays, none of which, insofar as it is known, was written after 1630" (1968, 61).

11. In this sense, the play follows Cervantine ambiguity as described by Johnson (1981), or indeterminacy as Simerka (1998) argues.

12. In Rojas's play the Roman Senate's "civilized" discussions contrast with the antagonism between those who would rule over Numancia. The bitter battles of the Numantians can evince a less-developed society: Megara, who calls himself "horror del cielo" (276), and Olonio with his "brazo fuerte" (290), nearly come to blows with Retógenes as to who is going to lead the city against the Roman invader. Although a seventeenth-century audience would admire Numancia's bellicose valor, they may also see them as "Bárbaros" (293), a term utilized by Megara himself.

13. There is a verbal conflict within Rojas's plays as to who represents Hercules, the Numantians or the Romans. In *Numancia destruida*, Retógenes sees himself as a Hercules battling Anteus, Cacus, Busiris, and Cerberus (418–29).

14. Although Zurbarán's Hercules cycle could have served as inspiration for the many references to the classical hero in Rojas's play, it was probably drawn too late for such an impact, since the play, according to MacCurdy (1968), should be dated around 1630.

15. The act will end with continued amorous skirmishes in which Cayo Mario is wounded under the light of Diana/the moon, a deity that avenges Florinda/Diana's abduction (vv. 2591–92). Curiously, Giulio Romano was fond of painting Diana as the moon. She thus appears in the "Sala del Sole" [Hall of the Sun] at the Palazzo del Te (the same palace that contains his *Hercules and the Hydra* and that may have prompted Rojas to foreground this labor). Giulio also painted a Diana/Luna at a second Mantuan location, the Palazzo Ducale.

16. Giulio Romano prepared the program and the consequent sketches for a tapestry series on the History of Scipio from 1532–5 (Salet 1978, 5, 11). This series was commisioned by the French monarch Francis I in order to exalt his own victories. For Hartt's opinion of these tapestries see (1958, 227–31).

17. This tale is found in Livy's *Histories* Twenty-six, 50, 1–12; Polybius's *History* Ten, 2, 19 and Valerius Maximus's *Memorabilia* Four, 3, 1 (Salet 1978, 46).

18. Here we might recall Botticelli's *Primavera*, which depicts the transformation of Chloris into Flora while Venus stands in the center of the painting.

19. Sumptuary proposals were passed and brothels were forbidden (Elliott 1986, 116–17).

20. According to Elliott, Olivares accompanied the king "on nocturnal expeditions round the streets of Madrid" (1986, 112).

21. "Assallés ce chastel! Gardés que nulles n'eschapperent entre vous, hommes, et que toit soit livré a honte!" (cited in Solterer 1995, 123). I would like to thank Isidro Rivera for pointing out this passage and Solterer's book.

22. The bold utilization of this myth reflects what Ann L. Mackenzie calls Rojas's desire to "dramatizar y poetizar lo nuevo, inaudito e inusitado" [1994, 19: dramatize and poeticize the new, the unheard of, the unusual]. Although her book is an effort to reexamine Rojas's historical plays among others (1994, 11), she does not study the *Numancia* plays.

23. Freud asserts: "the choice of object is restricted to the opposite sex, and most extra-genital satisfactions are forbidden as perversions" (1961, 60). In this brief history, Freud does not take into account the same-sex practices of the Greeks and Romans. On this topic see Cantarella (1992).

24. Plato rails against the myth of origins of same-sex love in the *Laws*, claiming that the Ganymede myth was created by the inhabitants of Crete to legitimize their sexual customs (Barkan 1991, 29). But Plato, "although himself a homosexual" (Cantarella 1992, 61), was not against relations between males. Rather, his objective was "the suppression of all passion" (Cantarella 1992, 62).

25. "Parmigianino and Giulio are responsible for more depictions of Ganymede than any other Renaissance artists" (Saslow 1986, 98). While in Mantua, Giulio drew seven compositions that included Ganymede (Saslow 1986, 137). In Spain, the figure of Ganymede was not absent. Together with many other mythological figures, he was painted on the ceiling of Juan de Arguijo's home in Sevilla (1601). For López Torrijos, the youth swept away by the eagle represents "el aspecto feroz que, en ocasiones, presenta al hombre la llamada o elección de los dioses" [1985, 106: the Savage aspect with which, on occasion, the call or choice of the gods confronts man.]

26. Vasari does not describe this hall in the Ducal Palace or the *Ganymede*, but Rojas could have seen one of the many drawings or prints of this mythological

figure. Vasari does mention the Hall of Troy (1991, 373). For the many mistakes made by Vasari in his descriptions of Tè and the ducal palace, see Rubin (1995, 131–5).

27. The Trojans are descendants of Dardanus, who was conceived in adultery by Jupiter and Electra.

28. Federico de Gonzaga, raised to the title of duke by Charles V in 1530, had the Palazzo del Te decorated for the emperor's visit (Tanner 1993, 116). The thundering Jupiter in the *Sala dei Giganti* "should be understood as a symbol of imperial power with which the Gonzaga house identified its fortunes" (Hartt 1958, 157–8). As Julia and Peter Bondanella state in their edition of Vasari's *Lives*, this hall was "conceived to honour the second visit of Emperor Charles V to Mantua in 1532" (1991, 568, n. 370). Tanner seems to argue that the Sala di Troia at the Ducal Palace also follows Spanish imperial ideals (1993, 116), although it was decorated by Giulio and assistants between 1536 and 1540.

29. The other two large frescoes are *The Rape of Helen* and *The Death of Laocoon*.

30. Hartt cannot explain the importance of Ganymede in this fresco, since he views the *sala* as "the triumph of Minerva and Vulcan over Venus . . . military virtues as compared with the worship of Venus" (1958, 181). I would argue that the *Sala di Troia*, like Rojas's plays, shows the relationship between eros and military conquest.

31. According to Ernst Curtius (1953, 170–71), there was a continuing debate throughout the Middle Ages as to what was the chief virtue of the epic hero, *sapietia* (Odysseus) or *fortitudo* (Achilles). This opposition, which is made clear in Rojas's plays, was one of the central conflicts of Cervantes's tragedy (de Armas 1994).

32. "pero vivirá su fama" [2. 2299: but his fame will live on].

33. Saslow assumes that since the *Danae* and the *Leda* were "commissioned as gifts for the emperor Charles" (1986, 70), so were the *Ganymede* and *Io*. All four were in Madrid by 1585 (Saslow 1986, 219 n. 12). According to Brown, the "frank sensuality" of the four paintings "made Philip uneasy, and he gave away two of them to his secretary, Antonio Pérez" (1991, 66).

WORKS CITED

Appianus. 1962. *Roman History.* Translated by Horace White. 4 vols. London: William Hernemann.

Barkan, Leonard. 1986. *The Gods Made Flesh: Metamorphosis and the Pursuit of Paganism.* New Haven: Yale University Press.

———. 1991. *Transuming Passion: Ganymede and the Erotics of Humanism.* Stanford: Stanford University Press.

Bloom, Harold. 1973. *The Anxiety of Influence.* Oxford: Oxford University Press.

Brown, Jonathan. 1991. *The Golden Age of Painting in Spain.* New Haven: Yale University Press.

Brown, Jonathan, and J. H. Elliott. 1980. *A Palace for a King: The Buen Retiro and the Court of Philip IV.* New Haven: Yale University Press.

Cantarella, Eva. 1992. *Bisexuality in the Ancient World.* New Haven: Yale University Press.

Cervantes, Miguel de. 1984. *Numancia*. Edited by Robert Marrast. Madrid: Cátedra.

Covarrubias, Sebastián de. 1987. *Tesoro de la lengua castellana o española*. Barcelona: Editorial Alta Fulla.

Curtius, Ernst. 1953. *European Literature and the Latin Middle Ages*. Translated by Willard R. Trask. New York: Harper and Row.

De Armas, Frederick A. 1974. "Classical Tragedy and Cervantes's *La Numancia*." *Neophilologus* 58: 34–40.

———. 1986. *The Return of Astraea: An Astral-Imperial Myth in Calderón*. Lexington: University Press of Kentucky.

———. 1994. "Achilles and Odysseus: An Epic Contest in Cervantes' *La Numancia*." In *Cervantes: Estudios en la víspera de su centenario*. Vol. 2. Kassel: Editio Reichenberger.

———. 1998. *Cervantes, Raphael, and the Classics*. Cambridge: Cambridge University Press.

De Armas Wilson, Diana. 1987. "Passing the Love of Women: The Intertextuality of *El curioso impertinente*." *Cervantes* 7: 9–28.

Domínguez Ortiz, Antonio, Concha Herrero Carretero, and José A. Godoy. 1991. *Resplendence of the Spanish Monarchy: Renaissance Tapestries and Armor from the Patrimonio Nacional*. New York: N. Abrams.

Dudley, Edward. 1995. "Goddess on the Edge: The Galatea Agenda in Raphael, Garcilaso, and Cervantes." *Calíope* 1: 27–45.

Elliott, J. H. 1986. *The Count-Duke of Olivares: The Statesman in an Age of Decline*. New Haven: Yale University Press.

Freud, Sigmund. 1961. *Civilization and Its Discontents, With a biographical introduction by Peter Gay*. Translated by Walter Strachey. New York: W. W. Norton.

Grant, Michael. 1993. *Constantine the Great*. New York: Charles Scribner's Sons.

Greene, Thomas M. 1982. *The Light in Troy: Imitation and Discovery in Renaissance Poetry*. New Haven: Yale University Press.

Gutiérrez Cortines Corral, Cristina. 1989. La fortuna de Giulio Romano en la arquitectura española. *Giulio Romano: Atti del Convegno Internazionale di Studi su Giulio Romano e l'Espansione Europea del Rinascimento*. Mantua: Gariplo.

Hartt, Frederick. 1958. *Giulio Romano*. Vol. 1. New Haven: Yale University Press.

Heiple, Daniel L. 1994. *Garcilaso and the Italian Renaissance*. University Park: Pennsylvania State University Press.

Hersey, George L. 1993. *High Renaissance Art in St. Peter's and the Vatican*. Chicago: University of Chicago Press.

Johnson, Carroll B. 1981. "*La Numancia* y la estructura de la ambigüedad cervantina." In *Cervantes: Su obra y su mundo*, edited by Manuel Criado de Val. Barcelona: Edi-6.

López Torrijos, Rosa. 1985. *La mitología en la pintura española del Siglo de Oro*. Madrid: Cátedra.

Mackenzie, Ann L. 1994. *Francisco de Rojas Zorrilla y Agustín Moreto: análisis*. Liverpool: Liverpool University Press.

MacCurdy, Raymond R. 1960. "The Numantia Plays of Cervantes and Rojas Zorrilla: the Shift from Collective to Personal Tragedy." *Symposium* 14: 100–20.

———. 1968. *Francisco de Rojas Zorrilla*. New York: Twayne.

Morales, Ambrosio. 1791. *Corónica general de España que continuaba Ambrosio de Morales cronista del rey nuestro señor don Felipe II*. Vols. 3–4. Madrid: Benito Cano.

Ovid. 1984. *Metamorphoses: Books IX–XV* Translated by Frank Justus Miller. Cambridge, MA: Harvard University Press.

Pagden, Sylvia Ferino. 1989. "Giulio Romano pittore e disegnatore a Roma." In *Giulio Romano*, edited by Ernst H. Gombrich, et al. Milano: Electa.

Panofsky, Erwin. 1969. *Problems in Titian*. New York: New York University Press.

Reid, Jane Davidson. 1993. *The Oxford Guide to Classical Mythology in the Arts, 1300–1990s*. 2 vols. Oxford: Oxford University Press.

Rojas, Fernando de. 1974. *La Celestina*. Edited by Bruno M. Daminani. Madrid: Cátedra.

Rojas Zorrilla, Francisco de. 1977. *Numancia cercada* y *Numancia destruida*. Edited by Raymond R. MacCurdy. Madrid: José Porrúa Turanzas.

Rubin, Patricia Lee. 1995. *Giorgio Vasari: Art and History*. New Haven: Yale University Press.

Salet, Francis, Bertrand Jestaz, and Roseline Bacou. 1978. *Jules Romaine: L'histoire de Scipion*. Paris: Editions de la Réunion des Musées Nationaux.

Saslow, James M. 1986. *Ganymede in the Renaissance: Homosexuality in Art and Society*. New Haven: Yale University Press.

Simerka, Barbara A. 1998. " 'That the rulers should sleep without bad dreams': Anti-Epic Discourse in *La Numancia* and *Aranco domado*." *Cervantes* 18.1: 46–67.

Simon, Kate. 1988. *A Renaissance Tapestry: The Gonzaga of Mantua*. New York: Harper and Row.

Solterer, Helen. 1995. *The Master and Minerva*. Berkeley: University of California Press.

Tanner, Marie. 1993. *The Last Descendants of Aeneas: The Hapsburgs and the Mythic Image of the Emperor*. New Haven: Yale University Press.

Tate, Robert B. 1954. Mythology in Spanish Historiography in the Middle Ages and the Renaissance. *Hispanic Review* 22: 1–18.

Tirso de Molina. 1991. *El burlador de Sevilla*. Edited by Alfredo Rodríguez López-Vázquez. Madrid: Cátedra.

Vasari, Giorgio. 1991. *The Lives of the Artists*. Translated by Julia Conaway Bondanella and Peter Bondanella. Oxford: Oxford University Press.

Virgil. 1978. *Eclogues, Georgics, Aeneid*. Translated by H. Rushton Fairclough. Cambridge: Harvard University Press.

Wind, Edgar. 1968. *Pagan Mysteries in the Renaissance*. 2d ed. New York: W. W. Norton.

Notes on Contributors

WILLIAM R. BLUE is Professor of Spanish at the University of Kansas. He is the author of *The Development of Imagery in Calderón's Comedias* (1983), *Comedia: Art and History* (1989), and *Spanish Comedy and Historical Contexts in the 1620s* (1996).

WALTER COHEN is Professor of Comparative Literature and Dean of the Graduate School at Cornell University. He is the author of *Drama of a Nation: Public Theater in Renaissance England and Spain* and is one of the four editors of *The Norton Shakespeare.*

ANNE J. CRUZ, Professor of Spanish at the University of Illinois, Chicago, received her Ph.D. from Stanford University. She has held offices in several Renaissance organizations, and is currently Treasurer of the Society for the Study of Early Modern Women. Her numerous publications on early modern literature and culture include *Imitación y transformación: El petrarquismo en la poesía de Boscán y Garcilaso de la Vega*, and four coeditions ranging from the Spanish Inquisition to Cervantes studies. She has recently completed a book on the Spanish picaresque novel.

FREDERICK A. DE ARMAS is Distinguished Professor of Spanish and Comparative Literature and Fellow of the Institute for the Arts and Humanistic Studies at Pennsylvania State University. In 1998 were published his *Cervantes, Raphael, and the Classics* and (ed.) *A Star-Crossed Golden Age: Myth and the Spanish Comedia*, the latter by Bucknell University Press. His other books include: *The Invisible Mistress: Aspects of Feminism and Fantasy in the Golden Age*, *The Return of Astraea: An Astral-Imperial Myth in Calderón*, (ed.) *The Prince in the Tower: Perceptions of La vida es sueño*, (BUP) and (ed.) *Heavenly Bodies: The Realms of La estrella de Sevilla* (BUP).

SIDNEY E. DONNELL received his Ph.D. from the University of Pennsylvania. A specialist in gender studies and early modern Spanish

271

theater, he is Assistant Professor of Languages at Lafayette College.

SALVADOR J. FAJARDO is Professor of Spanish at SUNY-Binghamton. His interests have included French Literature (his first book, *Claude Simon*, was a study of this new "novelist), and now he focuses principally on contemporary Spanish poetry. He has written books on Cernuda, Alberti, and Cervantes. He is currently at work on an edition of *Don Quixote* with James A. Parr.

THOMAS P. FINN is Assistant Professor of French at Angelo State University. Having earned an M.A. in Spanish and a Ph.D. in French, he has presented papers on Spanish and French literatures at conferences including the 1997 MLA. His publications include an article in *Laberinto* (1998). His dissertation on Molière's Spanish connections was published in 1998.

PERRY GETHNER is Professor of French at Oklahoma State University. He has published numerous critical editions and translations of early-modern French drama, including *The Lunatic Lover and Other Plays by French Women of the Seventeenth and Eighteenth Centuries*.

MARGARET GREER is Associate Professor of Spanish and Latin American Studies in the Department of Romance Studies at Duke University. Her publications include: *The Play of Power: Mythological Court Dramas of Pedro Calderón de la Barca* (1991); *La estatua de Prometeo of Pedro Calderón de la Barca: A Critical Edition* (1986); and *El teatro palaciego en Madrid, 1602–1707: Estudio y documentos* (coeditor with John E. Varey, 1997). She is presently completing a study of the novellas of María de Zayas y Sotomayor (*Desiring Readers: María de Zayas Tells Baroque Tales of Love and the Cruelty of Men*) and an edition of Calderón's play *Basta callar*.

SALVADOR OROPESA is Associate Professor of Spanish at Kansas State University. He has published numerous articles on twentieth-century Latin American literature and is author of *La obra de Ariel Dorfman: Ficción y crítica*.

JAMES A. PARR, Professor of Spanish at University of California, Riverside, has published *After Its Kind: Approaches to the Comedia* and *Don Quijote: An Anatomy of Subversive Discourse*, as well as editing a homage volume for Luis A. Murillo and two editions of *El burlador de Sevilla* (one version published in Spain, the other in the U.S.). He served as editor-in-chief of the *Bulletin of the Comediantes* from 1973 until 1999 and has just completed coediting an edition of *Don Quijote* for first-time readers.

AMY PAWL, Adjunct Assistant Professor of English at Washington University in St. Louis, teaches eighteenth-century English literature, directs the undergraduate writing program, and has previously published on Frances Burney and the reconstitution of the sentimental family.

BARBARA A. SIMERKA is Associate Professor of Spanish and Comparative Studies at the University of Texas, San Antonio. She has edited an anthology, *El arte nuevo de estudiar comedias: Literary Theory and Golden Age Spanish Drama* and with Christopher B. Weimer is cofounder and coeditor of *Laberinto: An Electronic Journal of Early Modern Hispanic Literatures*. She has published several articles using feminist and cultural materialist approaches to early modern literature and is also engaged in research on gender and ideology in contemporary chicana literature.

CHRISTOPHER B. WEIMER received a Ph.D. in Hispanic Language and Literature from Pennsylvania State University. He teaches Spanish and Humanities at Oklahoma State University. With Barbara A. Simerka, he is cofounder and coeditor of the online publication *Laberinto: An Electronic Journal of Early Modern Hispanic Literatures and Cultures*. His essays on both early modern and contemporary Hispanic theater have appeared in journals including *Bulletin of the Comediantes*, *Modern Drama*, *Estreno*, *Hispanófila*, and *Latin American Theater Review*.

AMY R. WILLIAMSEN is Associate Professor of Spanish at Arizona State University. She is a specialist in early modern Spanish literature and her books include *Co(s)mic Chaos: Exploring "Los Trabajos de Persiles y Sigismunda"* and *María de Zayas: The Dynamics of Discourse* (coedited with Judith A. Whitenack).

DIANA DE ARMAS WILSON is a Professor of English and Renaissance Studies at the University of Denver. She has published *Allegories of Love: Cervantes's "Persiles And Sigismunda"* (1991), and *Cer-*

vantes, *The Novel, and the New World* (forthcoming, Oxford UP). She has also coedited (with the late Ruth El Saffar) *Quixotic Desire: Psychoanalytic Perspectives on Cervantes*, and is currently sole editor for the new Norton Critical Edition of *Don Quijote*, using the Anglo-American translation by Burton Raffel.

Index